The Evolution of Natural Resources Law and Policy

Lawrence J. MacDonnell and Sarah F. Bates, Editors

AMERICAN BAR ASSOCIATION
Section of Environment,
Energy, and Resources

NATURAL RESOURCES
LAW CENTER
University of Colorado School of Law

Cover design by ABA Publishing.

Printed in the United States of America.

14 13 12 11 10 5 4 3 2 1

Library of Congress Cataloging-in-Publication Data

The evolution of natural resources law and policy / Lawrence J. MacDonnell and Sarah F. Bates, editors.
    p. cm.
  Includes bibliographical references and index.
  ISBN-13: 978–1-60442-430-0 (alk. paper)
  ISBN-10: 1-60442-430-3 (alk. paper)
  1. Natural resources—Law and legislation—United States—History. 2. Natural resources—Law and legislation—United States. I. MacDonnell, Lawrence J. II. Bates, Sarah F.
  KF5505.E94 2010
  346.7304'4—dc22   2009036371

Discounts are available for books ordered in bulk. Special consideration is given to state bars, CLE programs, and other bar-related organizations. Inquire at Book Publishing, ABA Publishing, American Bar Association, 321 North Clark Street, Chicago, Illinois 60654-7598.

www.ababooks.org

Summary of Contents

Contents

5 Better Ways to Work Together
Eric T. Freyfogle

6 Constitutional Law and the Future of Natural
Resource Protection
James R. May

II   *The Evolution of Resource Management*

8   Embracing a Civic Republican Tradition in Natural Resources Decision-Making   195
Mark Squillace

About the Editors

Lawrence J. MacDonnell is Professor of Law at the University of Wyoming College of Law. His substantive areas of work include water resources, energy and minerals, endangered species, and sustainable development of natural resources. Much of his work involves the interconnection between development and conservation—promoting environmentally beneficial development and use of land and natural resources.

Between 1983 and 1994 he served as the initial Director of the Natural Resources Law Center at the University of Colorado School of Law. Under his direction, the Center established nationally and internationally recognized programs of research, publication, and legal education and sponsored a visiting fellows program.

MacDonnell has worked in nonprofits, in private law practice, and as a consultant. His clients have included nonprofits, states, and private industry. MacDonnell has published extensively, primarily in the area of water law and policy. His publications include books, law review articles, and publications in other journals. Much of his writing has emphasized opportunities for changes in existing laws and policies to better meet contemporary needs.

Sarah F. Bates has written and spoken extensively on western water law and policy reform over the past two decades through research appointments with University of Montana and the University of Colorado, in her advocacy positions with Western Progress, the Grand Canyon Trust, and the Sierra Club Legal Defense Fund, and through her consulting work with groups such as the congressionally chartered Western Water Policy Review Advisory Commission.

Bates coauthored the book *Overtapped Oasis* with Marc Reisner in 1990, and has published four additional books (including *Natural Resources Policy and Law*, which she coedited with Lawrence MacDonnell), and numerous reports and articles. Her recent writings have focused on the nexus between land use planning and water law.

Bates is a graduate of the University of Colorado Law School (1988), where she subsequently returned to serve as the associate director of the Natural Resources Law Center from 1991 to 1993. She serves on the board of directors of the Montana-based Clark Fork Coalition and is a member of the advisory board of the Ruckelshaus Institute of Environment and Natural Resources at the University of Wyoming.

About the Contributors

Bruce Babbitt served as Attorney General of Arizona from 1975 to 1978, as Governor of Arizona from 1978 to 1987, and as Secretary of the Interior from 1993 to 2001. With degrees in geology, geophysics, and law, Babbitt was elected to statewide office as Attorney General on his first foray into elective politics at age 36. He subsequently served as Governor for nine years. As Governor, Babbitt brought environmental and resource management to the forefront in Arizona. He personally negotiated and steered to passage the Arizona Groundwater Management Act of 1980, which remains the most comprehensive water regulatory system in the nation. In addition, he was responsible for creation of the Arizona Department of Water Resources and the Arizona Department of Environmental Quality as well as a major expansion of the state park system.

Appointed Secretary of the Interior by President Clinton in 1993, Babbitt served for eight years, during which he led in the creation of the forest plan in the Pacific Northwest, restoration of the Florida Everglades, passage of the California Desert Protection Act, and legislation for the National Wildlife Refuge system. As a certified fire fighter, Babbitt brought his frontline experience to creating a new federal wild-land fire policy that emphasizes the role of fire in maintenance and restoration of natural ecosystems. He pioneered the use of habitat conservation plans under the Endangered Species Act and worked with President Clinton to create 22 new national moments, including the Grand Staircase–Escalante National Monument in Utah. Babbitt is perhaps best remembered by American school children as the Secretary who brought the wolves back to Yellowstone.

Babbitt is the author of *Cities in the Wilderness*, recently issued by Island Press, in which he lays out a new vision of land use in America. He currently serves as a Chairman of the World Wildlife Fund.

Babbitt resides in Washington, D.C., with his wife, Hattie, a former Ambassador to the Organization of American States. They have two children: Christopher, a lawyer residing in Washington, D.C., and T.J., a teacher in the Los Angeles public school system.

Federico Cheever is Director of the Environmental and Natural Resources Law Program and Professor of Law at the University of Denver College of Law. He began teaching there in 1993, specializing in environmental law, wildlife law, public land law, land conservation transactions, and property. Professor Cheever writes extensively about the Endangered Species Act, federal public land law, and land conservation transactions. He has recently coauthored a natural resources casebook, *Natural Resources Law: A Place-Based Book of Problems and Cases,* with Christine Klein and Bret Birdsong (2005). Over the years, Professor Cheever has represented environmental groups in cases under the Endangered Species Act, the National Forest Management Act, the National Environmental Policy Act, the Wilderness Act, and a number of other environmental laws. After graduating from Stanford University (BA/MA, 1981) and UCLA (JD, 1986) and clerking for Judge Harry Pregerson of U.S. Court of Appeals for the 9th Circuit in Los Angeles (1986–1987), he came to Denver as an Associate Attorney for the Sierra Club Legal Defense Fund (1987–1989). Between 1990 and 1993, he was an associate at the law firm Faegre and Benson.

Sally Fairfax is the Henry J. Vaux Distinguished Professor Emerita at the College of Natural Resources, University of California, Berkeley. She studied land conservation and management issues for almost 40 years prior to her retirement in 2008. She began her career as a close student of federal land agencies and soon turned to assessing alternative administrative regimes for managing resources in which the government shares management authority and power with diverse private groups. She is author or coauthor of numerous articles and books, including *Forest and Range Policy: Its Development in the United States* (with Samuel Trask Dana); *State Trust Lands: Their History, Management and Use* (with Jon A. Souder); *Conservation Trusts* (with Darla Guenzler); and *Buying Nature* (with Lauren Gwin, Mary Ann King,

Leigh Raymond, and Laura Watt). Her most recent work inquires into food systems and alternative foods in the San Francisco Bay Area. Fairfax has served as a member of numerous National Academy of Science boards, the Chair of the Board of the Central California Biosphere Reserve, the Title IX Coordinator for the Berkeley campus, and the Associate Dean for Instruction and Student Affairs in the College of Natural Resources, and has won many awards for distinguished teaching.

Robert L. Fischman is a professor at both the Maurer School of Law and the school of public and environmental affairs at Indiana University–Bloomington. Before joining the Indiana faculty in 1992, he taught at the University of Wyoming College of Law and served as Natural Resources Program Director and Staff Attorney at the Environmental Law Institute in Washington, D.C. He has taught in the environmental law programs at both Vermont Law School and Lewis and Clark School of Law. Professor Fischman has also been a senior research scholar at Yale Law School. He has written on public land management, endangered species recovery, environmental impact analysis, and global climate change. Fischman's books include *The National Wildlife Refuges: Coordinating a Conservation System through Law* (2003) and *Federal Public Land and Resources Law* (2007). Professor Fischman received his JD and MS from the University of Michigan in 1987 and his AB from Princeton in 1984.

Eric T. Freyfogle is the Max L. Rowe Professor of Law at the University of Illinois College of Law, where he has long taught courses on natural resources, property, wildlife law, land use planning, and environmental law and policy. His writings on nature and culture include over seven dozen articles and book chapters in scholarly and popular publications as well as several books, including *On Private Property: Finding Common Ground on the Ownership of Land* (Beacon Press, 2007); *Agrarianism and the Good Society: Land, Culture, Conflict, and Hope* (University Press of Kentucky, 2007); *Why Conservation is Failing and How It Can Regain Ground* (Yale University Press, 2006); and *The Land We Share: Private Property and the Common Good* (Island Press, 2003). His law school casebook, *Natural Resources Law: Private*

Rights and Collective Governance, was published by Thomson/West in 2007, and he is coauthor (with Dale D. Goble) of *Wildlife Law: Cases and Materials* (Foundation Press, 2nd ed. 2009) and *Wildlife Law: A Primer* (Island Press, 2009).

David H. Getches is Dean of the University of Colorado School of Law. In his more than three decades at Colorado Law, teaching before becoming Dean in 2003, Getches has become a national authority on natural resources and American Indian law issues. Prior to joining the faculty in 1979, he was the founding Executive Director of the Native American Rights Fund and spent several years in private practice. Professor Getches has had a prolific academic career. He has written casebooks, as well as books intended for a more general audience, and has published numerous articles and book chapters, including some written in Spanish and French. He served as the Executive Director of the Colorado Department of Natural Resources from 1983 to 1987, and was special consultant to the Secretary of the Interior in 1996. His current research focuses on the U.S. Supreme Court's Indian law decision-making, changing patterns of governance in water law, the law of the Colorado River, and indigenous water rights issues in Latin America.

Lisa Heinzerling is Professor of Law at the Georgetown University Law Center. She received an AB from Princeton University and a JD from the University of Chicago Law School, where she was editor-in-chief of the Law Review. She clerked for Judge Richard A. Posner on the United States Court of Appeals for the Seventh Circuit and for Justice William J. Brennan, Jr. on the United States Supreme Court. She served as an assistant attorney general in Massachusetts, specializing in environmental law. She has been a visiting professor at the Yale and Harvard law schools. She is the author, with Frank Ackerman, of *Priceless: On Knowing the Price of Everything and the Value of Nothing* (The New Press, 2004). She is currently on a leave of absence from Georgetown, serving as Senior Climate Policy Counsel to EPA Administrator Lisa P. Jackson.

Helen Ingram, Research Fellow at the Southwest Center at the University of Arizona, is a professor emeritus at both the University of

California at Irvine and the University of Arizona. Prior to 2006, she was Warmington Endowed Chair of Social Ecology at the University of California at Irvine. She holds a BA degree in government from Oberlin College and a PhD degree in public law and government from Columbia University. Her published works include 13 authored, coauthored, and edited books, and over one hundred articles and book chapters on public policy, policy design, water policy, environmental policy, and the politics of water in the southwestern United States and the U.S.-Mexico transboundary area. She is coeditor of *Water, Place and Equity* published in 2008, and coauthored the introductory and concluding chapters. She chaired a National Research Council panel for the committee on the Human Dimensions of Climate Change in the Division of Behavioral and Social Sciences that completed its work in 2008 and issued a report entitled *Research and Networks for Decision Support in the NOAA Sectoral Applications Research Program*. She also chaired the writing committee for the Climate Change Science Program (CCSP) 5.3 report released in 2008.

Robert B. Keiter is the Wallace Stegner Distinguished Professor of Law and Director of the Wallace Stegner Center for Land, Resources, and the Environment at the University of Utah S. J. Quinney College of Law. He holds a JD degree with honors from Northwestern University and a BA with honors from Washington University. He has taught at the University of Wyoming, Boston College, and Southwestern University, and served as a Senior Fulbright Scholar at Tribhuvan University in Kathmandu, Nepal. Professor Keiter teaches natural resources law, constitutional law, administrative law, and federal courts. His books include *Keeping Faith with Nature: Ecosystems, Democracy, and America's Public Lands* (2003); *Reclaiming the Native Home of Hope: Community, Ecology, and the West* (1998); *Visions of the Grand Staircase–Escalante: Examining Utah's Newest National Monument* (1998); and *The Greater Yellowstone Ecosystem: Redefining America's Wilderness Heritage* (1991). He has also written numerous book chapters and journal articles on the public lands and natural resource law, many addressing ecological management topics. Professor Keiter's board service includes the National Parks Conservation Association, Sonoran Institute, Greater Yellowstone Coalition, Rocky Mountain Mineral

Law Foundation, University of Utah's Institute for Clean and Secure Energy, and the University of Wyoming's Ruckelshaus Institute of Environment and Natural Resources.

Alexandra B. Klass is an Associate Professor of Law at the University of Minnesota Law School. She teaches and writes in the areas of natural resources law, environmental law, tort law, and property law. Her scholarly work includes publications in *William and Mary Law Review, Minnesota Law Review, Iowa Law Review, University of Colorado Law Review, Notre Dame Law Review, Wake Forest Law Review,* and *Ecology Law Quarterly.* Her recent scholarship includes a focus on the continuing role of state common law in today's federal regulatory state and an analysis of property rights and tort liability associated with the use of carbon capture and sequestration technology as a means to combat climate change. Prior to her teaching career, Professor Klass was a Partner at Dorsey and Whitney LLP in Minneapolis, where she specialized in litigating environmental law, natural resources law, and land use cases. She continues to represent clients *pro bono* in cases involving environmental law and land use matters. Professor Klass received her BA degree from the University of Michigan in 1988, and her JD from the University of Wisconsin Law School in 1992, where she was an articles editor for the *Wisconsin Law Review* and a member of the Order of the Coif. She clerked for the Honorable Barbara B. Crabb, Chief Judge of the U.S. District Court for the Western District of Wisconsin from 1992 to 1993. Professor Klass is a Member Scholar at the Center for Progressive Reform, http://www.progressivereform .org/.

Sarah Krakoff, of the University of Colorado Law School, is the coauthor of *American Indian Law: Cases and Commentary* (2008) (with Bob Anderson, Bethany Berger, and Phil Frickey) and is widely published in the areas of American Indian law and natural resources law. Her article examining the effects of federal law on the Navajo Nation's exercise of sovereignty, "A Narrative of Sovereignty: Illuminating the Paradox of the Domestic Dependent Nation" (*Oregon Law Review*) received the Jules Millstein Faculty Writing Award at the University of Colorado Law School in 2006. Professor Krakoff has also written about environmental ethics, public lands, and global warming. When Professor Krakoff first came to the Law School, she was the Director of the American Indian Law Clinic, supervising students in a range of federal Indian and tribal law matters. She succeeded in securing permanent University funding for the Clinic before moving to nonclinical teaching in 1999. Before coming to Colorado, Professor Krakoff was awarded an Equal Justice Works Fellowship to work on the Navajo Nation as Director of the Youth Law Project for DNA-People's Legal Services. Professor Krakoff clerked on the Ninth Circuit Court of Appeals for Judge Warren J. Ferguson from 1992 to 1993. She received her JD from Boalt Hall, University of California–Berkeley in 1991 and her BA from Yale University in 1986.

John D. Leshy is the Harry D. Sunderland Distinguished Professor of Real Property Law at the University of California, Hastings College of the Law in San Francisco, where he teaches property, constitutional law, various natural resources courses, and American Indian law. Previously he was Solicitor (General Counsel) of the Department of the Interior throughout the Clinton administration, special counsel to the Chair of the House Natural Resources Committee, a law professor at Arizona State University, Associate Solicitor of the Department of the Interior for Energy and Resources in the Carter administration, with the Natural Resources Defense Council (NRDC) in California, and a litigator in the Civil Rights Division of the Department of Justice in Washington, D.C. He chaired and co-chaired, respectively, the Interior Department transition team for the Clinton-Gore and Obama-Biden administrations. Leshy has published widely on public lands, water, and other natural resources issues, and on constitutional and comparative law, including books on the Mining Law of 1872 and the Arizona Constitution. He is coauthor of *Federal Public Land and Resources Law* (2007), currently in its sixth edition, and of *Legal Control of Water Resources* (2006), now in its fourth edition. He has litigated cases in state and federal courts, served on numerous commissions and boards, and since 2002 has been President and then Vice-Chair of the board of the Wyss Foundation, which supports land conservation in the intermountain West. He is currently on the Board of the Grand Canyon Trust and the Natural Heritage Institute, and has thrice been a visiting professor at Harvard Law School, from which he graduated in 1969 after earning an AB at Harvard College in 1966.

James R. May is a Professor of Law and Adjunct Professor of Graduate Engineering at the Widener University School of Law. Professor May teaches and publishes in constitutional, environmental, natural resources, hazardous substances, administrative, civil procedure, international environmental, environmental justice, hazardous wastes and substances, and engineering law. He directed the law school's Environmental and Natural Resources Law Clinic from 1992 to 2004. Professor May is also the founder and codirector of the law school's Master's of Marine Policy program, a joint program with the University of Delaware. Prior to law, he served as a Q clearance engineer on national defense projects. Professor May is the founder, past Executive Director, and President of the Mid-Atlantic Environmental Law Center, and cofounder and past codirector of the Eastern Environmental Law Center. Professor May was the founding chair of the ABA Section of Environment, Energy, and Resources Task Force on Constitutional Law, and was the Chair of the section's 38th Annual Conference on Environmental Law in March 2009. He has served as the Director of the Widener Institute at the MacQuarie University Environmental Law Centre in Sydney, Australia; Visiting Associate Director of the Institute for Public Representation and Visiting Professor at Georgetown University Law Center; summer faculty at Vermont Law School; and Visiting Fellow at the Environmental Law Institute. He has taught International Environmental Law in Sydney (four times) and Nairobi, Kenya. He earned his BS in Mechanical Engineering and his JD from the University of Kansas and his LLM from Pace University School of Law, where he was the Feldshuh Environmental Fellow.

James Rasband is Hugh W. Colton Professor of Law at Brigham Young University. Rasband teaches courses in public lands and natural resources law, water law, torts, and international environmental law. Prior to entering law teaching, he served as a law clerk to Judge J. Clifford Wallace of the U.S. Court of Appeals for the Ninth Circuit and practiced law at the Perkins Coie law firm in Seattle, Washington, where his practice focused on American Indian treaty litigation. Rasband has published extensively on public lands and natural resources law topics, with a particular focus on the public trust doctrine, the Antiquities Act, and wilderness issues. Along with Mark Squillace and Jim Salzman, he is the author of *Natural Resources Law and Policy* published by Foundation Press (2nd ed. 2009). Rasband is a graduate of Brigham Young University (BA, 1986) and Harvard Law School (JD, 1989), where he was also an editor of the *Harvard Law Review*.

Leigh Raymond is an Associate Professor of Political Science at Purdue University and is Associate Director of the Purdue Climate Change Research Center. Raymond's research and teaching focuses on the role of normative ideas in environmental policy, including work on market-based policies and endangered species protection on private lands. He is the author of *Private Rights in Public Resources* (RFF Press, 2003) and coauthor of *Buying Nature* (MIT Press, 2005). He has also published scholarly articles in a wide range of disciplinary journals including *Polity, Natural Resources Journal, Society and Natural Resources,* and *Science*.

William H. Rodgers, Jr. began teaching at the University of Washington School of Law in 1967, then spent seven years at Georgetown University Law School. In 1979, he returned to the University of Washington where he continues to teach today. Professor Rodgers specializes in natural resource law and is recognized as a founder of environmental law. He teaches environmental law and oceans and coastal law. Professor Rodgers is actively involved in the Berman Environmental Law Clinic. He has produced the first volume of his two-volume treatise entitled *Environmental Law in Indian Country* (Thomson West, 2005) and coauthored the recently published *The Si'lailo Way: Salmon, Indians and Law on the Columbia River* (Carolina Academic Press, 2006). He has been actively involved in the Exxon Valdez "reopener," including publishing "The Exxon Valdez Reopener: Natural Resource Damage Settlements, and Roads Not Taken" in the *Alaska Law Review*. The topics of his seminars have included Puget Sound, the

Duwamish River, Hanford, sacred Native American sites, and forest practices. Professor Rodgers was selected as the UW recipient of the Bloedel Professorship of Law from 1987 to 1992. In 1999, he was selected as the first University of Washington Stimson Bullitt Professor of Environmental Law and is serving his second five-year appointment.

J. B. Ruhl is the Matthews and Hawkins Professor of Property at Florida State University College of Law, where he teaches courses on environmental law, land use, and property. Professor Ruhl is a nationally regarded expert in the fields of endangered species protection, regulation of wetlands, ecosystem management, environmental impact analysis, and related environmental and natural resources fields. His extensive publications in these fields include recent articles in the *Stanford Law Review, Georgetown Law Review, Minnesota Law Review, Washington University Law Review,* and *Ecology Law Quarterly.* He is also coauthor of the recently published casebook, *The Law of Biodiversity and Ecosystem Management* (Foundation Press, 2nd ed. 2006), which is the first casebook to organize environmental law under these emerging themes, and *The Law and Policy of Ecosystem Services* (Island Press 2007), the first book-length treatment exploring the integration of ecosystem services into law and policy. Prior to entering full-time law teaching, Professor Ruhl was a partner in the law firm of Fulbright and Jaworski, LLP, practicing environmental and natural resources law in the firm's Austin, Texas office. He has also been a visiting professor at Harvard Law School and George Washington University Law School. Professor Ruhl received his BA (1979) and JD (1982) degrees from the University of Virginia, his LLM (1986) in environmental law from George Washington University, and his PhD (2006) in Geography from Southern Illinois University.

Mark Squillace is the Director of the Natural Resources Law Center and Professor at the University of Colorado Law School, teaching environmental law, water law, and advanced natural resources law. Before coming to Colorado, Professor Squillace taught at the University of Toledo College of Law where he was the Charles Fornoff Professor of Law and Values, and at the University of Wyoming College of Law where he served a three-year term as the Winston S. Howard

Professor of Law. In 2000, Professor Squillace took a leave from law teaching to serve as Special Assistant to the Solicitor at the U.S. Department of the Interior. In that capacity he worked directly with the Secretary of the Interior, Bruce Babbitt, on a variety of legal and policy issues. Professor Squillace also was former Director of Litigation for the Environmental Policy Institute in Washington, D.C., and for three years was Attorney Advisor for the Office of the Solicitor, U.S. Department of the Interior. He is a former Fulbright scholar and the author or coauthor of numerous articles and books on natural resources and environmental law including (with J. Rasband and J. Salzman), *Natural Resources Law and Policy* (2nd ed. 2008).

A. Dan Tarlock is a Distinguished Professor of Law at the Chicago-Kent College of Law and an Honorary Professor of Law at the UNESCO Centre for Water Law, Policy, and Science at the University of Dundee, Scotland. His teaching and research interests include land use controls, natural resources, international environmental law, and water law. He holds an AB and LLB from Stanford University and has previously been a permanent member of the faculties of the University of Kentucky and Indiana University, Bloomington. He has also visited at several law schools including the universities of Chicago, Pennsylvania, Hawaii, Kansas, Michigan, and Utah. He is the author of numerous articles and books on environmental law, land use controls and water law including *Environmental Protection: Law and Policy* (Aspen Publishing, 3rd ed. 2007) with W. Buzbee, R. Glicksman, D. Markell, and D. R. Mandelker; *Water Resources Management* (6th ed. 2009) with J. Corbridge, D. Getches, and R. Benson; and *Law of Water Rights and Resources* (1988 with annual updates). Professor Tarlock is a National Associate of the National Academies of Science and Engineering and has served on several National Research Council/National Academy of Sciences committees studying the protection and recovery of stressed aquatic ecosystems, including a ten-year review of the operation of the Glen Canyon Dam on the Colorado River and a study of the restoration of the Missouri River ecosystem, published as *The Missouri River Ecosystem: Exploring the Prospects for Recovery* (2002). From 2001 to 2004 he was a member of an NRC/NAS committee to assess the future of the U.S. Army

Corps of Engineers and contributor to the synthesis report, *U.S. Army Corps of Engineers Water Resources Planning: A New Opportunity for Service* (2004). In 1998, he was the chief writer for the Western Water Policy Review Advisory Commission report, *Water in the West*, which was one of the first major federal publications to examine the relationship between urban growth and water use. He is a special legal advisor to the Submissions Unit of the Commission on Environmental Cooperation in Montreal, Canada, which administers the NAFTA Environmental Side Agreement. He has lectured on the problems of ecosystem, natural resources, and river basin management in Austria, Australia, Brazil, Canada, China, Germany, Israel, Italy, Kazakhstan, Kyrgyzstan, the Netherlands, and Scotland as well as throughout the United States.

Introduction

When the renowned lawyer and former Interior Solicitor Clyde Martz was asked to teach a course on natural resources law at the University of Colorado Law School in 1947, the field was not even known as a discrete discipline. Undaunted, the newly appointed Professor Martz, fresh out of Harvard Law School, embraced the pedagogical challenge with the zeal that characterized his entire career. Soon thereafter, in 1951, Professor Martz published the first natural resources law casebook.

Today, less than 60 years later, in no small part because of Clyde Martz, natural resources law has emerged as a dynamic and challenging field with a rich and colorful history reaching back to the beginning of our nation. For those of us who work in the field, understanding the history of our land, water, and mineral resources informs our practice and enriches our appreciation of the challenges that still lie ahead.

In *The Evolution of Natural Resources Law and Policy*, leading scholars in the field use their considerable expertise to reflect on the past as a guide for the future. This book has two parts. The seven chapters that comprise part I are foundational. Chapter 1 begins with a historical tour through federal land policy as a prelude to describing three very different views of our natural resources future. Helen Ingram's "incremental vision" sees the future as evolving slowly from past policy. Leigh Raymond optimistically anticipates a change in property rights law that restores the primacy of public rights in public lands. And Sally Fairfax's less optimistic scenario sees climate change as limiting the ability of existing resource-based institutions to cope with the inevitable challenges that lie ahead.

Sarah Krakoff picks up in chapter 2 with climate change, using the daunting ethical questions that it poses as a lens to better understand ethical perspectives on natural resource issues. In her more hopeful assessment, Krakoff sees climate change as possibly forcing our society into a "deep version of sustainability . . . that proscribes . . . us from living beyond our ecological means."

In chapter 3, Lisa Heinzerling brings classical economic theory to bear on the polar bear—a species that has become iconic in the debate over global climate change. Heinzerling shows that any classical assessment of the economic value of the polar bear as a species, including its potentially high "non-use" value, is wholly undercut by economists' penchant for discounting the present value of the loss to reflect the fact that the loss will actually occur sometime in the future. Yet as Heinzerling cogently argues, discounting undermines the fundamental, long-term goals of laws like the Endangered Species Act.

In chapter 4, Alexandra Klass uses case studies on coalbed methane development and carbon sequestration to illustrate the continuing importance of tort and property law to the field of natural resources. In the coalbed methane study, Klass focuses on the discharge of groundwater from CBM wells, and questions the ownership of the water being discharged, and the damages that might occur from unregulated discharges of groundwater onto the surface of the land. The key issues for carbon sequestration, still unresolved in many states, concern the ownership of the pore space where CO_2 gas will be stored and the liability for gas that escapes.

In chapter 5, Eric Freyfogle highlights one of the chief problems with property rights in natural resources law—that they traditionally suffer either from being too clear or too vague. Rights that are too clear are inherently inflexible, and ill-suited to accommodate changing realities from events like climate change and population growth. They may also prove inadequate to reflect the public nature of certain property like water. Rights that are vague suffer from uncertainty, which makes it difficult for private actors to rely on them. Freyfogle also helps us understand how traditional mechanisms for resolving property rights disputes—especially litigation—are simply not adequate to address landscape-level resource issues and problems. He asks that we consider new mechanisms that are better suited to addressing modern notions of property.

In chapter 6, Jim May surveys the myriad problems that arise under the U.S. Constitution in natural resources law. Chief among these is the commerce clause—in both its active and dormant contexts—and the takings clause, which may limit federal power, and which, in the natural resources context, has special resonance for regulatory decisions.

In chapter 7, Rob Fischman examines the important role of federalism in the evolution of natural resources law. Fischman is particularly interested in statutory savings clauses and the varied approaches they take in sorting out the state/federal balance. Fischman concludes with a discussion of natural resources federalism that harkens back to the divergent views of the future set out in chapter 1. Fischman suggests that federalism might either take an incremental approach, which he labels as uniformitarian, or a less desirable approach, which he calls catastrophism. Like Fairfax, Fischman sees climate change as the most likely reason for catastrophic change. In the end, however, he sees money—more specifically, financial aid from the federal government to the states—as the driver for addressing future federalism issues.

In part II of the book, the foundational analyses give way to a review of thematic issues in natural resources law and policy. With chapter 8, Mark Squillace nicely bridges the two parts of the book with a discussion of natural resources decision-making processes. His goals are to explain those public processes used by the natural resource agencies to promote meaningful engagement between the public and decision makers, and to urge agencies to recognize and avoid processes that fail to achieve this important goal.

In chapter 9, James Rasband reminds us of the important role that names and labels play in public land use planning. The simple process of labeling lands as primitive, wilderness, multiple use, or recreational, influences not only the management policy for those lands, but also the public's perception of the lands and how they should be managed.

The protection of special places is the subject of chapter 10. Bob Keiter shows us how the debate over protection has evolved from a focus on enclaves like parks and refuges, to the "gathering consensus" that protected areas must encompass large landscapes and ecosystems. Inevitably land development and settlements already encroach upon these landscapes, and Keiter points the way to possibly "stitch[ing] the fragmented landscape together" through creative legislative initiatives and partnerships with state and local communities.

Bill Rodgers' exposition in chapter 11 of the discouraging lack of progress on the removal of the Elwha Dam is a case study in the perils of relying on nice-sounding ideas like adaptive management without insisting on firm commitments and decisive action. Especially compelling is Rodgers' critique of the funding of dam removal. He describes the removal of the Elwha dams as a "public-private partnership" where the "public assumes all risks and costs while private entities enjoy all profits and benefits." Rodgers advocates a Superfund-like model where the owner-operator of the dams pays for the cost of removal and restoration.

In chapter 12, J. B. Ruhl explores the sometimes divergent paths offered by endangered species protection under the Endangered Species Act, biodiversity conservation, and ecosystem management. Ruhl observes that while all three approaches have merit, only endangered species protection is supported by "hard law." Moreover, the "species-specific" approach of the ESA limits our ability to achieve the broader aims of ecosystem conservation. Still, he sees hope from the innovative approaches that have been taken under the ESA for more direct involvement by states and local governments in landscape-level initiatives.

Two of the most eminent scholars of water law, David Getches and Dan Tarlock, explore the "new realities" of western water law in chapter 13. While they lament the inflexible hold that the prior appropriation doctrine retains on the law, they nonetheless see the possibility that pragmatism and adaptive approaches may yet yield the water needed for changing consumptive and environmental needs.

The future of mineral development—especially on our public lands—is the focus of former Interior Solicitor John Leshy in chapter 14. Leshy describes a complex global market for minerals as the chief driver of modern federal mineral policy. While domestic supplies of oil and gas will never be sufficient to satisfy U.S. demand, reliance on foreign supplies is increasingly unrealistic, thus ensuring continuing pressure on domestic resources. And despite carbon pollution, demand for abundant domestic coal supplies will remain high for the foreseeable future.

Finally, in chapter 15, Federico Cheever offers a fitting close, by weaving together ideas from the earlier chapters in the course of describing forests and grasslands management. He does this by breaking the history of forest management into four phases. The first phase lasted through most of the nineteenth century and was dominated by privatization of forest lands. The second phase was characterized by the establishment of public reserves, beginning with the Yellowstone Park Act in 1872, and extending through the creation of vast forest reserves during the Teddy Roosevelt and Gifford Pinchot era. The second phase, as Cheever reminds us, was not about preservation of lands, but rather about using timber and other resources efficiently for the greatest good for the greatest number of people. The third phase, beginning in the early 1960s brought the environment and recreation into clearer focus. The current fourth phase is dominated by global issues, especially climate change, biodiversity conservation, and global demand for resources. Effectively coping with these issues will certainly require new legislation, but Cheever argues that meanwhile, much could be accomplished by reinvigorating the National Environmental Policy Act and restoring it to a prominent role in natural resource decision-making.

Beyond the tour that it offers through natural resources law and policy, *The Evolution of Natural Resources Law and Policy* includes various sidebars that deepen the reader's understanding of the issues and enhance the book's value as a teaching tool. Whatever your knowledge of natural resources policy, this book challenges you to think about our past and imagine a better future. One could scarcely ask more from any book about resource policy.

Bruce Babbitt
Washington, D.C., 2009

I

---

*Reflections on
Natural Resources
Law and Policy*

1

Historical Evolution and Future of Natural Resources Law and Policy

Sally Fairfax, Helen Ingram, and Leigh Raymond

I.   Introduction

The last time we gathered in Boulder to discuss the future of natural resources law and policy, the spot we now fill in this text was occupied by George Coggins and Clyde Martz. They talked about winners and losers, and it is not surprising that they did not agree. Martz lamented environmental constraints on commodity development, in what he characterized as an era of "environmental overreach," while Coggins gloated that the Reagan counter-reformation had failed.[1] Multiple use, a thin veil over the long path of commodity exploitation, was dead. The editors of the volume published afterward clearly agreed with Coggins—they appeared convinced that the "exploitation ethic" was giving way to an "ethic of sustainable use."[2] They concluded that conservation management of natural resources would benefit from the comprehensive approach called "integrated resources planning."[3]

Our analysis is different, concerned less about who wins and who loses than about who is in charge. We envision the future of natural resource law and policy in the context of Americans' evolving understanding of government. Our discussion emphasizes two concepts that have long been driving that evolution: science as a source of legitimacy for the growth of a centralized bureaucracy, and Americans' understanding of property and ownership. We draw a trajectory, mercifully brief, from the last 225 years and then use the patterns of that trajectory to suggest three paths of future evolution. We conclude with three sets of predictions for the future, ranging from the nearly utopian to the nearly apocalyptic.

We acknowledge one obvious weakness of our paper from the outset: when Clyde and George spoke at the Boulder meeting it was still conceivable to talk about natural resource law and policy as if it were a domestic issue. Clearly if such American exceptionalism were ever justifiable, it is no longer. But having tried to address that issue within the space limits assigned us, we better understand why their focus was purely domestic. We will try to avoid a too narrow perspective by referring occasionally to global trade and markets, transnational corporations, the WTO, and global environmental governance.

II.   The Trajectory Thus Far in Six Eras

A. The First Hundred Years

One important point from the first hundred years of American history is that lack of authority is no barrier to action. The centralization of water policy began as a manifestation of our first well-organized group of scientists. Surveyors and engineers attached to the U.S. Army gained power during the buildup to the War of 1812. Although the Corps was officially authorized to facilitate military construction, both Congress and the President soon appreciated the political advantages of civil improvements. Hence, subsidies are a second and durable element of our earliest resource law and policy.

Indeed, subsidizing the allocation and development of natural resources was a major element in the early growth of the federal government. Scholars have typically analyzed these developments in terms of the land and resources of western territories during the progressive era.[4] However, water development institutions and tools emerged earlier and perhaps more interestingly in our history.

Under the Articles of Confederation the central government was, as is well known, weak. The government was specifically not authorized to own land or manage water.[5] Nevertheless, the elaboration of central authority began early: limits on its powers did not stop the Confederated Congress from taking initial steps toward establishing the public domain and the Army Corps of Engineers. A series of General Land Ordinances in 1785 and 1787 constructed the durable architecture for management of the ceded state lands and the western two-thirds of the continent that became the public domain. The legislation accomplished this by providing a number of tools: the township and range system of rectangular surveys;[6] the reservation of one-third of all the gold, silver, copper, and lead mined in the new nation,[7] interim management and political organization of future states (which were to be carved from western lands that the new confederation was not technically allowed to hold); the basic notion of "equal footing" among old and new states; and the allocation of designated sections to the support of schools.[8] Lack of authority also did not deter the Congress from establishing federal water management.

The basic authorities changed significantly under the federal constitution. Not one, but two clauses in the 1789 document affect government-owned property, and the Fifth Amendment establishes a deeply contested relationship between government and private landowners. Of water, the Constitution says nothing. Yet interstate commerce sufficed as a stand-in for navigation, of which managing water proved to be an essential part.

Article I of the Constitution recognized the federal government's power to "make all needful rules" regarding the western territories. But the federal government's role was originally understood as limited to the rights of a "mere proprietor," enhanced by the Congress's responsibility for the "primary disposal of the soil."

Congress established the Treasury Department in 1789, assigning the Secretary duties that included executing "such services relative to the sale of the lands belonging to the United States, as may be by law required of him." The federal government began rather free-handedly as primary disposer of the soil and remained that way well into the twentieth century. It tried intermittently to raise funds by selling western land or to encourage orderly development by granting land to states and/or corporations. It also tried briefly, in the upper Midwest, to lease lead mines. Robert Swenson notes that early reservation of mineral lands attempted under the Articles reflected British assumptions concerning royal mines, but that in the transition from the Confederation to the Federation, this notion "died a natural death."

What made the death seem "natural," at the time that Swenson wrote, is of supreme interest: the notion of a right of "unilateral appropriation" of public property by private entities proved unstoppable. The 1841 Preemption Act allowed settlers to gain an exclusive, noncompetitive purchase right to land on the public domain in advance of the survey by removing it from nature and, in a wonderful Lockean diorama, putting the land to beneficial use by mixing their sweat with it. The idea would morph, of course, into a full-blown right to ownership through labor under the Homestead Act twenty-one years later.

Yet government authority over private property was limited in part by the Fifth Amendment, which concludes with an odd little add-on, "Nor shall private property be taken for public use, without just compensation." In the early days of the nation, however, this Constitutional protection was far less controversial than in the modern era.

Until the late nineteenth century, the dominant Fifth Amendment issue related to the justness of compensation. It was generally true, for example, that even when the government actually seized ownership of private land and put it to a public use, as in building a road on the "back 40," compensation was neither just nor required if the value created on the remaining property exceeded the value taken. In other words, the courts weighed "givings" against takings to assess a transaction's "justness." The idea of regulatory takings, and the divisible and fragmentary bundle of ownership rights it implied, would not arrive on the scene for more than one hundred years.

On the other hand, Congress expressed a powerful and continuing interest in water issues. Although the principle of reasonable use constrained riparian right holders under state law, state water policy was overlain by early assertions of federal authority. The interstate commerce clause and the war powers established in the Constitution allowed Congress to fortify coasts, clear and improve harbors, and engage in other "civic improvements." The Corps of Engineers was active during the Revolution, and Congress re-established the Corps and a military academy at West Point in 1802.[9] Thus water management was rooted in science long before George Perkins Marsh and the Progressive era. "Until 1866, the superintendent of the academy was always an engineer officer. . . . During the first half of the 19th century, West Point was the major and for a while, the only engineering school in the country."[10] The Corps of Engineers emerged as the only formally trained body of scientists in the new republic.

As part of the nation's small army, the Corps was available to serve the wishes of Congress and the executive branch. Enthusiasm for federal subsidies was a very early pattern in natural resource law and policy: as the Corps' own official history notes, "from the beginning, many politicians wanted the Corps to contribute to both military construction and works 'of a civil nature.' "[11] The familiar elements of the Corps' current profile were carved in stone by the 1824 Supreme Court ruling in *Gibbons v. Ogden*, which clarified that federal authority over interstate commerce included riverine navigation.[12] Arthur Maas has suggested that it is not always clear that the centralized authorities were serving national needs: state and local governments and diverse beneficiaries have long exhibited agility in deflecting federal programs to local priorities.[13] Nonetheless, the centralization of government authority through concentrated scientific expertise and subsidies began early in water.

B. After the Civil War: Industrialization, Western Expansion, and the Rise of the Corporation

After the Civil War, expectations about government changed dramatically. Rapid industrialization, economic growth, and the development of new, nation-spanning corporations pushed government in new directions. Americans' points of reference for life changed radically. Robert Wiebe has described the "nationalization, industrialization, mechanization, [and] urbanization," of the post–Civil War era in terms of pressure on the network of isolated "island communities" that comprised the United States before the War.[14] The new complexities disrupted the values of small-town community life for most Americans: "the network of relations affecting men's lives each year became more tangled and more distended."[15] Increasingly well-organized and diverse private interests lobbied Congress for programs that would meet their priorities. The lobbyists included both corporations seeking subsidies and citizens concerned with the rapid and sometimes wasteful exploitation of the nation's natural resources. Frequently the two overlapped: for example, those hoping to profit from increasingly subsidized federal irrigation projects[16] were also among the most vocal advocates of federal forest protection. Similarly, railroads seeking customers were equally effective in supporting and frequently managing national parks.

As the nineteenth century closed, an expansive reading of the ambiguous Article I property clause combined with the federal government's equally ambiguous Article IV power of "exclusive legislation" over forts, arsenals, and similar acquired land enabled the federal government to increase its control over its remaining western lands. Expanding and increasingly assertive federal land management agencies transformed the government from a mere proprietor of the public domain, first to a "proprietor plus" and ultimately to a sovereign in a series of court cases.[17] Parks, forests, and national monuments are among the most familiar manifestations of the central government's emerging willingness to reserve, retain, and manage large portions of the western landscape. Acquisition of land by the federal government for similar purposes was soon to follow.[18]

C. The Progressive Era

The standard story of the Progressive era is that it was a time of enlightened conservationists who fought for and won the right to retain and protect the public lands for the benefit of future generations. Our vision of this period is quite different: even as land disposition continued and intensified, "public ownership" of land became more acceptable as complex new tenure arrangements on public land and water multiplied.[19] The federal government's right to condemn land outside of the territories or the federal district was finally recognized in connection with Civil War battlefields in the late nineteenth century.

But reserved and newly acquired "public" lands were not always clearly under federal control. Many lands reserved as national forests were nominally owned by the government but effectively controlled by local livestock interests. In addition, such lands were subject to mineral locations under the 1872 General Mining Act. Other properties were more clearly controlled by the government, including some parks, but the resources were developed and marketed by private corporations. Other resources were reserved and then released, like Powell's cherished reclamation reserves. Thus, we see an enormous complexity in federal ownership and control over land emerging from the nineteenth-century forces of the Gilded Age during the Progressive era.

The status of federal interests in water was made substantially more complex. Federal subsidies regarding water development and irrigation took on new contours with the passage of the Reclamation Act. Federal authority was confused, however, by consistent flouting of the terms of the act. Moreover, the federal government appeared to have ceded authority to allocate water to the states. The apparent severance of the federal landowner's riparian water rights from the public domain lands made room for the ascendancy of state-administered prior appropriation systems in most western jurisdictions.[20] But the severance pattern is not clear.

Ironically, shortly after the federal government apparently divested itself of its riparian water rights, and as the *Lochner*-era courts stemmed the rising tide of unscientific social regulation, the courts also thwarted the corporate grasp of the Chicago waterfront and invented a federal quasi-appropriative water right to bolster federal land reservations for Native Americans. In *Illinois Central Railroad v. Illinois*, the Supreme Court held that the state legislature had a public trust concerning water and could not simply relinquish its responsibility to facilitate the wishes of industry.[21] In *Winters v. United States*, the Court held that federal authority over land, still shaky pending the 1911 decisions in *Light v. United States* and *United States v. Grimaud*, was sufficient to trump state appropriative law.[22]

Supporting this pastiche of new doctrine on both land and water was a deeply fragmented notion of property, elaborated from its Lockean roots to permit both federal landownership and corporate expansion. Government land retention in particular was underwritten by a new understanding of property that emerged along with the idea of a corporation. Where earlier the owner of a piece of property was generally considered to have something close to full control over its revenue and use, modern corporations—evolving particularly in the context of the railroads—pushed the law to recognize the growing division of labor between owners (the shareholders), who held the right to a company's revenue, and managers, who exercised primary control over the daily operation of the company. Supreme Court decisions giving private entrepreneurs something close to ownership of a particular legal environment considerably expanded the scope of private property beyond land and material goods.[23] To be sure, populist and progressive reformers contested many of these changes.[24] But the shifts in the legal notion of ownership were dramatic.

D. The Depression

The Progressive era's centralization and faith in scientific expertise peaked in the Depression, when the federal government began playing a more prominent role in natural resource planning. Although the Civilian Conservation Corps is frequently the referent here, the agricultural relief programs perhaps best mark the apex of federal power over land, water, and natural resources. This extreme expansion of federal authority was manifest in a new understanding of property: the government had the right, indeed the obligation, to adjust ownership patterns that were not socially and economically optimal. Federal power was used to create the Tennessee Valley Authority as a federal corporation, and while the form has not been copied, the idea persists today that river basin organizations should be an organizing concept that is layered over federal agencies' jurisdictions, states, and localities. At the other end of the planning spectrum, the Soil Conservation Service, a new agency established by President Franklin Roosevelt, launched a lasting program in watershed management that was often conflicting with other federal agencies and river basin planning.[25]

But even at the height of the New Deal, Progressive-era ideas were an overlay on our Lockean property tradition rather than a displacement of earlier understandings. For example, under the 1934 Taylor Grazing Act, the new Division of Grazing (soon renamed the Grazing Service) recognized the Lockean claims of historic range users when allocating access to the public grazing districts. The Division of Grazing rejected the Progressive ideal of distant, scientific, federal management—pushing instead for "democracy on the range" and an active system of advisory boards composed of local range users. The Division developed convoluted notions of title to allocate ownership of range improvements, and a shared tenure arrangement between federal government and private ranchers evolved.[26]

The emphasis in federal control over land was on centralized, scientific planning. The Bureau of Land Management (née Grazing Service) and even the tourism-managing National Park Service[27] have always suffered by comparison to the nominally scientific Forest Service. The science was not always apolitical, however. The Forest Service built its reputation largely on its success in suppressing fires, a practice that was recognized early on as inappropriate in many ecosystems.[28]

In the natural resources field, the momentum of centralized government science lasted through the first heady days of the 1970s when environmentalists followed the established path to Washington to address the growing concerns with air and water quality. But simultaneously, the environmentalists challenged government science in an early assault on federal land management: the clearcutting controversy.

E. 1970s: The Environmental Decade

The spectacular outpouring of environmental regulation at the federal level in the 1970s began with familiar conservation advocacy for protection of federally owned lands. But for the first time, a major goal of advocates was to include protecting lands from the federal scientists who managed them. The clearcutting controversy, culminating in the Monongahela case,[29] capped several decades of wilderness enthusiasts' efforts to put some areas of national forests beyond the reach of federal timber harvests. Similarly the National Trails System Act and the Wild and Scenic Rivers Act, both passed in 1968, continued what was effectively zoning on federal lands, with some small incursions onto private parcels as well.

But the real meat and potatoes of the era were statutes aimed not at commodities as traditionally defined but at "the environment"— air and water primarily, but also wildlife habitat and the threat of extinction. The vision of nature had shifted, as well, following *Silent Spring*—and Rachel Carson's depiction of the earth not as something to be conquered, à la Sir Edmund Hillary, but as a fragile spaceship requiring protection from humans' knowing and unknowing interventions.

With astonishing speed, the federal government passed one major statute after another in the post–Earth Day fervor, dramatically enhancing central authority over many aspects of our lives. Suddenly, scientific experts at the newly constituted Environmental Protection Agency were charged with setting acceptable levels of air and water pollution without regard to cost or industry concern. Progressive-era activists such as Gifford Pinchot would surely have been envious.

Yet simultaneously, the public lands agencies found themselves newly embroiled in public controversy and litigation. The National Environmental Policy Act, the National Forest Management Act, and the Federal Land Policy and Management Act exposed federal scientific agencies to intense public scrutiny and bogged down management in layers of contested planning processes. Thus, natural resource agencies were at the forefront of public advocates' efforts to erode the basis of federal authority. Centralized scientific bureaucracy gave way to a more participatory approach.[30] Even the newly minted EPA was soon subject to the same suspicious treatment, particularly during the administration of President Ronald Reagan.

Greater public access and local input cut both ways, however, as the Wise Use movement and the Sagebrush Rebellion followed quickly on the heels of the environmentalists' quest for greater access to federal decision making.[31] Yet another effort to give the federal lands "back" to the states flowered, requiring environmentalists to mount a surprising defense of federal land managers. The strength of local interests became even clearer when Jimmy Carter announced that he was cutting funding for eighteen ongoing water projects serving various state and local constituencies in the west. Even though seventy-four members of Congress had earlier expressed support for reform of water resources programs, the congressional reaction to the "hit list" was overwhelmingly negative. After a great deal of rancor, Carter eventually agreed to restore funding for half of the projects on the original list.

At the same time, the iron triangles of traditional politics—public agencies, local constituencies, and congressional committees whose members received water projects and other federal subsidies in their districts—witnessed significant change beginning to unfold. More arduous economic and environmental reviews were instituted, and a precedent of "no new starts" of additional water projects was established in 1981, although the Corps did continue to get money for "preauthorization studies."[32] The tougher standards of evaluation, along with the fact that most good dam sites had already been used, compelled many to believe that the era of big dams was over. Meanwhile somewhat lost in all this familiar rhetoric—central versus local, protect versus develop, and the more modern juxtaposition of "welfare cowboys" vs. "tree huggers"—were the beginnings of new complexities in the debate and on the land.

F. The Reagan Revolution

Reagan and his successors made room for markets in natural resource management, in part by presiding over a serious erosion of confidence in government control. While Reagan failed to dismantle the federal regulatory infrastructure of the 1970s, he was effective in undermining its credibility. The Democratic Congress and the environmentalist public spent much of the 1980s struggling to force government agencies to implement the laws passed in the previous decade. Meanwhile, the Spotted Owl dispute in the Pacific Northwest symbolized a growing belief that no matter what side you were on, something had gone seriously wrong with federal land management. The tuna–porpoise debates suggested, moreover, that perhaps it did not matter what Congress said in the face of ascendant global institutions like the World Trade Organization (WTO).

Not helping matters any was a growing sense of concern over whether federal scientists were really as nonpartisan or as competent as everyone had hoped. Critics of the public land agencies increasingly wondered if the federal scientists had the right ideas on basic issues from fire management to species conservation to pesticide use. Ever more prominent and more intense conflicts over good versus "junk" science helped to weaken public faith in scientific experts at all levels of government.

Thus, the 1970s legislation that brought comprehensive planning to the federal lands slouched in the 1990s through a series of slogans to become "ecosystem management." The terminological cosmetics briefly offered a way forward, but then ran aground on irreconcilable conflicts over such unscientific issues as the "desired future condition," as well as downsizing, inadequate funding of planned activities, and outsourcing basic management functions to the private sector.

G. Market-Based Resource and Land Management

Soon a large part of the conversation moved away from federal abuses on public lands to the topic of government abuses on any lands, public or private, and the need for better compensation for losses of private land value due to environmental regulations. Encouraged by a series of modest Fifth Amendment victories culminating in the 1992 decision in *Lucas v. South Carolina Coastal Council*, property rights advocates pushed for additional regulatory relief, and market-based alternatives to conservation were increasingly being promoted by free-market thinkers of the period.[33]

Into this breach stepped alternative agents of conservation pushing a market-based approach. Land trusts expanded rapidly, offering an ostensibly "private" path to conserving land while holding the government at arm's length (or at least hidden behind the green curtain). The land trusts' success appeared effective in responding to the increasingly successful property rights movement. Transactions that were nominally voluntary, compensated, and private helped to respond to growing criticism of government regulation. More generally, land trusts also appeared to offer ways to discourage regulators from enforcing environmental laws, turning even basic regulatory issues into opportunities for compensation to landowners.

Other market-oriented conservation efforts continued to expand: as a result, environmental groups now pay ranchers for livestock killed by endangered wolves, for example, and even try to bid on grazing permits and timber sales as conservation buyers. The agencies have also gotten on the market bandwagon, albeit haltingly, by charging greater fees for recreation users and by buying and selling lands to consolidate federal holdings while facilitating private development in rapidly growing areas, such as Las Vegas, that are hemmed in by federal lands. None of these efforts are without controversy, and the land consolidation program has been hampered by incompetence and chicanery in the land assessment process.[34]

Despite the outcry, bringing market incentives to bear on managing public lands did not effect a dramatic departure from public regulation or federal authority over the public estate. Attempts to move the federal lands to the states following the 1994 "Gingrich Revolution" in Congress went nowhere, as usual, and federal acquisition continued apace. Rumors of the demise of public regulation over private land were, as the saying goes, exaggerated.

Nevertheless, growing official reluctance to use the full force of regulation, especially on private lands, was increasingly evident, and the search intensified for more collaborative, and creative, alternatives to increasingly intractable conflicts.

H. A Mosaic of Actors Managing Land and Making Policy

The final piece of the trajectory, as our story nears the present, is characterized by its complexity. Hundreds of local groups organized around watersheds have tried, with uneven success, to manage their mixtures of federal and/or private lands better than commodity users or federal managers could do alone. Some have firmly excluded the feds from the process (e.g., the Quincy Library Group), while others have included them closely (the Land Trust Alliance), but they are all searching for more collaborative, less confrontational ways to manage natural resources that span various institutional boundaries. Meanwhile, new "virtual parks"—the Cosumnes River Preserve and the Blackfoot Challenge, to say nothing of Washington's home at Mount Vernon—are made up of public and private lands, using conservation easements and other tricks of the land trust movement to achieve conservation and recreation objectives in a less heavy-handed (and more economical) manner. Despite the best efforts of conservative politicians and their allies, there has been no swing back to a happier time of private rights ascendant. There has been instead a profusion of actors, arrangements, and institutions resulting in growing mosaics of conservation and use on the ground.

Water resources provide a good example of change toward the use of markets and market-like incentives in water management and illustrate the continuity of the federal role, newly cast as preventing Katrina-like flooding and promoting expensive environmental restoration and adaptive management projects. The mixture of old and new is nicely reflected in the movement of water from farms to cities through long-term leases and sales.

While today water is moved through market-like exchanges rather than through newly built projects, the parties are not individual buyers and sellers, but rather government entities such as cities, states, and irrigation districts. Large-scale regional programs involving multilevel governmental actors and nongovernmental organizations exist in a number of regions, including the California Bay Delta (CALFED), the Everglades, and the Chesapeake Bay. Regional governing arrangements have strongly institutionalized public participation and include environmental NGOs among their many partners. They embrace a new language of sustainability and even take into account climate change in their planning efforts. They have independent scientific advisory boards that are empowered to give public advice. At the same time, driven by fears of long-term drought and growing demand for water fueled by population growth in cities, new dams are the subject of serious discussions. In California, billions have been slated to bail out delta farmers and cities even though many of the levees to be fixed are privately owned.

Federal regulatory programs such the Endangered Species Act (ESA) continue to give the federal government considerable influence over water management, but the power is being exercised in far more collaborative and less intrusive ways. One example is the Environmental Water Account operating within CALFED. Under this program fish agencies acquire water reserves through markets, and they can release such water so as to avoid conditions with salmon or smelt that could trigger the ESA. Therefore, water contractors, cities, and agricultural districts are untroubled by surprises that would interrupt the reliability of water supplies or impose additional costs.[35]

III. Where Does Our Trajectory Take Us? The Next 50 Years

A. Review: So Where Are We Now, Approximately?

The federal role in natural resources law and policy has become increasingly complex. Our initial Lockean notions of property and limited government led to an early emphasis on market-based private disposition of land—but with public subsidies and government investment for water. Eventually, the need to suppress Native Americans and permit settlers and corporations to expand westward required a more active federal approach to land use. Scientific management gave this new assertion of authority political legitimacy.

Even at its apex, however, government authority over both land and water remained incomplete. The last gasp of federal command and control legislation passed in the 1970s was qualified by greater demands for public access and the shift in science from a government-dominated activity to competitive blood sport. Now, although markets and private rights seem to dominate, the current policy arena is actually a mix of public and private institutional arrangements that has become breathtakingly complex.

It is important to remember that some things never change: the quest for private profit from public resources, and reliance on the basic government tool of subsidies, either in the form of giveaways or regulations that burden the opposition.

Clearly the days are gone when scientists could promise simple answers to complex questions. The realities of disequilibrium ecology exacerbated by the uncertainties of climate change render all but the grossest observations of science—the earth is warming—too easily subject to strategically cultivated doubt to support management decisions.

But science is also perceived differently: Scientific management of natural resources, as practiced by natural resources agencies from the Progressive era—or a century earlier, if you look at the Army Corps of Engineers and water—until the close of the twentieth century, is a thing of the past. Science is now recognized as plural, uncertain, and branded by the contexts in which it is produced. For these and other reasons, centralized, bureaucratic dominance of decision making on the basis of privileged knowledge is no longer viable. Even so, the influence of science in decisions is likely to grow rather than wither away in our increasingly information-driven society. The need to find a scientific basis for all regulatory action has motivated the government to submit many of its scientific findings to reviews by ostensibly independent advisory bodies and to the National Academy of Sciences. Even the most emotion-laden of motivations, such as saving the planet, must be rationalized on the basis of a causal logic supported in some measure by science.

Private ownership of natural resources in the United States has also always been important, and that importance shows no signs of abatement. The Sagebrush Rebellion and the Property Rights Movement demonstrate the powerful hold property rights continue to have on the American imagination. Market mechanisms based on more or less secure property rights are now engaged for a wide variety of resource conservation goals, including controlling acid rain, protecting open space, and moving water from rural to urban water users.

At the same time, market transactions proceed in the context of government regulation. The case of water is illustrative. Even though water rights in the West are mainly governed by prior appropriation that allows senior water rights holders considerable discretion in water use, there have always been restrictions, often including the ties of water to land, provisions against waste, and an implicit and sometimes explicit requirement that the state government should protect the public trust. Trust obligations to Native Americans were enshrined in reserved water rights that exist without exercise and may be asserted as prior and more senior to allocated state water rights. In addition, under the rubric of the commerce clause, from time to time the federal government has greatly constrained private owners of wetlands and required limitations upon uses that pollute. The relationship between private landowners and public regulators follows a similar pattern. The result is an ever-expanding mosaic of ownership rights over natural resources.

B. Three Visions of the Future

Having reviewed this lengthy story of where we've been, where do we think we might be headed? Rather than offering a definitive answer, we take what is perhaps the easy way out by describing three visions of the future of natural resource management. Each one draws on important themes from the history we have told, but in different ways and with different emphases. Together they run the gamut from high optimism to deep skepticism.

1. The Incremental Vision

Helen's vision of the future continues the thinking outlined above by arguing that what is to come in natural resource management is, in short, more of the same. Property and markets have been used to allow the hollowing out of government: many government programs are now implemented by private firms nominally under government contract, and the commons—public land, water, and resources—are eroding. That is not to say that they will disappear. But it is to say that complex administrative arrangements with multiple public and private actors will advance while direct federal enforcement of federal standards continues to retreat. Conflict among agencies representing different geographical jurisdictions, river basin and watershed organizations, for instance, will continue—and, without the federal government as the final word, will perhaps become more intense.

Nor will science disappear as an element of government decision making. The science wars were once thought to discredit all science. Instead, controversy has seemed to democratize science so that citizen scientists collect their own data and do their own monitoring. Favorable science is no longer a trump card, but you still have to have some to have a winning hand. Think tanks, private consultants, and environmental group scientists with an abiding interest in their own employment will continue to lobby for laws that ensure the full employment of scientists, who will be educated in universities under the growing influence of enormous corporate donations. Expertise will play a continuing but more muddled role as experiential knowledge is increasingly recognized as legitimate. Moreover, the kinds of expertise now required in water management and other natural resources management will expand to include a wider roster of disciplines, ranging from engineering to life sciences to planning.

As sea levels rise and extreme weather events become more common, there will be extreme pressure to return to the construction of dams and levees, even though most environmentalists do not consider such projects as long-term solutions. Global climate change is expected to have devastating effects on ecosystems, and programs that manage ecosystems often involve expensive re-engineering and new construction of habitats to accommodate species that are fleeing habitats no longer hospitable to them. The use of federal tax dollars for a myriad of multifaceted projects enriching many private as well as public interests will continue and perhaps expand. It seems unlikely that recently installed public participatory mechanisms will be dismantled, but the water resources community has a long history of fashioning multipurpose projects that appeal to nearly every constituency.

More generally, natural resources governance will become a network activity that associates private property owners with NGOs and governmental actors at all levels. In these cases adherence to certain core beliefs or ways of knowing about resources motivates collective behavior that transcends the narrow self-interest of various parties. The problem in the future will be to build collaborative networks that function beyond organizational boundaries to take some positive action. The politics of gridlock is not good enough in an era of climate change.

2. The Optimistic View

Changes in property rights lie at the heart of Leigh's vision. Although we have described an era of growing preference for markets and strengthening private ownership powers, we have already noted that such changes are contested and complex. Moreover, a review of the recent past suggests that the association of a defense of individual property rights with robber baron behavior, or even strong economic self-interest, is not wholly accurate. Many property owners have agreed to voluntarily limit their use of their own lands in the name of habitat protection and environmental restoration. Environmental groups have demonstrated a willingness to establish land trusts that limit private use of the land. Private property owners have waxed enthusiastic about watershed associations and other institutions in which collective decisions are made in the name of preservation or environmental restoration.

Some, indeed, have suggested that we are moving toward a more ecological view of property, one in which the provision of ecological services by private land will be seen more as a duty than a favor.[36] We are skeptical of this line of thought, however much we might like it to be. Recent research suggests a deep-rooted belief in a Lockean notion of ownership.[37] While these views are more nuanced than they appear to be in the popular media, and reflect the landowners' sense of duty as "stewards" of private land, the prospects of growing acceptance for government regulation of private property strike us as dim.

That said, an interesting alternative trend may prove important. After years of blurring the distinction between public and private property, with public lands remaining subject to multiple private claims of control, there are a few signs that the public is asserting its right of collective ownership more strongly. Interestingly, those signs are occurring primarily in other contexts, vis-à-vis resources other than public lands in the western United States.

Fifteen years ago, at the birth of the first major U.S. emissions trading program with the 1990 Clean Air Act Amendments, the idea that government would do anything besides give away new rights to public resources was virtually unthinkable. That "grand policy experiment" allocated emissions permits for sulfur dioxide to existing polluters at no cost with nary a second thought. Although some criticized this action as a handout of free wealth to corporate polluters, the notion that government might do something different was never seriously entertained.[38]

More recent experiments regarding emissions trading of carbon dioxide in Europe include for the first time a small number of experiments with auctioning allowances rather than giving them away. More auctions are expected in a second phase of this program. Policy entrepreneurs have started talking actively about a national or global commons of resources that is owned equally by citizens of a given state or the world.[39] They assert, for example, that the atmosphere is owned by all citizens, not just those who currently exercise squatter's rights over its ability to absorb carbon dioxide, and they push for new distributions of public resources that generate revenue or other benefits for all citizens. More surprisingly, governments appear to be hearing this message: public officials refer to "public assets" in the atmosphere, and carbon-trading bills considered in Congress embrace a wide range of allocation options that go far beyond any squatter's rights model.

Most important for our purposes, this line of thinking puts the "public" back in public resources of *all* types, including, at least in theory, public lands. If the Progressive era was a time when "public lands" meant resources controlled by scientific experts in the federal bureaucracy, and the 1980s was a time when "public lands" meant lands controlled by private development interests, could the first decades of the twenty-first century be a time when "public lands" means lands actually controlled by and for citizens? A potentially naive and embarrassing argument to be sure, yet one that we cannot help but offer as a possibility in light of recent events and trends.

In this regard, we see yet another in a long series of ironic turns in the relationship between property as a natural right and the management of public lands in the United States. One of the things that makes Locke's view of property so appealing to many of his supporters is its relatively absolute and unchanging nature—ownership based on labor is a power that is in some sense "prepolitical," requiring recognition and due respect by any just government. While this private Lockean property right is not absolute in some Blackstonian sense, and remains subject to some regulation by government, it clearly has some normative punch expressed in government actions that protect it from more serious forms of interference and redistribution.

More recently, in the commons movement, we see a different "intrinsic" right to natural resources emerging, one based simply on equal human rights. Following in the footsteps of nineteenth-century property theorist P. J. Proudhon, those arguing for equal shares of natural resources cite an egalitarian vision of ownership in which no persuasive argument can be made for a distribution of at least some natural resources except on the basis of our common humanity. In this sense, their rejection of an intrinsic ownership right based on labor asserts a similarly firm and unchanging normative grounding for their conception of ownership. The only difference is that the foundation has become human need instead of productive labor. The key role of ownership continues, but in yet another guise. It is far too soon to proclaim the victory of this new conception of ownership, but it has certainly emerged as a serious player in recent environmental policy disputes related to climate change, minerals, and water.

At the same time, an opposing trend is clearly emerging on public lands. Explosive growth in recreational uses of various types has led to explosive conflicts among users. Snowmobilers now argue bitterly with cross-country skiers, off-road vehicle users spar with hikers, and everyone fights with conservation biologists over who gets to use what patches of public lands when. The result has been a fragmentation of those lands, with de facto or de jure "zoning" of national forests and recreation areas for particular activities, where everyone gets their little patch of paradise (except endangered species, who often end up holding the short stick). This hardly seems egalitarian or otherwise consistent with an emerging notion of common ownership over these resources, at least at first blush. But the tension may be less severe than it appears. Rather than favoring a select few users of the public lands, agencies are now exerting more authority over their parcels in order to provide something approximating access for everyone. Few uses, it seems, are to be excluded as each constituency claims their inalienable "right" to use part of the public domain.

3. A Pessimistic Alternative

Our final perspective is decidedly less optimistic. In Sally's narrative, global climate change will impose a new priority: resources will be managed to prevent the disasters related to global climate change. Parks and forests are, for example, already rushing to justify their existence in terms of carbon sequestration. However, neither governments nor corporations will be capable of managing the diverse and intensifying disasters to come; floods, fires, rising sea levels, dramatic changes in storm patterns, and repeated Katrinas are beyond the control—but not, of course, the exploitation—of science, government, and corporations.

Adopting this new goal will further discredit political decision making, which is already under assault for incompetence, corruption, and dishonesty. The challenges posed by climate change are of such magnitude, duration, and global distribution that familiar institutions, or even improved versions thereof, will be ill-equipped to deal with them. Their credibility will be eroded by their ineffectiveness. Indeed, if you throw in a wave or two of bird flu and other apparently pending pandemics, one might wonder whether our current institutions, or any institution, could survive.

The optimists among us believe in what might be called "perfect crises"—just enough wheels come off to force reforms in resource policies that will abate the crises. But it is not easy to envision institutions that can retain legitimacy and authority in the face of repeated demonstrations of irrelevance and incompetence, Katrina being a perfect example. History, particularly in the twentieth century, does not give many examples of confidence-building responses to crises great or small.

Although depressing tales of institutional failure abound, grasping for a parallel on the scale and duration of global warming almost inevitably turns the mind to the great plagues—a bad case scenario, although not the worst, perhaps. Between 1300 and 1440, as Barbara

Tuchman has written in *A Distant Mirror*, Europe's response to the spiraling death rates was marred by pillaging mercenaries, members of odd religious cults, and a whole host of unsavory actors. In our own ostensibly rational time, odd views of the world and where it came from are already confusing our understanding of scientific theories of evolution, theories that are far better demonstrated than global warming. The plague years do make us wonder what will survive in terms of rational processes when hell breaks loose, all over again, in all different places in the globe, and established institutions are largely incapable of preventing or addressing the results. It is pure optimism to presume that science, justice, and democracy will retain their status in the public lexicon of legitimacy when under severe environmental stress in the future.

Of course, the consensus is that the long-term effect of the plagues was democratizing: labor and time were scarce and their value enhanced. One author notes that technology substituted for both, the plague years having given us crossbows, guns, clocks, eyeglasses, and a new craving for general knowledge.[40] Clearly the period was followed by the Medicis' Florence, Brunelleschi's dome, Donatello's *Mary Magdalene*, Ghiberti's *Gates of Paradise*, and the Rome of Michelangelo and Leonardo da Vinci. Surely it is worth wading through another tough century or two for a similar subsequent flowering? On the other hand, human ingenuity has made the stakes much higher this time around, and it is harder to be as optimistic that the pessimist's scenario would have such a positive ending.

IV. Closing Word

We conclude our discussion of the future by underscoring the importance of the past. Patterns of globalization, corporate dominance, and enormous shifts in management resulting from assertions of different rights in land and water are nothing new. It is worth recalling that the North American continent was "discovered" by Europeans during an era of expanding global trade. When the same Europeans later came to settle—which required the imposition of European notions of ownership—much of the process was implemented by corporations acting specifically as governments. The Massachusetts Bay Company, the Hudson's Bay Company, and the railroads all played huge roles over several centuries. So we have experience with the tigers we are now astride. The future promises to shake our laws, policies, and institutions on an unprecedented scale and time frame. The challenge is to understand the past in ways that will allow us to help one another exercise improved judgment about the future.

Notes

1.   Clyde O. Martz, *Natural Resources Law: An Historical Perspective, in* NATURAL RESOURCES POLICY AND LAW: TRENDS AND DIRECTIONS 21–48 (Lawrence J. MacDonnell & Sarah F. Bates eds., 1993); George Cameron Coggins, *Trends in Public Land Law (A Title the Inaccuracy of Which Should Become Manifest), in* NATURAL RESOURCES POLICY AND LAW, *supra,* at 49–65.

2.   Lawrence J. MacDonnell & Sarah F. Bates, *Rethinking Resources: Reflections on a New Generation of Natural Resources Policy and Law, in* NATURAL RESOURCES POLICY AND LAW, *supra* note 1, at 19.

3.   *Id.* at 18.

4.   SAMUEL P. HAYS, CONSERVATION AND THE GOSPEL OF EFFICIENCY (1959).

5.   ROBERT WIEBE, THE SEARCH FOR ORDER, 1877–1920 (1968).

6.   HILDEGARD BINDER JOHNSON, ORDER UPON THE LAND: THE U.S. RECTANGULAR LAND SURVEY AND THE UPPER MISSISSIPPI COUNTRY (1976).

7.   Robert W. Swenson, *Legal Aspects of Mineral Resources Exploitation, in* PAUL W. GATES, HISTORY OF PUBLIC LAND LAW DEVELOPMENT (1968).

8.   A good place to start on the 1785–87 Ordinances is *in* PAUL W. GATES, HISTORY OF PUBLIC LAND LAW DEVELOPMENT 59 (1968). The minerals matters are better discussed in Robert W. Swenson, "Legal Aspects of Mineral Resources Exploitation," *in* HISTORY OF PUBLIC LAND LAW DEVELOPMENT, *supra,* at 701.

9.   U.S. Army Corp of Engineers: A Brief History, "Introduction," http://www .usace.army.mil/History/Pages/Brief/index.html (last visited Feb. 18, 2009).

10.   U.S. Army Corp of Engineers: A Brief History, "The Beginnings to 1815," http://www.usace.army.mil/History/Pages/Brief/02-beginnings/ beginnings.html (last visited Feb. 18, 2009).

11.   U.S. Army Corp of Engineers, *supra* note 9.

12.   Gibbons v. Ogden, 22 U.S. 1 (1824).

13.   ARTHUR MAAS & RAYMOND L. ANDERSEN, . . . AND THE DESERT SHALL REJOICE: CONFLICT, GROWTH AND JUSTICE IN ARID ENVIRONMENTS (1978).

14. WIEBE, *supra* note 5, at 12, 44.

15. *Id.* at 42.

16. W. E. Martin, H. M. Ingram & N. K. Laney, *A Willingness to Play: Analysis of Water Resources Development,* 7 W.J. AGRIC. ECON. 133 (1982).

17. Camfield v. United States 167 U.S. 518 (1897).

18. SALLY K. FAIRFAX, LAUREN GWIN, MARY ANN KING & LEIGH RAYMOND, BUYING NATURE: THE LIMITS OF LAND ACQUISITION AS A CONSERVATION STRATEGY, 1780–2004 (2005).

19. Leigh S. Raymond & Sally K. Fairfax, *Fragmentation of Public Domain Law and Policy: An Alternative to the "Shift-to-Retention" Thesis.* 39 NAT. RESOURCES J. (1999), *available at* http://ssrn.com/abstract=216819.

20. ROBERT G. DUNBAR, FORGING NEW RIGHTS IN WESTERN WATERS (1983).

21. 146 U.S. 387 (1892).

22. Winters v. United States, 207 U.S. 564 (1908); Light v. United States, 220 U.S. 523 (1911); United States v. Grimaud, 220 U.S. 506 (1911).

23. MORTON HOROWITZ, THE TRANSFORMATION OF AMERICAN LAW, 1870–1960: THE CRISIS OF LEGAL ORTHODOXY 151 (1992).

24. Cass R. Sunstein, *Lochner's Legacy,* 87 COLUM. L. REV. 873 (1987).

25. DONALD C. SWAIN, FEDERAL CONSERVATION POLICY, 1921–1933 (1963).

26. LEIGH RAYMOND, PRIVATE RIGHTS IN PUBLIC RESOURCES (2003).

27. RICHARD WEST SELLARS, PRESERVING NATURE IN THE NATIONAL PARKS: A HISTORY (1999).

28. See ASHLEY SCHIFF, FIRE AND WATER: HERESY IN THE U.S. FOREST SERVICE (1964).

29. West Virginia Division of the Izaak Walton League of America, Inc. v. Butz, 522 F.2d 945 (4th Cir. 1975).

30. RICHARD B. STEWART, THE REFORMATION OF AMERICAN ADMINISTRATIVE LAW (1975).

31. LAND RIGHTS: THE 1990's PROPERTY RIGHTS REBELLION (Bruce Yandle ed., 1995).

32. JEANNE NIENABER CLARKE & DANIEL C MCCOOL, STAKING OUT THE TERRAIN: POWER AND PERFORMANCE AMONG NATURAL RESOURCE AGENCIES (1996).

33. Lucas v. South Carolina Coastal Council, 505 U.S. 1003 (1992); TERRY L. ANDERSON & DONALD R. LEAL, FREE MARKET ENVIRONMENTALISM (rev. ed. 2001).

34. FAIRFAX, GWIN, KING & RAYMOND, *supra* note 18.

35. Helen Ingram & Leah Fraser, *Path Dependency and Adroit Innovation: The Case of California Water, in* PUNCTUATED EQUILIBRIUM AND THE DYNAMICS OF U.S. WATER POLICY (Robert Repetto ed., 2006).

36. Joseph L. Sax, *Property Rights and the Economy of Nature: Understanding Lucas v. South Carolina Coastal Council,* 45 STAN. L. REV. 1433 (1993); Eric T. Freyfogle,

The Owning and Taking of Sensitive Lands, 43 UCLA L. REV. 77 (1995), *reprinted in* 1996 LAND USE & ENV'T L. REV. (1997).

37. Leigh Raymond & Andrea Olive, *Landowner Beliefs Regarding Biodiversity Protection on Private Property: An Indiana Case Study*, 21 SOC'Y & NAT. RESOURCES 483 (2007).

38. RAYMOND, *supra* note 26.

39. Robert N. Stavins, *What Can We Learn from the Grand Policy Experiment? Positive and Normative Lessons from the SO2 Allowance Trading Program*, 12 J. ECON. PERSP. 69 (1997).

40. JOHN H. LIENHARD, ENGINES OF OUR INGENUITY NO. 123: THE BLACK DEATH, (Nov. 28, 2007), *available at* http://www.uh.edu/engines/epi123.htm.

2

Ethical Perspectives on Resources Law and Policy

Global Warming and Our Common Future

Sarah Krakoff

There was a time, not so long ago, when a book about United States resources law and policy would not have had a section on "Ethical Perspectives." In fact, the predecessor to this volume, published in 1992, did not have an ethics chapter. This is not because ethically based views about natural resources are a new phenomenon. Long before the arrival of Europeans, many indigenous communities throughout North America managed natural resources in accordance with ethical frameworks.[1] Further, some writers, including George Perkins Marsh and Henry David Thoreau, and even a few policy makers, such as John Wesley Powell and Gifford Pinchot, embraced ethical perspectives during the nineteenth and early twentieth centuries. Perhaps most prominently, writer and United States Forest Service officer Aldo Leopold drafted the thoughtful blueprint for many subsequent articulations of an environmental ethic when he penned *A Sand County Almanac*, published posthumously in 1949. Despite this history, ethical concerns had only a fleeting or marginal influence on United States laws and policies (whether federal, state, or local) until roughly the last half-century.

Since that time, there has been a flowering of ethical viewpoints about natural resources and a lively debate about their relative depth, accuracy, logic, and prescriptive tenacity. Some of the most contested issues are in regard to the extent of human obligations to other species and future generations. In addition, important concerns about equity among human communities have been raised by the environmental justice movement. In this chapter, we will consider ethical perspectives on natural resource issues in the context of the most pervasive environmental challenge humans have ever faced—global climate change. Global climate change heightens some of the difficulties inherent in applying conventional ethical frameworks to natural resource problems, yet it also provides a unique opportunity to unify and deepen some of the ethical approaches that have come to the fore in recent times. In particular, global climate change may provide the most urgent and salient opportunity to marry issues of justice and equity with ethical obligations to other species and future generations. The prescription to live sustainably, for the benefit of the least well-off human communities as well as for the earth as a whole, may finally be moving from the margins to center stage.

I.   What We Know About Global Warming

The International Panel on Climate Change issued its fourth set of assessment reports in 2007.[2] The reports, which reflect the consensus of hundreds of participating scientists who have reviewed thousands of studies on climate, concluded that "warming of the climate system is unequivocal," and further expressed "very high confidence" that human emissions of carbon dioxide (hereafter CO_2) and other heat-trapping gases since 1750 have caused the earth's surface temperature to rise. During that time, CO_2 the most important of the anthropogenic greenhouse gases, increased from a pre-industrial level of roughly 280 parts per million (ppm) to 379 ppm in 2005.

Some of the consequences of global warming are already in process. Ocean temperatures and sea levels are rising. Glaciers all over the world are retreating. In the Arctic, the name "permafrost" approaches the status of anachronism. In the western United States, wildfires are more frequent.[3] Spring is coming earlier in many regions, throwing nature's delicate timing into disarray.[4] Species that are dependent on

localized climates are disappearing.[5] Predictions of future effects include larger drought-affected areas; more frequent droughts and
floods; decreasing resilience of ecosystems; increasing threats of species extinction; increasing risks to coastal areas from rising sea levels
and floods; and increasing health risks to vulnerable populations due
to heat waves, changing disease vectors, malnutrition, and other local
weather events.[6]

From this objective assessment of global warming's causes and
effects, it is possible to discern the strands of ethical obligation that
emerge: What do we owe to human communities most susceptible to
the effects of climate change? What do we owe to other species likely
to be vulnerable or even to go extinct? Given that the IPCC reports
also clearly indicate that the predicted effects get significantly worse
beyond certain ranges of temperature increase, and that we have a
fairly limited time in which to prevent those increases from happening, what do we owe to future generations? These questions alone
would be enough to keep ethicists busy. Yet if we back up and incorporate some history about the evolution of scientific knowledge and
legal frameworks, further ethical dimensions emerge, including questions about relative responsibilities for curbing emissions and how those
responsibilities should translate into current reduction strategies.

II.   Evolution of Scientific and Political Certainty

The scientific hypothesis regarding the relationship between
CO_2 and the earth's temperature dates back to the late 1890s, when
the Swedish chemist Svante Arrhenius demonstrated that a decrease
in atmospheric CO_2 could have brought about an ice age and further
speculated that increasing levels of CO_2 due to coal-burning would
have a future warming effect.[7] In the late 1950s, scientists began to
document the concern that human activities, including significant
increases in CO_2 emissions, might be changing the way the atmosphere traps heat. In 1958, scientists Roger Revelle and Charles Keeling established a research station at the top of Mauna Loa in Hawaii,
from which they launched weather balloons and measured the amount

of CO_2 in the atmosphere.[8] The measurements revealed a striking trend of annual increases in CO_2 concentrations, which, coupled with the physics of how CO_2 and other greenhouse gases trap heat, supported the hypothesis that human emissions would cause increases in the earth's temperature.

By the late 1970s, the work of Revelle, Keeling, and others began to garner some political attention, and initial measures were taken by the U.S. government to explore the issue further. In 1978, Congress enacted the National Climate Protection Program, which required the President to establish a research program to investigate climate change.[9] One year later, the World Meteorological Organization (WMO) organized the first World Climate Conference, expressing concern about human effects on regional and global climate, and calling for global cooperation regarding science and policy planning.[10] As a result of these events and other catalysts to climate research, the science and politics of global warming took off in the 1980s. Climate modeling and documentation of the effects of warming became increasingly prevalent and more sophisticated. As early as 1988, climate scientist Jim Hansen testified before a United States Senate committee that there was a 99 percent probability that anthropogenic global warming had begun. The transnational causes and effects of this global phenomenon prompted corresponding calls for a global response. Recurrently, however, the United States played an obstructionist role. Despite increasing certainty of the problem and the serious consequences of delaying action, the United States' position was to forestall action in favor of further study.[11] In part due to the United States' insistence on more certainty, in 1988, the WMO and the United Nations Environment Programme created the International Panel on Climate Change (IPCC), whose charge is to summarize and synthesize the proliferation of scientific data into objective, non-prescriptive consensus reports that can be relied upon by policy makers.

The first IPCC assessment reports were published in 1990, and they, along with the primary research they synthesized, spurred the international negotiations that resulted in the Framework Convention on Climate Change (FCCC) negotiated at the Rio Earth Summit in 1992. The FCCC's main objective was to stabilize "greenhouse gas concentrations in the atmosphere at a level that would prevent dangerous anthropogenic interference with the climate system."[12] Just two of the developed countries, the United States and the Soviet Union, resisted binding timetables and targets for emissions reductions, yet their objections won out. The FCCC articulated only voluntary commitments to reduce greenhouse gas emissions to 1990 levels by 2000.

As the 1990s progressed, the European Union appeared to be the sole FCCC signatory likely to keep its emissions commitment, though this was due to economic downturns in the United Kingdom and Germany rather than to successful reductions programs. The United States, Australia, New Zealand, Japan, Canada, and Norway did nothing to meet their targets and continued to increase emissions. These failures led to the negotiation of the Kyoto Protocol in December 1997, which adopted quantified emissions reductions targets for developed countries but imposed no obligations on other countries during the compliance period. The Kyoto commitments are set to expire in 2012, with the expectation that new obligations will be agreed to for the future and that developing nations will eventually be brought into the reduction regime.

The story of the Kyoto Protocol has been often told, and three main themes emerge: first, that the United States (and, to a lesser extent, other developed countries) played a substantial role in weakening the Protocol's provisions, even though the United States ultimately renounced any participation in 2001;[13] second, that the Protocol is nonetheless an important first step toward negotiating a binding, enforceable, and global agreement; and yet, third, that the failure to achieve the Protocol's goals highlights the difficulty of stabilizing global climate change .[14] At the moment, it is unlikely that the fifteen European countries that signed the treaty will achieve the goal of an 8 percent reduction in greenhouse gas emissions from 1990 levels by 2012. Europe has developed a sophisticated system of carbon management, including caps on CO_2 and a trading system allowing for less efficient emitters to purchase carbon permits. But it has taken some time to determine which aspects of the European cap-and-trade system, as it is called, are working and which are susceptible to cheating and manipulation. It is now apparent, for example, that power companies lobbied for additional pollution permits, resulting in the dilution of the value of such permits. Rather than forcing companies to reduce emissions or buy more permits, the diluted permits allowed some companies to reap windfall profits by charging customers for the value of the permits without reducing emissions.[15] While some emissions reductions have been achieved, no country is on target to meet its Kyoto goals. Furthermore, just as in the pre-Kyoto setting, the countries responsible for the greatest emissions reductions are those from the former Eastern Bloc, whose plummeting economies required industrial closures and restructuring.[16]

Currently there is no clear sense of whether a post-Kyoto agreement with a sufficiently low emissions limit and enforceable compliance mechanisms will emerge. This ambiguity exists despite strong support for the view that we have a very limited time in which to stabilize atmospheric concentrations of greenhouse gases at a level (roughly 450 ppm) that will avoid dangerous consequences.[17] To the extent that there is disagreement within the scientific community, it tends to be about whether initial assessments of stabilization levels and their effects on average temperature increase were too optimistic.[18] Jim Hansen and others, for example, advocate stabilizing at 350 ppm, a level that we have already surpassed.[19] Yet most science and policy experts agree that to achieve any safe level of stabilization, global emissions have to level off this decade, and continue to decline prior to a rapid reduction by midcentury at the latest. A global regulatory regime that has the goal of achieving this, and thereby avoiding potentially catastrophic and unpredictable effects, must kick into high gear very soon.

There are some promising signs. In April 2007, the United Nations Security Council held its first-ever debate about global warming, catapulting the issue from its environmental niche into the realm of geopolitical stability. In addition, the United States finally appears to be on the verge of passing federal legislation limiting CO_2 emissions. Arguably, only hindsight makes it seem as if the United States behaved unethically by perpetuating a narrative of scientific uncertainty and using that narrative as the basis for political actions aimed at slowing and weakening global enforcement of emissions caps. But the fact remains: since 1988, when Jim Hansen apprised Congress of the seriousness and likelihood of the risk, two decades that could have been devoted to changing our emissions habits have been lost.

III.   Global Warming Beneficiaries and Victims

A full and deep discussion of the ethical dimensions of climate change must include facts regarding the disproportion between the countries that have contributed to global warming and the countries that will suffer the most acute effects. Developed countries, including most significantly the United States, are responsible for at least two-thirds of historical greenhouse gas emissions.[20] Yet underdeveloped and developing nations will experience more serious effects.[21] There are interrelated reasons for this. Many developing nations are located at latitudes that are more vulnerable to changes in surface temperature and its consequent effects on soil, water availability, and local weather. In addition, developing nations have fewer economic resources than developed nations to devote to adaptation measures. Further, many economies within developing nations are centered on local natural re-sources, the alteration or destruction of which will therefore have dra-matic economic and cultural effects. For African nations, for example, the IPCC Fourth Assessment Report expressed high confidence that, among other climate change effects:

- by 2020, between 75 and 250 million people will be exposed to an increase of water stress;
- local food supplies will be negatively affected by decreasing fish-eries in large lakes; and
- agricultural production, including access to food, will be severely compromised.

As the IPCC Fourth Assessment Report dryly concludes, "Africa is one of the most vulnerable continents to climate variability and change because of multiple stresses and low adaptive capacity." While the details vary greatly, the IPCC and other sources report a similarly disparate vulnerability for virtually all underdeveloped and developing regions.

Developed nations, by contrast, have not only benefited economically from their historical greenhouse gas emissions, they have also begun to spend some of that wealth on adaptation projects. For example, desalination projects are in the planning stages for arid regions in the United States and Australia. The Netherlands has begun to modify its infrastructure to prepare for rising sea levels, including constructing amphibious housing and planning for entire floating cities. And California and other western American states are well into planning processes to adapt their water storage facilities. So while global warming ultimately will be democratic, in that no country will be beyond its effects, wealthy nations will be less vulnerable initially and will be better able to manage the consequences.

Complicating equality issues even further, poor people, regardless of where they live, will suffer more from the effects of global warming. As Dale Jamieson has stated, "this pattern of the poor suffering most from extreme climactic events has been documented as far back as the 'little ice age' that occurred in Europe from 1300 to 1850."[22] In 2005, Hurricane Katrina highlighted the disproportionate effects of extreme weather on poor and minority populations in the United States. The lessons from Katrina are relevant regardless of whether that particular storm was intensified or caused by climate change, given the IPCC's predictions regarding increases in extreme weather, including heat waves, droughts, heavy precipitation, and tropical storms.

Yet another disproportionate effect is the potential disruption to, or even destruction of, communities who have particular social, economic, and spiritual ties to place. While some forms of adaptation are already inevitable for such communities, there will be a point at which adaptation is synonymous with cultural termination. For example, the Inuit communities of the polar region have framed as human rights violations the effects that are already in progress. In a petition against the United States (hereinafter Inuit Petition), filed before the Inter-American Commission on Human Rights, these communities allege violations of various international treaties and declarations stemming from the failure to take any steps to mitigate global warming.[23] As described in the petition:

> Inuit culture has developed over thousands of years in relationship with, and in response to, the physical environment of the Arctic. The Inuit have developed an intimate relationship with their surroundings, using their understanding of the arctic environment to develop a culture, including tools, techniques, and knowledge, that has enabled them to subsist and thrive on the scarce resources available.[24]

The Arctic region, which has experienced twice the rate of average temperature increase as the rest of the world, is already seeing palpable effects from global warming. The allegations in the Inuit Petition include the many ways in which these effects are interfering with Inuit subsistence harvest, travel, safety, health, education, and culture. The petition intersperses scientific data with direct observations by Inuit people. In the section on the negative effects of melting ice and snow, for example, the following comment is just one among many:

> "June, July, August, we used to be able to see the polar pack of ice, out in front of Barrow. That's no longer happening. Our people are going bearded seal hunting, walrus hunting, in the spring, are having to go farther and farther out to find game. . . . I'm one of those very unfortunate ones who didn't land any bearded seals this spring. My boys went out trying, and some of my crew members went out trying but they didn't land any."

The Inuit Petition also includes clear and poignant descriptions of how natural cycles are changing faster than human culture can adapt, resulting in the loss of key cultural practices, as well as vivid details about how other species are struggling and may be headed toward extinction.

IV. Environmental Ethical Frameworks and Global Warming

As the above context reveals, global warming presents questions not only about obligations that the global community owes to vulnerable populations, other species, and future generations; there is also the issue of whether developed nations, which have benefited from unregulated emissions, should have a greater duty to reduce global emissions today and in the future. Furthermore, should the responsibility of some countries, particularly the United States, be further heightened by obdurate behavior since the late 1980s, which may well have cost the entire world several precious decades during which unrecoupable progress might have been made?

Despite these various compelling reasons to see global warming in moral and ethical terms, many do not perceive it as a moral issue. According to Dale Jamieson, "A paradigm moral problem is one in which an individual acting intentionally harms another individual; both the individuals and the harm are identifiable; and the individuals and the harm are closely related in time and space."[25] The spatial and temporal dispersion that defines global warming makes these identifications and connections particularly difficult to make.

The difficulties are exacerbated by the fact that the behavior constituting the harm was, and for many still is, simply living a normal life in a wealthy, developed country. Consider my maternal grandparents. They drove two big Buicks for many years, lived in an apartment heated and cooled by fossil fuels, and, in their later years, flew all over the globe. It is quite possible that my grandmother never once took public transportation to get anywhere in her hometown of Columbus, Ohio. By living what they believed was a hard-earned, up-from-the-*shtetl*, American-dream of a life, they, along with similarly situated U.S. residents, have contributed to more than one-third of the global emissions that have put us in this climactic bind. Yet when they drove to the kosher butcher or boarded the plane to fly to Chile, they had no sense that they were contributing to a global crisis that would affect many future individuals and non-human species. In addition, the "harm" that they did cannot be disaggregated from the harms done by all other carbon emitters. We cannot trace my grandmother's CO_2 molecules to determine that they are the ones now causing the permafrost to melt, either theoretically (that is not how global warming works) or practically. Further, the victims of the harm my grandparents caused are dispersed in time and space. They are Inuit seal hunters today, island dwellers who may lose their homes in the twenty-first century, and perhaps residents of Manhattan several generations from now.

Increasingly emphatic statements by the IPCC (and the climate science community generally) about the causes and effects of global warming have begun to overcome these obstacles to perceiving global warming as a moral issue. While the link between facts and values may be forever fraught and contested, the more we know about the connections between our actions and their effects, the less difficulty we have accepting ethical constraints on our behavior. Edward O. Wilson put it slightly differently when he said, "When very little is known about an important subject, the questions people raise are almost invariably ethical. Then, as knowledge grows, they become more concerned with information and . . . more narrowly intellectual. Finally, as understanding becomes sufficiently complete, the questions turn ethical again."[26] Thus, despite the challenges of spatial and temporal dispersion, it is apparent that a moral vocabulary is emerging. People all over the world, including several prominent American politicians, are expressing concern for future generations, other species, and particularly vulnerable populations. These articulations correlate with the mounting scientific evidence of what we have wrought. Despite the ethical distance many may have to travel to get from the paradigm moral problem of "I knowingly hurt you," to "I, along with billions of others, am living my life in such a way as to deprive distant and/or future human beings and non-human species of a range of opportunities for an acceptable and/or flourishing life," we are beginning to make the trip. To better understand the conceptual tools required for this journey, we will briefly tour the ways in which various environmental ethical frameworks might assess global warming.

A. Hard and Soft Ecocentrisms

A variety of environmental ethical frameworks start from the position that values inhere in nature. The advantage of this starting point, from the perspective of natural resource protection and conservation, is that it avoids the pitfalls of justifying protection measures on the basis of actual or theoretical benefit to humans. Asserting that nature has value as a first principle does not, however, obviate dilemmas involving how to weigh harms to nature against harms to human individuals or communities. A range of ecocentric positions exist, some of which place all natural objects on equal moral footing with humans, and others that allow for more slippage. There are too many articulations of an ecocentric ethic to evaluate how each might assess global warming, but the following discussion should provide the reader with a sense of the parameters of ecocentric thought.[27]

1. Deep Ecology

The philosophy of "deep ecology," first articulated by Norwegian philosopher Arne Næss, is the strongest modern version of ecocentrism. Næss grounds deep ecology in the themes of self-realization and biocentric equality. He begins with the intuition that all human beings reach their highest state of self-realization through connection with nature. Nature, in all its complexity, is therefore a necessary condition for human flourishing, and preserving it is coincident with our own moral and aesthetic needs.[28] Bill Devall and George Sessions built on Næss's writings and formulated a platform of principles and prescriptions. "Humans have no right to reduce this richness and diversity except to satisfy *vital* needs," they state. "Policies must therefore be changed. These policies affect basic economic, technological, and ideological structures. The resulting state of affairs will be deeply different."[29]

Given these principles, deep ecologists would have no trouble defining global warming as a moral problem and would place serious restraints on human behavior in order to preserve the richness and diversity of other life forms. Species that are dependent on local climate conditions are already being affected. In addition to the well-publicized plight of the polar bears, some less-celebrated species have already gone extinct. Scientists attribute the disappearance of the golden toad in Costa Rica to global warming, and similar amphibious vanishing acts are occurring worldwide. Further, it seems clear that deep ecologists would not consider many of the emissions-producing activities, particularly those in developed nations, to be "vital human needs." It is conceivable that some activities in developing nations require increasing emissions, at least temporarily, and might be considered vital needs even by deep ecologists. But a stringent global cap, born largely by the world's largest emitters, calibrated to stabilize CO_2 at 450 ppm or less, seems entirely compatible with deep ecology's ethical framework.

Although it is consistent with the ethos of deep ecology to promote local and ecologically sustainable economies, deep ecology does not have much to say about achieving justice or equity among human communities. The assumptions of deep ecology include that a radical restructuring of our patterns of consumption will benefit developing nations and result in more egalitarian conditions for humans.[30] Yet the disproportionate impacts of global warming on poor nations, and poor people within all nations, would be, at best, a secondary concern. Therefore while deep ecology, with its strong articulation of biocentric equality, leads easily to a stringent regime of mitigation (i.e., reduction of greenhouse gas emissions), its principles do not provide us with any detailed guidance about how regulatory and other policy instruments might assist communities with adaptation, nor how mitigation might simultaneously encourage the growth of "green economies" for the least well off.

2. Aldo Leopold's Land Ethic

Aldo Leopold's Land Ethic, which sketched the philosophical arguments for including the "biotic community" in the realm of human ethical consideration, is the leading example of a more flexible ecocentric approach. Leopold was concerned that without a sense of the "rightness" of preserving natural systems for their own sake, we would destroy not only much that is beautiful, but much that ultimately is required for ecosystems to function. Waiting for or forcing an economic justification struck Leopold as both foolish and false: "One basic weakness in a conservation system based wholly on economic motives is that most members of the land community have no economic value. . . . When one of these non-economic categories is threatened, and if we happen to love it, we invent subterfuges to give it economic importance."[31] Further, Leopold understood that government regulation alone could not make up for the gaps in economic justification, and therefore that something that would restrain private individuals was required. Drawing on the nascent body of science that today we call conservation biology, Leopold described an ethical community that included all parts that are, or might well be, necessary to a functioning ecosystem—what he called the "Land Pyramid." The Land Ethic applies to that community, and is articulated as follows: "A thing is ethically right when it tends to preserve the integrity, stability, and beauty of the biotic community. It is wrong when it tends otherwise."

Given the serious effects of global warming on various biotic communities, it seems plain that the Land Ethic would require immediate and dramatic action to address global warming. The Land Ethic itself is therefore well suited to the problem, but in operation it is far different than Leopold imagined. Making an individual decision not to contribute to global warming is a very different kind of decision than refraining from making a destructive land use decision on your private property, in that the former has no chance of success absent the coordinated actions of the rest of the world. Leopold's thinking was complex, but in some ways the environmental problems he was facing were simpler. His sense that an ethic could substitute for excessive government bureaucracy now seems naive. Today, we need the ethic both to motivate our governments to act and to be receptive as individuals to government-coordinated solutions. On our own, we can choose not to drive big cars. But we cannot, as individuals acting alone, spur the development of alternative energy fast enough to reduce carbon emissions.

Unlike the deep ecology position, the Land Ethic does not hold that only "vital human needs" can justify the destruction of other members of the biotic community. Resources can be managed, used, and altered by humans, but they have a "right to continued existence,

and, at least in spots, their continued existence in a natural state."
Here, some might contend that Leopold does not give us any helpful
guidance in the global warming context. As Bill McKibben has suggested, there is, due to global warming, virtually no natural state any-
more.[32] Where, then, do we draw the line? If a thing is "wrong" when
it tends to destroy the integrity of the biotic community, then virtually all development since the dawn of industrialization has been
"wrong." To criticize the Land Ethic in this way, though, is largely to
miss the point. All but the most rigid and dogmatic of ethical systems
tend to falter when it comes to prescriptive precision. The flexibility in
the Land Ethic allows us to consider the "rightness" of our actions with
regard to non-human members of our community, and that consideration alone will often change the content of decisions. For example,
the National Environmental Policy Act (NEPA) has been interpreted to lack any substantive requirement to make environmentally
protective decisions, and its effectiveness has therefore been questioned.
But there is also convincing evidence that many anti-environmental
decisions have been avoided because of both strenuous advocacy under
NEPA and government self-mitigation pursuant to the statute.[33] If the
palpable and increasingly harsh effects of global climate change on
many plant and animal species were considered not just unfortunate
but "wrong," clear and decisive action would be a likely response. Yet
the flexibility also allows us to consider how and when to implement
mitigation strategies that balance human needs against the needs of
natural systems. This flexibility distinguishes the Land Ethic from
deep ecology, though beyond that distinction there is not much that
Leopold offers in terms of how to factor in human concerns. He did
not address issues of equity among human communities, and though
we might infer that Leopold would have favored principles of sustainability, his writings do not address these issues either.

B. Anthropocentric Views

Those who are troubled by the concept of anything having
value in itself, apart from our valuing of it, are more comfortable with
anthropocentric justifications for ethical obligations to the natural

world. Although anthropocentric justifications fall generally under some form of utilitarianism, some arguments are grounded in other philosophical approaches. For example, Joseph Sax's argument in *Mountains without Handrails* rested not on maximization of utility, but on the cultivation of human virtue.[34] Professor Sax eloquently put forth the case for preserving natural wild places because of the special opportunities they provide for human stimulation, engagement, and ultimately improvement. Still, the unifying theme of anthropocentric justifications is that the conservation of natural resources must, in some way, relate to human well-being or concerns.[35] Framing our obligations this way does not obviate the hard questions that exist in the ecocentric context. It simply displaces them onto the contested issues of what counts as human well-being or concern, and how that well-being or concern is best served.

For the purposes of this volume, it is not necessary to parse each argument about the proper grounding for an anthropocentric environmental ethic. Whether utilitarian, Kantian, virtue-based, or otherwise, ultimately the positions rest on how humans appreciate, or are improved or served by, nature. In addition, each of these positions, of course, considers the various ways in which people are harmed or otherwise affected by an environmental problem. Furthermore, the environmental justice approach considers the disproportion between environmental benefits and burdens for minority and disenfranchised communities. Therefore, to provide a rough and collective sense of all anthropocentric approaches, we will consider the effects both on nature and on humanity, from global warming. The effects on nature, as discussed above, are apparent in many parts of the world, where climate-dependant species and ecosystems are already harmed or are at risk of irreversible harm. To the extent that human health and aesthetic, spiritual, cultural, or other interests are linked to affected species or ecosystems, anthropocentric justifications require taking some action to mitigate climate change.

Global warming is already affecting human communities as well. The most intense harm caused by climate change will be borne by individuals who have lost or will lose their homes due to rising sea levels and extreme weather events, and by communities tied to particular climate-sensitive regions, such as the Inuit of the Arctic Circle.

As global warming progresses, people in developing countries will suffer drought, food shortages, increased vulnerability to disease, and more frequent and extreme weather events. The IPCC Fourth Assessment Report makes this threat clear; it also predicts increasing risk to and vulnerability of developed nations as temperature increases go beyond a certain range.[36]

Considering global warming from an anthropocentric environmental framework serves, it seems, only to heighten the conclusion that steps should be taken immediately to mitigate and reverse the upward trend of the earth's surface temperature. Not only is nature being harmed, but humans are suffering as a result. Furthermore, there are clear inequities in terms of which human communities will suffer the most and which ones have benefited the most from previous emissions. Ethicists who have focused on all of these aspects of global warming therefore recommend either a system of per capita emissions distribution, which would have the effect of radically redistributing current emissions from developed to developing nations, or some other subsistence-oriented basis for emissions allocation.[37]

V. Sustainability: Remarrying Humans and Nature

There is, in my opinion, largely only a theoretical difference between the most strenuous anthropocentric positions and the more flexible ecocentric views. Whether we start with the idea that non-human things have value in themselves, or we accept the idea that only humans are capable of registering and assigning value, at the end of the day it is the strength and depth with which humans act on those values that matters. While it is possible, therefore, to level a philosophical critique at deep ecology, for our purposes the more trenchant point is that very few people will act on the proposition of near-absolute biocentric equality. There is evidence, however, that the Land Ethic has taken hold in many quarters. Similarly, within the anthropocentric range of views, the idea that nature matters to us for aesthetic, spiritual, health-related, psychological, and short- and long-term economic reasons, and that we should therefore take steps to preserve it in various forms, is no longer a marginal view. Concepts from the environmental justice movement have also taken root in various legal and policy arenas, even if commitment to them has been uncertain and wavering in recent times.

Yet despite the local and global emergence of various versions of an environmental ethic, the United States has not internalized one as a matter of policy. There have been some important nods in that direction. But as Lisa Heinzerling discusses in chapter 3, the prevailing norm since the turn of the millennium has been an antediluvian (or ante–Earth Day, anyway) version of utilitarianism, which reduces all manner of values, obligations, and concerns to a unitary economic measure. This approach, derived from welfare economics, currently dominates a great deal of environmental and natural resource decision-making. The executive agencies of the federal government are required, for example, to apply cost-benefit analysis to a wide range of proposed agency actions.[38] Nature, in such a system, has no greater *a priori* ethical weight than the preference for a bigger ski area or a faster snowmobile ride. Some federal statutes, passed during the heady environmental moments of the 1960s and 1970s, do embody ethical obligations to nature. The boldest of these is the Endangered Species Act (ESA), which, on paper, requires some actions with regard to species preservation, irrespective of cost.[39] But even the ESA, despite its many success stories, has been melded to the realities of an economic system based on perpetual growth and development.[40]

What global warming may do is catapult us beyond this way of thinking. Addressing global warming will mean reconsidering what growth and development should consist of. The world within which growth can take place has always been defined by our ethics. We do not, for example, take into account the possible economic benefits of free labor from slaves or children when we consider whether or not to site a factory. Global warming makes visible the heretofore hidden exploitations that, if we were forced to think about them on a daily basis, should give us pause. For example, we might ask ourselves: is it really worth displacing other people from their families and homes just so I can drive a big car; does my ski trip to Canada really measure up against the last snows of Kilimanjaro? We might begin to evaluate our daily behavior in terms of its temporally and spatially dispersed, yet very real, effects.

Here too we are not starting from scratch. Sustainability, an approach both centuries old and recently articulated, marries the ethical insights from the environmental movement with those from the human rights framework. It embodies the ideas of viewing human and natural systems as interconnected and of meeting all human needs in a manner that supports the health of the environment. "Sustainable development" became a term of art after the World Commission on Environment and Development published the Brundtland Report. This publication explores environmental and development issues in tandem, and concludes that governments around the world must make simultaneous efforts to address poverty and environmental degradation so that the basic needs of humanity are not perpetually in tension with the long-term health of the environment. As the report explains:

> There has been a growing realization in national governments and multilateral institutions that it is impossible to separate economic development issues from environment issues; many forms of development erode the environmental resources upon which they must be based, and environmental degradation can undermine economic development. Poverty is a major cause and effect of global environmental problems. It is therefore futile to attempt to deal with environmental problems without a broader perspective that encompasses the factors underlying world poverty and international inequality.[41]

The report called on all nations of the world to integrate sustainable development into their policies by adopting eight principles: (1) to revive growth in order to alleviate poverty, both for equitable and environmental reasons (noting that poverty is a major cause of environmental degradation); (2) to change the quality of growth ("Revived growth must be of a new kind in which sustainability, equity, social justice, and security are firmly embedded as major social goals"); (3) to conserve and enhance the resource base ("sustainability requires the conservation of environmental resources such as clean air, water, forests, and soils; maintaining genetic diversity; and using energy, water, and raw materials efficiently"); (4) to ensure a sustainable level of population ("Population policies should be formulated and integrated with other economic and social development programmes—education, health care, and the expansion of the livelihood base of the poor"); (5) to reorient technology and manage risks; (6) to integrate environment and economics in decision-making; (7) to reform international economic relations; and finally (8) to strengthen international cooperation.[42]

A deep version of sustainability prescribes a way of living on the earth that allows each of us, in the company of nature, to thrive, but that proscribes any of us from living beyond our ecological means. These "ecological means" now include our greenhouse gas emissions, rendering unsustainable many activities and practices that until now were assumed aspects of life in the developed world.

Global warming has the potential to make sustainability, even in this more challenging form, go mainstream. The good news is that this moral shift does not require a brand new version of humanity. Those who are not sanguine about a "moral progress" narrative can take heart in the fact that we do not have to move forward; we can instead circle back. Paradigms of living within our ecological means, and considering it a moral and spiritual undertaking to do so, have been around a long time. As Justice William Brennan recounted, while dissenting in *Lyng v. Northwest Cemetery Association*, many Native American religious views "regard creation as an ongoing process in which they are morally and religiously obligated to participate. . . . Native Americans fulfill this duty through ceremonies and rituals designed to preserve and stabilize the earth and to protect humankind from disease and other catastrophes. Failure to conduct these ceremonies in the manner and place specified . . . will result in great harm to the earth and the people whose welfare depends upon it."[43] This is not a static, romanticized vision of people living in perpetual harmony with nature; rather it describes an ethical attitude that takes the form of daily habits and physical engagement, and is one that is strikingly well suited to the kinds of behavioral changes that will have to occur in a zero-emissions world. Many local communities committed to action on climate change have expressed these kinds of values, both in their positive laws and in their statements about why they are committed to addressing global warming. Notwithstanding the relative intransigence of national and international governing institutions, many people at local levels have begun to live as if they could indeed participate in the creation of a sustainable world.

VI. The Futility of Ethical Convergence?

The fact that there are strong and diverse ethical arguments in support of addressing global warming is of little consolation if we fail to act on them. Indeed, the internalization of an ethic often coincides with the cessation of argument about whether an ethical principle exists. For example, we still debate the ethics of abortion because it remains a contested moral issue. But for the most part, we no longer engage in arguments about the ethical pros and cons of slavery. And though it may be too sharp to point out, arguments about slavery ended only after the bloodiest war in which this nation has ever engaged. There will be no such war about whether to end global warming.

There may, however, be many skirmishes resulting from the scarcity of resources caused by global warming. What will "water wars" look like in the American West when average surface temperatures are anywhere from two to four degrees higher than they are now and heat waves are stronger and more frequent? How will the property rights of inland residents be affected when millions of their coastal neighbors have to be relocated? When and if we are faced with these enormous challenges, we will wish humanity had fought the war against global warming in time to stabilize it, thereby averting such intra-human conflicts. By the time the blood—let's hope it is only metaphorical—begins to spill on our own soil, it will be too late. Perhaps this, ultimately, is the role of ethics—to get us to act *before* it is obvious that doing so is in our own self interest. Because by the time it is, we will have forfeited the chance to be good and may be stuck with our own earthly version of natural resource hell. Global warming provides the over-arching material connections that can render the ethical paradigm of sustainability concrete, meaningful, and urgent. The facts, arguments, and concepts are all in place. All we need to do is act on them. If we do, we might find the world to be a better place simply because we are trying to make it so—even if global warming remains an ever-moving target.

Notes

1. *See* Rebecca Tsosie, *Tribal Environmental Policy in an Era of Self-Determination: The Role of Ethics, Economics, and Traditional Ecological Knowledge*, 21 VT. L. REV. 225 (1996).

2. *See* IPCC, 2007: CLIMATE CHANGE 2007: THE PHYSICAL SCIENCE BASIS, SUMMARY FOR POLICY MAKERS (S. D. Solomon et al. eds., 2007); IPCC, 2007: CLIMATE CHANGE 2007: IMPACTS, ADAPTATION AND VULNERABILITY. (M. L. Parry et al. eds., 2007); *all IPCC reports are available at* http://www.ipcc.ch/.

3. *See* A. L. Westerling, H. G. Hidalgo, D. R. Cayan & T. W. Swetnam, *Warming and Earlier Spring Increases Western U.S. Forest Wildfire Activity*, 313 SCIENCE 940 (2006), *originally published in* SCIENCE EXPRESS, July 6, 2006, http://www.sciencemag.org/cgi/content/abstract/313/5789/940

4. *See* Camille Parmesan & Gary Yohe, *A Globally Coherent Fingerprint of Climate Change Impacts Across Natural Systems*, 421 NATURE 37 (2003) (finding spring coming earlier by 2.3 days per decade and analyzing effects).

5. *See* Michelle Nijhuis, *What the Smallest Creatures Tell Us about Global Warming*, HIGH COUNTRY NEWS, Oct. 17, 2005, at 12–13.

6. IPCC, 2007: CLIMATE CHANGE 2007: IMPACTS, ADAPTATION AND VULNERABILITY, *supra* note 2, at 8–10.

7. TIM FLANNERY, THE WEATHER MAKERS 39–42 (2005).

8. *See* AL GORE, AN INCONVENIENT TRUTH: THE PLANETARY EMERGENCY OF GLOBAL WARMING AND WHAT WE CAN DO ABOUT IT 38–39 (2006).

9. *See* Massachusetts v. EPA, 549 U.S. 497, —, 127 S. Ct. 1438, 1448 (2007) (citing to 92 Stat. 601 (1978)).

10. *See* IPCC Brochure, 16 Years of Scientific Assessment in Support of the Climate Convention, Dec. 2004, *available at* http://www.ipcc.ch/pdf/10th-anniversary/anniversary-brochure.pdf.

11. *See* DONALD BROWN, AMERICAN HEAT: ETHICAL PROBLEMS WITH THE UNITED STATES' RESPONSE TO GLOBAL WARMING 97 (2002).

12. United Nations Framework Convention on Climate Change, art. 2, May 9, 1992, *available at* http://unfccc.int/essential_background/convention/background/items/1349.php.

13. *See* BROWN, *supra* note 11, at 36 (describing the U.S. role in weakening the protocol).

14. *See* Stephen M. Gardiner, *The Global Warming Tragedy and the Dangerous Illusion of the Kyoto Protocol*, 18 ETHICS & INT'L AFFAIRS 23 (2004).

15. *See* Stephen Castle, *Europe Moves to Make Big Polluters Pay for Emissions*, N.Y. TIMES, June 5, 2007, at C8.

16. *See* Cass R. Sunstein, *Of Montreal and Kyoto: A Tale of Two Protocols*, 31 HARV. ENVTL. L. REV. 1, 27 (2007).

17. *See* IPCC, 2007: CLIMATE CHANGE 2007: THE PHYSICAL SCIENCE BASIS, *supra* note 2, at 11.

18. *See* James Hansen et al., *Target Atmospheric CO_2: Where Should Humanity Aim?* 2 OPEN ATMOS. SCI. J. 217 (2008).

19. *See id.*

20. *See* Stephen M. Gardiner, *Ethics and Global Climate Change*, 14 ETHICS 555, 579 (2004).

21. *See* IPCC, 2007: CLIMATE CHANGE 2007: IMPACTS, ADAPTATION AND VULNERABILITY, *supra* note 2.

22. Dale Jamieson, *Adaptation, Mitigation, and Justice*, 5 ADVANCES ECON. ENVTL. RESOURCES 217, 227 (2005).

23. *See* Petition to the Inter American Commission on Human Rights Seeking Relief from Violation Resulting from Global Warming Caused by Acts and Omissions of the United States (submitted Dec. 7, 2005), *available at* http://www.earthjustice.org/library/legal_docs/petition-to-the-inter-american-commission-on-human-rights-on-behalf-of-the-inuit-circumpolar-conference.pdf.

24. *Id.* at 35.

25. *See* Dale Jamieson, *The Moral and Political Challenges of Climate Change, in* CREATING A CLIMATE FOR CHANGE: COMMUNICATING CLIMATE CHANGE AND FACILITATING SOCIAL CHANGE 475 (Susanne C. Moser & Lisa Dilling eds., 2007).

26. EDWARD O. WILSON, *The Conservation Ethic, in* BIOPHILIA: THE HUMAN BOND WITH OTHER SPECIES 119 (1984).

27. For a good overview and discussion of a range of positions, see PETER HAY, MAIN CURRENTS IN WESTERN ENVIRONMENTAL THOUGHT 41–57 (Indiana U. Press, 2002).

28. *See* Arne Næss, The *Shallow and the Deep, Long-Range Ecology Movement: A Summary*, 16 INQUIRY 95–100 (1973); Arne Næss, *Self-Realization in Mixed Communities of Humans, Bears, Sheep and Wolves*, 22 INQUIRY 231–41 (1984); Arne Næss, *Intuition, Intrinsic Value and Deep Ecology*, 14 THE ECOLOGIST 201–03 (1984); Arne Næss, *The Deep Ecology Eight Points Revisited, in* DEEP ECOLOGY FOR THE TWENTY-FIRST CENTURY 213–21 (G. Sessions ed., 1995).

29. BILL DEVALL & GEORGE SESSIONS, DEEP ECOLOGY: LIVING AS IF NATURE MATTERED 249–50 (1985).

30. *See* Arne Næss, *The Third World, Wilderness and Deep Ecology, in* DEEP ECOLOGY FOR THE 21ST CENTURY 397 (George Sessions ed., 1995); *see also* BILL DEVALL, SIMPLE IN MEANS, RICH IN ENDS: PRACTICING DEEP ECOLOGY (1988).

31. ALDO LEOPOLD, A SAND COUNTY ALMANAC AND SKETCHES HERE AND THERE (1949).

32. BILL MCKIBBEN, THE END OF NATURE (1989).

33. 42 U.S.C. §§ 4321–4370f (2000); See Bradley C. Karkainnen, *Whither NEPA?*, 12 N.Y.U. ENVTL. L. REV. 333, 348–49 (2004).

34. See JOSEPH SAX, MOUNTAINS WITHOUT HANDRAILS (1980); Sarah Krakoff, *Mountains without Handrails . . . Wilderness without Cellphones*, 27 HARV. ENVTL. L. REV. 417, 422–26 (2003).

35. See PETER HAY, MAIN CURRENTS IN WESTERN ENVIRONMENTAL THOUGHT 57–61(2002).

36. *See, e.g.,* IPCC, 2007: CLIMATE CHANGE 2007: IMPACTS, ADAPTATION AND VULNERABILITY, *supra* note 2, at 12 (noting that even regions, such as Northern Europe, where climate change will initially result in mixed, as opposed to negative, effects will eventually suffer over-all negative impacts as climate change continues).

37. *See* Gardiner, *supra* note 20, at 583–86 (discussing specific proposals about a just and equitable policy instrument for emissions reduction, e.g., Jamieson's per capita share based on 1990 population levels, or Singer's per capita share based on 2050 levels).

38. Exec. Order No. 13,422, 72 Fed. Reg. 2763 (Jan. 18, 2007) (requiring "market failure" assessment of all planned agency action, and annual cost-benefit analysis of all agency rules).

39. *See* Endangered Species Act, 16 U.S.C. §§ 1531–1544; Tennessee Valley Authority v. Hill, 437 U.S. 153 (1978).

40. *See* Amendments of 1978, 16 U.S.C. § 1536 (enacted/amended Nov. 10, 1978).

41. OUR COMMON FUTURE: WORLD COMMISSION ON ENVIRONMENT AND DEVELOPMENT 3 (1987), a*vailable at* http://www.un-documents.net/wced-ocf.htm.

42. *Id.* at 363–65.

43. Lyng v. Northwest Cemetery Protective Ass'n, 485 U.S. 439, 460 (1988) (Brennan, J., dissenting).

3

Why Care About the Polar Bear?

*Economic Analysis of Natural
Resources Law and Policy*

Lisa Heinzerling

Cost-benefit analysis is all the rage in pollution control law. So far, however, it has not played as significant a role in the evolution of natural resources law and policy. Perhaps this is because U.S. natural resources law has, as a whole, been characterized by quite weak standards and even weaker implementation. Because this economic tool is often applied, I believe, only to defeat regulation that might otherwise be thought a good idea, and because natural resources law has not been substantively threatening enough to prompt its deployment, cost-benefit analysis has not been a large feature of natural resources law.

Whatever the reason for its relative absence, would it be a positive development if cost-benefit analysis were used more often in the field of natural resources law? I will argue here that the answer is no. I will develop this argument by considering a specific case study: how economic analysis might evaluate public policies to protect the polar bear. I will suggest that none of the most important reasons to protect the polar bear will be meaningfully reflected in economic analysis.

I have picked the polar bear as my example because it presents a puzzle. I do not think it can be denied that the public cares a great deal about the fate of the polar bear. Consider the public's reaction to the threat to the polar bear posed by climate change. Many different factors have combined to focus public attention on climate change, but surely one of the items at the top of the list must be the widely circulated photos of apparently struggling, perhaps even drowning, polar bears. More than one person has told me that the photos changed her life—inspired her to change her driving habits, her patterns of consumption, and, in one case, even her professional purpose. If climate change has a face, it is the white-furred, black-nosed face of the polar bear.

Yet the overwhelming majority of us will never use a polar bear or even see one outside captivity. We will not eat its meat, wear its fur, or even travel to see it. Nor, in all likelihood, will we make any use of the Arctic marine resources—the ringed seal on which the polar bear feeds, the small fish and krill on which the seals feed, and so on down the ecological chain—that depend on the polar bear for their own flourishing and survival. Our economic relationship with the polar bear, conventionally speaking, is nil.

There are exceptions among us, to be sure. Despite the odds against them, the Inuit of Canada have maintained a close economic connection to the polar bear: They continue to hunt the polar bear for subsistence purposes. They sell polar bear pelts. And they even sell some of their hunting rights to trophy hunters, who pay up to $27,500 for the privilege of trying to kill a polar bear. In addition, growing numbers of tourists are traveling to the Arctic to observe the polar bear in its natural habitat.

Beyond these mainstream economic values lies the monetary value individuals place on "non-uses" of the polar bear, including having the option one day to see a polar bear in the wild, being assured that one's descendants will be able to make use (or non-use) of the polar bear if they wish, and simply knowing that the polar bear exists. These sources of value have produced exceedingly large estimates of the economic worth of species other than the polar bear. If similar non-use values obtained for the polar bear, the amounts would be huge and would greatly exceed the conventional economic value of this animal.

Thus, despite the rather narrow direct economic uses of the polar bear, it has the potential to have a gigantic monetary value. But that is assuming that non-use values are taken into account, which is by no means certain given current cost-benefit practices. Equally troubling for the polar bear's bottom line, moreover, is that the bear does not appear to be in imminent danger of extinction. Current research predicts that the polar bear, though doomed if we continue business as usual, will not actually become extinct for another 50 years or so. A government cost-benefit analysis, as it is currently practiced, would calculate the benefits of protecting the polar bear as of the time the bear would otherwise be materially harmed. If that date lies in the future, as it appears to for the polar bear, then the government would discount those benefits over the interval between the present and the time when the harm will occur. The theory behind discounting is that future costs and benefits are not as valuable as present costs and benefits. Discounting the value of benefits over a period as long as 50 years, particularly at the 7 percent rate favored by current government practice, will greatly diminish their apparent worth.

More fundamentally, asking what price we place on the very existence of the polar bear, and discounting that amount as if only money were at stake, misses the deepest and most profound reasons why we care about the polar bear. We can obtain very large economic values for the polar bear only by insisting that people reduce their admiration for and worries about the animal to monetary terms. But paradoxically, by doing so we denigrate the aesthetic, spiritual, and moral impulses that drive people to report such large monetary values for animals like the polar bear. Discounting the future worth of the species as if it were only money compounds this basic mistake.

My discussion proceeds as follows: First, I will say a few words about the polar bear itself: the animal, its habitat, and the threats it faces. Second, I will discuss the economics of the polar bear: how to calculate its worth both when we use it and when we don't. I will also discuss how the likely temporal remoteness of the polar bear's demise affects the economic value of the animal. Finally, I will explain how expressing the worth of the polar bear in economic terms adds next to nothing to our understanding of its real value to us and, in fact, subtracts a great deal. Cost-benefit analysis, in this context, is a way of *losing* information rather than generating it. As such, there is little to commend it.

I.   The Polar Bear

Evolved from the brown (grizzly) bear 100,000 or more years ago, polar bears now occur in 19 different populations in the Arctic.[1] The estimated 20,000–25,000 living polar bears can be found in five countries, often called the "polar bear nations": Canada, Greenland, Norway, Russia, and the United States. The polar bear is the largest living bear species and the largest land carnivore. It eats mostly ringed seals (and of these, mostly pups and their mothers), but it also eats other kinds of seals and sometimes walruses, narwhal, and belugas. Male polar bears live about 25 years, females often a few years longer than that. Females begin having cubs when they are five to six years old. Litters are small—typically two, rarely three, cubs. The cubs stay with their mothers until they are almost two and one-half years old. As a consequence of their late sexual maturity, small litters, and prolonged period before weaning, polar bears have a very low reproductive rate. The polar bear is regarded as a keystone species in its Arctic ecosystem, one that has a large influence on the ecological community in which it lives.

As land is to humans and water is to fish, the sea ice is to the polar bear. These animals are utterly dependent on sea ice, where they live most or all of their lives; this is, indeed, why they are considered marine mammals. They hunt from there, rest there, and mate there. Many of the polar bear's physical characteristics—from its water-repellant guard hairs to its paddle-like feet—are adaptations to the animal's life on the ice. Polar bears use the ice as a surface for moving from place to place, and must frequently adjust as shifting sea ice affects the distribution of the seal population on which they depend. In the areas where sea ice melts during the summer, the bears come ashore until the sea freezes over again. While on land, the bears typically live off their fat reserves, sometimes going as long as eight months without food.

It should come as little surprise, therefore, that changes in sea ice conditions due to climate change are expected to take a terrible toll on the polar bear. Since 1978, scientists have reported a decline of 7.7 percent per decade in late-summer Arctic sea ice and a decline of 9.8

percent per decade in perennial sea ice. It appears that the rate of decline has accelerated in recent years. The loss of sea ice has been accompanied by longer "melt seasons"; most dramatically, in 2005, the
melt season arrived approximately 17 days earlier than usual. About
half of existing climate models predict that Arctic summers will be
virtually ice-free by 2100.[2] Other researchers have predicted that the
Arctic will be ice-free by 2060 if warming trends follow their current
path.

The changes in sea ice affect the polar bear in many different
ways. Weight loss, lower reproductive rates, reduced survival rates for
cubs, starvation, and even drowning are among the consequences.
Moreover, as changes in the Arctic habitat affect the polar bear's prey,
the polar bear will be affected, too.

Climate change is not the only threat to the polar bear. Habitat
destruction due to other causes, such as oil and gas development, illegal hunting, and chemical contamination, is a concern, though the
impact of these causes—especially hunting—varies greatly depending
on the specific bear population under discussion. But in terms of long-
term survival of the species, climate change is the threat of greatest
concern. In the words of the head of the U.S. Department of the Interior upon announcing a proposal to list the polar bear as a threatened species under the Endangered Species Act, "the polar bear's
habitat may literally be melting."[3]

Does economics help us to understand why we should care? Can
it help us decide what to do?

II.   The Economics of the Polar Bear

There are several possible components of the economic value of
natural resources. First, most conventionally, is the value associated
with actually consuming or using the resource. If we buy a plate of
polar bear meat or a pelt of polar bear fur, we can look upon the market price of the meat or the fur as an indicator of its economic value.
Sometimes this calculation is complicated by the fact that the resource
is not directly sold in markets. Thus, for example, if we travel to the

Arctic to observe the polar bear in its natural habitat, our plane tickets have a market price but the animal itself does not. But by considering the price of travel, one can find at least some signal of the animal's economic value. Similarly, many natural resources play a role in ecosystems that, if the resources were depleted, would have to be performed, if possible, by equipment or technology, which itself has a market price. Therefore, one might also take the market prices of such equipment or technology as a sign of the economic value of the resource. This is, in simplified form, the economic component of the notion of "ecosystem services."[4]

Beyond these quite traditional, if complex, market values, many economists have also recognized that people place value on the protection of natural resources even when they do not use them. People are willing to pay, for example, to have the option to use a resource in the future, to know that their descendants and future generations will have the opportunity to use the resource, and for the simple knowledge that the resource is still here. Known in the jargon as "option," "bequest," and "existence" values, these amounts are impossible to measure using market behavior because no market activity is associated with them. We might care deeply about the polar bear, for example, and yet engage in no economic transaction that expresses our concern.

In these circumstances, economists have turned to the technique of contingent valuation,[5] which is, essentially, an elaborate opinion poll. Survey respondents are asked to report on the amount of money they are willing to spend to protect a particular natural resource. Results are tallied to estimate a monetary amount for the resource's non-use values. The numbers obtained in these surveys can be enormous; a famous contingent valuation study conducted in the wake of the Exxon Valdez oil spill, for example, concluded that as a nation we would be willing to pay as much as $9 billion to avoid the non-use losses associated with another similar spill.[6]

Using these various valuation techniques as our guide, what is the polar bear worth? Given the paucity of quantitative data on the economic value of the polar bear, I will not attempt a precise estimate here. Instead, I will simply describe the ways in which the polar bear's worth could be measured in economic terms and offer quantitative figures where they are available.

A. Use Values

The market for polar bear products (meat, fur, teeth, claws, etc.) has been strictly regulated since 1973, when the international Agreement on the Conservation of Polar Bears was signed by the polar bear nations. This agreement generally prohibits hunting, killing, and capturing polar bears, but makes an exception for "local people using traditional methods in the exercise of their traditional rights."[7] In the United States, polar bears are also protected by the Marine Mammal Protection Act of 1972, which generally prohibits hunting, killing, and capturing polar bears, yet allows Alaska native populations to hunt polar bears for subsistence purposes or to create and sell traditional handicraft and clothing.[8] Thus, despite international and domestic protections, the polar bear has several conventional economic uses. Some of these depend on killing the bear; others do not.

1. Nonexistence Values

Native populations in Canada, Greenland, and the United States may hunt polar bears; in Norway and Russia they may not. The native populations in Canada, Greenland, and the United States eat polar bear meat and fat; they make polar bear pelts into items like parkas or pants; and they use polar bear parts, such as teeth or claws, to make traditional handicrafts. Because subsistence uses of the polar bear for meat or other purposes do not entail an economic transaction, placing a dollar value on these uses would be somewhat complicated. In theory, certainly, one could price the value of replacement meat, for example, and thus derive a rough estimate of the economic value of polar bear meat. (Notice, however, how complicated things are even here: the Inuit eat polar bear meat for spiritual as well as physical sustenance; a pork chop wouldn't quite cut it as a substitute.) Other consumptive uses of polar bear parts do involve economic transactions. For example, handicrafts, such as jewelry, may be sold to tourists in Alaskan native villages, who may bring these items home.

In Canada and Greenland, native populations are permitted to sell a portion of their polar bear harvesting quotas to nonresidents. These rights come with a hefty price tag. Trophy hunters pay as much as $27,500 for the privilege of participating in a polar bear hunt, without a guarantee of success.[9] They, too, may bring their booty home with them. Some idea of the economic scale of this market can be gleaned from the fact that from 2002 to 2005, the United States granted 252 separate requests to import polar bear trophies.[10] Recent estimates indicate that trophy hunters bring approximately $2.9 million into the economy of Nunavut, the Canadian province that has the largest number of polar bears.[11]

2. Ecovoyeurism

The polar bear has economic value even when it is not dead. In the United States, the gross economic value of live bear viewing (including the brown bear as well as the polar bear) was estimated at $485 million in 1995.[12] If anything, it appears that this value has risen in recent years. Travel companies now offer Arctic "safaris" including "polar bear sightings (not guaranteed)," at a cost of as much as $20,000 per person.[13] Remarkably, some travel entrepreneurs have turned climate change itself into a tourist opportunity: islands in Norway's Svalbard archipelago, for example, advertise as destinations for witnessing the already dramatic effects of climate change on the Arctic.[14]

Polar bears are also zoo favorites. Knut, the polar bear cub born in late 2006, rejected by his mother, and raised by a Berlin zookeeper, has become a worldwide phenomenon. Knut has drawn over a million visitors, and shares of the company that operates the Berlin Zoo climbed over 100 percent in value in the first months of Knut's life.[15] Some observers speculated that the Knut "brand" could be worth as much as $13 million to the zoo.[16] Lesser-known polar bears also attract many visitors to zoos every year. As of February 2007, Polar Bears International estimated that there were 246 polar bears in captivity at 104 different zoos around the world.[17] And Baltimore's Magnet the polar bear won the computer game Zoo Tycoon's national "Beast in Show" award in 2001.[18] It is hard to know exactly what the economic value of captive and virtual polar bears says about the economic value of the polar bear as a species, but it is at least suggestive.

3. Ecosystem Services

Polar bears are the largest land predator in the Arctic, and indeed in the world.[19] Their status as a species affects all of the species situated below them on the ecological pyramid. Imbalance in the polar bear population would likely create imbalance in the seal populations they depend on, which would create imbalance in the krill and fish populations that the seals depend on, and so on down the pyramid. I am not aware of any attempt to measure the economic value of the polar bear's contributions to the Arctic ecosystem, and I will not make such an attempt here. The simple point for present purposes is that the polar bear's economic worth extends beyond the animal itself to include the ecosystem to which it contributes.

B. Non-Use Values

I am unaware of any economic research on the non-use value of the polar bear. There are, however, quite a few studies attempting to elicit the non-use value of other, similarly "charismatic" species. As noted above, these studies use the technique of contingent valuation to try to identify the value people place on species even when they do not use them. According to such studies, the average household would be willing to pay $216 to protect bald eagles, $173 to protect humpback whales, and $67 to protect gray wolves.[20] Extrapolated across the whole U.S. population, this means $23 billion for bald eagles, $18 billion for the humpbacks, and $7 billion for the wolves. To put these numbers in perspective, the total budget for the U.S. Department of the Interior—charged not only with protecting all threatened and endangered species, but also with managing about 500 million acres of public lands—was less than $11 billion in 2006. The numbers gleaned from contingent valuation studies also show that the non-use values associated with resources are often larger than the use values. In the case of the Exxon Valdez spill, the $9 billion figure gathered from the contingent valuation surveys dwarfed the $300 million in traditional economic damages claimed from the spill.[21]

We will return in a moment to the usefulness of contingent valuation studies in natural resources policy. For now, it seems safe to say that a contingent valuation survey for the polar bear would produce a number that would overwhelm the conventional economic value of eating, wearing, hunting, and viewing this animal. Yet it is not clear that the result of a contingent valuation study would be included in a government analysis of policies to protect the polar bear; the economic analysis of recent federal regulations aimed at protecting fish, for example, excluded non-use values.[22]

C. Polar Bear Futures

The U.S. Fish and Wildlife Service has listed the polar bear as a threatened species under the Endangered Species Act.[23] Although the Service finds that polar bear populations are already under stress due to climate change, the Service does not believe that the species is now in danger of extinction, the trigger for finding a species "endangered" rather than threatened. Rather, the Service believes that the polar bear is likely to become endangered—that is, will be in danger of extinction—"within the foreseeable future."[24] The Service defines the "foreseeable future" for the polar bear as approximately 45 years, which is three polar bear generations.[25] "Populations would be affected differently in the rate, timing, and magnitude of impact," the Service has written, "but within the foreseeable future, the species is likely to become endangered throughout all or a significant portion of its range due to changes in habitat."[26]

Federal guidelines for economic analysis direct agencies to apply a discount rate to costs and benefits that will occur in the future, on the theory that future costs and benefits are not as valuable as costs and benefits that occur today.[27] The guidelines state that 7 percent is the preferred discount rate, but that agencies should also show the results of analysis using a 3 percent rate. According to these guidelines, the federal agencies charged with protecting the polar bear would discount benefits over the interval between now and the time when those benefits would occur—that is, the time when the bear would otherwise perish.

Suppose that the economic value of preserving the polar bear is calculated to be $20 billion. Discounted at the preferred 7 percent rate over 45 years, this value shrivels to less than $1 billion in present-value terms. Even at a rate of 3 percent, the value shrinks to just over $5 billion. Therefore, because the polar bear is not expected to go extinct for decades, economic analysis as currently practiced by federal agencies would, through the use of discounting, take a huge chunk out of whatever monetary value could be attached to the protection of the species.

D. The Limits of Economic Analysis

The polar bear appears to be worth very little in conventional economic terms. A small number of individuals are willing to pay a great deal to hunt or to view the polar bear, but most people will never use or even see one of these animals in the wild. If values similar to those obtained for other popular species applied to the polar bear, the polar bear's non-use value would be high. Yet current guidelines on economic analysis call for a dramatic reduction in this value through discounting. It appears, therefore, that economic analysis would tell us that the polar bear is not worth very much. But this answer cuts against the intuitive grain; if the polar bear doesn't matter much to us, it is hard to make sense of the species' salience in public awareness of and discourse on climate change. Perhaps economics does not tell us, after all, why we care about the polar bear. Moreover, even if economic analysis—discounting and all—somehow produced a monetary valuation for the polar bear that seemed commensurate with the public's level of concern, would it be helpful in deciding what to do about the bear? I believe the answer is no.

III. Why We Care

There are several reasons why economic analysis will not give us a meaningful answer about what natural resources, including the polar bear, are worth to us. These reasons include: the "public goods" character of most natural resources, the importance of the future in valuing natural resources, the interconnectedness of natural resources, the possibility of irreversibilities and discontinuities in effects on natural resources, and the moral dimension of natural resources protection.

A. Public Goods

Natural resources are classic examples of public goods, "not available for purchase in individual portions."[28] I cannot buy the polar bear's survival through my own behavior; even if I spend extra money on a Prius to decrease my carbon footprint, someone else can buy a Hummer and completely offset the effects of my actions. Even natural resources that have some characteristics of private goods (and many do) often bear traits that are in the nature of public goods. If I buy timber rights to a forest, for example, I can exclude others from taking the lumber away from me. But by cutting down the trees, I harm the water flows, species habitat, natural beauty, and other "goods" that are bound up in the forest along with the timber. These are the kinds of things that are difficult to reduce to private ownership and difficult to protect on an individual basis.

The public goods character of natural resources poses a difficulty for this type of economic analysis, which asks people, individually, what they are willing to pay to protect a resource. If I am the rational character that economic analysis assumes (and prefers) me to be, I will pay nothing individually to protect a common resource, since I have no expectation that my expenditure will do any good. Economic analysts, in fact, have long asserted that rational people will not sacrifice anything, individually, to protect resources held in common.[29] However, even if I am willing to spend nothing on my own to protect a common resource, this does not mean that I am unwilling to spend money on a collective effort to protect that resource. The former response might reflect nothing more than an expectation that the expenditure will be futile. As Frank Ackerman and I paraphrased a point by Amartya Sen, "if your willingness to pay for a large-scale public initiative is independent of what others are paying, then you probably have not understood the nature of the problem."[30]

One might reasonably wonder, then, what economic analysts are thinking when they design surveys aimed at eliciting individuals' willingness to pay (WTP) to protect public goods. Since analysts also try to design these surveys and interpret the results by reference to standard economic theory, one would expect them to assume that no one would pay anything, individually, to protect a commonly held resource. But the analysts have not been deterred. The way they have tried to skirt this problem is by formulating the survey questions to mimic a collective decision. They ask, for example, how much survey respondents would be willing to pay in additional taxes to protect a resource.[31]

There is evidence, however, that survey respondents are not fooled by this gambit. Researchers who have explored the motivation behind responses to contingent valuation surveys have found that people have a hard time valuing public goods in isolation from consideration of what other people would do, even when questions are framed in terms of collective choices. Detailed interviews of participants in a survey designed to assess the value of an important marsh in England revealed that a number of participants' answers were influenced by their sense that their own individual monetary contribution would not protect the marsh. "[W]hat good would it be," asked one participant, "if I had said 'oh yes, I'd give a thousand pounds?' I mean, in isolation that is absolutely no good anyway, is it?"[32] Other participants expressed a desire for a truly collective process of decision making, informed by "local knowledge and local values," but in which experts also played a role.[33] In another study, respondents were asked to state their willingness to pay for policies to address climate change.[34] While doing so, they were also asked to "think aloud" about their responses to the survey questions. Several respondents stated that they were unsure what their individual contribution would imply for the general problem of climate change, and others stressed the importance of a collective effort: "[I]f you're paying you feel it has to be part of a joint effort with everyone else, it can't just be selectively done."[35]

In attempting to elicit economic values for goods not traded in markets, therefore, contingent valuation has not solved the problem of public goods; it has merely glossed over it. Many survey respondents have been clever enough to see the device of asking about increased taxes for what it is: a way of pretending that public goods can be valued by individuals acting in isolation from one another. Economic analysts, to be sure, have been hard at work trying to design valuation studies that will capture the collective reflection many respondents have been so anxious to see. But the closer contingent valuation comes to collective deliberation, the further it moves from the central economic tenets on which it was founded. More fundamentally, once contingent valuation becomes a means for people to decide, together, on collective means and ends, then one must seriously ask what role this technique has to play in shaping policy. After all, collective deliberation on collective means and ends lies at the heart of our government structure. Yet a major consequence of cost-benefit analysis has been to upend the legislative products of that structure, that is, to question the goals laws set by referencing individuals' supposed preferences. But if the practice of contingent valuation is to make the technique look like a public referendum, why not skip contingent valuation and have the referendum? Or why not skip contingent valuation and respect the laws in place?

Strangely, instead of asking the question this way, some researchers have suggested that perhaps a "democratically legitimized" dialogue should precede contingent valuation to make more likely the production of "well-founded estimates of WTP."[36] This strikes me as just exactly backward. Democratic deliberation is not a tool that serves WTP; WTP is a tool that—in theory—serves democratic deliberation.

In any event, the public-goods character of many natural resources (including the polar bear as a species) ensures that accounts of individuals' willingness to spend will reveal little about the resources' real worth. Cost-benefit analysis using such accounts will give us bad information.

B. The Future

One of the central struggles in natural resources policy has been between those who favor short-term exploitation and those who favor long-term preservation. The trouble with cost-benefit analysis in this context is that it inherently, but almost invisibly, favors the former perspective. Discounting—universally favored among cost-benefit analysts—makes protection of natural resources into the far future seem like a bad idea. Yet discounting is also a quite arcane methodology, difficult for a layperson to understand or even to discern in operation. Thus, cost-benefit analysis with discounting could undo the case for long-term preservation of natural resources, without most people even understanding why.

This result would be directly contrary to a central thrust of U.S. natural resources law. Every major modern U.S. law on natural resources is written with an eye on the far future. None of these laws dictates the short-term exploitation of natural resources at the expense of long-term protection. To be sure, in operation, these laws have often condoned, if not encouraged, short-term destructive use. But their aspirations are mostly to the contrary.

Consider, for example, the Endangered Species Act, under which the polar bear may soon be protected. This law does not require temporary protection for listed species, only for as long as seems convenient. Rather, it contemplates and seeks to ensure the continued existence of species into the indefinite future.[37] This is a law built for the long haul. By trivializing the benefits of protecting species into the far future, discounting mocks the very premises of the Endangered Species Act.

The same is true of numerous other modern natural resource laws. The laws protecting national parks,[38] national monuments,[39] and wilderness areas[40] likewise aspire to long-term protection of natural resources. Even other, less overtly preservationist laws at least take long-term protection as a central theme. The Multiple-Use Sustained-Yield Act of 1960, for example, aims to protect sustainability of the forest resource into the indefinite future.[41] The Federal Land Policy and Management Act has a similar goal for other public lands.[42] Examples abound. The basic point is this: modern U.S. laws on natural resources were written in the hope of protecting these resources, not just for our generation, but for many generations to come. They do not have an expiration date on which protection of natural resources becomes undesirable.

Discounting is inconsistent with this forward-looking purpose. It puts a large (probably crushing) thumb on the scales in favor of short-term exploitation over long-term preservation. Cost-benefit analysis using the technique of discounting—that is, all cost-benefit analyses currently undertaken by the federal government—will systematically undercut the case for long-term protection of natural resources. Perhaps equally bad, it will do so underhandedly, in a way only experts (or very motivated and numerate laypeople) can understand.

C. Interconnectedness

Economic analysis tries very hard to isolate particular commodities and to ensure that the value of these commodities is not entangled, in the valuing group's mind, with other commodities. Thus, economic analysts trying to figure out what the polar bear is worth would work hard to make sure that their estimates did not include values for ringed seals, krill, or the Arctic itself. A significant part of the literature on contingent valuation, in fact, has focused on ways to avoid this kind of misestimation—or, in the view of economic analysts, overestimation.

But the polar bear eats the ringed seal, the ringed seal eats krill, and all of these species depend on a stable Arctic environment for their survival. At the same time, "the Arctic," as we have come to know it, includes, as central constituents, the polar bear, the seals, and the ice that is melting under their feet. Economic analysis does not work well without reductionism—practitioners of contingent valuation contend that in order to work tolerably well, valuation questions must be precise, targeted, and limited—but the reductionism it insists on does not exist in the real world. You cannot have the polar bear without the Arctic, and you cannot have the Arctic without the polar bear. Thus asking how much the polar bear, in isolation, is worth is an unrealistic and possibly meaningless exercise. As Aldo Leopold famously put a similar idea: "Everybody knows . . . that the autumn landscape in the north woods is the land, plus a red maple, plus a ruffed grouse. In terms of conventional physics, the grouse represents only a millionth of either the mass or the energy of an acre. Yet subtract the grouse and the whole thing is dead."[43]

Many respondents in contingent valuation surveys understand this point, just as they understand the concept of public goods. Some respondents recognize that nature cannot be separated into discrete chunks, with each valued as if it were not part of a greater whole.[44] Similarly, they understand that the specific resource being valued is often just one "inseparable part" of a larger environmental issue.[45] Stated another way: "Butterfly species in the Amazon are becoming extinct because of the loss of habitat. The only way to save one species is to save them all by saving the forest as well."[46] The idea makes a good deal of sense, yet contingent valuation surveys continue to strive to isolate the specific resource of concern from its larger context. This cannot help but befuddle numerous respondents and lead to strangely acontextual estimates of value.

D. Irreversibilities and Discontinuities

Economic analysis is designed to evaluate problems at the margins, to discern the effect of small changes in outcomes on the prices of various commodities. Economic analysis is also tailored to stable problems, with predictable signs and magnitudes. Neither of these features makes it well suited to natural resources policy.

Consider again the Endangered Species Act. The goal of the law is to ensure that species do not become extinct. Extinction is not a problem at the margin. Figuring out what the survival of a species is worth is not the same as deciding what one polar bear, or ten, or one hundred, are worth. Rather, it means deciding what avoiding a world entirely devoid of polar bears is worth. Coupled with discounting, economic analysis is not a good way to make this kind of decision. Discounting, like economic analysis more generally, assumes stable problems. Irreversibilities and discontinuities are inconsistent with this comfortable mindset.

One way to appreciate how little economic analysis has to say about irreversible and/or discontinuous calamities is to examine the way it goes about valuing human lives. Economists have long conceded that it is not possible to place an economic value on certain death. If asked what they would pay to avoid certain death, most individuals would pay whatever they had; in that case, "willingness to pay" would measure only ability to pay and would be a poor reflection of true value. If asked what they would accept to allow certain death, most individuals would be unlikely to make a deal, opting instead to go on living; in that case, economic analysis would come up with no useable number at all. For these reasons, economists long ago turned to the device of "statistical lives" to measure the value of human life. A statistical life is a collection of small risks in a population such that, when totaled together, they will result in one death; for example, one million risks of one in one million add up to one statistical life (or death). That economists have resorted to this contrivance—which ends up measuring the value only of risk, not of life—is one important indication that economic analysis does not work well when it comes to irreversible and discontinuous events, like death.

Certainly, not all natural resource problems present issues of irreversibility and discontinuity, but many do, including, among others, the extinction of species, the destruction of original wilderness, and the contamination of land and other resources with persistent and, for all purposes, permanent toxins. In these cases, which are numerous, economic analysis will fall short in valuing the resources at stake.

This problem is more than technical. It is not just that economic analysis, as presently constituted, has a hard time dealing with irreversibilities and discontinuities. It is also that, particularly with respect to irreversibilities, a thoroughly non-economic perspective comes into play. Consider this passage from Peter Matthiessen's *Wildlife in America*:

> The finality of extinction is awesome, and not unrelated to the finality of eternity. Man, striving to imagine what might lie beyond the long light years of stars, beyond the universe, beyond the

void, feels lost in space; confronted with the death of species, enacted on earth so many times before he came, and certain to continue when his own breed is gone, he is forced to face another void,
and feels alone in time.[47]

Profound anxieties and longings come to the fore when one contemplates the prospect of irreversible loss. These anxieties and longings are
not well reflected—nor even much respected—in economic analysis.

E. Morality

The moral dimension of natural resources protection is complex
and subtle, ranging from belief in the rights of other living things not
to suffer at our hands, to metaphysical questions about humans' place
in the universe. I cannot describe all of its intricacies here. I hope to
show, however, that economic analysis slights this moral dimension and
thus fails to grasp a large part of the reason we protect natural resources
in the first place.

Contingent valuation has the best hope of capturing the moral
dimension of natural resource valuation. It is hard to see how market
values—for example, the price we pay for polar bear trinkets, or the
airfare for a visit to polar bear habitat—reveal any kind of moral
stance. To be sure, we might value the trinket or the visit because of
the reverence we feel for the species, and reverence—much like hu-
mility borne of an appreciation of our own small place in the
universe—has a moral dimension. But the market cost of the symbols
of our reverence must pale in comparison to the worth of the object of
our reverence. To say otherwise would be like saying that the price of
rosary beads signals the value of Catholicism to their owner. The
moral dimension of natural resource valuation is captured, I think,
not so much in the ways we use or consume natural resources, which
can be reflected in market exchanges, but more in the ways we do not
use them. This is where contingent valuation comes in. As we have
seen, it is the only method for identifying non-use values.

Yet even here, economic analysis falls short. Respondents in
contingent valuation surveys frequently express moral qualms about

"buying" or "selling" natural resources, and these qualms confound the results of the surveys. Some respondents express moral outrage by stating an exceptionally high willingness to pay for natural resource protection. Others, interestingly, express the same kind of sentiment by refusing to pay anything at all.[48] Either way, the estimation of economic value is unsettled by the presence of respondents who recoil at the very prospect of monetary valuation in this setting.[49]

Some scholars have argued that the presence of moral impulse in responses to contingent valuation surveys renders the whole enterprise meaningless from an economic perspective. They believe that respondents giving voice to such impulses are "purchasing" not a public good, but "moral satisfaction," and that "[t]he amount that individuals are willing to pay to acquire moral satisfaction should not be mistaken for a measure of the economic value of public goods."[50] Or, put another way, existence values should be used in economic analysis only if "people's individual existence values . . . reflect only their own personal economic motives and not altruistic motives, or sense of duty, or moral obligation."[51] As Michael Hanemann has trenchantly observed, however, "[t]his criticism hardly comports with the standard view in economics that decisions about what people value should be left up to them. . . . When estimating demand functions for fish prior to Vatican II, no economist ever proposed removing Catholics because they were eating fish out of a sense of duty. Nor, when estimating collective choice models, do we exclude childless couples who vote for school bonds because they lack a personal economic motive."[52]

Hanemann's critique seems on target as far as it goes. Indeed, it strikes me as nothing short of bizarre that in a world where economists would most certainly include the sale of Chanel's $260,000 handbag in a calculation of gross domestic product, without questioning whether a hunger for status through conspicuous consumption reflects "a measure of the economic value" of the handbag, moral values would be barred from admission into the economic sphere.[53] Yet I think Hanemann does not go far enough. Contingent valuation simply cannot process individuals' unwillingness to put nature up for sale. If individuals feel very strongly about protecting natural resources, at some point their willingness to pay will be bounded by and reflective of only their ability to pay. Or, as noted above, individuals who feel very strongly might refuse to participate in the economic valuation at all, reporting an answer of "zero" that completely misrepresents the true worth of the resource to them.

Worse still, economic valuation itself compounds the moral uneasiness associated with depletion or destruction of natural resources. When we give a price at which we would be willing to "sell" the polar bear, or we say that we are unwilling to pay above a certain price to "buy" the protection of the bear, we become complicit in the species' demise. Economic valuation is not a way out of the moral dilemmas surrounding natural resource protection; it is a way of creating new ones.

IV. Conclusion

Cost-benefit analysis has not yet steamed through natural resources policy the way it has through the policy of pollution control. Given its popularity in the latter context, however, it is worthwhile to consider the wisdom of extending its use to natural resources law and policy. I have argued that this would not be a good idea. Using the polar bear as my example, I have shown that the conventional economic value of a species the public appears to regard as extremely valuable is probably quite low. Moreover, even if the value derived from economic analysis were high, economic analysis would miss many of the reasons why we might care about the polar bear and thus would provide a poor reflection of true value. Public goods, the future, natural interconnectedness, irreversible and discontinuous events, and the moral dimension are all poorly captured, if captured at all, by economic analysis. Yet these characteristics and consequences lie at the heart of the resource protection mission. Cost-benefit analysis captures the small things tolerably well but misses the large ones. The picture it gives of value is distorted, and we are better off, and have better information, without it.

Notes

1. The discussion in this section draws primarily upon two sources: Ian Stirling, Polar Bears (1988); Fish and Wildlife Service, Endangered and Threatened Wildlife and Plants; 12-Month Petition Finding and Proposed Rule to List the Polar Bear (Ursus maritimus) as Threatened throughout Its Range, 72 Fed. Reg. 1068, 1068 (Jan. 9, 2007) [hereinafter Listing Proposal].

2. IPCC, 2007: Climate Change 2007: The Physical Science Basis, Summary for Policy Makers 16 (S. D. Solomon et al. eds., 2007), available at http://www.ipcc.ch.

3. U.S. Department of the Interior, Interior Secretary Kempthorne Announces Proposal to List Polar Bears as Threatened under Endangered Species Act (Dec. 27, 2006), http://www.doi.gov/news/06_News_Releases/061227.html.

4. See, e.g., Peter Morton, The Economic Benefits of Wilderness: Theory and Practice, 76 U. Denv. L. Rev. 465 (1999).

5. For an excellent introduction to and defense of contingent valuation, see W. Michael Hanemann, Valuing the Environment Through Contingent Valuation, 8 J. Econ. Persp. 19 (1994).

6. Frank Ackerman & Lisa Heinzerling, Priceless: On Knowing the Price of Everything and the Value of Nothing 156 (2004).

7. Agreement on the Conservation of Polar Bears, art. III(d), Nov. 15, 1973, 27 U.S.T. 3918, 13 I.L.M. 13 (1974).

8. 16 U.S.C. § 1371(b).

9. Katherine Harding, Putting a Chill on the Polar Bear Hunt, Globe and Mail (Canada) (Apr. 3, 2007).

10. Listing Proposal, supra note 1, at 1084 Table 2.

11. Harding, supra note 9.

12. R. H. Lemelin, Conservation Strategies in North American Bear Viewing Areas—A Comparative Analysis of Management Policies in Connection With Bear Observation Activities in Bear Congregation, in Proceedings of the 9th Annual Graduate Leisure Research Symposium. 2001: A Leisure Odyssey (University of Waterloo, Ontario), May 2001.

13. Journey to the Edge of the Arctic with the Great Canadian Expedition Package from the Hilton Toronto, Hudson's Bay Company, and Moccasin Trail Tours Luxurious Travel Package Promises Height of Luxury, Peak of Adventure, CCNMatthews Newswire, May 16, 2007.

14. Arctic Islands Pitch Climate Tourism, Sydney Morning Herald, May 17, 2007, available at http://www.smh.com.au/news/World/Arctic-islands-pitch-climate-tourism/2007/05/17/1178995330288.html.

15. Andreas Hippin, Berlin Zoo Stock Jumps on "Knut" Polar Cub Brand Bets, Bloomberg News, Apr. 3, 2007, available at http://www.bloomberg.com/apps/news?pid=20601100&sid=adjAaVeZ5wRU&refer=germany.

16. Hippin, supra note 15.

17. This calculation was based on information provided by Polar Bears International, at http://www.polarbearsinternational.org/zoos-with-polar-bears.

18. *Baltimore Bear's Animal Magnetism Earns Stardom, Job Offer,* GameZone, Dec. 13, 2001, http://pc.gamezone.com/news/12_13_01_10_20AM.htm.

19. Stirling, *supra* note 1, at 23.

20. Ackerman & Heinzerling, *supra* note 6, at 159.

21. *Id.* at 154–55.

22. *Id.* at 172.

23. 73 Fed. Reg. 28,211 (May 15, 2008).

24. 16 U.S.C. § 1532(20).

25. Listing Proposal, *supra* note 1, at 1070–71.

26. Listing Proposal, *supra* note 1, at 1094.

27. OMB Circular A-4, at 32, *available at* http://www.whitehouse.gov/OMB/circulars/a004/a-4.pdf.

28. Lisa Heinzerling & Frank Ackerman, *Pricing the Priceless: Cost-Benefit Analysis of Environmental Protection,* 150 U. Pa. L. Rev. 1553, 1566 (2002).

29. William F. Baxter, People or Penguins: The Case for Optimal Pollution 34 (1974).

30. Heinzerling & Ackerman, *supra* note 28, citing Amartya Sen, *The Discipline of Cost-Benefit Analysis,* 29 J. Legal Stud. 931, 949 (2000).

31. Hanemann, *supra* note 5, at 24; *see also* Ty Raterman, *On the Role of Preferences and Values in Public Decisions,* 33 Social Theory & Practice 251, 260 (2007) (suggesting that the way out of the dilemma posed by Sen is to ask each respondent "what amount she would be willing to pay if she had an assurance that everyone else would pay that amount as well").

32. Judy Clark et al., *"I Struggled with This Money Business": Respondents' Perspectives on Contingent Valuation,* 33 Ecol. Econ. 45, 50 (2000).

33. *Id.* at 56.

34. Henrik Svedsäter, *Economic Valuation of the Environment: How Citizens Make Sense of Contingent Valuation Questions,* 79 Land Econ. 122 (2003).

35. *Id.* at 129; *see also* David A. Schkade & John W. Payne, *How People Respond to Contingent Valuation Questions: A Verbal Protocol Analysis of Willingness to Pay for an Environmental Regulation,* 26 J. Envtl. Econ. & Mgt. 88, 99 (1994)

36. Svedsäter, *supra* note 34, at 134.

37. *See, e.g.,* 16 U.S.C. § 1531(b) (declaring purpose of statute to be conservation of species and ecosystems on which they depend, without any temporal qualification).

38. *See, e.g.,* National Park Service Organic Act, 16 U.S.C. § 1 (purpose of national parks, monuments, and reservations "is to conserve the scenery and the natural and historic objects and the wild life therein and to provide for the enjoyment of the same in such manner and by such means as will leave them unimpaired for the enjoyment of future generations").

39. Antiquities Act of 1906, 16 U.S.C. § 431 (providing for "proper care and management" —without temporal limit—of designated "historic landmarks, historic and prehistoric structures, and other objects of historic or scientific interest" situated on the public lands).

40. Wilderness Act of 1964, 16 U.S.C. § 1131(a) ("it is hereby declared to be the policy of the Congress to secure for the American people of present and future generations the benefits of an enduring resources of wilderness").

41. 16 U.S.C. § 529 (forest resources to be developed for purpose of achieving "multiple use and sustained yield"); *id.* at § 531(b) ("sustained yield" is "the achievement and maintenance in perpetuity of a high-level annual or regular periodic output of the various renewable resources of the national forests without impairment of the productivity of the land").

42. 43 U.S.C. § 1743(b) (Secretary of the Interior directed to manage public lands so as "to prevent unnecessary or undue degradation of the lands").

43. ALDO LEOPOLD, A SAND COUNTY ALMANAC 146 (Oxford Press 1966).

44. N. A. Powe et al., *Mixing Methods within Stated Preference Environmental Valuation: Choice Experiments and Post-Questionnaire Qualitative Analysis*, 52 ECOL. ECON. 513, 517 (2005).

45. Svedsäter, *supra* note 34, at 125.

46. Arild Vatn, *Environmental Valuation and Rationality*, 80 LAND ECON. 1, 6 (2004), quoting W. Schulze et al., *Methodological Issues in Using Contingent Valuation to Measure Non-use Values*, EPA/DOE Workshop Paper, Herndon, VA (1994).

47. PETER MATTHIESSEN, WILDLIFE IN AMERICA 22 (Viking Press 1959).

48. Thomas H. Stevens *et al.*, *Measuring the Existence Value of Wildlife: What Do CVM Estimates Really Show?*, 67 LAND ECON. 390, 397 (1991).

49. *Id.* at 399; Clark et al., *supra* note 32, at 60.

50. Daniel Kahneman & Jack L. Knetsch, *Valuing Public Goods: The Purchase of Moral Satisfaction*, 22 J. ENVTL. ECON. & MGT. 57, 69 (1992).

51. Paul Milgrom, *Is Sympathy an Economic Value? Philosophy, Economics, and the Contingent Valuation Method*, in CONTINGENT VALUATION: A CRITICAL ASSESSMENT 431 (J.A. Hausman ed., 1993).

52. Hanemann, *supra* note 5, at 33.

53. *See* Ylan Q. Mui, *Exclusive Statute: It's in the Bag*, WASH. POST, at D1 (Aug. 21, 2007).

4 | The Growing Influence of Tort and Property Law on Natural Resources Law

Case Studies of Coalbed Methane Development and Geologic Carbon Sequestration

Alexandra B. Klass

I.   Introduction

This chapter considers the present-day role of tort and property law on natural resources law. It attempts to show through two case studies that regardless of today's drift toward federal statutes and regulations, the role of state tort and property law in the development and allocation of natural resources is important and growing.

Natural resources law has always been both rooted in the common law and moving toward capture by the federal regulatory state. With the growth of federal statutes and public regulation governing mining, oil and gas, protection of endangered species, and environmental review of public projects and private projects on public lands, natural resources law has come to resemble the field of environmental law, which has long been dominated by public law and the regulatory state. But whether the topic is natural resources law or environmental law, space remains within and between the statutes. In some cases, that space was intentional to allow state statutory law or common law to continue to serve a role in governing resources. In other cases, the space was unintentional, arising out of new technologies or new resource concerns that were never contemplated by Congress. In those circumstances, stakeholders turn to state tort law and property law to resolve disputes, allocate rights and responsibilities, and balance public needs and private interests.

Even in environmental law, a field dominated by the regulatory state, there has been a noticeable shift back to relying on tort and property law to resolve modern problems. Local governments have brought common law tort claims and state statutory tort claims against industry to recover for chemical contamination of public water supplies.[1] States have brought common law nuisance actions against power plants and automobile manufacturers to obtain injunctive relief or to recover for damages associated with greenhouse gas emissions.[2] Local governments and states have brought nuisance claims against paint manufacturers to force remediation of lead paint in buildings.[3] In all these examples, federal environmental laws do not provide redress for injured parties and do not allocate rights and responsibilities; state common law and state statutory law are there to fill in the gaps.

As this chapter will show, this "gap-filling" role for state tort and property law is as important in the field of natural resources law as it is in environmental law. In other words, state tort and property law are not only a part of the history of natural resources law, but they are also part of its future. Moreover, state tort and property law do not serve a role only when there is a new type of resource technology or a new natural resource problem that was not contemplated or addressed by Congress. Instead, state tort and property law can and should continue to provide rights and remedies where Congress has addressed an issue on a national level but left significant room for state and local variations in remedies and resource allocation.

State tort and property law, and particularly state common law, is not a substitute for effective statutory regulation of natural resources. Regulation, when done right, can balance preservation and development interests and level the playing field among natural resource developers. Without regulation, rights can only be asserted through expensive, case-by-case lawsuits that result in a patchwork of different judge-made rules within and between jurisdictions. However, before regulation in a particular area, and even after regulation is put in place, there remains an important role for state tort and property law.

This chapter explores this issue through two case studies. The first case study looks at coalbed methane (CBM) development in the Powder River Basin of Montana and Wyoming. The second case study explores the developing technology of geologic sequestration of carbon dioxide for the purpose of limiting greenhouse gas emissions. These case studies illustrate the continuing importance of tort and property law when it comes to new forms of natural resource development that are not currently part of the federal regulatory structure. At this time, state tort and property law are virtually the only laws governing these areas. This landscape will change as regulation catches up and begins to occupy the field. But that occupation likely will not, and should not, be complete. Instead, while state tort and property law may diminish in scope, they will remain important bedrocks of the regulation and may also provide rights and remedies beyond the regulation. In this way, state tort and property law can remain important components of the law even in areas that generally come to be considered part of the federal regulatory state.

II. Coalbed Methane, Split Estates, Property Rights, and Tort Claims

To address growing energy demands, there has been a push to develop more of the estimated 30 trillion cubic feet (tcf) of CBM gas that underlies the Powder River Basin in eastern Wyoming and Montana. This resource spans approximately 14 million acres, much of which is held in "split-estate," meaning the land surface and the mineral rights are in separate ownership. Split-estate ownership of federal public lands began in the early 20th century with the Stock-Raising Homestead Act of 1916 and the Taylor Grazing Act of 1934, through which the federal government retained mineral rights to land when it conveyed the surface rights for ranching and agricultural use. The federal government owns most of the mineral rights in the Powder River Basin and leases these rights to oil and gas companies. Currently, there are over 15,000 CBM wells operating in the Powder River Basin with 20,000–50,000 more expected in the next ten years.

In order to release the methane gas from the coal seam, the developer must first remove and discharge the groundwater. As a result, significant amounts of water are discharged to surface streams and ditches, often resulting in conflicts with ranchers who do not want the water, which is saline and can damage certain crops and hayfields. Cumulative CBM water production from 1987 though December 2004 was over 380,000 acre-feet (2.9 billion barrels), while annual CBM water production in 2003 was 74,457 acre-feet (577 million barrels). Total production of CBM water across all Wyoming coal fields could total roughly 7 million acre-feet (55 billion barrels) if all of the recoverable CBM gas in the projected reserves of over 30 tcf were produced.

Disputes between mineral rights holders and surface owners in the West have existed as long as lands have been held in split-estate. In recent years, however, the rate of development, the spacing and frequency of wells, and the need to discharge large amounts of groundwater has created new conflicts between surface owners and mineral rights holders in the Powder River Basin. Under common law, on split-estate lands the mineral estate is dominant. This means that CBM developers can make use of the surface to access and develop the CBM resource even if it interferes with surface uses, often with minimal compensation for damages in the absence of negligence or a contractual agreement to the contrary. In addition, CBM developers, like all mineral development companies in both Montana and Wyoming, can exercise the private right of eminent domain to take surface lands above the mineral estate as well as neighboring property for water discharge, roads, drilling, ditches, and other activities in connection with developing the resource. This can result in an imbalance of power between mineral developers and surface owners.

These problems are exacerbated by the fact that there is very little in the way of a federal or state regulatory system to address the CBM water discharge problems, particularly in Wyoming. Under federal water quality regulations for oil and gas operations, groundwater may be discharged directly to the surface from oil and gas operations in western states (west of the 98th meridian) where the produced water is of good enough quality for livestock watering or agricultural use and is put to such use. Wyoming law designates CBM water as a beneficial use and allows discharge to the surface by permit. These water discharge permits are routinely issued on the grounds that the water is of good enough quality for livestock watering or agricultural use, even when the surface owner indicates it does not intend to put the water to that use.

Moreover, in both Wyoming and Colorado, state regulators have refused to create a system to regulate the quantity of water discharged in connection with CBM development. Landowners in Colorado sued the state engineer for his refusal to exercise jurisdiction over permitting of CBM wells. Similarly, Wyoming's governor rejected rules enacted by the state Environmental Quality Council governing water discharge associated with CBM operations. The governor rejected the rules on grounds that they were an attempt to regulate water quantity, not water quality, and that only the state engineer could regulate water quantity issues. For his part, the state engineer has also declined to regulate the quantity of water discharged from CBM operations. In Wyoming, landowners and environmental groups that have been urging environmental regulators to enact rules and standards on CBM water discharge contend that they "have been left in a regulatory gap."[4]

Although regulatory efforts to address CBM development are beginning in some states, they are far from mature. As a result, there is a space in the regulatory framework that was established to govern oil and gas. This framework simply does not address the problems unique to CBM development, particularly the issue of water discharge. In this regulatory void, affected parties turn to tort law and property law to assert their rights and resolve disputes. A review of how the stakeholders frame the issues in these disputes and how courts are beginning to resolve them provides insight into not only the use of tort and property doctrines, but also how those doctrines remain vibrant in the field of natural resources law. There have been significant developments in both the common law and state statutory law to shape tort and property doctrines that create rights and provide remedies in the context of this new area of natural resource development. The following sections first discuss common law developments and then move to state statutory developments.

A. Common Law Developments

Landowners in Wyoming, where much of the CBM development has occurred, have brought high-profile trespass and nuisance
lawsuits based on the flow of CBM water into ephemeral streams
causing damage to trees and agriculture. These lawsuits show that just
like in the field of environmental law, stakeholders rely on tort and
property law to create a framework for resolving natural resource
disputes in the absence of federal regulation.

For instance, in *Williams v. Maycock*, a case in Wyoming state
court, Williams proposed to develop CBM gas pursuant to mineral
rights on Maycock's land.[5] In order to extract the gas, Williams wished
to pump out the groundwater and drain it through two creeks, which
it argued were "watercourses" under Wyoming law. If the creeks were
watercourses, then Williams would not need to condemn and pay for
the land because the watercourses were owned by the state, not Maycock. The district court ruled in October 2005 that CBM waters
were "waters of the state," that if the creeks were watercourses, they
were subject to the state's easement for water flow, and thus payment
to Maycock via condemnation was not required. The district court
later ruled in March 2006 that the creeks were too ephemeral to constitute watercourses, and thus Williams could pump water onto those
lands only if it condemned them and paid just compensation to Maycock. In the absence of taking the lands through condemnation, the
discharge of water would constitute a trespass and would support liability for damage to Maycock's meadows. Williams then began proceedings to condemn an easement to flow water in the drainage across
Maycock's ranch.

In a similar case in Wyoming, *The PeeGee Ranch v. Devon Energy
Prod. Co.*, Devon began discharging CBM water into ephemeral
drainages that flowed through the plaintiff's property and into the
Powder River in 2000.[6] The plaintiff alleged damages to trees on his
property and sued Devon for trespass. The court dismissed the claims
after a trial on the grounds that: (1) the Wyoming State Engineer's
Office had designated the discharge of water for CBM production
purposes to be a beneficial use of groundwater; (2) Devon received a
permit to discharge CBM water into the drainage; (3) water legally

placed in natural watercourses, even water produced from CBM, is water belonging to the state, and the state enjoys an easement across all private property for state water flowing through those watercourses and for the purpose of managing waters of the state; (4) the drainages at issue were "natural watercourses" subject to the state's easement; and (5) the plaintiff's ranch was subject to the state's easement and thus the discharge of water into the state's easement did not constitute a trespass on the plaintiff's land.

Lawsuits have also been brought for interference with drinking water wells. In *Cole v. J.M. Huber Co.,* the plaintiffs had drinking-water wells on properties north of Sheridan, Wyoming that were drilled and permitted several years before Huber began CBM operations on surrounding lands.[7] In the course of drilling hundreds of CBM wells in the area, Huber began producing millions of gallons of water from the coal seams in which the plaintiffs' wells were located. Soon after, the plaintiffs alleged, the wells began producing methane gas instead of water. The plaintiffs sued Huber under theories of trespass and negligence seeking diminution in value to property, emotional distress damages, and punitive damages, among other relief.

What is notable about these cases is how the parties and the courts rely on basic tort and property law doctrines to resolve disputes that have resulted from new technologies, new energy policies, and new energy needs. The parties and the courts have very little in the way of federal or state statutes or regulations to guide their arguments and decisions. Instead, these cases are decided with reference to the state law of public easements, water rights, and tort doctrines of trespass and nuisance. In this way, common law tort and property doctrine serve a crucial role in addressing new natural resource challenges. Just as the history of natural resources is grounded in basic common law doctrines, its future remains closely tied to those doctrines.

B. Statutory Developments

The preceding section shows the continuing importance of the common law of tort and property in addressing new natural resources challenges in the area of CBM development. But state tort and property law does not develop only through the common law; it also develops through state statutory law. Just as the courts have shaped common law tort and property doctrines to address CBM disputes, state legislatures also have altered state tort and property law to reallocate rights between surface owners and mineral owners. These developments are discussed below.

1. Reasonable Use and Surface Owner Accommodation Laws

Until recently, the law had been fairly settled with regard to the rights of mineral owners versus surface owners. The mineral estate was the dominant estate, and the mineral owner had the right to use that portion of the surface estate reasonably necessary to develop the severed mineral interest. Moreover, the owner of the mineral rights was not liable for surface damage in the absence of negligence unless there was a contractual agreement to pay damages or a statute providing a right to damages.

Starting in the 1970s, however, some courts began to adopt forms of the "accommodation doctrine" which required mineral owners to "accommodate" surface owners to the fullest extent possible. This meant that if the method of developing mineral rights would preclude or impair surface uses, and there were reasonable alternatives available to develop the mineral rights that would not preclude or impair surface uses, such reasonable alternatives must be used. Any interference with surface rights that could have been avoided through reasonable alternatives constituted a trespass and entitled the surface owner to damages.

These judicial developments were limited to a few states, however, and relied on a case-by-case determination to allocate rights and responsibilities between mineral owners and surface owners. This problem was exacerbated as the CBM development boom created more frequent conflicts between surface owners and mineral developers. These growing tensions encouraged state legislatures to step up and reallocate property rights through so-called "split-estate laws" or "surface owner accommodation laws." These laws tend to codify common law accommodation doctrines, allow for recovery of surface damages even in the absence of operator negligence, and grant additional leverage to surface owners in negotiating where and how CBM and other gas development on their lands will occur.

Some of these statutes impose strict liability for surface damages and specifically allow for restoration costs. These statutes also provide additional bargaining rights for surface owners. For example, in 2005, Wyoming enacted the Surface Owner Accommodation Act, which gives additional protection to surface owners during oil and gas development. Key provisions state that oil and gas operators must (1) "reasonably accommodate" existing surface uses; (2) give 30 days' written notice prior to obtaining access to private lands and beginning oil and gas operations; (3) pay landowners compensation for economic losses caused by oil and gas activity, including lost land value, loss of value of improvements, and loss of production and income; and (4) attempt to negotiate a surface use agreement with landowners regarding the planning of oil and gas activities that affect private surface lands and if negotiations fail, obtain a bond from the State Oil and Gas Conservation Commission to access private lands in split estate.[8]

New Mexico and Colorado enacted split-estate laws in 2007.[9] In a news article reporting on New Mexico's law, Governor Bill Richardson was quoted as saying that the law shows the state is "an energy producer with sensitivity to the land and property rights and property owners."[10] The increase in split-estate legislation is another example of how property law and tort liability have been altered to respond to tensions over a new type of natural resource development. In this case, the problem is addressed not in the courts through common law but by state legislatures rebalancing property and tort rights.

2. Eminent Domain Reform and Natural Resources Development

Eminent domain reform is another area where states have focused on reallocating property rights to address resource conflicts. Much has been written about the state legislative reaction to *Kelo v. City of New London*, a case in which the Supreme Court held that the taking of private property to promote economic development was a "public use" and thus did not violate the Fifth Amendment to the U.S. Constitution.[11] As a result of the case, which outraged the public, over 30 states have enacted statutory or constitutional reforms to limit the ability of state and local governments to engage in "economic development" takings except in cases of severe "blight," nuisance, or violation of public health standards.

In the interior West, however, eminent domain reform has also been used to readjust property rights between surface owners and mineral owners. In natural resource–rich states like Wyoming and Montana, private oil and gas companies can use the power of eminent domain to condemn private lands associated with oil and gas development. These condemnation rights include the power to condemn land for easements for drilling and production of oil and gas; for the construction of roads; and for the location, construction, maintenance, and use of reservoirs, drains, ditches, and other means of discharging water associated with oil and gas development. As CBM development has increased in the Powder River Basin, the more frequent use of eminent domain for the discharge of CBM wastewater has fueled the push for eminent domain reform.

In 2007, Wyoming enacted eminent domain reform that focused not solely on *Kelo*-type urban renewal projects; it also focused on providing new landowner rights in the context of condemnation proceedings for natural resource development. Some of the Wyoming statutory provisions include requiring new negotiation protocols between condemning parties and landowners, attorneys' fees for landowners if the condemning party refuses to negotiate in good faith, and use of comparable sales for easements and other property interests to define fair market value for rural lands. A newspaper article reporting on the legislation declared that property owners in the state "are demanding reform of the state's eminent domain laws to protect what they say might be a dying Western value."[12] The article goes on to describe the battle as one between the booming energy economy and the need for smart growth and land preservation. This legislation shows Wyoming using statutory reforms of state property laws to address the perceived imbalance of power between mineral companies and landowners in the context of CBM development.

3. Summary

CBM development has an impact on private property that is different from traditional oil and gas development. Existing laws cannot address problems unique to CBM development, such as the rapid increase in the amount of development and the massive amounts of water discharged in the process. Regulation of water quantity limits in connection with CBM development is still rare or nonexistent in most states. In the meantime, the parties, courts, and legislatures are working through tort and property law to resolve ongoing disputes between surface owners and CBM developers. In states with significant CBM development, notably Wyoming, there are reallocations of tort and property rights through the courts, as well as legislative efforts to address surface rights and eminent domain reform. These reallocations will likely continue until policymakers create a regulatory framework specific to CBM development. Even if a regulatory framework is created, tort and property law remain tools to address the inevitable spaces that will remain in any regulatory system.

CBM development shows how tort and property law evolve with changing conditions. The *Maycock* case built on existing easement and water law to establish a public easement for CBM operators to flow water in established watercourses. Likewise, as land-use conflicts increase as a result of CBM development in a more populated West, courts and legislators in many states have adopted the accommodation doctrine to reallocate rights between surface owners and mineral developers.

CBM development raises important issues of tort and property law where natural resources are removed from the subsurface and released into the environment. The next case study is a mirror image: it focuses on tort and property issues where natural resources are removed from the environment and released into the subsurface.

III. Geologic Carbon Sequestration, Property Rights, and Tort Claims

One of today's most pressing environmental problems is the need to address increasing levels of carbon dioxide (CO_2) in the atmosphere in order to prevent global warming. One of the technologies being developed to deal with increasing concentrations of CO_2 in the atmosphere is Carbon Capture and Sequestration. This technology drastically reduces emissions from power plants and industrial sources by capturing CO_2 emissions and sequestering them in deep geologic formations for long periods of time. The sequestration portion of this system is known as Geologic Carbon Sequestration (GS). Areas for potential CO_2 sequestration include oil and gas fields, saline aquifers, and coal seams. These formations have provided natural storage for crude oil, natural gas, brine, and CO_2 for millions of years. GS technologies would attempt to take advantage of these natural storage capacities to reduce CO_2 emissions.

A Department of Energy report released in 2007 indicates very large capacity across the United States and Canada for storing CO_2 and other greenhouse gases produced at power plants and other industrial sources.[13] The Powder River Basin in Wyoming alone is estimated to have the capacity to sequester 13.6 billion metric tons of CO_2.[14] Several GS projects are under way or planned in Canada, the United States, and other countries. Over the past several years, Congress, the Department of Energy, other federal agencies, and the private sector have invested significant resources to research and develop GS technology.

What does this have to do with tort and property law? Possibly, a great deal. The long-term storage of CO_2 poses significant potential risks to human health and the environment as a result of surface leakage or sub-surface migration. It is critical to establish in advance as precisely as possible where tort liability, financial responsibility, and ownership interests will rest among corporate developers, state and federal governments, and other interested parties. Because of these competing property interests, there is a significant potential for trespass, nuisance, strict liability, and negligence claims similar to those brought in cases where CO_2 is injected into oil reservoirs for enhanced recovery. State and federal statutes will provide a framework for tort liability and will delineate property interests, but undoubtedly, there will be spaces in that system, which will make common law tort and property doctrines equally important to this endeavor.

For instance, many of the potential areas for GS are in the western United States, where split-estate lands predominate. As a result, GS offers the same potential for conflicts between surface owners and subsurface owners as CBM. Who is liable if the gas escapes? Who owns the gas and for how long? Does ownership change if the gas moves? The next sections review the applicable common law foundations as well as recent legislative efforts to more precisely define ownership and liability issues related to GS.

A. Common Law Issues: Fugitive Resources and Property Rights

As far back as the middle of the nineteenth century, there have been disputes over who owns subsurface oil and gas, when interference with oil and gas constitutes a trespass or conversion of a property right, and who owns oil and gas that has been recovered and then reinjected into the subsurface for storage or enhanced oil recovery purposes.[15] The body of common law that developed around these issues forms a potential basis to resolve disputes over the injection and storage of CO_2. While state and federal statutes and regulations will almost certainly create a regulatory system governing these issues, this system will be set against a backdrop of the common law, which will inevitably be put to use in interpreting the statutes and filling in the gaps within the statutes.

In the early twentieth century, courts found it difficult to apply traditional ideas of ownership to substances that could not be seen from the surface and moved seemingly on their own accord. As a result, early courts often drew analogies to legal doctrines governing ownership of water, wild animals, and other "fugitive resources." This resulted in a body of case law that held that a landowner did not own oil and gas in place beneath the land until it was reduced to "possession." Such law also held that an owner lost title to oil or gas if it was reinjected (placed back "into the wild") for storage purposes and that the owner was not liable for trespass of that oil or gas on neighboring property because of the lack of ownership. This denied the landowner any protectable property interest in oil or gas being drained to other tracts and also discouraged the use of underground storage reservoirs as a safe and economical means of holding oil and gas after production. As stakeholders and courts developed more sophisticated knowledge about the movement of oil and gas, most courts rejected the analogy to wild animals and held that once previously extracted oil or gas is stored in defined underground reservoirs, title to the oil or gas is not lost and remains with the person or company placing the oil or gas in storage.

Once that shift occurred, the question arose: under what circumstances would the owner of re-injected oil or gas be liable for trespass or other tort liability if the oil or gas migrated and interfered with neighboring property or persons? Generally, if substances injected into a reservoir for storage or for enhanced oil recovery cause damage to neighboring property, the injector is liable. In some cases, though, courts have found that a trespass in the absence of damage is not actionable and that a trespass is not actionable where public policy favors the injection.

Cases refusing to find a trespass based on public policy favoring injection of dry gas or salt water for enhanced oil recovery are particularly instructive. For example, in *Phillips Petroleum Co. v. Stryker*, the Alabama Supreme Court in 1998 reversed a $27 million jury verdict in favor of the plaintiffs who had claimed that the defendant wrongfully injected dry gas into the ground that migrated onto the plaintiffs' property and allegedly drained the natural gas from their property.[16] The supreme court held that there was no actionable trespass because the defendants had injected the dry gas to obtain secondary recovery of oil and gas resources within an area the state oil and gas board had approved as "unitized" for oil and gas recovery.

The court found that state public policy supported unitization of areas for oil and gas recovery and also supported secondary recovery to promote the efficient collection of oil and gas, prevent waste, and avoid the drilling of unnecessary wells. The court found that the plaintiffs had never sought to have their properties included in the approved unit despite notice of the proposed unitization of the oil and gas field, and that to hold the defendant liable for draining "would run counter" to the state's policy regarding secondary recovery unitization.

Likewise, in the 1962 case *Railroad Commission v. Manziel*, the Texas Supreme Court held that water injected into a well for secondary recovery purposes pursuant to a state agency order does not constitute a trespass if the injected water moves across lease lines and interferes with neighboring oil and gas wells.[17] The court reasoned that it was state policy to encourage secondary recovery operations to increase the ultimate recovery of oil and gas, and that "secondary recovery programs could not and would not be conducted if any adjoining operator could stop the project on the ground of subsurface trespass."[18]

The development of GS will inject CO_2 into the subsurface on a scale that dwarfs current injection of CO_2 or other substances for storage or enhanced oil recovery purposes. However, as a matter of common law, courts will be forced to look to the precedent created in traditional oil and gas operations and will attempt to apply that precedent to a new technology on a new scale. In the same way that courts moved away from analogies to wild animals as public policy began to favor reinjection and storage of oil, gas, and water, courts may also need to create new common law frameworks to address the needs of GS. It is likely that public policy favoring reduction of greenhouse gas emissions will weigh in favor of applying liability sparingly as a common law matter, as has been done in the past with traditional oil and gas operations. Because of the scope and scale of GS, however, courts undoubtedly will be working with more than just common law tools. The large amounts of money at stake will encourage corporate interests and government entities to create statutes and regulations to allocate property rights and assign liability for CO_2 injected into the subsurface. Efforts to create such a statutory structure are discussed below.

B. Statutory Issues: Indemnity and Permitting

There is no federal program that currently regulates GS and CO_2 injection, although some small-scale CO_2 storage projects have been permitted under the EPA's Underground Injection Control Program created under the Safe Drinking Water Act of 1974. Federal and state legislators, however, are fully aware of the importance of defining property rights and tort liability in advance of implementing GS projects. Recent efforts to enact GS legislation are instructive and show a recognition of the importance of property rights and tort liability in the development of this new technology.

For instance, over the past few years, there has been an initiative to build the world's first integrated sequestration and hydrogen production research power plant. This project, called FutureGen, was structured as a $1 billion public/private partnership made up of member power companies working with the U.S. Department of Energy (DOE) to build the world's first coal-based, zero-emission electricity and hydrogen production facility. The DOE evaluated four candidate sites in Illinois and Texas, and FutureGen then chose Mattoon, Illinois as the project site. A critical component of the project, as well as other similar projects, is the storage of CO_2 in geologic formations; a portion of the CO_2 may also be used in enhanced oil recovery operations where oil reserves are currently unrecoverable but can be "unlocked" using CO_2.

A review of federal and state legislation in connection with the FutureGen project provides insight into the significant tort and property issues associated with GS. For instance, in 2006, the U.S. House of Representatives considered a bill to authorize and appropriate funds for the FutureGen project "to demonstrate the feasibility of the commercial application of advanced clean coal energy technology, including carbon capture and geological sequestration, for electricity generation."[19] One of the failed amendments to that bill was to allow the Secretary of the Department of Energy to "indemnify the consortium and its member companies for liability associated with the first-of-a-kind sequestration component of the project," with indemnity extending to any legal liability arising out of "the storage or unintentional release" of sequestered emissions. The proposed indemnification contained exceptions for gross negligence and intentional misconduct, and limited the U.S. Government's aggregate liability to $500 million for a single incident.[20]

The two state finalists for the FutureGen project, Illinois and Texas, were in keen competition for the project, which would bring cutting-edge coal research, hundreds of jobs, and a new market for local natural resources including but not limited to coal. As part of that competition, both states began a race to enact legislation to enhance their bids as the host site, including offering freedom from tort liability through statutory indemnification and transfer of property rights in CO_2. Texas enacted legislation in 2006 providing that the state would acquire title to CO_2 captured by a clean coal process, thus releasing the owner of the project from any liability after capture of the CO_2.[21]

In 2007, additional bills were introduced in the Texas legislature to strengthen those indemnification provisions and make clear that "once the State of Texas assumes ownership of CO_2, the [FutureGen] Alliance will be protected from tort liability."[22] According to a press release from the Railroad Commission of Texas, the purpose of the indemnity provisions was to move "Texas significantly ahead in the national competition for FutureGen because no other state has identified a suitable answer to this important question."[23]

Illinois attempted to provide similar assurances to the Alliance. In 2007, Illinois approved legislation to offer liability protections similar to those enacted in Texas in order to "compete" with Texas and put Illinois "on an even playing field."[24] In January 2008, the Department of Energy announced that it was withdrawing support from the FutureGen project in favor of investing in multiple projects across the country.[25] Even if continuing attempts by the Illinois Congressional delegation fail to revive the project,[26] the legislative efforts by Illinois and Texas during the life of the project reflect the debate over how to structure tort and property law in the context of GS.

States, particularly in the West, not competing for any specific GS-related projects still have a significant and immediate interest in legislation governing GS because many of these states will be major repositories for CO_2 generated by such projects. As a result, these states must consider whether they need legislation to create permitting systems and other regulatory frameworks to govern the massive amounts of CO_2 that will be stored under their lands. Several states have enacted legislation governing GS since 2007, and Wyoming has enacted legislation vesting ownership of subsurface pore space in the surface owner but reaffirming that the mineral estate remains dominant.[27] This shows the beginnings of an attempt to create a regulatory system that will create and allocate property interests, provide parameters for a permit system, and delineate liability.

All of the legislation introduced or enacted illustrates the importance of property law and tort law in the creation of new natural resource technologies to address global warming. Unlike CBM development, which implemented a new technology without resolving many of the unique tort and property issues in advance, governments and private parties are attempting to use legislation to create parameters prior to implementing GS technology. There are obvious reasons for the different approaches. CBM development more closely resembles traditional oil and gas development, can be implemented on a well-by-well basis with modest up-front investment, and has its primary impact in only a handful of states. GS, by contrast, is part of a significant public/private endeavor involving major corporate interests and the federal and state governments and has massive start-up costs. Under those circumstances, much more work will be done in advance to allocate rights and determine who will be responsible for liabilities associated with GS projects. Nevertheless, there is a level of sophistication that seems to be missing from the legislative efforts of Illinois and Texas to provide the broadest indemnity provisions for liability associated with GS. As GS technology development continues, one hopes to see a fuller discussion of the risks of GS and how they should be allocated. Releasing corporate investors from liability may not be the only answer. This discussion can and should look to some of the policy principles that underlie our tort and property system both in the common law of oil and gas storage and beyond.

IV. Conclusion

The CBM development and GS technology case studies illustrate the continuing importance of tort and property law in the development of natural resources law. These current natural resources issues show how easy it is for gaps to exist in a regulatory system. In those circumstances, stakeholders can and should rely on tort and property doctrine to assert their rights and impose responsibilities for the use of resources and land. In addition, state statutory reforms can address new issues and local conditions more quickly than the common law or federal agency action. Moreover, the role for tort and property law does not end with congressional or agency action. When all eyes focus on new regulation, it is important not to lose sight of the role tort and property law can continue to play, not only as the historic base of regulation but as a continuing vehicle for creating and applying legal doctrine.

The tort and property issues associated with GS are less mature than those present in the area of CBM development because GS is far less developed as a natural resource technology. It is clear though that both GS and CBM development present critical concerns of ownership, trespass, allocation, and property rights in the context of natural resources development. As GS technology and policy develops, lawmakers and stakeholders can learn from the tort and property disputes in the CBM arena. Regardless of the sophistication of the technology, stakeholders must consider the tort and property law issues that will be central to GS development. These issues can be addressed through a combination of statutory, market, and common law forums. As the law evolves to encompass new technologies and resources, new technologies and resources must fully consider existing tort and property frameworks.

Notes

1. *See, e.g.,* In re MTBE Prod. Liab. Litig., 379 F. Supp.2d 348, 361 (S.D.N.Y. 2005).

2. *See, e.g.,* Connecticut v. American Elec. Power Co., 406 F. Supp. 2d 265 (S.D.N.Y. 2005); California v. General Motors Corp., No. C06-05755 MJJ, 2007 WL 2726871 (N.D. Cal. Sept. 17, 2007). *See also* Alexandra B. Klass, *Tort Experiments in the Laboratories of Democracy,* 50 WM. & MARY L. REV. 1501 (2009) (discussing suits brought by states to address harm associated with greenhouse gas emissions and climate change).

3. *See, e.g.,* State v. Lead Industries, 951 A.2d 428 (R.I. 2008) (dismissing state's public nuisance claim against paint manufacturers); Katie J. Zoglin, *Getting the Lead Out: The Potential of Public Nuisance in Lead-Based Paint Litigation, in*

CREATIVE COMMON LAW STRATEGIES FOR PROTECTING THE ENVIRONMENT 339 (Clifford Rechtschaffen & Denise Antolini eds. 2007) (discussing public nuisance suits brought by states and municipalities to address harms of lead paint in residential buildings).

4.   *See* Letter from Gov. Dave Freudenthal to EQC regarding Final Rules for Water Quality Division, April 23, 2007; Tripp Baltz, *Wyoming Governor Rejects Rules on Water Produced by Coal Bed Methane Operations*, BNA DAILY ENV. REP. No. 79, at A-10 (April 25, 2007).

5.   Williams Prod. RMT Co. v. Maycock, Civil No. 26099 (Wyo. Dist. Ct.).

6.   Case No. 26607 (filed Wyo. Dist. Ct., March 19, 2007).

7.   Case No. 06-CV-0142-J (Wyo. Dist. Ct., Amended Complaint filed Jan. 2007).

8.   WYO. STAT. §§ 30-5-401–410.

9.   *See* N.M. Stat. Ann. §§ 70-12-1 to 70-12-10 (2008), Colo. Rev. Stat. §§ 34-60-127 (2008). North Dakota and Montana statutory law also provide for surface owner compensatory damages resulting from oil and gas operations. *See* N.D. CENT. CODE § 38-11.1-04 (2006); MONT. CODE ANN. § 82-10-504 (2007).

10. *See* Deborah Baker, *Surface Protection Bill Signed Into Law*, FREE NEW MEXICAN (March 8, 2007).

11. 545 U.S. 469 (2005).

12. *See* Dustin Bleizeffer, *Property Power Struggle*, CASPER STAR-TRIBUNE (Jan. 1, 2007).

13. *See* DOE, CARBON SEQUESTRATION ATLAS OF THE UNITED STATES AND CANADA 13-115 (2007). *See also* Alexandra B. Klass & Elizabeth J. Wilson, *Climate Change and Carbon Sequestration: Assessing a Liability Regime for Long-term Storage of Carbon Dioxide*, 58 EMORY L.J. 103, 119–20 (2008) (providing details on subsurface storage capacity for CO_2).

14. Dustin Bleizeffer, *State Has Vast Capacity for CO_2 Sequestration*, CASPER STAR TRIBUNE (April 5, 2007).

15. *See* OWEN L. ANDERSON ET AL., HEMMINGWAY OIL AND GAS LAW AND TAXATION 29–30 (4th ed. 2004).

16. 723 So. 2d 585 (Ala. 1998).

17. 361 S.W.2d 560 (Tex. 1962).

18. *Id.* at 568.

19. *House Grapples with Granting FutureGen Companies CO_2 Liability Relief*, INSIDE GREEN BUS, June 29, 2006, http://carboncontrolnews.com/index.php/igb/show/house_grapples_with_granting_futuregen_companies_co2_liability_relief (quoting an amendment by Rep. Jerry Costello of Illinois to H.R. 5656, which was floated and then withdrawn).

20. *Id.*

21. *See* TEX. NAT. RES. CODE Ch. 119 (enacted as Tex. H.B. 149 (2006)).

22. *See* Press Release, Railroad Commission of Texas, *House Energy Committee Unanimously Approves 2007 FutureGen Legislation* (April 11, 2007).

23. *See* Press Release, Railroad Commission of Texas, *Williams: Legislation Improves Texas Chance to Win FutureGen* (May 16, 2006).

24. *See* Kate Clemens, *Illinois Senate Passes Bill to Help Land FutureGen Plant*, THE NEWS-GAZETTE (March 22, 2007). *See also* Ill. S.B. 1704 (2007); Ill. H.B. 5825 (2006) (requiring state attorney general to appear and defend an operator of a clean-coal project in civil proceedings commenced against the operator from the escape or migration of injected carbon dioxide and requiring the state to indemnify the operator except in cases of intentional, willful or wanton misconduct).

25. *See* Steven D. Cook, *DOE Pulls Support for FutureGen Project, Will Fund Carbon Capture at Multiple Sites*, DAILY ENVT'L REP. (BNA) No. 20, at A-1 (Jan. 31 2008).

26. In March 2009, the Department of Energy announced it was reviewing its earlier decision to abandon the FutureGen project and that it may proceed with a modified plan. *See* Ben Geman, *DOE Taking "Fresh Look" at Future-Gen, Energy Chief Says*, N.Y. TIMES, March 5, 2009.

27. WYO. STAT. § 34-1-152; Wyo. H.B. 57 (2009). For more information on which states have enacted GS legislation and the provisions of that legislation, see Alexandra B. Klass & Elizabeth J. Wilson, *Climate Change, Carbon Sequestration, and Property Rights*, 2010 U. ILL. L. REV. (forthcoming).

5

Better Ways to Work Together

Eric T. Freyfogle

Natural resources law is under stress today, as most observers recognize. Many of its pressures come from the messy, frustrating methods we use to resolve resource-related disputes. Other stresses stem from the difficulties of shifting resources to higher and better uses, and coordinating activities at landscape or watershed scales. Tempers run high; litigation is slow and costly; land planning, it seems, never ends. Into the tempest has come the call to unleash the market. Yet, market forces often do little to lessen core problems, and measures taken to improve the market's functioning carry costs of their own. Meanwhile, pressures mount to increase regulatory constraints, mostly to promote some vision of common good. Such constraints, in their turn, trigger cries about invaded property rights if not socialism.

So where should we be headed? Are there ways to improve natural resources law to better meets our needs: to help shift resources to higher and better uses, to improve environmental outcomes, and to facilitate coordination at landscape levels?

My claim in this essay is that the central resource challenge of our day relates to the poorly functioning ways in which we make collective resource-use decisions. It has more to do, that is, with our landscape-governance systems, than it does with either inaptly defined private rights or any failure by lawmakers to put more of nature into private hands. To address this central challenge, I contend, we need to come up with better ways of governing the landscapes that we inhabit; better ways of performing the essential, functional task of re-adjusting land- and resource-use practices so that they sensibly reflect our evolving priorities.

I call this issue "collective governance," but the term needs using with care. Governance doesn't mean only civil government as we know it. It also includes a wide array of other arrangements by which people collectively make decisions and resolve disputes about the physical landscapes they inhabit. Such arrangements could work at various spatial scales, with local governance operating subject to guidance generated on a larger spatial scale. They could exhibit features that blend the public and private as we now know them. And they certainly could (and should) blur the artificial lines among the functions of *defining* resource entitlements, *adjudicating* resource disputes, and *regulating* the ways people use what they own—functions that, in fact, overlap considerably. Finally, new governance arrangements could, in one place, integrate a variety of natural resource uses and users, mixing and coordinating multiple activities and actors in a shared landscape.

In the future, legal scholarship ought to pay less attention to individual resources (that is, water, minerals, forage, timber, and the like) and think instead in *functional* terms, about how natural resources law works overall. We would do well to set aside our dominant conceptual model of the way resources law is structured: that private resource users possess distinct private rights, which they can exercise and which courts, when asked, will enforce and protect. To be sure, there *is* a distinction between private rights set by law and the judicial enforcement of them. The law does define property rights, and people do turn to courts for protection. When we look closer, however, we see that enforcement mechanisms are really part and parcel of the process of defining the rights—sometimes the more important part. We also see that property and natural-resources "laws" and "regulations" aren't really all that different. Regulations are a form of law. They help define private rights, working together with statutes and the common law. Indeed, it is simplistic and distorting to assert that individuals possess distinct property rights that government then regulates. The situation is more complex, legally and politically; the functional roles are more blurred.

Property rights ultimately are creatures of law. They are defined by the combination of all laws—from local to federal, common law to constitutional—that apply in a given time and place. And the making of these laws, and hence the reconfiguration of private rights, goes on endlessly, generation upon generation. Common law and statutes that prescribe the basic terms of private property rights blend indistinguishably into detailed regulations, which, in turn, blend into litigation and the other means by which resource conflicts are resolved and patterns of resource use, re-adjusted. Substance and process run together, as they always have. It is a messy, integrated system, just as alive and dynamic as the natural world itself. We need to understand this system, as a system, better than we do. And we need to conceive ways of improving it.

As scholars, lawyers, and judges we could benefit from a better understanding of how all of these seemingly different functions and activities blend together—the overlapping functions of lawmaking, regulating, enforcing, managing, and reassigning. These days, we have difficulty shifting natural resources to better uses and coordinating resource practices at various spatial scales. We need to see that these challenges don't relate to just one of the law's functions and activities. They relate to all of them, and to their constant interaction. A fresh approach to the situation could help us see better what's going on and what we might do.

I.   Where We've Been

Natural resources law is the body of law that has arisen to help channel and arrange our uses of nature. It doesn't make sense for people to use their common landscapes without coordination. A better approach is to divide nature into pieces and to turn control of the pieces over to particular users and groups. Natural resources law defines the kinds of private rights users can have in their pieces. It prescribes what specific parts of nature they will control, how they might use their parts, and how much protection they'll enjoy against interference.

The most common way of studying natural resources law is to examine laws resource by resource—water, oil and gas, wildlife, timber, forage, and the like. A rather different approach is to study the subject on a function-by-function basis.[1] Natural resource law typically performs a number of recurring functions. It specifies the particular part of nature that's involved, prescribes use rights in it (however vaguely or precisely), and then allocates the rights in some way. The law also sets rules governing the duration of the rights (including rules on forfeiture, abandonment, and condemnation) and explains whether the owner can transfer and divide the rights. In the case of land—best understood, perhaps, as a number of resource use rights bundled together rather than as a distinct thing—the law gives an owner substantial freedom to carve out limited use rights in the land and then to make the rights available to other users. As landowners exercise that delegation of managerial power, carving out and conveying discrete resource rights to other people, they necessarily engage in the same rule-making tasks. They set the terms of the use rights that they'll convey, describe the particular rights, define their duration and transferability, and so on.

Largely by necessity, the law performs these various functional tasks in all resource settings. The law's precise terms—the rules it prescribes for particular resources—differ a fair amount from resource to resource. A water-use right, for instance, contains different elements than a recreational-use right. The law's functions, though, are largely the same, and the various options that lawmakers have available, with respect to each function, are in fact rather limited. By studying natural resources law function by function, not resource by resource, we get a new look at issues. We see challenges that recur in setting after setting. And we see linkages among the key functions that are otherwise easy to miss.

Much of our natural resources law came together in the nineteenth century, the era when the United States settled its continent. Liberty, understood as individual economic opportunity, enjoyed high favor. So did private property, gradually redefined to allow more intensive land uses. Economic growth was a prime goal, for Americans collectively and for most citizens individually. The continent was vast, and it made sense in settling it to unleash the individual energies and desires of settlers. Guiding settlement was a belief that the common good was best fostered by allowing individuals to use nature as they saw fit, subject only to rules to reduce direct conflicts. Landscapes would become whatever they would become, the result of countless decisions by countless owners.

The natural resources law that emerged during this era of expansion often featured precise rules regarding the physical dimensions and components of land- and resource-use rights. That is, physical boundaries (for example, the dimensions of hardrock mining claims or place-of-use rules in water law) were sometimes quite clear. At the same time, the law often used vague principles to prescribe how owners could use their bounded bits of nature. Originally, private law featured a general do-no-harm rule to resolve resource-use conflicts. In time, *sic utere tuo* gave way to the now-popular language of reasonable use. Resource owners could act as they saw fit so long as their actions were reasonable under the circumstances. Vague resource-use limits worked well enough while resources were plentiful, direct conflicts were few, and the community itself didn't care much about what people did. But times would change. The drawbacks of such laws would soon become clear.

Though the overall development of twentieth-century resources law is familiar, its implications may not be. America's westward expansion reached the coast; free lands declined in quantity and quality; resource competition stiffened. On federal lands in particular, the law authorized multiple, physically overlapping resource uses by different private actors. Inevitably, resource conflicts became more numerous. New, ecologically based values gained strength, as did a new understanding of nature's interconnectedness. Early in the century the call went out to manage resources sustainably. Only over time did we realize how difficult that challenge was, ecologically, politically, and economically. On the nation's rivers, a variety of instream-flow uses began to draw widespread support. Meanwhile, concerns about wildlife called attention to the need to manage habitat and to constrain wildlife harvesting over large spatial scales. The effects of diverse human activities in river corridors stimulated a similar recognition of the need for collective waterway planning. As cities and populations grew, resource uses from the previous century no longer made sense. Lawmakers shrewdly took steps to limit new resource allocations to uses that satisfied public interest criteria. It no longer seemed wise to let private owners do as they pleased.

Perhaps the most important trend taking place during this time was the public's intensifying interest in the ways private owners used their lands and discrete resources. The philosophy of laissez faire no longer held sway. In many resource contexts, the law had no choice but to get involved in conflicts among private actors, given the public implications of private actions. Legal disputes routinely arrived in court, pitting one resource owner against another or one resource owner against multiple neighbors. Courts had to decide whom to favor, and, in doing so, it only made sense to take into account public values and needs. A growing ecological awareness heightened these legal disputes, as it became more apparent how resource-intensive activities often caused damaging, wide-spread ecological ripples. To varying degrees, lawmakers took note. Several states enacted forestry practices statutes. More imposed limits on mining and oil drilling. Water users were pressed to reduce waste, while new laws limited development in wetlands and floodplains and on barrier islands. Farmers were induced to control soil erosion. Various state and local governments imposed limits on activities along waterways, and wild species were reintroduced and habitat protected.

II. Where We Are

To survey where things now stand we can cast our net widely, looking at developments in a variety of resource settings. In part III we can draw our observations together, identifying trends and isolating what might well be the key resource challenge for coming decades.

A. The Precarious Plight of Wildlife

For generations, courts have explained how wildlife is owned by the people collectively, with the state entrusted to manage creatures for the good of all. Animals need places to live and food to eat, on private lands as well as public. They are hurt by habitat degradation—by contamination, fragmentation, and the disruption of ecological processes. Inevitably, resource conflicts arise when these publicly owned animals live on private land. Loosely, the situation is legally akin to an easement to use land privately owned by another—a right to hunt, for instance, to cut timber or to divert water. What right does the public have to protect wildlife located on private land? Can the public, as owner of the animals, legitimately restrict not just direct takings of animals but indirect harms and habitat degradation?

Wildlife cases are becoming more common and will likely increase in intensity as well. Conflicts under the Endangered Species Act are the most visible, along with cases involving damage caused by wildlife. Many citizens call for greater protections for wildlife, direct and indirect. On the other side, private landowners complain about legal restrictions that interfere with land-use options.

How might we resolve these wildlife disputes, given the immense variation of physical settings and wildlife needs? Could we attempt to define exactly what we expect of landowners, in terms of making room for wildlife? Or is there so much variation—among landscapes, species, and communal needs—that lawmakers by necessity would have to deal with challenges in vague terms, as Congress did when it told the U.S. Forest Service simply to manage its forests to preserve the diversity of wild species? Instead of telling landowners precisely what they can and cannot do, might we, for instance, impose upon them a vague, general duty to do their fair share to promote regional wildlife populations?

B. The Vagueness of Riparian Rights

Throughout the eastern half of the United States water conflicts are on the rise, with a rapid ascent looming. Many conflicts relate to diversions and water allocation. Other conflicts deal with water quality, while still others relate to physical modifications of waterways. As revised in the nineteenth century, the common law addressed such conflicts by directing riparian owners to exercise their rights "reasonably," a standard that required (on paper at least) due recognition of the equal rights of other riparian users. Most states also addressed water conflicts by limiting the use of water to the riparian tract and within the watershed of origin. However, these place-of-use limits soon came under attack because, though they accomplished what was intended, they undercut socially worthy water uses that took place away from riparian lands. Place-of-use rules favored water uses occurring on riparian tracts, even over more socially valuable alternatives away from the river. As for the basic reasonable use rule itself, which governs all riparian uses, it has provided scant guidance as to what water uses are allowed and where.

In most states that recognize riparian rights, a conflict over the exercise of such rights must go to court for resolution under the normal rules of civil litigation. When a court ultimately issues a ruling, it resolves the specific dispute at hand (an adjudicative function) and thereby enhances the clarity of rights that the riparian owner possesses (a second, lawmaking function). Litigation, it hardly needs saying, can be time-consuming and expensive. This is particularly true when the factual inquiry ranges widely, as it can in disputes about the reasonableness of competing water uses.

Civil litigation is not an efficient way to resolve water conflicts. It is particularly deficient when time is urgent. Consider, for example, the case of the irrigator who draws water from a river during time of drought; the river is at low flow, pollution levels are concentrated, and aquatic life is under stress. An environmental group or state agency moves to halt on-going diversions to protect the river. How useful is it to tell the complainant to go to court to initiate a full-blown lawsuit addressing reasonableness? How sensible is it to propose litigation that will consume weeks, months, or even years?

C. The Rigidity of Prior Appropriation

Water conflicts in prior appropriation jurisdictions arise constantly, some between competing users, others involving public entities and conservation groups. Whole-stream adjudications, dragging on for years, are perhaps the most notorious and wearisome. One is tempted, surveying the landscape of conflict, to chalk it all up to water shortages and to mounting conflict over how water is best used. The assessment is fair as far as it goes, but by digging deeper we discover that the governance methods themselves—the methods of clarifying rights and adjudicating disputes—are also much to blame.

Prior appropriation took shape in response to water scarcity and to the need, in the West, to promote water uses that diverted water far from any riparian tract. As the new law of prior appropriation developed in arid states, the rights of water users gained ever greater precision. Water owners knew precisely how and where they could use water and when they could complain about interferences by other water users, senior and junior. The aim of the law was twofold: to promote the most efficient and repeated uses of water possible (what was termed "conservation") and to encourage investment in water-using activities by giving even junior users a high-level of legal protection. Water was a valuable commodity. Clarity and high protection, lawmakers believed, would promote its most full and efficient use.

At the time, this reasoning made sense. In retrospect, though, it contained a major flaw.

The problem with the prior appropriation system is that it defines water rights so precisely, and fits individual rights together so snugly, that it creates in arid lands the waterway equivalent of highway gridlock. In theory, no user can change the nature or place of his water use if the change would interfere with the water rights of others. Transfers become exceedingly difficult due to this no-harm rule and to the factual complexity and costs of litigation. Lawmakers have further stimulated the full, repeated use of water by limiting the export of water outside watersheds—another obstacle to resource reallocation and thus a further cause of gridlock.

The problem, looking back, is that nineteenth-century law-makers didn't take into account the likelihood that social needs for water would change over time; they didn't consider that the water uses of the first appropriators might seem socially unreasonable a century or more later. Lawmakers devoted little apparent thought to the inevitable need to reallocate water over time, as circumstances and values evolved. Had they foreseen this predictable need they could have modified their water-rights system to facilitate reallocation. Instead, they forged a scheme that offered maximum clarity of rights and maximum individual protection—in perpetuity, rather than for a limited term. The effect was a legal system that inhibited efforts to accommodate new desires.

In much of the West water is now stuck in uses of low economic value. And it makes little sense to expect the market to remedy things when the law imposes such severe limits on the market's functioning. We could radically revise water law to allow the most senior users to transfer their water more easily. But we could do that only by reducing severely the property-rights protections of junior users. That is, we could make senior rights easier to sell, particularly to distant buyers, only by slashing the very security of water rights that early lawmakers strove so hard to install.[2] The possibility of doing this remains as an option to promote reallocation. Before we exercise it, though, we ought to consider the alternatives.

D. Mineral Estates and the Loss of Clarity

In much of the country land ownership is fragmented between the owner of the surface and a separate owner of the land's underlying minerals. Mining, of course, often requires a miner to alter the land surface, disrupting or undercutting the activities of surface owners. Sometimes the miner can accommodate surface activities by revising mining operations in one way or another. Many conflicts, though, are unavoidable.

Consistent with the pro-development ethos of the era, nineteenth-century law forestalled these disputes by setting a clear rule of priority.

The miner's wants and actions were legally superior when it came to using the surface, at least when the miner's conduct was "reasonably necessary." The mineral estate, that is, was dominant; the surface estate servient.

The twentieth century saw a marked resistance to this crisp rule of dominance. One line of attack questioned whether the most destructive surface uses by miners were really necessary (an issue sometimes submitted to a local jury rather than a judge). Another approach was to require miners to leave enough minerals in place to provide subsurface support for existing buildings. Many states added requirements that miners compensate for the surface damage they caused, even when they had the right to impose damage without permission. More recently, states have interjected vague accommodation duties, which require miners to minimize disruption of preexisting surface activities when they can reasonably do so. Administrators and local officials, in turn, have gotten into the act with a wide array of regulations and ordinances that ban mining in specified places, impose limits on water contamination, and require surface restoration when mining ends. On federal lands, miners are hampered by extensive regulations limiting their ability to disturb the surface.

These various legal changes evidence a distinct frustration with the common law's simple rule of surface-use priority for miners. The common law rule was indeed clear and firm. Parties knew where they stood. Today, the situation is more complex. Importantly, this complexity has come by reducing the law's clarity. No longer do parties know clearly where they stand. Rights and liabilities have evolved to become more vague.

E. Drainage Law's Move to the Middle

Even as water shortages expand geographically, tensions mount over the ability of land- and resource-owners to drain water from their lands and otherwise alter hydrologic cycles. The problem is especially contentious in flat areas of the Midwest, where landowners generations ago formed drainage districts to help move rainwater off farm fields, thereby allowing spring planting to begin on time. In other regions, drainage is criticized for causing surface subsidence, water pollution, and wildlife habitat degradation.

Drainage law began in a simple, easy-to-understand form. Landowners in some states had freedom to drain as they saw fit; diffuse water, these states ruled, was a "common enemy." In others, landowners were obligated to leave the land's natural drainage unaltered. Landowners, it was said in these latter states, enjoyed the right to have water flow on and under their lands as nature provided, without disruption by others. The former approach allowed nearly unlimited drainage, the latter allowed almost none. In either instance the law was clear and disputes, presumably, manageable. However, both approaches have come under attack. Most states have moved from an extreme to a more moderate position, allowing some drainage but halting actions causing undue harm. The result seems socially sensible in that it allows landowners to use land efficiently while protecting them from unreasonably disruptive drainage by neighbors.

These new drainage rules, though, have the effect of reducing the law's clarity, leading to greater uncertainty for all landowners. As in other resource-use settings, clarity has given way to vagueness and flexibility. The situation became even more complex as conservation interests gained awareness of the ecological costs of moving floodwater downstream quickly. Drainage had distinct ill effects, despite its benefits; it increased flooding after rains, eroded stream banks, and degraded riparian habitat. The fast movement of water gave water flows less time to cleanse themselves of pollutants. Water that would have percolated slowly through the soil instead rushed downstream rapidly, worsening droughts in drier times. Low flows were lower. Aquatic life suffered.

The issue of drainage has become a slumbering beast, little noticed by urban scholars. One day it will awaken. Today's vague rules, standing alone and with civil litigation as the only dispute-resolution mechanism, will not resolve the problems.

F. Making Room for Fire

Across the West and elsewhere, fires have become regular news. A fire that consumes a landscape offers vivid testimony of ecological interconnection. Fire-control policies on federal lands have drawn contentious litigation for years.[3] A newer concern is the protection of private lands, reflecting an increasing recognition that society should take steps to reduce fire dangers to people, buildings, and activities. The dominant policy for generations was to halt fires and keep them from happening. The folly of that approach has now become apparent. We need controlled fires, sometimes often.

Fire is not an economic resource in any familiar sense. But similarities exist with wildlife, drainage, and even water allocation. Fire also fits into considerations about ecosystem "services" and the wisdom of sustaining them. Land can now be managed to respect or mimic natural fire regimes, thereby promoting ecological health. Or, as it has been, it can be managed to interfere with natural fire regimes. Fire, accordingly, can be seen as a type of land use, akin to uses of land by migrating animal herds and slow moving waters.

American law has hardly begun to develop a law that treats fire as potentially good. But it needs to come, and it will. The challenges of promoting good fires while controlling bad ones will certainly resist easy legal solution. Indeed, the efforts of even the wisest lawmakers may be overwhelmed if their lawmaking goal is to prescribe clearly, by law, when landowners can and cannot interfere with fire regimes. An alternative legal approach toward fire seems called for, one that matches flexibility with greatly improved methods for making landscape-scale decisions.

III. Ongoing Trends

We have typically gone about dealing with disputes over land and discrete resources by defining private rights by law and then letting owners use and negotiate as they see fit. When conflicts develop, we either open the courtroom doors to litigation or create a regulatory body to avert conflicts. Legislatures occasionally also get involved, sometimes by tinkering with existing laws, and sometimes by setting up new agencies or making extensive alterations. Statutory and regulatory changes, though, have typically not altered the basic legal arrangement, which features (i) individual rights, (ii) courts that entertain private disputes and enforcement actions, and (iii) government bodies that "regulate" what resource owners can do. Functionally, that is, the law seems to prescribe what owners possess, courts exist to enforce rights and the limits on the rights, and regulators cut into private rights by limiting their exercise. That's the system as we conceive it.

Keeping these traditional functions in mind, how might we characterize the resource challenges described in the previous section? What problems do we have with these various bodies of resources law? And are there patterns to the problems that might point the way to solutions?

A. The Troubles with Clarity

The apparent assumption of generations of lawmakers has been that property rights are best defined with clarity, whenever possible. The more clear the rights, the better owners know where they stand. Disputes are easier to resolve, and perhaps fewer in number. The virtue of clarity was presented starkly in the familiar wildlife case of *Pierson v. Post*, the case of the fox on the unoccupied beach.[4] The court's majority saw wisdom in a clear rule of capture, based on actual physical possession. A clear, easy to apply rule, the court announced, would reduce litigation and help keep the peace. In dissent, Justice Livingston argued for a more subtle, factually complex inquiry that took into account a hunter's intent and apparent ability to capture the hunted animal. Under Livingston's rule, it was harder to know whether a hunter in hot pursuit did or did not gain ownership of an animal. But this factual messiness was necessary, Livingston asserted, to yield a legal rule that sportsmen would consider fair. The complex rule produced a socially better outcome.

This simple clarity-versus-fairness trade-off provides a way to begin drawing together what we know about natural resources law, past and future. Justice Tompkins and his majority won the day in 1805.

But Livingston's policy preference has enjoyed rising favor. Again and again, clarity of rights has given way to greater factual complexity and fairness. Clarity has also given way to other competing policy rationales, including economic development, the protection of settled expectations, and the promotion of community and ecological welfare. Clear rules, it appears, too often produce bad results. Pressures have mounted to change them.

B. The Troubles with Vagueness

As clarity has declined, vagueness has rushed in. With it, though, has come a rising inability to resolve resource disputes quickly and efficiently. When we don't know what rights people possess, it is harder to adjudicate conflicts. This difficulty increases as we deem more factors legally relevant.

One virtue of vagueness is that it facilitates efforts to plan and coordinate resource uses at the landscape scale. When private rights are precisely defined, planning and regulation seem to cut into the rights by limiting their exercise. Regulations, that is, more *visibly* cut into property rights when private rights are clear. When, instead, private rights are defined vaguely (in terms of "reasonable use," to use the familiar instance), planning and regulation seem to pose less conflict. A regulation can seem legitimate to the extent it halts an activity that is, in some sense, unreasonable.

On the other side, vaguely defined rights pose a grave question about institutional powers, along with the obvious problems of messiness in dispute resolution. When the law defines a private right vaguely—for instance, the reasonable use of water, reasonable drainage, reasonably necessary surface uses by miners—who is supposed to decide which activities are reasonable? Is this a judicial question alone? Can regulators and legislators, instead or in addition, make their own decisions? And is it a question of law rather than fact? We're having trouble answering these questions. One cause of the trouble, perhaps the biggest cause, is that we don't see clearly what the questions entail in functional terms.

C. Wildlife, Again

Consider again the case of wildlife on private land. The problem we have protecting these animals is that landowner rights are rather clearly defined. Landowners at law are free to use their lands as they see fit, destroying habitat and physically excluding wildlife. It is a legal arrangement that calls out for change as a matter of public policy. Yet (as we asked above), how might we change this rule if we wanted to do so? How might we redefine landowner rights; how might we prescribe legal limits on the ways landowners can harm animals?

Given the enormous factual complexity of landholdings, any redefining of landowner rights would surely have to paint with the broadest of brushes. It would likely entail something like a new duty on all landowners to take "reasonable steps" to make room for wildlife or to fulfill some sort of "fair share" burden of allowing wildlife to inhabit the land.[5] The predictable downside of such a rule is that it would be so vague that it would give landowners little notice and outsiders no benchmark for judging performance. It would inevitably foster knotty, frustrating litigation centered on the key, vague terms. Still, the needs of wildlife are simply too diverse and complex to allow for clear laws that tell landowners exactly what they can do. The physical circumstances of lands are simply too varied.

If we are going to protect wildlife on private land, it cannot be by precise rules, set in advance, guiding landowner behavior, nor can it be by some vague rule imposing a duty on landowners to accommodate wildlife. Neither approach makes sense. Clear rules, given the complexities, are simply impossible. Vague rules, standing alone, are unworkable. Where, then, are we to head?

D. Riparian Rights

As for riparian rights, the current, vague law of reasonable use provides little guidance as to what landowners can and cannot do. It produces intractable litigation in the instances in which people are financially willing to turn to courts. Again, though, it seems infeasible to establish a clear rule that tells landowners exactly what water uses they can undertake. Riparian law has long featured one clear rule: water can only be used on the riparian tract. That rule, though, has seemed unwise and in many states is largely gone. The influential Restatement of Torts judges all water uses based on their reasonableness, without regard for location.[6] In operation this standard is so inclusive of the factors considered, and so vague in their interaction and summation, that it leaves everyone confused and guessing. Is a given water use reasonable under the Restatement? In truth, no one can say.

The way riparian rights really work, of course, is that litigated disputes turn on specific facts and get sent to a finder of fact to resolve. That fact finder is handed a laundry list of factors to consider and, after retreating behind closed doors, somehow comes up with an answer: yes, the water use is reasonable, or no it is not. The key point here is this: The law (reasonable use) does not really resolve the dispute in any *substantive* sense. Instead, it supplies a *process* that frames the inquiry and then turns the issue over to a fact finder. Armed with vast discretion, the fact finder decides who gets to do what. As it does so, the fact finder is not enforcing or protecting private rights so much as determining the content of the rights—which is basically a law-making function. And this takes place in a procedural setting that is drawn out, expensive, and unpredictable.

As a method of dispute resolution and rights clarification, civil litigation over riparian rights deserves a failing grade. (It rates even lower as a method of water planning.) The law's chief defect lies not in poorly defined individual property rights; those are inevitable and have their virtues. Instead it lies in the poorly designed enforcement/clarification process. Having defined private rights vaguely for rather good reasons, we lack prompt, communally responsive ways to decide, on the ground, who gets to do what.

E. Other Resources

In the context of prior appropriation, it is again useful to describe our current plight in functional terms. The law once embraced clarity of private rights (and still does in many settings). In time, it became apparent, as it routinely does, that clear private rights come at a high cost. In arid lands this cost has been bad and inflexible water-use practices. Water is stuck in low-valued uses without good ways to reallocate it. Based on what we have seen, a redefinition of water rights to make them more vague (most likely, by giving teeth to some sort of reasonable or beneficial use standard) would not, without additional action, improve things overall. Perhaps senior users in such a regime would become better able to sell their rights for use elsewhere and in new ways, despite the resulting harms to junior users. But it would be hard to know whether senior users could do that, given the law's vagueness. Water litigation could become even more awkward than it is. With private rights unclear the market would work no better.

In the case of mining, the shift from clarity to increased vagueness continues apace, albeit slowly. Miners are yielding some of their once total dominance in using the surface, as critics second-guess whether particular surface activities by miners are "reasonably necessary" and call for expanded duties of accommodation. We can anticipate that, should this trend continue, we'll end up in a legal place where neither miners nor surface owners really know with assurance where they stand. Disputes will become harder to resolve. Landscape planning will float as a distant dream.

Drainage law, as we have seen, is following a similar course. Clarity is giving way to vagueness. Lawmakers pushing aside the old, clear rules are converging on a vaguely defined middle position. Increasingly, landowners can drain if their activities, under the complex circumstances, are reasonable. Added atop the vague reasonableness principle are various statutes, regulations, and drainage authorities. Drainage disputes have become more complex, legally and factually. Typically the only current way to resolve them is through drawn-out litigation, which is to say, by commencing a time-consuming, expensive, frustrating legal proceeding.

As for the final illustration, fire regimes, we have hardly gotten a start. In some forest settings landowners are directed to clear vegetation around dwellings to reduce the risk of burning. Otherwise landowners are typically free to remove trees or not as they see fit. Ideally, we might imagine landscape-scale planning that designates areas where fires will be allowed to burn without interference, planning that might also take account of such resource-related issues as wildlife habitat and natural water purification. But we are a long way from such planning, and a long way also from an understanding of land-owner rights that makes such planning sensible.

IV. The Upshot

We can draw several conclusions from the preceding discussion. First, lawmakers are in a real bind when it comes to prescribing the elements of resource rights. When resource rights are defined clearly they become inflexible, inhibit planning and coordinated action, and otherwise suffer from various problems—mostly because they either fail to require resource owners to act sensibly or actually inhibit owners from doing so. At least in some settings (prior appropriation water law for instance) clear entitlements make market transfers harder, not easier. On the other side, vaguely defined rights have defects of their own. Private actors do not know where they stand. Conflicts are more numerous even if litigation is rare. Institutional roles are unclear.

Second, without regard for how precisely or vaguely we define resource rights, private litigation in court is simply not a sound way to resolve disputes. And it is virtually useless as a setting to coordinate land- and resource-use activities on larger spatial scales. Imagine the challenge of coordinating land and resource uses so as to restore more natural water flows in a river or to turn a river corridor into a better passageway for wildlife. A judicial forum offers little promise.

Third, nature's own dynamism, changing patterns of settlement and resource use, and various other factors have together led many observers to call for land management at the ecosystem or landscape scale; that is, at a scale typically well above the individual land parcel. At the moment, only government agencies can undertake this kind of work. And in doing so they are greatly hampered by private property rights. Planning agencies are openly resisted, culturally and politically, in large parts of the country. Even more ambitious than ecosystem planning is the related call for adaptive land management, in which managers and users keep tabs on changing conditions and modify land-use patterns accordingly. At the moment, we lack good ways to engage in such management except on individually owned parcels with single owners in charge.

Fourth, particularly as we place higher value on "ecosystem services," we find ourselves routinely wanting to promote multiple resource uses on pretty much all tracts of land, private and public.[7] Many particular resource activities do not involve people entering onto private land. They deal instead with wildlife populations, water drainage, and fire regimes; that is, with natural processes that we ought to respect more than we have. (Who knows, though, we might be closer than we realize to a day when, like Britain, we open up rural lands to qualified public wandering rights—thereby partially returning to the days of antebellum America when private rural lands were open to public uses.[8]) In any event, there are multiple reasons why it makes sense to coordinate private activities on large spatial scales, taking account of multiple resource activities. Again, we lack good ways to do that today.

These quickly sketched observations lead us toward a conclusion. All of these considerations, it turns out, point in a single direction. Plain and simple, we need better ways of coming together at the landscape scale to make resource-related decisions. (For an example, see the sidebar to this chapter.) We need better ways to discuss and decide how we might tinker with our land- and resource-uses so as to accomplish a long, shifting list of resource-related goals. We cannot restore sound wildlife populations or contain exotics except by coordinated action. We cannot restore natural water flows, create recreational trails or make room for occasional fires without similar coordinated action. With such coordination we can undertake wide-ranging grazing practices. We could develop ways to control polluted water runoff without forcing farmers to give up all chemical usage. And, we could concentrate residential and other intensive development so as to reduce infrastructure costs and enhance landscape aesthetics.

Looking ahead, the chief need in natural resources law is to develop new mechanisms to undertake such collective discussion, planning, and implementation.[9] In designing these governance structures, we have many options—more than we might realize. We need not use as models simply government bodies that we already know. When appropriate, we can craft regimes that are firmly linked to the knowledge, ideas, and values of users. Regimes could, for example, resemble a typical homeowners association as much as they do any civic government. They could be no larger than a half-dozen ranchers who have pooled their lands for common management, to enhance economic returns and foster ecological health. The options are many. Experimentation should be the order of the day.

In all likelihood, the governance regimes that work best will be ones that blur functional lines and work in ways that seem to defy easy categorization. By providing a forum for resolving disputes relating to resource uses, they will clarify for a time the options of various users and thus participate in the law-making process. They will certainly engage in something that resembles regulation, but it might well be regulation developed by the users rather than imposed by outsiders. As they go about their work, the governing bodies will likely play a role in resource reallocation over time—not as a full substitute for market transactions, but by helping readjust resource uses to make reallocation more feasible. Looking on these new arrangements from a distance, it might well prove difficult one day to distinguish between a person's property rights as individual owner and the power the person exercises as a member of the governing group. Certainly a successful governance regime will be one in which participants understand the ways they and their private holdings are interconnected with all that surrounds them. Good land use and good living cannot take place in isolation.

In a crowded world that presses against the land's carrying capacity, we simply must find ways to coordinate our uses of nature better than we do—flexible, adaptive ways that engage the knowledge and desires of users while working to sustain larger wholes. The day is gone when we can simply define private rights, allocate them to individual owners, and then let them live as they see fit. A much different model is needed, one in which private rights are embedded into governance regimes whose flexible work transcends old functional categories. It is work very much worthy of our top legal minds.

Managing the Lake

In 1999, the Indiana Supreme Court faced a legal dispute relating to the use of Lake Julia, a 22-acre non-navigable water body located in Lake County. The dispute had to do with rights to use the surface of the lake. One long-time user wanted to continue using the lake surface for a variety of intensive recreational endeavors, including waterskiing. The user, however, owned only one-half acre of land underneath the lake—about 2.5 percent of the total. The remainder of the lake bed was owned by other littoral landowners. Landowners controlling a majority of the lake bed formed a property owner's association, which desired to impose restrictions on the lake surface in the form of binding covenants. The proposed restrictions included a ban on all motors except small battery-powered electric motors. The long-time user resisted, claiming a prescriptive easement over the entire lake surface.

For various reasons the Indiana court denied the claim of a prescriptive easement based on lengthy use of the lake surface for boating and skiing.[10] The foundation of the court's ruling, though, was the basic common law governing access to the lake surface. At common law, owners of land around the lake owned to the center of the lake, unless their deeds provided otherwise. With the ownership of a piece of the lake bed came the right of exclusive control over the water surface above the land. Lake Julia, then, was controlled by a number of landowners who each possessed exclusive rights in a portion of the lake. No one enjoyed the right to use the entire lake surface. The property owner's association, accordingly, could not ban all motorboats on the lake. On the other hand, the long-time user possessed only the right to use the water surface above its half-acre of land. Legal rights were clear; the lake was fragmented.

A decade earlier, the same issue had come before the Illinois Supreme Court.[11] The lake was larger (240 acres) and the surrounding owners more numerous. One of the owners sought to open a marina on the lake and invite members of the public to rent boats. The problem for surrounding owners was the number of boats. The Illinois court, like the Indiana one, began by reciting the common law of non-navigable water bodies. Only surrounding owners could use the lake, and they could use it only on the water above the lake-bed that they owned. This rule struck the Illinois court as misguided, and the court decided to alter it. The court set aside the common law rule and adopted instead the rule prevalent in civil law systems. Under the civil law system, each surrounding landowner has a right to use the entire lake surface, subject to the requirement that all uses be reasonable under the circumstances. The owner of the proposed marina, accordingly, had the right to use the entire lake surface and could invite guests to come on and make use of that legal right. On the other hand, the marina owner's total use of the lake, including activities by all guests, had to comply with the reasonable-use limit. The Illinois court sent the dispute back to the trial level to undertake a factual determination about the reasonableness of the proposed use.

The case of the non-navigable lake illustrates the challenges faced in many areas of natural resources law while highlighting an important trend in lawmaking. The original common law set private rights with clarity. The result was to fragment lakes in ways that hampered the sensible use of them. Full use required successful negotiations and agreements among all landowners—sometimes possible, sometimes not. The defects of this approach became apparent, particularly in the instance of larger lakes with large numbers of users. Aware of the defects, the Illinois court decided to redefine private rights. It did so by shifting from a clear regime to one of near total vagueness. Under the reasonable use rule, landowners could all use the lake. But they faced difficulty deciding what uses were and were not permissible. In the event of a dispute that the landowners could not resolve among themselves, the only option was to go to court to engage in factually difficult litigation. The law provided little to no guidance, either for neighbors trying to negotiate a settlement or for judges and juries. The Illinois court, that is, opened up the lake to more uses, but did not provide a good mechanism for deciding disputes. The court got rid of one problem—the inability for people to use the entire lake—but added a new one, a vagueness in private rights and thus an enhanced difficulty in resolving disputes.

Both the Indiana and Illinois courts assumed that the way to resolve such disputes at law was to define private rights and then make courts available to enforce the rights. It is easy to see, though, a better way. When the common law rule is followed, landowners can use the entire lake surface if they can assemble and agree on terms. Similarly, the civil law rule works well when landowners can get together and decide among themselves what reasonable use shall mean. Both systems work well when land-owners can agree; neither works well when they cannot. This observation points to a third, perhaps better approach to dealing with such disputes—and the many disputes like them that arise in natural resources law.

What if the aim of the law was not to define private rights in the best way, but instead to provide a framework for landowners to manage the lake most successfully? That is, what if lawmakers thought about methods of collective governance and crafted legal rules that facilitated its emergence in the form of a lake management association? A number of issues would immediately arise. In all likelihood the association should have power to form and act without requiring unanimous approval of all landowners. But what sort of super-majority consent would be fair? What powers should the association have? Could it go beyond controlling surface uses of the lake to take steps to promote wildlife habitat and protect water quality? Might it have some say in uses of surrounding land, perhaps to limit the use of lawn chemicals? In any event, the association would effectively perform a variety of related, intermingled functions. It would regulate uses of the lake and, in the process, clarify landowner rights. It would resolve disputes. And as it changed rules over time it would play a role in resource reallocation—perhaps by restricting uses of the lake in certain places to provide improved habitat for fish spawning and waterfowl nesting.

If the use of a lake affected only the surrounding owners, we might, in drafting a lake management law, leave management issues entirely to the owners. But lakes do form parts of hydro-logic systems and wildlife depend on them. Thus we'll likely want outsiders to have some role in the lake management. That role could take the form of representation in the management association, or instead (and perhaps more likely), it might take the form of power reserved within government to prescribe standards for lake management that consider hydrologic inter-connection and wildlife factors.

The case of the non-navigable lake provides a straight-forward illustration of many of today's natural resources challenges. Like many landscapes, lake surfaces can be used in multiple ways, some involving human entry, others related to fish, wildlife, and ecological functions. It is simply not conceivable for lawmakers sitting in a state capital, or even a county seat, to prescribe by law exactly what each landowner should and should not be able to do. Similarly, it does not work well to prescribe rights vaguely and then rely on courts to sort things out. A better approach is a well-constructed governance regime, led by lakefront property owners and subject to guidance that seeks to protect the public interest—a governance regime that would blur the public-private divide while intermingling the various legal functions of defin-ing property-rights, adjudication, regulation, and reallocation. The new horizon for natural resources scholars is to help fashion such governance regimes.

Notes

1. ERIC T. FREYFOGLE, NATURAL RESOURCES LAW: PRIVATE RIGHTS AND COL-LECTIVE GOVERNANCE iii–vii, 1–6 (2007).
2. Eric T. Freyfogle, *Water Justice*, 1986 U. ILL. L. REV. 481.
3. Robert Keiter, *The Law of Fire: Reshaping Public Land Policy in an Era of Ecology and Litigation,* 36 ENVTL. L. 301 (2006).
4. Pierson v. Post, 23 Cai. R. 175, 2 Am. Dec. 264 (N.Y. Sup. Ct. 1805).
5. DALE D. GOBLE & ERIC T. FREYFOGLE, WILDLIFE LAW: CASES AND MATERI-ALS 1407–1422 (2002).
6. RESTATEMENT (SECOND) OF TORTS §858 (1979).
7. Eric T. Freyfogle, *Goodbye to the Public-Private Divide,* 36 ENVTL. L. 7 (2006).

8. MARION SHOARD, THIS LAND IS OUR LAND: THE STRUGGLE FOR BRITAIN'S COUNTRYSIDE (London: Gaia Books Ltd., 1997); ERIC T. FREYFOGLE, ON PRIVATE PROPERTY: FINDING COMMON GROUND ON THE OWNERSHIP OF LAND (Boston: Beacon Press, 2007), chapter 2, "The Lost Right to Roam."

9. FREYFOGLE, *supra* note 1, at 607–737.

10. Carnahan v. Moriah Property Owners Ass'n, Inc., 716 N.E.2d 437 (Ind. 1999).

11. Beacham v. Lake Zurich Property Owners Ass'n, 123 Ill. 2d 227, 526 N.E.2d 154 (1988).

6

Constitutional Law and the Future of Natural Resource Protection

James R. May

The use and protection of natural resources are often influenced by developments in constitutional law. Throughout U.S. history, the Supreme Court's constitutional pronouncements have helped shape natural resources policy. This influence may well increase in the coming years, as the country faces new and difficult environmental and energy challenges. How the Court interprets the breadth of Congress's power under the Constitution may affect the allocation of authority and responsibility to address natural resource concerns. Does the Constitution afford the federal government sufficient authority to protect natural resources? Should Congress rely upon the Commerce Clause, the General Welfare Clause, the Treaty Clause, or the Property Clause when it seeks to develop national natural resource programs? Or does the Tenth Amendment inhibit Congress's exercise of authority? Equally important is whether the role of state governments will be encumbered by the Court's application of the dormant (or negative) Commerce Clause. Other constitutional doctrines have been—and are likely to remain—pivotal in the evolution of natural

The author thanks Sam Kalen for his comments and Angela Whitesell and Gina Serra for additional research and proofreading.

resources law and policy, including the protection of property rights and the law of standing, as well as a host of additional lower profile constitutional issues.

The Constitution lies at the core of natural resource policies. It sets the boundaries for federal and state authority to exploit or protect natural resources. At the federal level, this includes defining the extent to which Congress may conserve rare species or regulate pollutant releases from mineral extractions on private property. Constitutional questions likewise infuse state actions designed to control the precursors of climate change or the interstate movement of energy, carbon allowances, natural resources, and wastes. Courts are left to mediate constitutional challenges and decide whether the litigants belong there in the first place.

Constitutional law doctrines often dictate what Congress, states, and individuals can and cannot do with natural resources. For the nation's first century and a half, nearly all of the U.S. Supreme Court cases involving natural resources turned on constitutional issues, such as the reach of the Commerce, Contract, Property, Enclave, Takings, and Due Process Clauses, and the Nondelegation and Incorporation doctrines. For the next half-century, however, until the dawn of the modern natural resources era, state and federal laws respecting natural resource protection and disposition seldom collided with constitutional principles.

The last three decades have again witnessed a sea change. Constitutional issues now often occupy center stage in federal and state efforts to protect land, air, water, species, and habitat. As Robert Fischman examines in chapter 7 of this book, most issues surrounding the extent to which Congress and the states can protect natural resources arise in the crucible of federalism under our republican system that "split the atom of sovereignty."[1] Accordingly, the subject of whether natural resource protection is better served by federal or state authorities has been much debated. Suffice it to say that the Tenth Amendment provides states with wide latitude to regulate in spheres not withheld or retained. Yet there are substantial constitutional restraints on state authority, including the dormant Commerce and Supremacy Clauses, and as Eric Freyfogle discusses in chapter 5, the Takings Clause.

This chapter examines how constitutional law shapes natural resources law in the United States. Following a brief background, part I identifies and discusses the various constitutional law developments affecting the scope of Congress's power to regulate the use of natural resources. It focuses primarily on the Commerce Clause (in conjunction with the corresponding case study) and the concomitant extrinsic limits on such authority, including principles of federalism and the Tenth Amendment, as well as the diminished Nondelegation doctrine. Part II does the same for state authority and the dormant Commerce and Supremacy Clauses. Part III then examines several dynamic constitutional doctrines that tend to thwart implementation of natural resources laws, such as standing, the Takings Clause, and the Eleventh Amendment. Part IV canvasses a variety of underutilized constitutional provisions and doctrines influencing the past and future development of natural resource policy, including the Treaty, Compact, General Welfare, Due Process, and Property Clauses, and the First Amendment, and even less controversial provisions, such as the Enclave Clause.

Part V concludes that constitutional law does not address natural resources law and policy except in an ad hoc fashion when the Court believes it is necessary to address some other issue—such as standing or the Eleventh Amendment. As Robert Glicksman and I have observed, rather than reflecting any clear constitutional thread in natural resources law, the outlook for constitutional jurisprudence in this area is a surrogate for wider debates about government regulation of human activity in the United States.[2] At bottom are 220-year-old questions of who decides who can do what, when, and where under the U.S. Constitution.

Most of these questions elide easy answers. After all, as Chief Justice John Marshall observed nearly 200 years ago, "we must never forget that it is *a constitution* we are expounding."[3] The legacy of jurisprudence from the Rehnquist Court and early indications from the Roberts Court suggest that constitutional law will continue to shape natural resources law and policy for many years to come.

The future of natural resource protection may well hang in the balance. The Court often seems to tilt against natural resource protection. This tilt is most likely a result of the property-rights and federalism hue that imbues our founding document.

I. Sources of and Limits to Congressional Authority over Natural Resources

Most congressional authority to regulate natural resources, especially resources not on federal lands, stems from the Commerce Clause. Yet, the Tenth Amendment, and less so the Nondelegation doctrine, have the potential to cabin the exercise of congressional authority over natural resources.

A. Congressional Authority Under the Commerce Clause

A majority of the nation's core natural resources laws rely on the Commerce Clause, which provides that "[t]he Congress shall have the power . . . [t]o regulate Commerce . . . among the several states."[4] These laws include the National Environmental Policy Act, the Clean Air Act, the Clean Water Act, the Endangered Species Act, the Resource Conservation and Recovery Act, the Safe Drinking Water Act, and the Comprehensive Environmental Response, Compensation, and Liability Act, to name but a few.

In some ways, natural resources law and Commerce Clause jurisprudence share a point of origin. One of the Supreme Court's first cases construing congressional authority under the Commerce Clause involved natural resources. In 1823, the Court held that Congress's authority to restrain the alienation of land from Native Americans and the disposition of natural resources therein stems from the Commerce Clause.[5] The next year, the Court upheld Congress's broad Commerce Clause authority to regulate competing use of navigable waterways notwithstanding countervailing state laws. The Court found that Congress may regulate "those internal concerns which affect the states generally; but not to those which are completely within a particular state, which do not affect other states."[6] Writing for the Court in both cases, Chief Justice Marshall maintained that in a representational democracy it is the voting public's job, and not the Court's, to curtail or redirect congressional action.

For about the next century, the Court rarely concluded that Congress exceeded its authority under the Commerce Clause, and when it did so, the cases did not involve the use and disposition of natural resources. But this changed during the throes of the industrial revolution, when the Court invalidated numerous congressional efforts to regulate natural resources under the Commerce Clause. The invalidated congressional acts attempted to control the use of natural resources at the point of manufacturing or production within a state, such as restricting monopolies in the sugar industry,[7] limiting the extent to which children and sometimes women could work the fields and factories to convert natural resources into commercial products,[8] setting prices in the coal and oil industries, or empowering coal and oil workers to engage in collective bargaining regarding maximum hours, minimum wages, pensions, and health care.[9]

This trend reversed in 1937, when the Court by a bare majority upheld congressional authority under the Commerce Clause to regulate unfair labor practices in manufacturing and production in the steel industry, because it has a "close and substantial relation to interstate commerce."[10] Four years later, the Court held that Congress's Commerce Clause authority extends to intrastate activities that have a "substantial effect" on interstate commerce.[11] And the next year, the Court allowed Congress to regulate noncommercial use of natural resources, such as wheat grown for home consumption, if such individual activities could, in the aggregate, affect interstate commerce.[12]

Given this expansive backdrop, for the next four decades natural resource laws were seldom subject to Commerce Clause challenges. When they were, the Court found Congress to have acted within their authority. In *Hodel v. Virginia Surface Mining & Reclamation Ass'n, Inc.*, for instance, the Court held that the Commerce Clause provided Congress with authority under the Surface Mining Control and Reclamation Act to require private mining companies to restore private lands located entirely within a state.[13] The Court determined that the appropriate inquiry is whether Congress has a "rational basis" to find that a state activity substantially affects interstate commerce, not whether it actually does. Concurring, Justice Rehnquist ominously noted that Congress cannot regulate commerce "to the nth degree."

Recent Commerce Clause jurisprudence supports Rehnquist's view. In *United States v. Lopez*, the Supreme Court held that the Commerce Clause permits Congress to regulate in three areas; that is, channels and instrumentalities of interstate commerce, and those activities that "substantially affect" interstate commerce.[14] And in *Morrison v. Olson* it described the "substantially affects" component as a function of whether (1) the underlying activity is "inherently economic," (2) Congress has made specific findings as to effect, (3) the law contains a jurisdictional element, and (4) whether the overall effects of the activity are actually substantial.[15]

While thus far *Lopez* and *Morrison* have not upset federal authority over natural resources, they nevertheless have the potential to profoundly impact federal natural resources law, particularly such programs as the Endangered Species Act (ESA). On the heels of *Lopez*, the D.C. Circuit decided that Congress has Commerce Clause authority under the ESA to protect an endangered fly that exists predominantly within a single state.[16] Following *Morrison*, the Fourth Circuit held in *Gibbs v. Babbitt* that the ESA's prohibition on the "taking" of an individual endangered red wolf in North Carolina does not exceed Congress's authority under the Commerce Clause.[17] Over a stinging dissent, a majority of the court found that protecting endangered red wolves satisfies *Morrison*, because tourism and the potential of a pelt market make regulation inherently economic in nature. (For more about the *Gibbs* case, see the case study at the end of this chapter.)

Likewise, the Fifth Circuit upheld Congress's Commerce Clause authority to apply the ESA to land development that would harm federally protected spiders and insects that neither inhabit nor cross state borders.[18] In addition, the D.C. Circuit upheld Congress's authority to provide ESA protection to intrastate toads that do not facilitate economic opportunities like tourism.[19] The Supreme Court denied petitions for certiorari each time it was sought in these cases, which might suggest it is not yet inclined to extend *Lopez* and *Morrison* to regulation of natural resources.

A broader reading of the Commerce Clause was also suggested in *Gonzales v. Raich*.[20] There, the Court upheld an aspect of the federal Controlled Substances Act, which prohibits in-state sale and distribution of marijuana notwithstanding state laws that permit in-state sale for medical purposes if prescribed by a physician. In a decision by Justice Stevens, the Court held that it was not necessary to decide "whether respondents' activities, taken in the aggregate, substantially affect interstate commerce in fact, but only whether a rational basis exists for so concluding."[21]

Whether courts adopt the *Raich* or *Lopez* and *Morrison* standard of review could profoundly impact natural resources law. It is easier to show that Congress has Commerce Clause authority to protect species, habitat, and water quality under *Raich* than it is under *Lopez* and *Morrison*. For example, in *Alabama–Tombigbee Rivers Coalition v. Kempthorne*, the Eleventh Circuit upheld Congress's authority under the Commerce Clause to allow federal wildlife agencies to list as a protected species the last remaining population of the Alabama Sturgeon, a noncommercial species that exists only within the State of Alabama.[22] Applying *Raich*, the court maintained that "when a general regulatory statute bears a substantial relation to commerce, the *de minimis* character of individual instances arising under that statute is of no consequence." Notwithstanding the lack of an inherently economic activity and congressional findings of impact, the court easily held that Congress *could* have had a rational basis for concluding that protecting endangered species, in the aggregate, substantially affects interstate commerce. That the ESA bears a substantial relation to commerce, the court found, is reflected in the $5–6 billion spent annually on illegal trade in rare plants and animals; the "incalculable" value of genetic heritage; the unknown value of safeguarding species and genetic diversity for medical, agricultural, and aquacultural purposes; and the tens of billions of dollars in annual expenditures associated with hunting, fishing, birding, tourism, and other economic activities. Thus, the court concluded, "Congress was not constitutionally obligated to carve out an exception" for intrastate species or noncommercial species from the ESA's "comprehensive statutory scheme."

Some have also argued, based on *Lopez* and *Morrison*, that Congress lacks the authority to regulate waters that are not historically navigable-in-fact. But applying *Raich*, the Tenth Circuit found otherwise in *United States v. Hubenka*.[23] There, the court held that the Commerce Clause authorizes the U.S. Army Corps of Engineers to regulate the dredging and filling of non-navigable tributaries that flow downstream into navigable waters.

The record thus shows broad support among the federal appellate courts for congressional authority to regulate intrastate activities under the Commerce Clause. Nevertheless, the validity of congressional authority under the ESA—and other federal natural resource acts—is hardly secure. The composition of the Court has changed since *Raich*. Justice O'Connor cast the deciding vote in *Raich*, but her successor, Justice Alito, seems inclined to view federal authority more narrowly. Moreover, Chief Justice Roberts, who was not involved in *Raich*, rather famously remarked in dissent in *Rancho Viejo* that the Commerce Clause does not provide Congress with authority to protect a "hapless toad that, for reasons of its own, lives its entire life in California."[24]

In addition, context matters. The majority Justice Stevens mustered in *Raich,* involving controlled substances like marijuana, may not hold when the subject of regulation is a noncommercial, intrastate species with no inherent economic value, particularly when Congress has not made specific findings that loss of individual species has a "substantial effect" on interstate commerce. Finally, the Court also has employed *Lopez* and *Morrison's* constrained view of Commerce Clause authority as a tool of statutory construction to limit the jurisdictional reach of other natural resources and environmental laws. For example, in *Solid Waste Agency of Northern Cook County v. U.S. Army Corps of Engineers (SWANCC)*, the Court passed on an opportunity to decide whether the Corps' and EPA's interpretation of the Clean Water Act as requiring a permit for discharge into an isolated, intrastate water not adjacent to a navigable waterway exceeds Congress's authority under the Commerce Clause.[25] Instead, the Court found that the Corps' and EPA's use of the so-called Migratory Bird rule to establish jurisdiction exceeded the reach of the Act's definition of "navigable waters." But the Court noted that a contrary interpretation would raise "significant constitutional questions" under the Commerce Clause.

The tenuous grip *Raich* has on Commerce Clause jurisprudence was on display again in *Rapanos v. United States*.[26] Like *SWANCC*, *Rapanos* raised a question about the scope of the Corps' authority to regulate dredge and fill discharges. In *Rapanos*, the key discharges were on wetlands that were adjacent to non-navigable tributaries of "navigable waters." Notably in *Rapanos*, Justice Kennedy's concurrence, which provided the key vote for remanding the case, relied on *Raich* for the proposition that "when a general regulatory statute bears a substantial relation to commerce, the *de minimis* character of individual instances arising under that statute is of no consequence."[27]

As recent cases under the Commerce Clause cast doubt about Congress's ability to protect natural resources, particularly rare plants and animals, habitat, and water, the constitutionality of natural resource laws may hinge more frequently on other less emphasized sources of congressional authority, like the Treaty, Property, and General Welfare Clauses, discussed in part IV.

B. Limits on Congress's Authority over Natural Resources

Federalism and the Tenth Amendment present the principal constraints on Congress's authority to regulate natural resources not on federal lands. The largely defunct Nondelegation doctrine could also influence the future of congressional authority over natural resources.

1. Federalism and the Tenth Amendment

The Tenth Amendment supplies potential limits on Congress's authority to enact natural resources laws, particularly in "traditional areas of state and local authority," such as land use or public health. It preserves the "dignity" and sovereignty of the states by providing that "the powers not delegated to the United States by the Constitution, nor prohibited by it to the States, are reserved to the States."

Thus far, Tenth Amendment jurisprudence has only curtailed natural resource programs that upset political accountability and diminish state dignity. In *New York v. United States*, the Court held that

Congress may not "commandeer" state political or personnel resources by requiring a state to "take title" of its own low-level radioactive waste if it fails to arrange for proper disposal under federal law.[28] Courts have been reluctant, however, to find that Congress has commandeered state resources under other circumstances. For example, a federal court rejected a state claim that the Magnuson-Stevens Fishery Conservation and Management Act violates the Tenth Amendment by compelling participation in a regional management council that set quotas on the seasonal catch of fish.[29] Another court rejected a state's Tenth Amendment claim that the ESA "commandeers" state resources by requiring it to engage in conservation efforts.[30] Moreover, the Supreme Court held, by a bare majority, that the EPA's rejection of a state's determination of what constitutes "best available control technology" did not unduly infringe upon state prerogatives under the Clean Air Act's system of cooperative federalism.[31]

It does not appear that the Tenth Amendment will be a significant impediment to congressional efforts to promote natural resource policies in the future.

2. Nondelegation Doctrine

The Nondelegation doctrine is rarely endorsed, but remains available as a limit on Congress's authority to vest administrative agencies with wide authority to implement natural resource laws. The doctrine stems from Article I of the Constitution, which vests "all legislative" authority in Congress, and presumably not in agencies charged with implementing national policies. Nonetheless, while Congress may not "delegate" legislative authority to agencies that administer federal law, legislation that provides an "intelligible principle" to guide the exercise of agency discretion will be upheld. The relevance to natural resources law is acute, as many federal programs governing the administration of public lands provide agencies with considerable discretion in managing those lands for the public interest or to achieve multiple but possibly inconsistent uses.

Other than in the midst of the New Deal in the 1930s, the Court has seldom found that Congress has failed to provide an "intelligible principle." Most recently, in 2001, the Court declined an opportunity to use the doctrine to strike a provision of the Clean Air Act that charges the EPA with the duty to set national ambient air quality standards as "requisite" to protect public health and welfare. In *Whitman v. American Trucking Ass'n*, the Court unanimously rejected the nondelegation challenge, holding that "requisite" falls "comfortably within" the Court's nondelegation jurisprudence.[32]

However, it would be foolhardy to think that the Nondelegation doctrine—while in desuetude—is bereft of meaning. For example, while Justice Thomas concurred in *American Trucking*, he all but invited a test case challenging other statutory provisions granting general authority to federal natural resource and environmental agencies. In addition, *American Trucking* reversed a contrary opinion from the D.C. Circuit Court of Appeals, usually the second most influential court in cases involving agency action and natural resources and environmental law.[33] The Court's recent appointees, Chief Justice Roberts and Associate Justices Alito and Sotomayor, have not yet weighed in about the nondelegation doctrine.

II.   Sources of and Limits to State Authority over Natural Resources

The Tenth Amendment generally provides the justification for state authority to regulate the use and disposition of natural resources off federal lands. The dormant Commerce Clause and the doctrine of federal preemption generally constrain such authority.

A. State Authority over Natural Resources

As the Tenth Amendment "reserves" state authority in areas neither reserved for Congress nor withheld from the states, many states have adopted extensive laws governing natural resources, especially as needed to fill in gaps left by federal regulation. Constitutional law, however, is occasionally employed by opponents of such legislation as a means to prevent state regulation.

B. Limits on State Authority over Natural Resources

The dormant (or "negative") Commerce Clause and Supremacy Clause also limit state efforts to regulate natural resources.

1. Dormant Commerce Clause

In the absence of federal laws, many states, counties, and municipalities have enacted legislation either to protect natural resources from toxic wastes or to conserve resources for state purposes. Yet, the Court has invalidated many such efforts under the dormant Commerce Clause. The idea that the Commerce Clause contains a "dormant" or "negative" aspect arguably originated in a natural resources case. Chief Justice John Marshall coined the phrase "dormant Commerce Clause" in *Willson v. Black-Bird Creek Marsh Co.*, a case allowing Delaware to issue a license to block navigation of the Black-Bird Creek, absent a countervailing federal law.[34]

Today, the phrase "dormant Commerce Clause" is most often used to describe limits on a state's authority to adopt laws or policies that discriminate against interstate commerce. For example, the Court has struck down a ban on the importation of dangerous out-of-state waste,[35] higher tipping fees or surcharges for wastes generated out-of-state,[36] and waste flow control ordinances prohibiting landfill operators from accepting out-of-state waste or requiring all county waste be processed at the county's facility.[37]

State efforts to sequester natural resources for the benefit of their own residents are also vulnerable to dormant Commerce Clause objections. Several early cases upheld such state laws. *Geer v. Connecticut* upheld a state law prohibiting the out-of-state shipment of game birds killed within the state.[38] Likewise, in *Hudson County Water Co. v. McCarter* the Court upheld a state's prohibition on the out-of-state transportation of water from state rivers and lakes.[39] As recently as 1950 the Court rejected a commerce clause challenge to a state law designed to conserve state supplies of natural gas by regulating prices.[40] The Court, however, has overruled both *Geer* and *Hudson County*. The modern view is illustrated by such cases as *Hughes v. Oklahoma*, which overturned an Oklahoma law prohibiting the transport of minnows caught in the state for sale outside the state,[41] and *Sporhase v. Nebraska,* which struck down a Nebraska statute that restricted withdrawal of groundwater from any well in the state for use in an adjoining state.[42]

In similar fashion, the Court has also rejected state efforts to control commerce in energy and fuels. In 1982, for example, the Court struck down a state law that prohibited the export of energy generated within the state.[43] It has also invalidated other state initiatives awarding tax credits for in-state ethanol production,[44] or requiring that in-state power plants burn in-state-mined coal.[45]

Hughes establishes the general test for dormant Commerce Clause cases involving state regulation of natural resources. First, the court asks "whether the challenged statute regulates evenhandedly with only 'incidental' effects on interstate commerce, or discriminates against interstate commerce. . . . "[46] If the statute regulates even-handedly, it is generally upheld unless the burden on commerce is excessive.

But where a statute discriminates, it is usually struck down unless the state can show that it is seeking to accomplish a legitimate local purpose that cannot be accomplished by less discriminatory means.[47] For example, the Court upheld restrictions by the State of Maine on the importation of bait fish where the state demonstrated that such fish might carry diseases that were not detectable, but that could adversely impact native fish species.[48] However, it struck down an additional fee imposed by the State of Alabama for the disposal of hazardous waste generated outside the state on the ground that it discriminated against interstate commerce.[49] While the state may have had legitimate concerns about the total amount of waste disposal in Alabama, those concerns could have been addressed by less discriminatory means.

The Court has also recognized that where a state acts as a market participant, rather than as a market regulator, the dormant Commerce Clause places no limits on state activities. But this exception does not allow the state to apply burdens on commerce beyond the market in which it participates. For example, Alaska was not allowed to claim the market participant exception for the sale of state timber that was subject to the requirement that the buyer partially process the timber prior to shipping it out of state.[50]

Public facilities that regulate natural resources for public benefit may enjoy wider latitude under the dormant Commerce Clause. In

United Haulers Association, Inc. v. Oneida-Herkimer Solid Waste Management Authority, a plurality of the Court decided that a county's flow control ordinance—requiring that all solid waste generated within the county be delivered to the county's publicly owned solid waste processing facility—does not violate the dormant Commerce Clause.[51] Relying on *Pike v. Bruce Church, Inc.*, the plurality concluded that facilities operated by public hands for "public good" directed at goals other than mere protectionism have greater leeway to control the flow of wastes.[52] Cases applying *United Haulers* thus far suggest that the constitutional prospects of local flow-control regimes involving publicly owned facilities have been enhanced.[53] *United Haulers* may also signal judicial receptivity to local flow control ordinances not involving "clearly public facilities."[54] However, relying on *Oneida's* focus on safety, the district court recognized broad state discretion to identify legitimate state ends respecting waste disposal.

The Court's skepticism toward state regulation of the flow of natural resources and energy is unlikely to change anytime soon, and may become an even more problematic issue as states address climate change and the development of renewable energy sources. Only former Chief Justice Rehnquist regularly dissented from the string of cases applying the dormant Commerce Clause to strike down state natural resource laws. He chided his brethren for failing to "acknowledge that a safe and attractive environment is the commodity really at issue," reasoning that "[s]tates may take actions legitimately directed at the preservation of the State's natural resources, even if those actions incidentally work to disadvantage some out-of-state waste generators."[55] Rehnquist also argued that federal courts should presume—as with quarantine laws—that state conservation laws are a rational means to achieve legitimate state ends that have but incidental effects upon interstate commerce.[56] Moreover, Rehnquist believed that federal courts should defer both to state legislative and judicial findings supportive of a nonprotectionist impetus behind state waste control laws.[57]

2. Supremacy Clause and Preemption

The Constitution's Supremacy Clause provides that "[t]he Constitution and the Laws of the United States which shall be made in

Pursuance thereof . . . shall be the Supreme Law of the Land."[58] Thus, the Constitution authorizes federal natural resources laws to displace inconsistent state laws. In 1819, in a case involving use of navigable waterways, the Court made its earliest pronouncement on the subject and held that federal law usurps inconsistent state laws that may "retard, impede, or burden" federal operations.[59]

Absent specific intent to preempt, the modern Court has held that Congress may preempt state law implicitly by "field" preemption, where Congress occupies a field of interest so pervasively that preemption is assumed, or when state law "conflicts" with federal law.

While the Court held that a comprehensive regulatory scheme involving natural resources may occupy the field and thus implicitly preempt federal common law,[60] it has generally been receptive to state efforts to supply common law causes of action involving the use or protection of natural resources.[61]

Courts have been especially skeptical of claims that federal law implicitly preempts state laws concerning natural resources. In *Exxon Shipping Co. v. Baker*, the Court held that the federal Clean Water Act does not preempt punitive damages under maritime law.[62] Other courts have concluded that federal law does not expressly or impliedly preempt state-imposed fleet fuel-efficiency requirements,[63] or tailpipe restrictions on greenhouse gas emissions.[64]

Moreover, the Court often tends to find that state actions concerning energy production, water allocation, and disposition of natural resources are not preempted absent an express preemption provision, a clear indication of a pervasive federal regime, or some actual federal-state conflict. In 1983, for example, the Court held that congressional regulation of the field of nuclear safety did not preempt California's moratorium on new nuclear power plants absent safe and reliable methods for disposal of high-level radioactive waste.[65] And in 1978, the Court held that Congress did not intend to displace the application of state water law to the distribution of water behind a federally constructed dam.[66]

On the other hand, state activities that impinge on federally occupied spheres of activity may be implicitly preempted. For example, the Court has held that federal legislation governing the issuance of fishing licenses preempts a state's effort to limit the ability of outsiders to fish in the state's territorial waters.[67] And while the Court held that the Federal Power Act comprehensively regulated hydroelectric power and preempted a state's ability to set minimum stream-flow requirements and protect fish populations,[68] it nevertheless refused to cabin a state's effort to regulate hydroelectric development and protection of natural resources when acting under the Clean Water Act.[69]

Looking ahead, the prospect of preemption continues, given the wide swath cut by federal natural resources laws. Numerous state laws fill in both the wide and the interstitial fissures left by federal natural resources law. Most states have myriad natural resources laws that apply to activities that adversely affect ecosystems or diminish property values. Most states have comprehensive statutory programs that regulate pollution inputs into water, air and soil; regulate the use of state natural resources, such as wildlife, minerals, and forests; and have common or codified laws, such as nuisance, trespass, and negligence, to provide remedies for those harmed by excess pollution or imprudent land use resulting in injury to persons or property. Many local governments also have laws governing the use of natural resources. Preemption issues, then, will continue to influence the development of natural resources laws at the state level.

III. Constitutional Doctrines That Diminish Implementation of Natural Resource Laws

Several constitutional doctrines diminish the implementation of natural resources laws. Of these, the most prominent are constitutional standing, the Takings Clause, and the Eleventh Amendment.

A. Standing

The doctrine of standing has had a pervasive and deeply imbedded influence on natural resources law. The standing doctrine constrains the extent to which litigants can enforce federal natural resources laws. Article III extends "judicial authority" to "Cases . . .

and Controversies." In general, the Supreme Court has construed this provision to require that a plaintiff show a personal injury that can be traced to the defendant's conduct and redressed by a judicial remedy.[70] In 1972, the Court recognized non-economic aesthetic and environmental interests as legally cognizable "injuries" that can serve as a sufficient basis for constitutional standing under Article III.[71] More recently, in *Friends of the Earth v. Laidlaw Environmental Services*, the Court made clear that it is injury to a person, and not the environment, that matters, thus obviating any need to show environmental degradation to support constitutional injury.[72] An association has standing when (1) its members would otherwise have standing to sue in their own right; (2) the interests it seeks to protect are germane to the organization's purpose; and (3) neither the claim asserted nor the relief requested requires the participation of individual members in the lawsuit.[73]

Despite these limits, standing doctrine should not prove an insurmountable bar to plaintiffs in natural resources cases. For example, a federal appeals court found that a citizen group that regularly uses Yellowstone National Park has constitutional standing to challenge construction of a coal-fired electric plant whose emissions reduce visibility.[74] Others have found that plaintiffs concerned about the effects of climate change have standing to enforce compliance with the National Environmental Policy Act.[75] And still others have recently shown receptivity to standing based on governmental failure to abide by statutorily required procedures in natural resources laws.[76] In *Summers v. Earth Island Institute*, the plaintiffs contended that certain regulations established by the U.S. Forest Service were invalid because they were not preceded by advance notice and an opportunity for comment and administrative appeals as mandated by the Forest Service Decision Making and Appeals Reform Act.[77] The Court held that Earth Island lacked standing to challenge the application of these regulations nationwide because it had voluntarily settled the portion of the lawsuit pertaining to its only member who suffered actual injury in fact that was "concrete and particularized."

States may enjoy wider latitude to demonstrate constitutional standing in cases involving natural resources law. In *Massachusetts v. EPA*, the Court held that states are entitled to "special solicitude" in standing analysis in cases involving state efforts to protect natural resources.[78] There, the Court recognized Massachusetts' potential shore-line loss as a legally cognizable injury in allowing it to challenge the EPA's failure to regulate greenhouse gas emissions. Individuals, on the other hand, must still show a tight "geographic nexus" between the claimed injury and the federal action.[79]

B. Takings

As discussed more fully in chapter 4, the Fifth Amendment, which the Fourteenth Amendment incorporates to the states, forbids the government from "taking private property for public use without just compensation." The concept of "regulatory" takings (for instance, by conserving species or in-stream flows) first arose in *Pennsylvania Coal Co. v. Mahon.*[80] Justice Holmes, writing for the Court, held that a state's regulation that goes "too far"—in this case, by prohibiting mining coal that might cause surface subsidence—could amount to a taking.[81]

Determining whether a law constitutes a regulatory taking involves a balancing approach that turns on how closely the impact of the challenged regulation resembles a physical occupation of the regulated property. In *Penn Central Transportation Co. v. New York City,* the company argued that the New York City Landmarks Preservation Law of 1965 constituted a regulatory taking.[82] The law allowed the city to designate structures and neighborhoods as "landmarks" or "landmark sites," thus preventing Penn Central from building a multistory office building atop Grand Central Terminal. The Court disagreed, finding that the city's restriction was substantially related to the general welfare of the city. In *Penn Central,* the Court weighed three factors to determine whether a government regulation requires compensation: (1) "the economic impact of the regulation on the claimant," (2) "the extent to which the regulation has interfered with distinct investment-backed expectations," and (3) the "character of the governmental action," that is, whether it amounts to a physical invasion or merely affects property interests through "some public program adjusting the benefits and burdens of economic life to promote the common good."

The Court has applied the *Penn Central* factors in a series of cases involving natural resources. A leading case is *Lucas v. South Carolina Coastal Council*.[83] There, Lucas bought two beachfront residential lots on which he intended to build single-family homes. Shortly thereafter, the state enacted a law aimed to protect barrier islands that barred Lucas from erecting permanent residences. The Court held that depriving a landowner of all economically viable use of property goes too far and constitutes a regulatory taking *per se*, unless such use constitutes a nuisance under the state's traditional common law.

Even preexisting state laws can go too far and constitute a compensable taking. In *Palazzolo v. Rhode Island*, Anthony Palazzolo owned a waterfront parcel of land in Rhode Island, most of which was salt marsh subject to tidal flooding.[84] State law enacted prior to him acquiring the property designated state salt marshes as protected "coastal wetlands." Palazzolo claimed that the state's subsequent denial of his multiple requests to develop the property constituted a regulatory taking because it had deprived him of "all economically beneficial use" of his property. The Court upheld his claims, even though he acquired the property after the state law went into effect. Justice Kennedy, writing for the court, held that a contrary ruling would "in effect, put an expiration date on the Takings Clause . . . [depriving] [f]uture generations [of] a right to challenge unreasonable limitations on the use and value of land."

Normal regulatory delays that temporarily deprive an owner of all economically beneficial use of property do not necessarily constitute a taking. In *Tahoe Sierra Preservation Council, Inc. v. Tahoe Regional Planning Agency*, the government imposed two moratoria on development while it prepared a comprehensive land use plan.[85] The moratoria lasted a total of about 32 months. The landowners claimed that during its duration the moratoria constituted a deprivation of all economically viable use of land. The Court disagreed. Applying the *Penn Central* factors, it concluded that the delay did not constitute a taking, noting that a categorical rule that any temporary deprivation of all economic use constitutes a taking—no matter how brief—would impose unreasonable financial burdens due to normal, foreseeable delays in processing land use applications.

The Court has wrestled with how closely its takings jurisprudence ought to track substantive due process jurisprudence. In *Agins v. City of Tiburon*, the Court declared that government regulation of private property constitutes "a taking if it does not substantially advance legitimate state interests."[86] This standard is analogous to the standard of review the Court uses in deciding whether a governmental law deprives one of a fundamental right to substantive due process.

After applying it for two decades, the Court subsequently abandoned the standard of review endorsed in *Agins*. In *Nollan v. California Coastal Commission*, the Court struck down a state requirement that certain beachfront property owners in California maintain along their property a public pathway that provided access to the beach.[87] The Court held that while maintaining public access is a legitimate state interest, the means chosen did not substantially advance this end, and constituted a compensable regulatory taking. Likewise, in *Dolan v. City of Tigard*, the Court rejected the City's effort to require Dolan to set aside part of her land for a greenway along a nearby creek to help alleviate surface runoff and for a pedestrian/bicycle path to relieve traffic congestion, in exchange for allowing her to expand her store and pave her parking lot.[88] The Court held that the City had failed to show an "essential nexus" between the ends (reducing erosion and traffic) and the means chosen to achieve them.

More recently, in *Lingle v. Chevron U.S.A.*, the Court considered a takings challenge arising out of a cap on the rent oil companies could charge dealers leasing company-owned service stations.[89] Chevron and others argued the cap constituted a regulatory taking because the means chosen (limiting rent charges) did not "substantially advance" a legitimate state aim. Writing for a unanimous Court, Justice O'Connor denied the claim. In an effort to "correct course," the Court held that the "substantially advances" test announced in *Agins* was akin to substantive due process analysis and does not apply in the takings context. Instead, takings challenges should be assessed based on the severity of the burden caused by the regulation, not how well the regulation furthers governmental interests.

Looking ahead, takings jurisprudence will continue to impact natural resource law significantly, especially in constraining state actions. Government agencies are acutely aware of the potential to pay large compensatory awards for denying or delaying permission to develop property, or for imposing conditions on property use. For example, the U.S. Court of Claims awarded $14 million to farmers who alleged that federal limits on water withdrawn from the Sacramento–San Joaquin Delta to conserve Chinook salmon and delta smelt and their habitat constituted a compensable regulatory taking.[90] The same court, however, recently rejected a claim that prohibiting the development of jurisdictional wetlands constitutes a compensable taking of the most economically valuable use of the property.[91]

Changes on the Court could substantially impact the Court's Fifth Amendment jurisprudence. Many Fifth Amendment regulatory takings cases over the last 30 years were decided by a bare majority. Therefore, a philosophical disagreement from either Chief Justice Roberts or Justice Alito that departs from their predecessors could have profound impacts on natural resources law. Initial cases from the Roberts Court suggest some hesitation to expand takings jurisprudence any further at this point. In *John R. Sand & Gravel Co. v. United States*, the Court rejected claims that the EPA's installation and repositioning of fences around a contaminated site constituted a taking of the plaintiff's leasehold rights for its adjacent mining operation.[92] It found dispositive that the claimant had failed to file the claim within the statute of limitations provided by federal law under the Tucker Act. Likewise, in *Wilkie v. Robbins*, it rejected a claim by the owner of a Wyoming ranch who asserted that the Bureau of Land Management's treatment of him following his refusal to grant the agency an easement across his property constituted a compensable taking.[93] The Court found that there were alternate remedies, and it lacked standards for determining when the government's tactics "demanded too much and went too far."[94]

C. Eleventh Amendment

Under the Eleventh Amendment, "[t]he Judicial power of the United States shall not be construed to extend to any suit in law or equity, commenced or prosecuted against one of the United States by

Citizens of another State." Absent express consent, states are virtually immune from legal action in federal court, including lawsuits to force compliance with federal natural resource programs. The Eleventh Amendment clearly limits federal jurisdiction in actions based on diversity. A century ago, the Court extended this prohibition to federal court actions based on federal question jurisdiction as well. In 1986, the Court upheld the constitutionality of the Comprehensive Environmental Response, Compensation, and Liability Act insofar as it permitted suits against the states for monetary damages in federal court.[95] The Court has made clear, however, that Congress may not subject states to federal question lawsuits without state consent, in federal court,[96] in state court,[97] or before federal agencies.[98]

This creates a potential obstacle to citizen suits to redress violations of federal natural resources laws by state agencies. For example, the Surface Mining Control and Reclamation Act (SMCRA) allows citizens to sue state and federal mining agencies to enforce its provisions, including bonding provisions and requirements to protect water quality. Thus, in *Bragg v. West Virginia Coal Ass'n*, citizens brought an action to forestall the practice of filling valleys with excess spoil or waste rock from mountaintop mining.[99] The citizens sued state and federal officials to enjoin them from issuing permits in the absence of the sufficient financial assurances SMCRA requires, including funding to protect affected streams. The Fourth Circuit dismissed the action. It held that SMCRA's "exclusive" delegation of permitting to a state transforms SMCRA requirements into state standards, which cannot be enforced in federal court.[100] Notwithstanding the decision in these cases, an argument remains that states waive their claim to immunity when they voluntarily seek approval to operate a program pursuant to a federal law like SMCRA.

The Court's Eleventh Amendment jurisprudence also has hampered implementation of federal whistleblower protection laws designed to protect state employees who report a state agency's transgressions from federal natural resources laws, including appropriations to states to administer federal natural resource programs.[101]

State officials are still subject to federal causes of action for prospective injunctive relief, a tack left available under *Ex Parte Young*.[102]

Thus, the Eleventh Amendment does not prevent a court from requiring a state official to comply with federal natural resource laws.

Eleventh Amendment jurisprudence will likely continue to hamper efforts to enforce natural resources laws against states. This is especially true if Chief Justice Roberts and Justice Alito share Justice Rehnquist's solicitude for states' rights.

D. Political Question Doctrine

While the Political Question doctrine has not traditionally impeded implementation of natural resource laws, recent decisions suggest it deserves to be watched closely in the future, at least concerning climate change. In *Marbury v. Madison*, Chief Justice Marshall lamented the "irksome" and "delicate" questions that are inherently political and out of reach to the judiciary.[103] And in 1962, the Court held that matters demonstrably committed to a coordinate branch of government, or that lack ascertainable standards, or could otherwise result in judicial embarrassment, are nonjusticiable "political questions."[104] For example, the Court has recognized that executive power over foreign affairs, impeachment, and treaty abrogation are political questions into which courts "ought not enter the political thicket." The Court declined to engage arguments inviting analysis under the Political Question doctrine in holding that the federal Clean Air Act provides the EPA with authority to regulate emissions of so-called greenhouse gases from new motor vehicles.[105] Nonetheless, several federal courts have recently turned to the Political Question doctrine in deciding that cases involving climate change are nonjusticiable. For example, federal courts in California and New York have dismissed state public nuisance actions brought to address the effects of climate change against U.S. auto manufacturers[106] and coal burning power plants,[107] electing not to "enter the global warming thicket." Much remains to be seen about how the doctrine may affect natural resources laws in this and other contexts.[108]

IV. Additional Constitutional Sources of and Limitations to Natural Resources Law

Various other provisions warrant attention when considering the future of natural resources law. These include the Treaty, General Welfare, Compact, Due Process and Property Clauses, and the First Amendment, as well as a few other constitutional attributes. Each has the potential to assume a more central role in the future of natural resources law.

A. Treaty Clause

The Treaty Clause is an underutilized source of congressional authority to enact natural resource laws. It provides that the executive branch "shall have power, by and with the advice and consent of the Senate, to make Treaties, provided two thirds of the Senators present concur."[109] After a Treaty is approved, Congress has the power under the Necessary and Proper Clause "to make all laws which shall be necessary and proper for carrying into execution . . . all . . . powers vested by this Constitution in the Government of the United States."[110] Because of the Supremacy Clause (discussed above), these laws effectively preempt any conflicting laws enacted by states. There is some jurisprudence that suggests that the Treaty Clause invests Congress with the authority to force state adherence to federal natural resource laws enacted pursuant to validly ratified treaties, irrespective of the limitations otherwise imposed by the Tenth Amendment. The leading case involves the Migratory Bird Treaty Act (MBTA). Congress enacted the MBTA to facilitate enforcement of a treaty between the United States and Great Britain to protect a number of migratory birds in the United States and Canada. Missouri claimed the treaty infringed upon rights reserved by the Tenth Amendment. The Court disagreed. In *Missouri v. Holland*, Justice Holmes, writing for the Court, upheld Congress's authority to enact legislation pursuant to a treaty that governed a traditional state function like hunting.[111] The Court found that the Treaty Clause, when coupled with the Necessary and Proper Clause, provided Congress with authority to infringe upon state sovereignty in ways it could not under the Commerce Clause alone.

In the future, the Treaty Clause may play a greater role in supplying authority for natural resource laws enacted pursuant to an underlying treaty. This is especially so for the ESA, which, as discussed above, is subject to persistent challenges under the Commerce Clause. Congress enacted the ESA in part to implement aspects of the Convention on the International Trade in Endangered Species of Wild Fauna and Flora, and the Western Convention on Nature Protection and Wildlife Preservation.

The decision of *Missouri v. Holland* suggests that the Treaty and Necessary and Proper clauses may offer a better source of constitutional authority for natural resource laws such as the ESA.[112] This also suggests a possible advantage for Senate ratification and congressional implementation of other treaties designed to level the playing field in the use of natural resources, such as the United Nations Convention on the Law of the Seas.

Bilateral treaties may also play a more substantial role in the future of water use and natural resources protection. In 1909, the United States and Canada entered into the International Boundary Waters Treaty, which established the International Joint Commission to help resolve disputes regarding waters shared by the two countries, including the Great Lakes. Disputes between the countries about water use could prove to become more significant, particularly with a warming planet and the loss of the polar ice caps. Thus far, however, federal courts in the United States have declined to entertain disputes about boundary waters, finding such matters to be constitutionally committed to foreign policy and thus not justiciable.

B. General Welfare Clause

The General Welfare Clause is another provision that provides a potential basis for promoting natural resource values. It allows Congress to "provide for the common defense and General Welfare of the United States" and has been construed to authorize Congress's taxing and spending powers.[113] Further, Congress may achieve its general welfare goals by attaching conditions to the receipt of federal funds, provided they are not coercive.[114]

The Land and Water Conservation Fund (LWCF) offers a good example of a federal spending program that benefits natural resources.[115] Established in 1964, the LWCF has provided hundreds of millions of dollars in grants to federal, state, and local governments to acquire land, water, and related resources for recreational, wildlife, and aesthetic purposes that benefit the public.

The General Welfare Clause's imprint on natural resources can also be problematic. This is perhaps best reflected by the work of the Bureau of Reclamation, which has sponsored many large water development projects throughout the western United States under the auspices of the General Welfare Clause and the Reclamation Act of 1902.[116] Without the Bureau, much of the western United States would still be undeveloped desert. Between 1902 and 1981, the federal government invested $7.3 billion in Bureau projects to construct about 350 diversion dams, more than 15,000 miles of diversion canals, and about 50 hydroelectric plants, including the Hoover Dam.

C. The Compact Clause

The Compact Clause of the U.S. Constitution provides that "no state shall, without the consent of Congress . . . enter into any agreement or compact with another state."[117] States have entered into more than 200 compacts, 26 of which involve allocating interstate waters.[118]

Historically, water resource allocation has been the area where regional issues warranted an appreciation of the Compact Clause. For example, the Colorado River Compact of 1922—the first interstate water compact—includes seven states and has had a substantial influence on water resources allocation among those states. As our climate changes and demands for fresh water resources grow, disputes among states sharing interstate waters are expected to increase dramatically, including in areas, like the southeastern United States, that have historically had ample water supplies. Georgia, Florida, and Alabama, for example, have waged a pitched and unresolved battle over water rights to the Apalachicola-Chattahoochee-Flint river system for two decades.

The Court is generally loath to get involved in state disputes about water, pushing by fiat or filibuster for interstate compacts.[119] To aid in this effort, the Utton Transboundary Resources Center began work in 2004 to develop a Model Interstate Water Compact.[120]

D. Procedural Due Process

The Fifth Amendment, which applies to the federal government, and the Fourteenth Amendment, which applies to the states, provide that no individual "shall be deprived of . . . property without the due process of law." Generally, due process protects only traditional property rights. Nonetheless, because natural resources law frequently involves the issuance of permits and enforcement actions for violating permits or other legal requirements, due process rights abound. The amount of process that is due may vary with the scope of the right, but most federal and state agencies that regulate natural resources, including land, air, and water resources, afford parties who are directly impacted by agency decisions with procedural rights to contest those decisions. Less process is usually due when the use of natural resources poses a threat to health or safety. In *Hodel v. Virginia Surface Mining and Reclamation Ass'n*, the Court upheld several provisions of SMCRA against procedural due process challenges.[121] SMCRA permits the Secretary of the Interior to issue an order for immediate cessation of mining when he or she determines that conditions pose a serious threat to public health and safety or the environment. The Court held that this process did not violate the coal producers' procedural due process rights to an expedient hearing prior to issuance of the order.

Furthermore, failure to meet statutory requirements can extinguish a claim of deprivation of procedural due process. In *United States v. Locke*, the Court upheld the constitutionality of statutes providing for the automatic termination of vested property rights upon the failure to comply with statutory conditions.[122] The Federal Land

Policy and Management Act requires mining claimants to rerecord claims every year with the Bureau of Land Management "*prior to December 31*" (emphasis added). When a mining claimant re-recorded a claim *on* December 31, the owner lost the claim that he had worked for more than twenty years. The Court held that no further process is required.

E. The Property Clause

The Property Clause authorizes Congress to make all "needful" rules concerning federal land, which constitutes about 28 percent of the country. In 1897, the Court analogized Congress's power under the Property Clause to state police power, lest federal property be at the mercy of the states. Since then, the Court interpreted the scope of this authority to be "virtually without limitation."[123] With this authority, Congress has enacted numerous laws allowing for development, use, and exploitation of natural resources on federal lands.

Other provisions of the Constitution have also allowed Congress to exercise relatively unquestioned authority to protect natural resources on federal enclaves under the Enclave Clause.[124] Congress also has authority to "acquiesce" to Presidential power to "reserve" natural resources on federal land.[125]

F. The First Amendment

The First Amendment prohibits Congress from passing laws "respecting an establishment of religion, or prohibiting the free exercise thereof." In the natural resources context, First Amendment claims typically arise in the context of public land management. In a leading case on the Free Exercise Clause, *Lyng v. Northwest Indian Cemetery Protective Association,* various parties contested the Forest Service's plans to permit timber harvesting and road construction in an area of national forest that was traditionally used for religious purposes by members of three Native American tribes in northwestern

California.[126] The Court held that the Free Exercise Clause protects an individual from certain forms of governmental compulsion, but it does not give an individual a right to dictate government conduct, even if that conduct might significantly interfere with one's religious practices. Thus, the timber harvesting and road construction were allowed to go forward.[127]

Unlike free exercise cases, Establishment Clause cases typically arise where the government seeks to protect resources of religious significance and someone objects to that protection on the ground that the government is promoting religion. For example, in *Mount Royal Joint Venture v. Kempthorne*, the Department of the Interior withdrew about 20,000 acres of public mineral estate from mineral location and entry, in part to protect areas of traditional spiritual importance to Native Americans.[128] The court found, however, that the Secretary had also articulated secular purposes for the withdrawal, including the protection of aquifers and the environment. Consequently, the court concluded that the withdrawal did not primarily affect religious interests and thus did not foster excessive government entanglement with religion in a manner that would violate the Establishment Clause.[129]

V. Conclusion

Constitutional law provides the foundation for modern natural resources law, but it also raises obstacles for both federal and state agencies seeking to protect or exploit natural resources. The recent rise of federalism principles will likely place increased pressure on the Court to limit federal power both by narrowly construing the Commerce Clause and by reading the Tenth and Eleventh Amendments more expansively. On the other hand, the dormant Commerce Clause and the Supremacy and Takings Clauses will challenge states in their efforts to protect their own natural resources. Emerging constitutional principles in this field, including the Treaty, Compact, General Welfare, Due Process, and Property Clauses, as well as the First Amendment, are likely to play more significant roles in the future.

Protecting Reintroduced Red Wolf
Populations in North Carolina

Richard Lee Mann had no interest in becoming the impetus for a test case contesting the constitutional limits of Congress's authority to protect endangered species. With his family, he owned a cattle farm nestled next to the Alligator River National Wildlife Refuge not far from the Great Smoky Mountains National Park in northeastern North Carolina. His cattle were his stock and trade, his family's livelihood, his children's future. He erected fences to contain them and keep them from wandering. These barriers, however, worked better at corralling his cattle than at protecting them from predators that harassed, attacked, and killed the young, old, and infirm in the lot. He anguished about both the fate of his cattle and the bottom line.

After another night's sleep interrupted by howling wolves, barking dogs, and bleating calves, Mr. Mann reached his limit. Shortly after sunrise on a crisp fall day in October 1990, he set out to even the score. A trail of rendered livestock led him to his nemesis, an adult red wolf, which he pursued and dispatched on his property. While he did not catch the wolf in the act of harming or threatening his cattle, Mr. Mann feared that its natural tendencies made preemptive action necessary.

Thousands of native red wolves formerly ranged throughout much of the United States east of the Mississippi River. By the 1960s, however, humans had nearly extinguished them. Hence, in 1967 the U.S. Fish and Wildlife Service (FWS) determined that the red wolf was endangered. Then, in a last-gasp effort to fend off extinction, it trapped the last remaining red wolves that roamed the Texas-Louisiana border and placed them into an experimental captive breeding program under the Endangered Species Act (ESA), in hopes of releasing progeny into the wild.

As part of the re-introduction program FWS released four pair of red wolves into the Alligator River National Wildlife Refuge. In little more than a decade the population of wild red wolves in the area grew about tenfold; this growth was partly due to ESA protections that provide that people may not "take" red wolves, that is, "harass, harm, pursue, hunt, shoot, wound, kill, trap, capture, or collect" them, or "attempt to engage in any such conduct" unless, according to FWS rules, "wolves are in the act of killing livestock or pets . . . and the taking is reported within 24 hours."

Unfortunately for Mr. Mann, the red wolf he shot was protected under the aegis of the FWS's reintroduction program. He did not shoot it while it was in the act of killing livestock or pets, and he did not report the episode. Federal criminal charges ensued, and Mr. Mann pled guilty to violating the ESA.

Local and state officials leapt to Mr. Mann's defense. The North Carolina Department of Agriculture filed a formal protest against the program. The state legislature enacted a bill that expressly countenanced Mr. Mann's act, entitled, "An Act to Allow the Trapping and Killing of Red Wolves by Owners of Private Land."

Joined by sympathetic counties and public officials, Mr. Mann brought a federal lawsuit claiming that the FWS's application of the ESA against him exceeded Congress's authority under the U.S. Constitution in several ways explained in this chapter. Mr. Mann claimed that the Commerce Clause does not allow Congress to prohibit him from killing a wild animal on his property, even one that is designated as "endangered" under federal law. Mr. Mann maintained that his taking of a lone red wolf does not "significantly affect" interstate commerce under the Supreme Court's interpretation of that clause in *Lopez* and *Morrison*. He also alleged that a contrary construction would demean North Carolina's traditional authority under the Tenth Amendment to manage wild animals and that the ESA does not preempt North Carolina's law that allows for killing red wolves on private property.

In *Gibbs v. Babbitt,* the U.S. District Court for the Eastern District of North Carolina disagreed with Mr. Mann.[130] It held that red wolves are "things in interstate commerce" because they move across state lines, and "substantially affect" interstate commerce due to the interest of tourists, academics, and scientists. The court also reasoned that federally protected animals are not a resource traditionally managed by states. Mr. Mann and his co-plaintiffs appealed to the U.S. Court of Appeals for the Fourth Circuit.

A divided panel of the Fourth Circuit affirmed, holding that Congress could possess a rational basis for determining that the taking of red wolves—which includes killing a single animal— might "substantially affect" interstate commerce.[131] The court held that taking wolves is an inherently commercial activity. Tourists, academics, and scientists visit North Carolina to witness red wolf "howling events," resulting in attendant commerce of about $170 million annually. Moreover, the court observed, wolves are inherently things in interstate commerce due to the value of their pelts, which can fetch as much as $300. The query, the court reasoned, is not whether the loss of an individual wolf "substantially affects" interstate commerce, but instead whether losses "in the aggregate" might do so. The court had no trouble holding that losses of individual red wolves—in the aggregate—substantially affects interstate commerce.

It also held that protecting rare and wandering wildlife is not traditionally a state matter and that preventing Congress from doing so would "work a rent" in our federal system.

A stinging dissent complained that the majority of the panel had turned its back on the sum and substance of *Lopez* and *Morrison* and the Tenth Amendment. It posited that Congress has no business prohibiting the killing of an individual wolf on private land authorized under state law and that "the negative limits of the Commerce Clause do not wax and wane depending upon the subject matter of the particular legislation under challenge." The Supreme Court denied Mr. Mann's petition for certiorari.[132]

In a mark of poetic justice of sorts, Mr. Mann's federal sentence included 32 hours of community service constructing housing for red wolves who were to be reintroduced into the Alligator River Wildlife Refuge. The FWS presently estimates that about 100 red wolves now populate the area. By some accounts, existing habitat and prey base in the forests in the northeastern United States could accommodate another 2,000 red wolves, vastly compounding the potential for comparable constitutional conflict.

Notes

1.   U.S. Term Limits v. Thornton, 514 U.S. 779 (1995).

2.   James May & Robert L. Glicksman, *Justice Rehnquist and the Dismantling of Environmental Law,* 36 ENVTL. L. REP. (ENVTL. L. INST.) 10585 (2006) (hereinafter, *"Dismantling of Environmental Law"*).

3.   M'Culloch v. State of Maryland, 17 U.S. 316 (1819).

4.   U.S. CONST. art. I, § 8.

5.   Johnson v. McIntosh, 21 U.S. 543 (1823).

6.   Gibbons v. Ogden, 22 U.S. 1 (1824).

7.   United States v. E.C. Knight Co., 156 U.S. 1 (1895).

8.   Hammer v. Dagenhart, 247 U.S. 251 (1918).

9.   Carter v. Carter Coal Co., 298 U.S. 238 (1936); Panama Ref. Co. v. Ryan, 293 U.S. 388 (1935).

10. NLRB v. Jones & Laughlin Steel, 301 U.S. 1 (1937).

11. United States v. Darby, 312 U.S. 100 (1941).

12. Wickard v. Filburn, 317 U.S. 111 (1942).

13. Hodel v. Va. Surface Mining & Reclamation Ass'n, Inc., 452 U.S. 264 (1981).

14. United States v. Lopez, 514 U.S. 549 (1995).

15. Morrison v. Olson, 529 U.S. 598 (2000).

16. Nat'l Ass'n of Homebuilders v. Babbitt, 130 F.3d 1041 (D.C. Cir. 1997).

17. Gibbs v. Babbitt, 214 F.3d 483 (4th Cir. 2000).

18. GDF Realty Investments v. Norton, 326 F.3d 622 (5th Cir. 2003).

19. Rancho Viejo, LLC v. Norton, 323 F.3d 1062 (D.C. Cir. 2003), *petition for reh'g en banc denied,* 334 F.3d 1158 (D.C. Cir. 2003).

20. Gonzales v. Raich, 545 U.S. 1 (2005).

21. *Id.* at 19.

22. Alabama–Tombigbee Rivers Coal. v. Kempthorne, 477 F.3d 1250 (11th Cir. 2007).

23. United States v. Hubenka, 438 F.3d 1026 (10th Cir. 2006).

24. Rancho Viejo, LLC v. Norton, 323 F.3d 1062 (D.C. Cir. 2003), *petition for reh'g en banc denied,* 334 F.3d 1158 (D.C. Cir. 2003) (Roberts, C.J., dissenting).

25. Solid Waste Agency of N. Cook County v. U.S. Army Corps of Engineers, 531 U.S. 159 (2001).

26. Rapanos v. United States, 547 U.S. 715 (2006).

27. *Id.* at 783.

28. New York v. United States, 505 U.S. 144 (1992).

29. Connecticut v. United States, 369 F. Supp. 2d 237, 241–42 (D. Conn. 2005).

30. Wyoming v. U.S. Dep't of the Interior, 360 F. Supp. 2d 1214 (D. Wyo. 2005).

31. Alaska Dep't of Envtl Conservation v. U.S. Envtl Prot. Agency, 540 U.S. 461 (2004).

32. Whitman v. Am. Trucking Ass'n, 531 U.S. 457 (2001).

33. American Trucking Ass'n v. U.S. Envtl Prot Agency, 175 F.3d 1027 (D.C. Cir. 1999).

34. Willson v. Black-Bird Creek Marsh Co., 27 U.S. 245 (1829).

35. Philadelphia v. New Jersey, 347 U.S. 617 (1978).

36. Fort Gratiot Sanitary Landfill, Inc. v. Mich. Dep't of Natural Res., 504 U.S. 353 (1992); Oregon Waste Sys., Inc. v. Dep't of Envtl. Quality, 511 U.S. 93 (1994).

37. C & A Carbone, Inc. v. Clarkstown, 511 U.S. 383 (1994).

38. Geer v. Connecticut, 161 U.S. 519 (1896).

39. Hudson County Water Co. v. McCarter, 209 U.S. 349 (1908).

40. Cities Serv. Gas Co. v. Peerless Oil & Gas Co., 340 U.S. 179 (1950).

41. Hughes v. Oklahoma, 441 U.S. 322 (1979).

42. Sporhase v. Nebraska, 458 U.S. 941 (1982).

43. New England Power Co. v. New Hampshire, 455 U.S. 331 (1982).

44. New Energy Co. of Ind. v. Limbach, 486 U.S. 269 (1988).

45. Wyoming v. Oklahoma, 502 U.S. 437 (1992).

46. Hughes v. Oklahoma, 441 U.S. 336 (1979).

47. *Id.*

48. Maine v. Taylor, 477 U.S. 131 (1986).

49. Chemical Waste Mgmt., Inc. v. Hunt, 504 U.S. 334 (1992).

50. South-Central Timber Development, Inc. v. Wunnicke, 467 U.S. 82 (1984).

51. United Haulers Ass'n, Inc. v. Oneida-Herkimer Solid Waste Mgmt. Auth., 127 S. Ct. 1786 (2007).

52. Pike v. Bruce Church, Inc. 397 U.S. 137 (1970).

53. *See, e.g.,* Lebanon Farms Disposal v. County of Lebanon, 538 F.3d 241 (3d Cir. 2008) (County flow control ordinance requiring waste generated within the county be carried to a specific, publicly owned disposal facility does not contravene dormant Commerce Clause).

54. *See, e.g.,* Quality Compliance Services, Inc. v. Dougherty County, Georgia, 553 F. Supp. 2d. 1374 (M.D. Ga. 2008) (ordinance requiring disposal within county limits—excluding the plaintiff's out-of-state station—does not violate the dormant Commerce Clause).

55. Chemical Waste Mnftrs. v. Hunt, 504 U.S. 334, 349–50 (1992)(Rehnquist, C.J., dissenting).

56. *See Dismantling of Environmental Law, supra* note 2, at 10597–99.

57. *Id.*

58. U.S. Const. art. VI, cl. 2.

59. Gibbons v. Ogden, 22 U.S. 1 (1824).

60. Milwaukee v. Illinois, 451 U.S. 304 (1981).

61. *See, e.g.,* International Paper Co. v. Ouellette, 479 U.S. 481 (1987).

62. Exxon Shipping Co. v. Baker, 128 S. Ct. 2605, 2617 (2008).

63. Engine Manufacturers Ass'n v. South Coast Air Quality Mgmt. Dist., 498 F.3d 1091 (9th Cir. 2007).

64. Green Mountain Chrysler Plymouth Dodge Jeep v. Crombie, 508 F. Supp. 2d 295 (D. Vt. 2007).

65. Pacific Gas & Elec. v. State Energy Comm'n, 461 U.S. 190 (1983).

66. California v. United States, 438 U.S. 645 (1978).

67. Douglas v. Seacoast Products, Inc. 431 U.S. 265 (1977).

68. California v. FERC, 495 U.S. 490 (1990).

69. PUD No. 1 of Jefferson County v. Washington Dep't of Ecology, 511 U.S. 700 (1984).

70. Lujan v. National Wildlife Fed'n, 497 U.S. 871 (1990).

71. Sierra Club v. Morton, 405 U.S. 727 (1972).

72. Friends of the Earth v. Laidlaw Envtl. Services, 528 U.S. 167 (2000).

73. Hunt v. Washington State Apple Adver. Comm'n, 432 U.S. 333, 343 (1977).

74. Nat'l Parks Conservation Ass'n v. Manson, 414 F.3d 1 (D.C. Cir. 2005).

75. Earth Island Inst. v. Ruthenbeck, 459 F. 3d 954 (9th Cir. 2006); Friends of Earth, Inc. v. Watson, No. C02-4106, 2005 WL 40071 (N.D. Cal. Jan. 6, 2005).

76. Lemon v. Geren, 514 F.3d 1312 (D.C. Cir. 2008) (under the National Environmental Policy Act); Salmon Spawning & Recovery Alliance v. United States, 523 F.3d 1338 (D.C. Cir. 2008) (Endangered Species Act).

77. 555 U.S. —, 129 S. Ct. 1142 (2009).

78. Massachusetts v. EPA, 549 U.S. 497 (2007).

79. Nuclear Info. and Res. Serv. v. Nuclear Regulatory Comm'n, 457 F.3d 941 (9th Cir. 2006).

80. Pa. Coal Co. v. Mahon, 260 U.S. 393 (1922).

81. *Cf.* Keystone Bituminous Coal Ass'n v. DeBenedictis, 480 U.S. 470 (1987) (state statute restricting mining that resulted in surface subsidence was not a taking).

82. Penn Cent. Transp. Co. v. New York City, 438 U.S. 104 (1978).

83. Lucas v. S.C. Coastal Council, 505 U.S. 1003 (1992).

84. Palazzolo v. Rhode Island, 533 U.S. 606 (2001).

85. Tahoe Sierra Pres. Council, Inc. v. Tahoe Reg'l Planning Agency, 535 U.S. 302 (2002).

86.   Agins v. City of Tiburon, 447 U.S. 255 (1980).

87.   Nollan v. Cal. Coastal Comm'n, 483 U.S. 825 (1987).

88.   Dolan v. City of Tigard, 512 U.S. 374 (1994).

89.   Lingle v. Chevron U.S.A., 544 U.S. 528 (2005).

90.   Tulare Lake Basin Water Storage Dist. v. United States, 49 Fed. Cl. 313 (Fed. Cl. 2001).

91.   Brace v. United States, 72 Fed. Cl. 337 (Fed. Cl. 2006), *aff'd,* No. 2007-5002, 2007 WL 2947319 (Fed. Cir. Oct. 10, 2007).

92.   John R. Sand & Gravel Co. v. United States, 128 S. Ct. 750 (2008).

93.   Wilkie v. Robbins, 127 S. Ct. 2588 (2007).

94.   *Id.*

95.   Pennsylvania v. Union Gas Co., 491 U.S. 1 (1989).

96.   Seminole Tribe of Fla. v. Florida, 517 U.S. 44 (1995).

97.   Alden v. Maine, 527 U.S. 706 (1999).

98.   Fed. Mar. Comm'n v. S.C. State Ports Auth., 535 U.S. 743 (2002).

99.   Bragg v. W. Va. Coal Ass'n, 248 F.3d 275 (4th Cir. 2001), *cert. denied,* 534 U.S. 1113 (2002).

100. *See also* Pa. Fed'n of Sportsmen's Clubs v. Hess, 297 F.3d 310 (3d Cir. 2002).

101. *See, e.g.,* R.I. Dep't of Envtl. Mgmt. v. United States, 304 F.3d 31 (1st Cir. 2002) (barring federal administrative action by whistleblower who alleged retaliation for complaining about Rhode Island's implementation of Solid Waste Disposal Act); Taylor v. U.S. Dep't of Labor, 440 F.3d 1 (1st Cir. 2005). *See also* Vermont Agency of Natural Res. v. United States *ex rel.* Stevens, 529 U.S. 765 (2000) (upholding standing to bring qui tam action under False Claims Act for false submissions to EPA, but dismissing the action on statutory grounds).

102. *Ex parte* Young, 209 U.S. 123 (1908) (ordering a state official to comply with federal law on ground that he lacked constitutional authority to commit unconstitutional act).

103. Marbury v. Madison, 5 U.S. 137 (1803).

104. Baker v. Carr, 369 U.S. 186 (1962).

105. Massachusetts v. EPA, 549 U.S. 497 (2007).

106. California v. Gen. Motors Corp., No. C06-05755, 2007 WL 2726871 (N.D. Cal. Sept. 17, 2007).

107. Connecticut v. Am. Elec. Power Co., 406 F. Supp. 2d 265 (S.D.N.Y 2005).

108. *See, e.g.,* Comer v. Murphy Oil, USA, Inc., No. 1:05-cv-436, (S.D. Miss. Aug. 30, 2007) (dismissing under the Political Question doctrine state law nuisance cause of action based on enhanced effects of climate change), *appeal docketed,* No. 07-60756 (5th Cir. 2007).

109. U.S. CONST. art. II, § 2, cl. 2.

110. U.S. CONST. art. I, § 8, cl. 18.

111. Missouri v. Holland, 252 U.S. 416 (1920).

112.   *See, e.g.,* Shields v. Babbitt, 229 F. Supp. 2d 638 (W.D. Tex. 2000), *vacated sub nom,* Shields v. Norton, 289 F.3d 832 (5th Cir. 2002) (holding ESA valid under Treaty and Necessary and Proper Clauses).

113.   U.S. CONST. art. I, § 8; United States v. Butler, 297 U.S. 1 (1936).

114.   South Dakota v. Dole, 483 U.S. 203 (1987).

115.   16 U.S.C. §§ 4601 *et seq.*

116.   *See* United States v. Gerlach Live Stock Co., 339 U.S. 725, 738 (1950).

117.   U.S. CONST. art. I, § 10, cl. 3.

118.   *See* Jerome C. Muys et al., *Utton Transboundary Resources Center Model Interstate Water Compact,* 47 NAT. RES. J. 17, 21 (2007).

119.   *See, e.g.,* Vermont v. New York, 417 U.S. 270, 277 (1974); Muys et al., *supra* note 118, at 27.

120.   Muys et al., *supra* note 118, at 27.

121.   Hodel v. Va. Surface Mining and Reclamation Ass'n, 452 U.S. 264 (1981).

122.   United States v. Locke, 471 U.S. 84 (1985).

123.   Kleppe v. New Mexico, 426 U.S. 529 (1976).

124.   Fort Leavenworth R. Co. v. Lowe, 114 U.S. 525 (1885).

125.   Midwest Oil Co. v. United States, 236 U.S. 459 (1915).

126.   Lyng v. Nw. Indian Cemetery Protective Ass'n, 485 U.S. 439 (1988).

127.   *See also,* Wong v. Bush, 542 F.3d 732 (9th Cir. 2008) (Coast Guard's "security zone" that prohibited plaintiff from blockading certain waters surrounding Kauai, Hawaii, finding restriction content-neutral; time, place and manner restriction that left ample alternative channels of expression; and that demonstrators may not "cordon off" an area and "force" others to listen).

128.   Mount Royal Joint Venture v. Kempthorne, 477 F.3d 745 (D.C. Cir. 2007).

129.   *See also* Access Fund v. U.S. Dep't of Agric., 499 F.3d 1036 (9th Cir. 2007) (affirming lower court's upholding of the U.S. Forest Service's ban on climbing a sacred rock by members of a Native American Tribe because the ban had a secular purpose and lacked impermissible religious motivation).

130.   Gibbs v. Babbitt, 31 F. Supp. 2d 531 (E.D.N.C. 1998), *aff'd,* 214 F.3d 483 (4th Cir. 2000).

131.   Gibbs v. Babbitt, 214 F.3d 483 (4th Cir. 2000).

132.   Gibbs v. Babbitt, 214 F.3d 483 (4th Cir. 2000), *cert. denied,* Gibbs v. Norton, 531 U.S. 1145 (2001).

7

The Federalism Dynamic in Natural Resources Law

Robert L. Fischman

I. Introduction

One can scarcely conceive of a more important topic for under-standing the evolution of natural resources law than federalism. It is both ubiquitous and essential. Power sharing arrangements are part of the organic legislation for all of the federal land systems except the national parks. They are key elements in the exercise of regulatory authority as well. Because private land use control is the last outpost of near-exclusive state/local jurisdiction, the federal government needs state partners to achieve any federal objective where control-ling soil disturbance is key. With ecosystems crossing boundaries of federal lands, even the traditional proprietary functions of natural resources law increasingly depend on federal arrangements. Though less strong than land use control, pervasive state management of water and wildlife also means that state cooperation is necessary for achiev-ing most federal objectives concerning those resources. Land, water,

Parts of this chapter are drawn from Robert L. Fischman and Angela M. King, *Savings Clauses and Trends in Natural Resources Federalism*, 32 WILLIAM & MARY ENVIRONMENTAL LAW & POLICY REVIEW 129 (2007).

and wildlife concerns encompass all of the great resource disputes that federal law seeks to resolve.

This chapter examines how the federalism dynamic plays out in natural resources law. Though important constitutional issues remain unresolved concerning the outer boundaries of state and federal power, the focus of this essay is the manner in which federalism is hammered out and practiced by legislatures, agencies, and the courts interpreting statutes. It is on this level of implementation that most of the exciting developments unfold.

As I have explored at length elsewhere, the distinguishing aspects of federalism based on resource management compared with that based on pollution control are its site-specific variation and discretionary disparities.[1] Although fealty to subsidiarity and respect for state interests are universally expressed values, in practice the substantive preference of a state has as much to do with the weight a federal agency will afford that preference as does the legal or policy framework for a particular resource.

Federalism is to environmental law what scope of review is to administrative law: a pervasive, indispensable doctrine defined concisely in ways that give little insight into how it actually works. It takes five minutes to explain federalism but a lifetime to understand its dynamic on the ground. Nothing better captures this elusive aspect of federalism than the statutory savings and cooperation clauses that this chapter analyzes.

Though commentary abounds on particular components of federalism policy, especially placed-based collaboration, there exists little scholarship building a framework for understanding the kinds of federalism operating in natural resources law. This chapter concentrates on the descriptive challenge of cataloging the federalism dynamic, particularly in public land management. Part II reviews the distinctive kinds of federalism found in natural resources law, and highlights how they differ from the pollution control style of federalism. Part III builds upon this framework to highlight the recent trends that set the direction for policy innovations in natural resources federalism. Part IV bores into the common statutory savings clauses that establish the broad scope of federal arrangements. It provides a taxonomy for understanding the types of legislative formulations. It then analyzes the

interpretive approaches courts may employ to make sense of the statutory savings language. The case study discussed in the sidebar, the
controversy over managing elk in the Jackson Hole area of Wyoming,
illustrates the federalism dynamic in public land and wildlife management. It also shows how a statutory savings clause can provide a state
with traction to advance its interests. Part V concludes with general
thoughts about the future of federalism in natural resources law.

II. The Distinctive Types of Natural Resources Federalism

Federalism in environmental law is most often associated with
the model pervasive in pollution control, which is narrowly circumscribed around state permitting and standard setting overseen by the
federal government to assure compliance with national minimum
criteria. Natural resources law, in contrast, employs a wider array of
cooperative tools, including place-based collaboration, state favoritism in federal process, and federal deference to state process.

Place-based collaboration tailors decision making about the environment to a specific region. Rather than impose a uniform model
for interaction, place-based collaborations grow from the particular
circumstances of the locus and nature of a dispute. The chief strength
of this approach is that it brings a wide range of stakeholders and
regulatory jurisdictions together to engage in holistic management.
Place-based collaborations are one of the most popular current approaches to cooperative federalism in natural resources law. Place-
based collaboration softens the command-and-control requirements
that typically bind parties in environmental law; instead, it employs
more flexibility to create a watershed-, jurisdiction-, or habitat-
specific approach. It also helps satisfy many of the criteria for ecosystem management. A favorite example was the CALFED Bay-Delta
program to manage fish and other resources in the Sacramento River
Delta, until the effort collapsed in 2005. More recently, the U.S. Fish
and Wildlife Service (FWS) issued an incidental take permit in 2005
endorsing a tri-state effort to manage the lower Colorado River's

aquatic habitat. But place-based collaborations risk local capture and may frustrate coordinated management of public lands systems. Widely debated examples include the board Congress created to operate the Valles Caldera National Preserve as a national forest unit and the cooperative agreement outsourcing much of the management of the National Bison Range to the Confederated Salish and Kootenai tribal governments. The clearest, and longest-term, recent trend in natural resources law has been reliance on more place-based collaborations. This is a bipartisan enthusiasm.

State favoritism in federal process is a coordinating tool that reserves an enhanced role for states in federal environmental decision-making. Though it does not guarantee that the state view will prevail, federal agency decision-makers have a responsibility to at least document their consideration of the state's view and to explain why it did not prevail. The state's direct avenue to assert its interests is often not open to other stakeholders in the federal decision. The organic acts for the national forest, national wildlife refuge, and Bureau of Land Management (BLM) land systems all employ this tool in their comprehensive planning mandates. For instance, the BLM must coordinate with state and local governments in the development of land use plans "to the extent consistent with the laws governing the administration of the public lands."[2]

The George W. Bush administration was particularly enamored of state favoritism, as exemplified by the now-suspended roadless rule. The 2005 rule invited state governors to petition the Forest Service to promulgate special rules establishing management requirements for roadless areas within the state. The rule bound the Forest Service to act on the state petition within a definite time frame, but reserved federal national forest management authority. The roadless rule's version of procedural favoritism was inspired by the Wild and Scenic Rivers Act, which provides an alternative to congressional river designation where a governor applies to the Secretary of the Interior for administrative designation of rivers protected under state law.

Federal deference to state process is created when legislation specifies that a state policy, standard, or plan—if adopted in accordance with certain procedures—will be employed by the federal government in its own national decisions. While procedural favoritism gives states an advantage over other stakeholders in asserting their interests in federal decision-making, this third category—federal deference—provides greater assurance that the federal government will actually comply with the state position. The best statutory example of this approach to cooperative federalism is the Coastal Zone Management Act's consistency criterion. But it also pops up in public land management. For example, federal public lands routinely embrace state hunting regulations as a default rule;[3] even the FWS regards state-permitted takes as per se appropriate for national wildlife refuges.[4] Because federal deference to state process is the strongest restraint on federal activities, it has not been a particularly attractive tool for any administration recently. As the next part explains, the political power driving federal natural resources policy prefers rhetorical allegiance to state interests rather than binding commitment.

III. Policy Directions

Enlisting state and local interests to support federal aims has been official policy at least since the New Deal, especially in watersheds (basins). However, it has never been a doctrine of purity. Administrations and Congress have always picked and chosen compliant states for deference and pushed aside states seeking competing objectives from resource management. In a recent example, the "cooperative conservation"–themed Bush administration denied New Mexico's proposal to protect wildlife through restrictions on oil and gas development on the Otero Mesa, reflecting a judgment about politics and the priority of energy resource development. That is consistent with the tradition of selective use of federalism in natural resources policy. Like all administrations, the Bush administration found other state wildlife initiatives—such as brucellosis vaccination on the National Elk Refuge—more palatable to its centralized policy agenda.

While the two-term, recent era of the George W. Bush administration does not depart from historical patterns of pragmatic federalism, it does display three distinctive attributes. First, it hyped up the rhetoric of federalism with great discipline and consistency. Interior

Secretary Norton's motto of the four Cs—communication, consultation, and cooperation in the service of conservation—became something of an incantation necessary to legitimize agency action within the department. This rhetoric matured in the 2004 executive order promoting "cooperative conservation."[5] Both versions of cooperative conservation are considerably broader than federalism because they embrace direct federal partnerships with landowners, businesses, and NGOs. Federalism partners must include a tribe, state, or local government unit. Still, the federalism discourse, including its suggestions of devolution, downsizing, and outsourcing, provides a flavor of the policies favored by the administration.

Second, the Bush administration pushed some innovation of federalism tools. The example discussed above, the 2005 roadless rule, while not without precedent, nonetheless established a high-profile template for managing federal conservation systems in accordance with principles that vary by state preference. Another example of novel federalism is a 2006 FWS policy for managing the National Wildlife Refuge System that extends to certain state actions the umbrella immunity of "refuge management activity," a category exempt from both the compatibility and appropriateness analyses that are otherwise necessary before approving an activity on a refuge. State game management may be deputized as refuge management through a memorandum of understanding between a state wildlife agency and a FWS regional office, a document that is not subject to any particular public oversight or participation. Such programs as predator control, or even hunting rules, may circumvent the public hearing and environmental analysis otherwise used to ensure that activities fulfill the proper national objectives. Both examples employ state favoritism without establishing criteria for adopting the state position. They also involve purely administrative initiatives, eschewing legislative reform.

The third recent trend arises from what a water lawyer might call the "reliction" of national interest in many environmental concerns. As federal leadership recedes, states may enter to fill the void. States have a newfound assertiveness in regulating the environmental impacts of public land mineral development, especially the effects of drilling on split estates, as the federal government has tilted toward favoring production as a preeminent goal. More well-known are the state and multi-state initiatives to reduce emissions of greenhouse gases such as carbon dioxide. It is important to note, however, that federalism is not a zero-sum game. States may aggressively assert control over even those aspects of natural resource management for which the federal government retains an active engagement. Most statutes preempt only certain or weaker kinds of state rules, not the entire field. Conversely, recession of federal leadership does not mean necessarily that states will expand their interest. The simultaneous retreat from noise control in the 1970s reflected decisions at both the state and national levels that the issues did not merit close attention.

IV. The Meaning of Savings Clauses

Describing the large-scale structure of natural resources federalism or summarizing recent trends in its implementation only goes so far in providing a fine-tuned understanding of the relationship between law and federalism policy. This part delves into statutory savings clauses, which have long set the tone for integrating state concerns and procedures into federal programs. A statutory savings clause seeks to delimit the degree to which a federal agency should pursue national objectives at the expense of a state's different view. It provides a statement, and sometimes a mechanism, for incorporating state interests notwithstanding a statute that seeks to implement a uniform federal program.

A. A Taxonomy of Savings Clauses

Savings clauses approach the protection of state (or tribal) prerogatives in a variety of ways. Some statutes have a single section that bundles together all of the savings promises, while others have separate sections for each savings program. In general, however, it is useful to divide savings clauses (which may be sections or parts of sections) into two types: jurisdictional and cooperative.

Jurisdictional savings clauses focus on the line separating federal from state power. All savings clauses implicitly address this separation, but the true jurisdictional clauses carve out distinct areas for either federal action or state authority. The jurisdictional savings clauses are particularly important in regulatory statutes and less prominent in public land management legislation.

The most famous example of a jurisdictional savings clause establishing the reach of a national regulatory program is the Federal Power Act's clause giving the Federal Power Commission (now the Federal Energy Regulatory Commission) its mandate to regulate interstate sale and transmission of electricity.[6] The seminal 1945 Supreme Court decision in *Connecticut Light and Power* limited the Commission's jurisdiction more narrowly than Congress's possible range of delegated Commerce Clause authority because of the savings clause's description of those aspects of the electric market "affected with a public interest."[7] This principal jurisdictional clause of the Act circumscribes the outer bounds of federal agency authority.

An important subset of jurisdictional savings clauses carve out a specific area of state law that Congress preserves despite a preemptive statutory program. The most common type of state law savings clause affirms the continued availability of state common law causes of actions notwithstanding federal regulation. For instance, the Federal Boat Safety Act preempts state "law or regulation," but the savings clause "does not relieve a person from liability at common law or under State law."[8]

Unfortunately, many savings clauses appear agnostic when faced with real federalism disputes. The best example is the Wilderness Act's provision on state water law: "Nothing in this chapter shall constitute an express or implied claim or denial on the part of the federal Government as to exemption from State water laws."[9] Such a clause can cause more litigation and controversy than it resolves, but it may be an essential element in the legislative compromise allowing passage of the law.

Cooperative savings clauses are particularly important in public resource management. They go beyond the sorting and separating of powers to describe how the two levels of government should work together. For instance, the Federal Land Policy Management Act

(FLPMA) requires federal resource management plans to be "consistent with State and local plans to the maximum extent [the Interior Secretary] . . . finds consistent with Federal law and the purposes of this Act."[10] Consistency review under FLPMA has a regulation of its own that describes a substantive test and procedure for determining when the BLM will accept the recommendations of a Governor on a plan. This state favoritism finds expression in national forest and national wildlife refuge planning as well.

Hybrid savings clauses combining features of jurisdiction and cooperation are common. For instance, the Clean Water Act's "Wallop Amendment" states that:

> It is the policy of Congress that the authority of each State to allocate quantities of water within its jurisdiction shall not be superseded, abrogated or otherwise impaired by this chapter. It is the further policy of Congress that nothing in this chapter shall be construed to supersede or abrogate rights to quantities of water which have been established by any State. Federal agencies shall co-operate with State and local agencies to develop comprehensive solutions to prevent, reduce and eliminate pollution in concert with programs for managing water resources.[11]

Though it concludes with a cooperative savings clause, the jurisdictional issue has played the more important role in shaping the interpretation of the Clean Water Act and other regulatory statutes.

In contrast, public land legislation, because it focuses on particular federal tracts, tends to generate fewer jurisdictional disputes. For example, though the organic act for the refuge system contains a similar hybrid savings provision, the cooperative clause has played the more important role in interpretation. The refuge savings provision states:

> Nothing in this Act shall be construed as affecting the authority, jurisdiction, or responsibility of the several States to manage, control, or regulate fish and resident wildlife under State law or regulations in any area within the System. Regulations permitting hunting or fishing of fish and resident wildlife within the System shall be, to the extent practicable, consistent with State fish and wildlife laws, regulations, and management plans.[12]

The refuge system savings provision illustrates the self-contradictory tone of many of these perplexing formulations. Though eschewing the split personality of some other clauses that neither affirm nor deny key propositions about the division of power, the second sentence of the provision does seem to contradict the facial meaning of the first sentence. If nothing in the organic act for national wildlife refuges truly affects state authority to regulate wildlife (first sentence), then why would the federal government be regulating hunting in ways that may be inconsistent with state law (second sentence)? Partly for this reason, the refuge savings provision can only be useful for its cooperative component.

B. Judicial Interpretation of Savings Clauses

What should we make of these instructions to cooperate with states while fulfilling legislative missions circumscribed by "saved" state authorities affecting water, wildlife, fish, intra-state interests, or common law causes of action? Courts have been answering versions of this question since the New Deal. However, each decade bears a new harvest of slightly different savings clauses. And, recent conflicts have revived interest in the meaning of the congressional commands. One of the most important engines that will drive the future development of federalism in natural resources law is judicial interpretation of savings clauses.

There is a continuum of interpretations of savings clauses from almost vanishingly weak to relatively strong drivers of agency structure and procedure. To date, the vast majority of decisions fall on the weak side, creating a consensus in the judiciary that Congress does not mean to command or limit very much with savings clauses. However, hints of change, particularly from the 2002 Tenth Circuit decision of *Wyoming v. United States*, may indicate possible movement toward a stronger version of savings clauses.[13] In order to see how courts understand savings clauses, I divide interpretations into two categories, weak and strong, each of which has three variations. A caveat is in order, however. Many court decisions, especially *Wyoming*, mix together several of the approaches. Parts of *Wyoming*, for instance, support at least three of the options described below. This section begins with the weakest interpretive option and moves toward the strongest extreme.

1. Weak Interpretations

The weak interpretations all share the characteristic of contributing nothing to the actual disposition of a case. General principles of statutory interpretation, preemption analysis, and administrative law subsume weak interpretation under the more broadly applied judicial rules of decision. Most opinions that have considered savings clauses fall into this category.

a. Hortatory

One can hardly read a savings clause without detecting a whiff of apple pie. A common, honest interpretation of the savings clause is that it is a mere exhortation of good politics: pay attention to local attitudes, particularly as reflected in state policy. In the public land context, this interpretation would mean that Congress intended to instruct agencies to be good neighbors when they can. Because this weakest of interpretations does not force an agency to do or show anything, it provides almost no traction for judicial relief. A hortatory interpretation is most likely for a savings clause in an introductory section of a statute, laying out broad, ambitious, and conflicting goals.

An example of this approach can be found in *Riverside Irrigation District v. Andrews*.[14] In that case, various water districts challenged the decision of the U.S. Army Corps of Engineers (Corps) to require an individual permit application for the construction of a dam. Because building the dam would require deposition of fill material into waters of the United States, Section 404 of the Clean Water Act (CWA) required a permit from the Corps.[15] The irrigation districts argued that the dam construction fell within one of the categories of nationwide permits that the Corps created in CWA regulations. The regulations included certain conditions that, if met, allow the nationwide permit to apply automatically. The Corps determined that the water districts did not satisfy the conditions and, therefore, were required to obtain an individual permit through a public hearing and notice process.

Specifically, the Corps found that the discharge would "destroy" a species protected under the Endangered Species Act—the whooping crane. The Corps did not conclude that the fill activity itself would adversely affect the whooping crane's habitat. Instead, the Corps determined that the reservoir created by the dam would result in the depletion of stream flow because of increased consumptive use, and that this depletion would adversely affect the whooping crane's habitat downstream. The water districts claimed that the Corps exceeded its authority in considering water quantity and indirect effects. However, the court found that specific provisions of the CWA statute and regulations required consideration of all effects on the "aquatic environment" resulting from the fill, not just factors related to water quality. The water districts claimed that the Corps' denial violated the CWA's Wallop Amendment (discussed in part IV.A above as an example of a hybrid savings clause) by impairing the state's ability to allocate water within its jurisdiction. The court, citing *Connecticut Light and Power Co. v. Federal Power Commission*, held the Wallop Amendment to be "only a general policy statement" unable to invalidate the clear and specific grant of jurisdiction given to the Corps.[16] In the absence of a jurisdictional limitation within the specific provisions authorizing the fill permit program, the court upheld the Corps, despite the rhetoric of the savings clause. The Supreme Court unequivocally endorsed this interpretation in *PUD No. 1 of Jefferson County v. Washington Department of Ecology*.[17]

b. Confirmatory

The next step for a court looking for somewhat more content in a savings statement is to interpret it to mean that the ordinary principles of conflict preemption apply. In other words, Congress did not attempt to preempt the entire field. This interpretation is a bit stronger than a mere policy suggestion, but generally adds nothing to an understanding of the statute. In environmental law, there is scarcely any legislation that preempts an entire field, and the rare exceptions are clear about their scope. Hence, an interpretation that ordinary principles apply merely confirms what a court would do in the absence of a savings clause. Generally Congress need not specify that any ordinary principles of statutory analysis apply—by definition the ordinary ordinarily applies. The most fundamental canon of statutory interpretation on preemption assumes "that the historic police powers of the States were not to be superseded by the Federal Act unless that was the clear and manifest purpose of Congress."[18] The confirmatory approach to savings clauses simply reads the statute to acquiesce to this ordinary assumption favoring state prerogatives. Still, there may be some justification for the belt-and-suspenders approach of making absolutely sure that courts and agencies understand the scope of delegated authority.

A good example of this approach is *National Audubon Society v. Davis*, which held that the national wildlife refuge system's organic act preempts state regulation of trapping on federal lands within the system.[19] The National Audubon Society, in an effort to protect birds from predation, challenged the application of "Proposition 4," a popularly adopted California law that sought to protect the welfare of animals by banning the use of certain types of traps. The court characterized the dispute as one between "bird-lovers" and "fox-lovers," but more fundamentally the litigation amounted to a determination of the relative scope of state wildlife management on federal lands. The state prohibition on certain types of traps, including leg-hold traps, conflicted with federal refuge administration, which employed leg-hold traps. The court found this to be a situation of direct conflict and therefore preempted the state law. Congressional authority under the U.S. Constitution's Property Clause authorized the delegation of refuge management authority to the Fish and Wildlife Service. That delegated power did not contain any limitations with respect to traps. Therefore supremacy trumped the state law. The court reached this result notwithstanding the Refuge Improvement Act's savings provision. *National Audubon Society v. Davis* interpreted the provision to endorse the Tenth Circuit's interpretation of the statute "as reflecting Congress's intent for ordinary principles of conflict preemption to apply."[20]

c. Documentary

Beyond mere advice and ordinary principles of preemption, the next option for a court is to interpret a savings clause to require the agency to put something in the record showing consideration of state views. Like the confirmatory approach, this does not add much of substance to the scope of review ordinarily applicable under the Administrative Procedure Act. However, particularly given the importance of state favoritism as a widely used tool of natural resources federalism, this option attractively matches the literal terms of many savings clauses.

For example, in *Richardson v. Bureau of Land Management* the governor of New Mexico challenged the adoption of a BLM Resource Management Plan Amendment dealing with oil and gas leasing on federal lands in southern New Mexico, including Otero Mesa.[21] Though the litigation involved many statutory challenges, the important one for federalism is the allegation that the bureau violated the FLPMA cooperation clause because the amendment conflicted with a state water plan, two state wildlife management plans relating to species recovery, the New Mexico Noxious Weed Management Act, and State Water Quality Control regulations. The court held that although FLPMA encouraged cooperation and commanded the BLM to consider state plans, the BLM retained deference to determine whether or not the state plans were consistent with federal goals. The court held that the judiciary should overturn a BLM decision only where there is a clear and specific conflict between a federal land use plan and a specific state plan. In this case the court held that the alleged conflicts were based on mere general statements, "likely" effects, and unspecified interference. Thus, all that FLPMA required of the BLM was to take the state plans into account and address differences of opinion in the administrative record. In other words, the savings clause "requires that BLM pay attention to the suggestions, concerns, and land use plans of a state;" but "BLM was entitled to decide that as a policy matter it preferred its own proposal, and the Court is not in a position to question that policy decision."[22] This interpretation of the savings clause restates the basic principles of administrative law under the Administrative Procedure Act.

2. Strong Interpretations

Strong interpretations add something to the judicial analysis that might influence the outcome of a dispute. A strong interpretation means that a savings clause adds a factor into litigation that would

otherwise be absent or less important. The three approaches described below map out the territory for courts seeking greater traction from savings provisions. Strong interpretations remain scarce in
the reported decisions, but the versions described below remain feasible options for a court seeking to promote state deference to greater
effect.

a. Interpretive

Savings clauses can be read to resolve ambiguities in a statute in
favor of state interests. Where Congress did not precisely address the
issue, the interpretive rule would put a finger on the scale in favor of
deference to the state. Of course, there are almost always other factors, such as legislative history and textual analysis, to consider in
understanding the meaning of a statute. Therefore, this principle of
interpretation may not be dispositive. But, it would be in play.

Although there do not appear to be any judicial opinions employing the interpretive approach in resolving disputes over savings
clauses, the approach is analogous to the *Chevron* principle of administrative law. In *Chevron U.S.A. v. Natural Resources Defense Council*, the
Court decided that where a statute does not precisely address a question at issue, the judiciary should interpret the legislation in a way that
defers to the consistent judgment of the implementing agency.[23] As
applied in the federalism context, the interpretive approach would fill
lacunae and imprecisely anticipated circumstances by deferring to
state decisions. Just as the *Chevron* rule is justified by the preeminent
role that agencies play in making policy, the interpretive approach to
finding meaning in savings clauses would be justified by the default
and traditional dominance of state interests in controlling land, water,
and wildlife.

The Supreme Court's interpretation of the McCarran Amendment's federalism-minded authorization for the United States to be
"joined as a defendant" in state general stream adjudications is an example that approaches the strong interpretive approach. In both *Colorado River Water Conservation District v. United States* and *Arizona v. San
Carlos Apache Tribe*, the Court resolved issues not precisely addressed
by the Amendment in a manner that fulfills the "underlying policy,"
which required constructions favoring states over the United States

(as trustee for tribes).[24] Reed D. Benson has accurately characterized these holdings as elevating policy above text.[25]

Another example involving federal administration of water law comes from an interpretation of the savings clause in the 1902 Reclamation Act, which presents an easy case for strong construction because it is less discretionary than most of the more recent savings clauses discussed in this chapter. Section 8 of the Reclamation Act states that:

> Nothing in this Act shall be construed as affecting or intended to affect or to in any way interfere with [state water laws. . . . The] Secretary of the Interior, in carrying out the provisions of this Act, shall proceed in conformity with such laws.[26]

In *California v. United States*, the Court interpreted this savings clause as an example of "cooperative federalism" even though that term was not a part of the legal argot of 1902.[27] In a ringing endorsement of deference to states, Justice Rehnquist, speaking for the majority, derived the principles of federalism not solely from the constitution and relevant statutes, but also from the lived experience of national development through manifest destiny. As part of the Central Valley Project, the U.S. Bureau of Reclamation applied to California for water appropriation permits in order to impound a reservoir behind the New Melones Dam. The state agency in charge of water permits granted the Bureau's application but subject to twenty-five conditions. The most contentious condition prohibited full impoundment until the United States could show firm commitments (e.g., through a specific plan) for the use of the water. The federal government challenged the state's power to impose the conditions and the Court ruled for California. Limiting the dicta of earlier cases interpreting the Reclamation Act, Justice Rehnquist held that the United States must follow state conditions unless an explicit statutory provision conflicts with them. Absent an expressly inconsistent provision in the statute, the savings clause compels the federal government to accept the judgment of states in implementing reclamation policy.

b. Scrutinizing

The most intriguing kind of strong interpretation triggers a heightened scope of review when federalism disputes lead to challenges of agency action. Like the interpretive approach, the scrutinizing approach understands a savings clause as bending ordinary principles of administrative and procedural law. This category raises the bar considerably for an agency to justify its actions in light of a disagreement about resource management with a state. The scrutinizing approach may be thought of as a kind of *State Farm* analysis requiring better reasoning than courts normally demand from an agency because of a special circumstance. In *State Farm*, the special circumstance was the reversal of a prior agency position.[28] In the federalism context, the special circumstance would be a savings clause with a bite.

Though *Wyoming* contains statements that employ the hortatory and confirmatory approaches to interpreting savings clauses, they do not explain the outcome of the case as well as the scrutinizing approach. The case applied the refuge organic act's savings provision, discussed in part IV.A. In *Wyoming*, the court used the scrutinizing approach to place an unusually heavy burden of proof on the FWS to show the inefficacy of the vaccination approach advocated by the state. In sending the case back to the district court to make a finding of whether the administrative record sufficiently justified the FWS refusal of Wyoming's request, the Tenth Circuit strongly hinted that the record would fail the application of the scrutinizing test it established.

Wyoming had repeatedly requested permission from the FWS to conduct a vaccination program on the National Elk Refuge (NER) in order to suppress brucellosis in bison. The court recognized that, under ordinary circumstances, deference to agency action is appropriate when "scientific and technical judgment within the scope of agency expertise" is at issue. But the court found the cooperative federalism concerns reason to reduce deference.

The court criticized what it perceived to be a federal indifference to Wyoming's legitimate interests:

> The problem is that after an extended period of time, the FWS still appears unable or unwilling to make any judgment regarding the biosafety and efficacy of Strain 19 as applied to free ranging elk. But the law requires answers. For instance, the FWS has never explained why the State's proposal would "stand as an obstacle to the accomplishment and execution" of federal objectives.[29]

The court held that the FWS's failure to make a judgment regarding the effectiveness of Strain 19 after more than a decade and the parties' inability to reach common ground on the issue did not satisfy the statutory savings clause. Although the court agreed that the first sentence of the savings clause seemed to give the state sweeping authority in the management of wildlife, the act taken as a whole did not support the state's assertion of power. The court cited the second sentence of the savings clause, the savings clause's legislative history, and the overall mission of the NWRS to deny the state's sovereign claim. The second sentence of the savings clause directs the FWS to act consistent with state laws, regulations, and management plans only "to the extent practicable." The legislative history indicated that the savings clause preserved "the status quo," leaving difficult jurisdictional disputes for the courts to determine on a case-by-case basis. And the state's claim would be inconsistent with the mission of the NWRS to provide a network of refuges managed in a consistent, national system.

Even though these factors did not support the state's interpretation, the court recognized that Congress meant the savings clause to serve a purpose. The court affirmed that the FWS had the authority to block state vaccination on the refuge, but insisted that the decision must be reached through real cooperation:

> The FWS's apparent indifference to the State of Wyoming's problem and the State's insistence of a "sovereign right" to manage wildlife on the NER do little to promote "cooperative federalism." Given the [refuge organic act]'s repeated calls for a "cooperative federalism," we find inexcusable the parties' unwillingness in this case to even attempt to amicably resolve the brucellosis controversy or find any common ground on which to commence fruitful negotiations.[30]

This approach reverses the general rule that the burden is placed on the party proposing to conduct an action on federal land to show that the action will be consistent with relevant standards.

After establishing that the FWS had the authority to make the decision, the court next turned to the question of whether the decision itself was correctly made. The court interpreted the refuge organic act to suggest that cooperative federalism limits FWS decision making. The court emphasized the concept of cooperative federalism and the need for the parties to work together in reaching a result.

A related, but not congruent, example of heightening the scope of review comes from *Wilderness Society v. Tyrrel*.[31] In that decision the court remanded a Forest Service timber sale based on a violation of one of the savings clauses in the Wild and Scenic Rivers Act.[32] That provision requires an agency administering a segment of the wild and scenic rivers system to "cooperate with" state water pollution control agencies to diminish pollution. The California Department of Fish and Game, California Department of Conservation, and an official from a regional water quality control board all raised concerns about the effects of the proposed timber sale on water quality. The Forest Service environmental impact statement dutifully included these critical comments, but the agency ultimately dismissed them. Instead, the Forest Service chose to rely on best management practices to reduce pollution from logging. The resulting record of decision did not say anything other than acknowledge lack of proof that best management practices would actually succeed in protecting water quality. The court found the record showed Forest Service *consultation*, but not *cooperation*, with the state. The key distinction for the court was the necessity for the service to carry a heavier burden to show why the state's concerns were misplaced and why the state's approach would not be the better option. Though the court of appeals overturned aspects of the district court decision, it did not upset the scrutinizing interpretation of the savings clause.[33]

c. Structural

If courts were to strengthen further the state's position in applying a savings clause, they might adopt a structural interpretation. This would require the agency to have some framework in place for cooperative management. An example of such a structure is the BLM rule describing state consistency, partly at issue in the Otero Mesa case.[34] The test of the structure's adequacy would be whether there exists real sharing of authority in a manner described by a savings clause.

This interpretation is absent from the case reporters in part because the savings clauses are so vague and enigmatic. A court employing a structural interpretation of a savings clause would have to overcome thirty years of judicial precedent hostile to the imposition of administrative requirements that go beyond what the Administrative Procedure Act compels. *Vermont Yankee Nuclear Power Corp. v. Natural Resources Defense Council* ended the effort of the D.C. Circuit to impose additional administrative procedures where needed to fulfill the overarching goals of statutes.[35] The structural approach would revive the activist, pre-1978 tradition in the name of federalism.

A structural approach would move beyond the reactive federalism of simply responding to a state request and toward constructive federalism where partners together create a management regime. Place-based collaboration, such as management of the Valles Caldera, employs constructive federalism through a structure for cooperation. Importantly though, the structure comes not from a savings clause, but from a detailed statutory blueprint. In the end, a savings clause likely cannot serve as a firm enough foundation for true structural federalism.

Judge Brimmer's decisions overturning the Clinton administration's rules protecting roadless areas in the national forests and prohibiting snowmobile recreation in Yellowstone National Park, however, do approach structural federalism by closely scrutinizing how agencies treat states in the NEPA process. In preparing an environmental impact statement (EIS) under NEPA, federal agencies follow the Council on Environmental Quality regulations, which establish the structure for the analysis. The regulations allow agencies engaged in consideration of a federal action triggering the EIS requirement to select a state agency affected by a proposed action or possessing special expertise to participate as a "cooperating agency."[36] Cooperating agencies take on special projects in their area of expertise and work with the lead agency in conducting the analysis.[37] In the snowmobile case, Judge Brimmer found that the lead agencies did not sufficiently involve the cooperating state agencies in the development of alternatives and did not delegate any meaningful duties to them.[38] In the roadless rule case, Judge Brimmer found that the lead agency did not sufficiently justify denying cooperating agency status to Wyoming.[39] Both decisions evince a deeper level of scrutiny of federal interaction with states in the NEPA process and suggest a greater obligation to cooperate with states than the statute or Council on Environmental Quality regulations expressly provide.

3. Conclusion

The abstract and broad language of savings clauses, especially cooperative provisions, allow courts as well as agencies to see in them a mirror of their own conceptions of cooperative federalism. Although courts mostly continue to interpret the savings clauses using one of the three weak approaches, recent cases illustrate the attraction of stronger interpretations. The three strong approaches give states an advantage in court that they would not otherwise have. In particular, the *Wyoming* opinion on vaccinating elk and the Brimmer decisions on the roadless rule and the snowmobile ban in Yellowstone, show courts using statutory and regulatory hooks of federalism to prompt federal reconsideration of state interests in public land management. In the National Elk Refuge case, the court helped prompt a comprehensive review in order to facilitate federal management more responsive to state objectives. Is this the future of natural resources law federalism? The next part sets out to answer that question.

V.   The Future of Natural Resources Law Federalism

The concept of uniformitarianism was promoted in the eighteenth century by James Hutton, the founder of modern geological science. Uniformitarianism postulates that the Earth's history can be understood by studying the geologic processes at work today. This stands in contrast to catastrophism, which postulates that disruptive changes fundamentally reorient the course of the future. The principle that the geologic past operated under the same laws and conditions as are currently observed helped displace biblical flood theories.

A uniformitarian approach to predicting the future of federalism would assume that the trends discussed in part III would continue into the foreseeable future. Such a continuation would result in:

1. the continued proliferation of diverse but weak federal invitations for state participation in natural resources decision-making;

2. a steady rise in state sophistication and assertiveness on natural resources issues; and

3. more frequent treatment of tribes as states for cooperative federalism purposes.

However, looming over such a prediction of steady movement in the current direction is the prospect of abrupt changes in natural resources law to adapt to climate change. Already resource managers face daunting challenges to respond to current sea level rise, asynchronous modification of migratory habitat, and warming of the high latitudes. The next few decades promise more significant disruptions to business-as-usual in natural resources law. The phenomenon of climate change may well upset the uniformitarian assumptions. Then catastrophism would be a better guide to predicting the future of cooperative federalism, but there is little certainty in what that would mean. President Obama is responding to climate change with more assertiveness than prior administrations. Most commentators stress that adaptation will require larger spatial and longer temporal scales for resource management. This suggests that the federal government may assert a more dominant role in natural resources law simply because larger scales demand more cross-boundary thinking. On the other hand, spatial scale coordination—say, through watershed management—will require closer cooperation with tribal, state, and local jurisdictions that control land use, water consumption, and wildlife conservation.

Even though climate change may of necessity prompt more cooperative federalism, the history of prognostication counsels caution when projecting an imminent golden era of good feelings. For decades, commentators have cited place-based collaborations as the flourishing future of resource management.[40] While the tools for such efforts have certainly improved in the past quarter-century, they have not significantly altered the national direction of natural resources law. Increasingly, skeptics like Robert L. Glicksman have documented ways in which cooperative federalism has faltered.[41]

The prediction in which I have the most confidence is that money will continue to drive federalism efforts. Money is an engine for intergovernmental relations in two respects. First, as a matter of equity, the federal government owes an obligation to state and local governments that carry disproportionate burdens of public land policy. The perpetual negotiations over payments in lieu of taxes, and especially funding for local schools, indicate how much respect the federal government has for outstanding promises to sustain communities that miss out on property tax revenue due to federal resource management policy. It is unrealistic to expect local communities to cooperate with federal objectives without federal appropriation of a fair return to jurisdictions that bear special burdens because of the United States' tax immunity. Second, and more pervasively, money is the key inducement for states to cooperate with federal policy priorities. Whether conservation grants for area-wide wildlife plans, appropriations for pollution abatement programs, or specific earmarks for place-based collaborations—such as the CALFED project in the Sacramento River Delta—money greases the skids for participation, compromise, and concluding negotiations in program development. When the federal government promises significant funding for implementation, a cooperative effort is far more likely than when the government offers little more than recognition.

Federalism's asymmetry is an important attribute of its fascination and complexity in natural resources law. Federal and state legal activity may act in tandem, in opposition, or independently of each other. Increased federal involvement in, for example, oil and gas development does not necessarily displace state law—it may in fact increase local regulation. Also, states are not miniature versions of the federal government. The inherent, sovereign police powers that undergird state regulation of land, water and wildlife significantly differ from the constitutional powers of Congress to regulate interstate commerce and make rules to manage federal property. Moreover, Congress does not act independently from states. Congress (especially the Senate) itself comprises state delegations. Particularly in public land management, affected state congressional delegations have an enormous influence on federal programs focused on particular land units. These essential differences drive the comparative advantages that promise continued potential for improved resource management through cooperation. Shifts in politics are not likely to dramatically change this fundamental differentiation. While natural resources federalism is cloaked in rhetoric, its vital center remains rooted in law.

State Vaccination on the National Elk Refuge

Some of the largest concentrations of elk in North America occur in Jackson Hole, Wyoming. The elk herd there has averaged 14,600 over the past several years, but is currently closer to 13,000. Approximately 7,000 elk winter on the National Elk Refuge (NER). The federal government recently completed an environmental impact statement (EIS) to decide how many elk (and bison) the federal lands should support, and what management tools ought to ensure the health of the herd. This recent study caps nearly a century of intensive efforts to maintain elk, sometimes with federal and state agencies locking horns.

The state of Wyoming has a distinctive tradition of winter elk feeding, with origins in the history and culture of Jackson Hole. When elk populations were being extirpated in the late 1800s and early 1900s, Jackson residents wanted to protect the elk from "tusk hunters" and commercial hunting operations. At the same time, the ranching in and around Jackson reduced the elk's native winter range. This development combined with the area's geography to confine the elk herds in the winter. In addition, severe winters made foraging difficult and left substantial numbers of elk dead. In response, local citizens and organizations, as well as state and federal officials, began feeding the elk in the winter of 1910–1911 to reduce mortality rates and minimize the damage to ranchers' hay. In 1912, Congress provided money for the purchase of a winter range for the 20,000 elk in the area. This area became the National Elk Refuge.

While many states have emergency protocols in place to prevent the decimation of elk herds, no state has more than a couple public feeding stations. By contrast, the state of Wyoming has built on the experience of Jackson Hole to create twenty-three public feeding stations in the western part of the state. Winter feeding maintains herd populations, compensating for the decline in natural winter feeding habitat or providing food where little native range existed. However, a high concentration of elk creates problems of its own. It increases the risk of major disease outbreaks. Increased populations also cause more damage to vegetation on the feeding grounds, resulting in harm to wildlife dependent on healthy stands of shrubs and trees. Unusually low winter mortality rates require hunting programs and reduce food for predators, scavengers, and detritivores. And, most notably for federalism law and policy, high levels of brucellosis in the elk and bison herds accompany the high concentration of the animals around winter feeding stations.

In *Wyoming v. United States*, the state challenged the Fish and Wildlife Service (FWS) refusal to permit the state to vaccinate elk on the refuge against brucellosis. Brucellosis is a bacterial borne pathogen that infects the reproductive organs and lymphatic systems of ungulates. Most commonly, the disease causes spontaneous abortion in females during the first pregnancy following infection. Brucellosis is usually spread by the consumption of infected tissue, or contaminated feed or water. Thirty percent of the wild elk in western Wyoming have brucellosis. The concentration of elk in winter feeding grounds perpetuates the disease because herds are in close contact during the birthing period. Elk rarely infect domestic cattle with brucellosis under natural conditions, but concentration of herds raises the risk.

In 1997, Wyoming requested that the FWS allow state vaccination, at state expense, using "Strain 19." The state feared the loss of its brucellosis-free status for livestock, which would limit market access and increase costs to both ranchers and the state. However, the FWS claimed the state did not demonstrate the efficacy of Strain 19. Instead, the service claimed to be able to avoid the spread of the disease through feed-line management. More specifically, the FWS began replacing hay with alfalfa pellets, and disbursed the feeding locations. However, Wyoming persisted in its efforts to vaccinate, eventually turning to federal courts. In 2002, an important decision in the litigation from the Tenth Circuit prompted new discussion of the legal attributes of cooperative federalism and a new path for elk management in Jackson Hole.

The Tenth Circuit viewed the legal claims of both the federal and state governments as overreaching. The state made sovereignty claims and asserted concurrent, if not exclusive, authority over wildlife management on the NER. The FWS asserted unlimited discretion under the National Wildlife Refuge System Improvement Act (NWRSIA) to manage wildlife on the refuge. According to the court, the state claimed that the FWS acted outside its authority under NWRSIA in refusing to permit the state to vaccinate because of Tenth Amendment constraints. However, the court held that the Constitution, not a federal statute, determines whether the Tenth Amendment reserved a power to the states.

Although the court recognized that states historically had the power to manage wildlife on federal lands within the state, this historic ability resulted from congressional acquiescence, not from the Constitution. The Property Clause empowered Congress to exercise jurisdiction over federal lands within a state, and the NWRSIA did just that for refuges. Whether or not the state was able to manage wildlife on federal lands within the state depended upon the extent to which Congress exercised its Property Clause power in enacting NWRSIA. The court held that the FWS did have the authority to block state vaccination on the National Elk Refuge, but that the FWS may not have properly exercised that authority. The court paid particular attention to the statutory savings clause in seeking a clearly justified explanation for the federal government's denial of Wyoming's request. The Tenth Circuit remanded to the district court the factual finding of whether the administrative record adequately supported the federal decision.

Rather than continue to litigate the case, the Bush administration settled by agreeing to conduct an initial environmental
assessment on an interim vaccination program. After issuing a
Finding of No Significant Impact, elk vaccinations began in
early 2003 and would continue until the federal government
completed a more comprehensive analysis of elk and bison management in Jackson Hole. But the vaccines were too late for
Wyoming to retain its brucellosis-free certification. The U.S.
Department of Agriculture revoked the certification in 2004.
Wyoming regained its brucellosis-free status in 2006.

The federal government completed the comprehensive EIS
and adopted a new elk management plan in 2007. The Wyoming
Game and Fish Department (WGFD) served as a cooperating
agency and partner on the EIS, which considered six alternatives. Under Alternative One few changes would occur in the
management of the elk and bison herds, therefore, the high prevalence of brucellosis would continue. Alternative Two would
greatly reduce active management of the herds on refuge lands
and phase out supplemental feeding over ten to fifteen years.
Brucellosis prevalence would be reduced over time by more
natural, dispersed, winter densities. Alternative Three would actively manage the herds on refuge lands and reduce supplemental feeding over ten years, providing it only during the severest
winters. Under this Alternative, brucellosis would be reduced as
the concentrations of the herds decreased and more effective
techniques and vaccinations were developed. Alternative Four
would adaptively manage both refuge and park lands, emphasiz-
ing the improvement of winter, summer, and transitional range.
This Alternative would allow WGFD to vaccinate the herds
against brucellosis "as long as logistically feasible." Alternative
Five would heavily manage the herds on refuge lands and
permit WGFD to vaccinate elk and bison. This Alternative
would provide supplemental feeding in all but the mildest
winters, decreasing disease outbreaks by spreading out feed
and changing feed locations. Alternative Six would adaptively
manage the herds on refuge lands to improve winter grazing
habitat. Brucellosis prevalence would decrease over time as

concentrations decreased and new techniques and vaccines were developed.

The federal government chose Alternative Four in the 2007 elk management plan. The new plan emphasizes four goals: habitat conservation, sustainable populations, numbers of elk and bison, and disease management. These goals are to be implemented through a "structured framework, in collaboration with the WGFD, of adaptive management actions that include established criteria for progressively transitioning from intensive supplemental winter feeding." However, the EIS neither describes the "structured framework" nor defines the criteria for winter feeding. Fundamental aspects of the plan include population management, vegetation restoration, continuous monitoring, and public education programs. The state's objective of maintaining an elk herd of approximately 11,000 will be achieved through the cooperation of the FWS, National Park Service, and WGFD. Although management actions will not be designed to facilitate vaccination, the WGFD is permitted to vaccinate the herds as long as logistically feasible. The plan does not promise to end supplemental feeding, but merely articulates a desire to move away from supplemental feeding in good winters. The federal choice in elk management was to pick the least definite alternative, allowing for the greatest flexibility in the coming years. This kind of adaptive management coincides with maximal discretion for the agency.

All stakeholders in the elk management process claim healthy elk populations as their objective. The disagreement focuses on whether continued winter feeding with vaccination is the best way to achieve that end. In his review of the brucellosis controversy fifteen years ago, Robert Keiter observed a divide in professional culture between range scientists and wildlife biologists. While range scientists are comfortable with intensive management that includes vaccination and slaughter, wildlife biologists tend to favor populations that fluctuate wildly in response to natural conditions. Professor Keiter attributed the division to divergent professional views of the relationship between people and nature. Range scientists emphasize that science can and should be able to improve nature. Wildlife biologists focus on park and wilderness settings as excellent opportunities to observe nature's ways, providing valuable baseline scientific data. The dispute with the WGFD belies this simple dichotomy. Instead of backing the natural regulation policy usually favored by wildlife biologists, the WGFD aligned with the livestock ranchers to support intensive management of brucellosis through vaccination. This is partly a reflection of the political power the livestock and hunting sectors wield in Wyoming state government. It is also related to the fiscal realities faced by the WGFD, which derives much of its budget from hunting licenses: elk are prime game in Wyoming. The state is as interested in maintaining high numbers of huntable elk as it is in keeping its livestock brucellosis free. And easily watchable or huntable elk sustain an important aspect of the Jackson Hole tourism economy.

Many of the federal wildlife biologists and environmental groups, led by the Greater Yellowstone Coalition, oppose any elk management plan that fails to set strict timetables for phasing out vaccination and clear criteria for the circumstances justifying supplemental winter feeding. Without firm commitments to end winter feeding, they fear that the inertia of the current feeding practices will perpetuate the unhealthy high concentrations of winter elk populations. They favored Alternative Six because it established a more definite deadline of five years for terminating winter feeding. While philosophically disposed to prefer natural variations in elk populations, the environmental groups also rely on scientists and the Animal Plant Health Inspection Service's findings that infectious diseases will be more likely to affect elk maintained by winter feeding. The vaccinations do not eliminate brucellosis, and sometimes fail to contain it. Looming on the horizon is the spread of a devastating chronic wasting disease that may sweep through concentrated elk populations and decimate herds. For supporters of Alternative Six, Wyoming created the brucellosis problem through its aggressive winter feeding programs and should address the problem by removing the underlying cause rather than rely on a risky strategy of vaccination that neither eliminates elk brucellosis nor protects against other infectious risks and habitat degradation caused by crowding. In 2008, a coalition of conservation groups challenged the 2007 management plan in federal court.[42] The complaint argues that the plan violates both the mandate to "maintain biological integrity, diversity, and environmental health" and the conservation mission to sustain "healthy populations of . . . wildlife" from the 2007 Refuge Improvement Act.[43] As this chapter goes to press, the court has not yet ruled on the suit.

Many hunters remain concerned by the winter program's increased risk of chronic wasting disease. Still, some hunting groups support winter feeding to maintain greater opportunities for bagging elk: Sportsmen for Fish and Wildlife staged a "Hay Day" in December 2006 to draw attention to its claim that the NER was underfeeding the wintering elk. The group attracted publicity when it delivered sixty tons of unsolicited hay to the NER in a convoy with a police escort. The longtime NER Manager, Barry Reiswig, who thinks that protecting more acres of natural winter habitat is the lynchpin of elk conservation, candidly commented that:

> Right now, we have millions of acres of public land with mule deer and antelope on it, but elk are barred from ever going there. Instead, they are kept on these postage stamps (the feed grounds), time bombs for disease. The stock growers are not economically powerful, but they have political power, and they have kept the fish and game from buying any more winter range.[44]

Notes

1. Robert L. Fischman, *Cooperative Federalism and Natural Resources Law*, 14 N.Y.U. ENVTL. L.J. 179 (2005).
2. 43 U.S.C. § 1712(c)(9).
3. 43 U.S.C. § 1732(b).
4. 16 U.S.C. § 668dd(m).
5. Exec. Order No. 13,352, 69 Fed. Reg. 52,989 (Aug. 30, 2004).

6.   16 U.S.C. § 791(a).

7.   324 U.S. 515, 517 (1945).

8.   46 U.S.C. § 4301.

9.   16 U.S.C. § 1133(d)(6).

10. 43 U.S.C. § 1712(c).

11. 33 U.S.C. § 1251(g).

12. 16 U.S.C. § 668dd(m).

13. Wyoming v. United States, 279 F.3d 1214 (10th Cir. 2002).

14. Riverside Irrigation Dist. v. Andrews, 758 F.2d 508 (10th Cir. 1985).

15. 33 U.S.C. § 1344.

16. Conn. Light and Power Co. v. Fed. Power Comm'n, 324 U.S. 515 (1945).

17. PUD No. 1 of Jefferson County v. Wash. Dep't of Ecology, 511 U.S. 700, 719–21 (1994).

18. Rice v. Santa Fe Elevator Corp., 331 U.S. 218, 230 (1947).

19. Nat'l Audubon Soc'y v. Davis, 307 F.3d 835 (9th Cir. 2002).

20. *Id.* at 854.

21. Richardson v. Bureau of Land Mgmt., 459 F. Supp. 2d 1102 (D.N.M. 2006).

22. *Id.* at 1120–21.

23. Chevron U.S.A. v. Natural Res. Def. Council, 467 U.S. 837 (1984).

24. Colo. River Water Conservation Dist. v. United States, 424 U.S. 800, 810 (1976); Arizona v. San Carlos Apache Tribe, 463 U.S. 545, 570 (1983).

25. Reed D. Benson, *Deflating the Deference Myth*, 2006 UTAH L. REV. 241, 272.

26. 43 U.S.C. § 383.

27. California v. United States, 438 U.S. 645, 650 (1978).

28. Motor Vehicle Mfrs. Ass'n of U.S. v. State Farm Mut. Auto. Ins. Co., 463 U.S. 29 (1983).

29. Wyoming v. United States, 279 F.3d 1240 (10th Cir. 2002).

30. *Id.*

31. Wilderness Soc'y v. Tyrrel, 701 F. Supp. 1473, 1488–89 (D. Cal. 1988).

32. 16 U.S.C. § 1283(c).

33. Wilderness Soc'y v. Tyrrel, 918 F.2d 813 (9th Cir. 1990) (overturning district court on the basis that a comprehensive management plan is not required in order to conduct land management activities), 53 F.3d 341 (1995) (denying plaintiffs' attorneys' fees).

34. 43 C.F.R. § 1610.3-2.

35. Vt. Yankee Nuclear Power Corp. v. Natural Res. Def. Council, 435 U.S. 519 (1978).

36. 40 C.F.R. § 1508.5.

37. 40 C.F.R. § 1501.6.

38. Int'l Snowmobile Mfrs. Ass'n v. Norton, 340 F. Supp. 2d 1249, 1262 (D. Wyo. 2004); 65 Fed. Reg. 80,908, 80,916 & 80,920 (Nov. 22, 2000).

39. Wyoming v. U.S. Dept. of Agric., 277 F. Supp. 2d 1197, 1221 (D. Wyo. 2004), *vacated,* 414 F.3d 1207 (10th Cir. 2005).

40. *See, e.g.,* Charles F. Wilkinson, *A View toward the Future: Lessons from Tahoe and the Truckee, in* NATURAL RESOURCES POLICY AND LAW: TRENDS AND DIRECTIONS (Lawrence J. MacDonnell & Sarah F. Bates eds., 1993).

41. Robert L. Glicksman, *From Cooperative to Inoperative Federalism: The Perverse Mutation of Environmental Law and Policy,* 41 WAKE FOREST L. REV. 719 (2006).

42. Defenders of Wildlife v. Kempthorne, No. 1:08-cv-00945 (D.D.C. June 3, 2008).

43. *Id.* (citing 16 U.S.C. §§ 668dd (a)(4)(B) & 668ee(4)).

44. Hal Herring, *Predator Hunters for the Environment,* HIGH COUNTRY NEWS, June 25, 2007.

II

*The Evolution
of Resource
Management*

8

Embracing a Civic Republican Tradition in Natural Resources Decision-Making

Mark Squillace

The public's right to participate in government decisions is rarely questioned today. The public expects to be granted an opportunity to become involved in agency proposals, and government agencies tout their commitment to participation at all levels. Public processes abound and consume substantial portions of agency resources. Yet too often, the public's role lacks meaning. Even where agencies start with good intentions, the public process often becomes a rote exercise, tolerated but not embraced by the agency, and endured by the public as a necessary step on the path toward litigation.

This chapter offers a prescription for making public processes more meaningful in the context of policy decisions impacting natural resources. It begins by tracing the history of public participation in government action. It then reviews the arguments that support public participation, as well as several reasons that may counsel against it. Participation processes will surely endure, but a better appreciation of the challenges they present can help agencies tailor their processes to be more meaningful.

The chapter then analyzes the theoretical foundations for public participation, concluding that the civic republican tradition offers the only viable approach for meaningfully engaging the public in natural resources decision-making. Various modes of participation are then evaluated in light of the civic republican model, with suggestions for modifying these processes to enhance their utility in engaging the pubic. Finally, the chapter discusses some of the ongoing problems with current public processes and suggests possible reforms.

I.   A Brief History of Public Participation

Upon leaving the Constitutional Convention in 1787, Benjamin Franklin was asked what sort of government the delegates had created. He famously replied, "A republic, if you can keep it." Franklin was promoting the idea that a democratic republic requires not merely the consent of the governed, but also, most critically, the active engagement of an informed citizenry. Yet, despite increasingly sophisticated methods of communicating and engaging, including electronic mail, interactive web sites, talk radio, and cable television, the level of public discourse often disappoints. A brief tour of the American experience with participatory government is offered here in an effort to place in context the evolution of public participation in natural resources policy.

American history is replete with examples of public involvement influencing government behavior. *The Federalist Papers*, a series of 85 essays written by James Madison, Alexander Hamilton, and John Jay, is one of the earliest examples and illustrates how writing alone can influence important government policy—in this case, the American Constitution itself.

Public demonstrations and civil disobedience have also played a prominent role in influencing American policy, from the Boston Tea Party to the civil rights and anti-war movements in the 1960s. Contemporary examples of civil disobedience in the context of natural resources and environmental policy are also easy to find. Edward Abbey's celebrated 1975 book, *The Monkey Wrench Gang*, spawned a whole new vernacular, from "monkey wrenching" to "ecotage" to ecoterrorism. And Julia "Butterfly" Hill famously took up residence in an ancient redwood tree that she named "Luna" to prevent a logging company from cutting it down.

Litigation has also played a prominent role in influencing policy, and this has been especially true in the context of natural resources and environmental policy. The Supreme Court's decision in *Sierra Club v. Morton* was a nominal loss for the environmental group that brought the action, but it established the principle that parties could go to court to redress aesthetic injuries.[1] Beginning in the 1970s with the passage of the Clean Air Act, Congress also authorized private citizens to file lawsuits on behalf of the public to redress violations of environmental laws. The proliferation of lawsuits brought by an ever growing number of national and local environmental and conservation groups attests to their popularity as a vehicle for fostering the protection of environmental values, and few would question their significant role in influencing public policy.

In the American system, Congress was designed as the most prominent body for engaging the public in a meaningful dialogue over government policy. "We, the people," would elect wise leaders from our communities to represent us in the "people's branch," and these elected, local representatives would engage their constituents in a discussion of the issues of the day. These exchanges would help inform and influence representatives' views, thereby resulting in better decisions. Given this design, it is ironic that Congress has evolved into one of the least accessible venues for public engagement. Somewhere along the way, perhaps because of the enormous growth in our population, or perhaps because our representatives were spending more and more time raising money for their next campaign, our representative democracy stopped working as it was intended.

In fairness, many members of Congress hold regular town hall meetings and engage their constituents in these settings. But these open forum events do not lend themselves to engaging a representative on a particular issue in a sustained and meaningful way. Direct access to your local congressional representative or senator is far more likely to be available (through his or her staff) only for particular matters, like securing a lost Social Security check. Meaningful engagement with a member of Congress on particular legislation or policy issues is largely relegated to the people with personal or political connections— primarily, the lobbyists and interest groups with positions on issues consistent with those of the legislator. Individual constituents lack sufficient access to have any meaningful ability to influence legislative policy.

Another irony in the evolution of our system is that the demise of participatory democracy at the legislative level coincided with a flowering of public process in the executive branch. In 1958, in an address at Harvard Law School, Bernard Schwartz famously decried administrative agencies as the "headless fourth branch of government." But even as he spoke, the times and the laws were changing. If members of Congress were becoming less connected to their constituents, they were at least insisting that government agencies take public views into account. The most important vehicle for promoting accountability in the executive branch is the Administrative Procedure Act (APA), enacted in 1945.[2] The APA divides agency actions into two categories—rules and orders—and demands that agencies adhere to specific processes for each.

For orders, which generally involve agency decisions on particular matters such as permits, licenses, or enforcement action, the APA establishes *adjudicatory* processes.[3] Orders can be either *formal* or *informal*. Formal orders, which normally involve actions affecting significant property rights or other constitutionally protected rights, are subject to detailed, trial-type hearing requirements that are designed to ensure both fairness and transparency. In the natural resources context, formal orders might include, for example, a mining claim contest, the revocation of a lease for noncompliance with the lease terms, or a citation and fine for unlawful off-road vehicle use. Informal orders are commonplace on public lands because decisions affecting those lands often implicate only public, rather than private rights. Decisions to sell timber from public lands, to make lands available for oil and gas leasing, or to close public lands to off-road vehicle use are typically informal orders that are subject only to minimal process requirements under the APA.

Rules, which are defined to include "agency statement[s] of general or particular applicability and future effect designed to implement, interpret, or prescribe law or policy," can also be formal or informal, but the vast majority of agency rules, and virtually all rules impacting public lands and natural resources are of the informal variety.[4] Informal agency rules include all forms of generalized agency standards and instructions, such as agency manuals, instruction memoranda, and "notice and comment" rules scheduled for codification in the Code of Federal Regulations. Generally, all agency rules are subject to publication requirements, and most significant rules are subject to notice by publication in the Federal Register and an opportunity for public comment.

In addition to the procedures established under the APA, Congress passed the Freedom of Information Act in 1966, making government documents available to anyone unless the documents fall within one of nine enumerated exemptions.[5] The act has been amended several times, most importantly perhaps in 1996 with the passage of the Electronic Freedom of Information Act Amendments. These amendments require that agencies make most rules and significant decisions available electronically, and they have helped to promote nearly universal access to a wide range of government documents.

In the context of engaging the public in decisions impacting natural resources, several other laws play an important role. Most prominent among these is the National Environmental Policy Act (NEPA), which requires federal agencies to prepare environmental impact statements (EIS) on "major federal actions significantly affecting the quality of the human environment." Although NEPA requires EISs only for major actions, it also requires agencies to "study, develop, and describe appropriate alternatives to recommended courses of action in *any* proposal which involves unresolved conflicts concerning alternative uses of available resources."[6] The Council on Environmental Quality (CEQ) regulations, which establish binding NEPA standards for all federal agencies, implements this latter requirement by requiring agencies to prepare environmental assessments (EAs) in most cases where EISs are not required.[7] In fact, while federal agencies prepare only a few hundred EISs each year, they prepare many thousands of environmental assessments in accordance with the CEQ's NEPA rules. Public participation is not necessarily required for an EA but it is routinely granted; the EA/EIS process has become the vehicle through which the public participates in actions involving many other federal laws, including, for example, consultation under the Endangered Species Act for federal actions that might impact listed species,[8] and the assessment of federal undertakings that might impact historic properties as provided under the National Historic Preservation Act.[9] Beyond any requirements that may apply under NEPA, public participation is also mandated by the major public land use planning laws, including the National Forest Management Act,[10] the Federal Land Policy and Management Act,[11] and the National Wildlife Refuge Administration Act.[12]

The major environmental laws also provide myriad vehicles for public participation, including the processes for issuing permits. For example, the Clean Air Act requires the stationary source permit application process to include "public notice" and "an opportunity for public comment and a hearing."[13] Likewise, the Clean Water Act requires notice and an opportunity for a hearing before issuing "dredge and fill permits" under section 404[14] or "point source discharge" permits under section 402.[15] Thus, the opportunity for public comment in decisions impacting natural resources is nearly universal for major agency decisions, and commonplace for many less significant decisions as well.

II.   The Reasons for and the Problems with Public Participation

Nobel laureate Amartya Sen has ably described the reasons for promoting public engagement:

> [D]emocracy's claim to be valuable does not rest on just one particular merit. There is a plurality of virtues here, including, first, the *intrinsic* importance of political participation and freedom in human life; second, the *instrumental* importance of political incentives in keeping governments responsible and accountable; and third, the *constructive* role of democracy in the formation of values and in the understanding of needs, rights, and duties.[16]

As Sen suggests, participation can and often does serve important utilitarian values. It helps ensure that agency officials are accountable for their actions, and by educating both the public and the agency it can help promote better agency decisions. It also serves important civic functions by engaging and sometimes even empowering citizens who become involved in the democratic process. An effective public process can help build trust between agencies and the public, making it less likely that the agency will face litigation over its decision.

But participation is not without its problems. Process can be used to delay agency decisions. It can be tedious, expensive, and time-consuming. To avoid or minimize these problems agencies must carefully describe projects or discrete aspects of projects in a manner that more directly elicits public input on key unresolved issues. They can also design the processes to reflect the available time and expertise of interested parties. If a proposal is too broad or complex and the agency is unwilling or unable to define it in a manner that can meaningfully engage the public, the agency will likely be disappointed in the response it receives.

Even when the public is willing to engage the agency on policy proposals, the process can be counterproductive if the agency's support for it is disingenuous or half-hearted. If the public perceives, rightly or wrongly, that its comments are being ignored, the public may become alienated from the agency, and mistrust and resentment will build on both sides. Such mistrust will also encourage a sense on the part of the public that its only recourse is with the courts. Thus, participation has its pitfalls, and agencies would be well advised to consider them, both when deciding whether to allow participation and in designing the processes to be used. (For a poignant example of this, see the sidebar to this chapter.)

In addition to the more process-oriented problems associated with public participation, substantive problems arise as well. In particular, concentrated and powerful private interests can use public process in a manner that overwhelms the public interest. Public choice theory predicts that such "rent-seeking" behavior on the part of private parties is an inevitable consequence of our economic and political system. Agencies must design their processes to overcome this problem, perhaps by finding ways to better identify and balance public interests against concentrated private interests. They might even need to limit the processes used to avoid giving undue advantage to those private interests. James Buchanan and Gordon Tullock, two of the early architects of public choice theory, offer a compelling argument against process where the public interest is relatively easy to discern:

> If the "public interest" or the "common good" is something that can be determined with relative ease, and if individual participants in collective choice act so as to promote this "common good" rather than their own interests, there seems to be little rational support for the many cumbersome and costly institutions that characterize the modern democratic process. Under such conditions the delegation of all effective decision-making power to a single decision maker, and an accompanying hierarchy, may appear perfectly rational. If some means can be taken to insure that the dictator will, in fact, remain "benevolent," the argument becomes even stronger.[17]

Thus, agencies must take care not to allow process to interfere with the agency's ultimate responsibility to act in the public interest.

III. Public Participation Before Administrative Agencies Under Different Decision-Making Models

The responsibility for setting government policy is generally entrusted to Congress, the legislative branch of government. But early on, the Supreme Court bowed to the reality that agencies should be allowed to exercise some level of delegated responsibility to flesh out that policy. In particular, the Court held that Congress could delegate legislative power to government agencies if it established an "intelligible principle" to guide the exercise of the agency's discretion.[18] Yet, despite striking down several New Deal–era laws on the grounds that they failed to establish adequate guidance for the regulatory agency, the Court has generally deferred to congressional delegations even where the delegated powers are quite broad.[19] For example, in *Yakus v. United States*, the Court upheld the Emergency Price Control Act of 1943, which authorized the Office of Price Administration to set "generally fair and equitable" rent and price ceilings.[20]

As administrative agencies began to exercise policy-making authority, commentators and critics began to consider various theories to justify or explain agency approaches. Mark Seidenfeld has analyzed four different theories to explain agency behavior.[21] The "transmission belt" model views agencies as merely conduits for congressional choices. Under this model, agencies do not exercise independent political judgment but merely implement the congressional will. A second model relies on agency expertise to justify the delegation of power to the agency. A third approach—pluralism—invites agencies to make policy choices by reflecting the values of interested organizations and individuals. Finally, civic republicanism relies upon our republican roots by asking agencies and engaged citizens to set aside their personal preferences and work together deliberatively to act in the broader public interest. With the exception of the "transmission belt" approach, which does not recognize the agency as a policymaker, these approaches are explored in greater detail below. For the reasons that follow, however, civic republicanism offers the only viable platform from which to exploit the advantages that public participation offers, including a meaningful role for the public in government decision making.

A. Reliance on Experts

Modern concepts of public participation in agency actions arose in part, at least, as a response to the perceived excesses of the Progressive era of the early twentieth century and the burgeoning government bureaucracy that arose out of the New Deal. The Progressive era was a time of reliance on government experts who were entrusted with the authority to act in the public interest and make the "best" decisions, based on sound scientific and policy analysis. This approach is reflected in modern policy instruments like cost-benefit analysis and risk analysis, and in the management style of utilitarians like Gifford Pinchot. Pinchot's approach is illustrated by his statement that the goal of conservation should be to produce "the greatest good of the greatest number for the longest time."[22] Viewing important policy questions through the lens of expert analysis allowed policymakers to claim a normative approach toward decision making. Under this view, science and logic would always yield the "right" decision.

While superficially appealing, most decisions are not purely dependent on facts or science. They also reflect moral or value judgments that can figure heavily into policy decisions. (See chapter 3 in this volume.) So, for example, when the U.S. Environmental Protection Agency sets ambient air quality standards at a level designed "to protect the public health" with "an adequate margin of safety," it is essentially applying science to inform its value judgment about what level of pollution is "safe."[23] That value judgment requires an exercise of discretion. As the Supreme Court itself has recognized, "safe does not mean risk-free."[24] Likewise, wildlife experts generally agree about population trends and data with respect to particular wildlife species, but they often disagree about whether those trends suggest that the species is in danger of extinction and thus subject to listing under the Endangered Species Act.

Beyond the fact that experts are often not well suited to making policy decisions, a decision-making approach that relies on experts cannot hope to achieve the intrinsic, instrumental, and constructive advantages that public participation offers. These limitations led to calls for greater transparency in government decision making and additional opportunities for public engagement on the values-based issues that proposals raised. Ultimately, this led to passage of the APA.

B. Pluralism

A pluralist approach views policy choices not in terms of right or wrong decisions but rather as a problem of negotiating among competing interests to achieve a "good" result. The role of the agency in this model is simply to serve as an arbiter among the competing interests. While pluralism superficially appeals to democratic ideals, its goal is not to achieve any semblance of the public good, but rather to promote a politically acceptable result gleaned from the individual preferences of private individuals and organizations. Pluralism makes no normative judgment about the moral value of the result. It is "good" simply because it emerged from a market-like political process. Moreover, as Cass Sunstein has argued, pluralism allows "bad preferences" to emerge from the process because it is "indifferent among preferences."[25]

Pluralism owes much of its appeal to a sense that it promotes utilitarian solutions. In theory, establishing a free market from which to assemble and distill ideas should point the way toward pragmatic decisions. But pluralism wrongly assumes that the government actors can best serve the public by simply aggregating and accommodating private interests. For various reasons, this assumption does not withstand scrutiny.

First, the pluralist approach risks giving undue weight to the views of the limited number of private parties who are involved in the process. Of course, this is a risk inherent in any public participation process, but it is more problematic in the context of a pluralist approach since the outcome depends so substantially on the views of those who participate. Efforts can be made to assemble parties that represent a broad spectrum of views, but it is often not possible to engage all points of view. Moreover, those involved in the process are generally motivated to protect their own private interests. While organizations with missions to protect the public interest can sometimes balance the influence of private interest groups, the focus of a pluralist process is on reaching a political accommodation as something like a surrogate for the public interest, without actually weighing the decision against a normative, public interest standard. In addition, because it is far more efficient to organize and represent a large, concentrated, private interest than it is to organize a diffuse public, public choice theory predicts that the concentrated private interests will be better positioned to participate effectively, and thus more likely to prevail in a pluralist process, even where the public interests are plainly at odds with this result.

Pluralism may also push agencies toward decisions that are perceived to be acceptable to the largest segment of the public. Unfortunately, majoritarian choices are not necessarily good choices from the perspective of the public interest. They often impinge on the interests of unrepresented or underrepresented minorities. Moreover, they cannot even be fairly justified as popular choices. Kenneth Arrow has shown that it is impossible to discern public preferences when more than two choices are available, as is so often the case with natural resource proposals.[26] This is not to suggest that the agency should ignore plurality views, but it does advise caution in justifying decisions in any substantial part on this basis.

Pluralist approaches are not especially good at bringing out the best features of public participation. While they may help agencies to find creative solutions to problems, they often reward private enterprise more than civic virtue. This can be problematic where the goal is to promote the public interest. Moreover, a pluralist approach sometimes allows agencies to avoid accountability for their decisions by effectively passing the responsibility for the decision to private parties.

Collaborative decision-making processes often reflect pluralist values, and they are increasingly popular with government agencies. But agencies charged with the responsibility to act in the public interest should be wary of using these processes without adequate safeguards in place. In the best case, the process will involve a collaboration among private and public interests, inevitably leading to a compromise of the latter. In the worst case, private interests will dominate the process, and agency actions will not even remotely reflect the public good.

C. Civic Republicanism and Deliberative Democracy

"Civic republicanism" takes a fundamentally different approach to government decision making than either of the alternative approaches. Unlike the expert approach, civic republicanism views agencies as neither the sole nor even the chief source of expertise. And unlike pluralism, it does not assume that the best government decisions are those distilled from the private preferences of individuals and groups. Rather, in keeping with the republican tradition, the civic republican ideal asks private citizens to demonstrate "civic virtue" by subordinating their private interests and instead working, through a deliberative process and meaningful engagement, toward decisions that are in the public interest. The process may very well require the assistance of experts, and it will most likely need to wrestle with political realities and private interests, but its ultimate goal is to promote the public good.

While acknowledging that republican approaches vary, Professor Sunstein has argued that they all embrace four common themes: (1) they are deliberative; (2) they promote political equality; (3) they are designed to achieve a definable, common good; and (4) they require participants to engage in the process, not as parties with private interests, but as citizens committed to the public interest. It is no coincidence that they also achieve all of the virtues of public participation extolled by Amartya Sen: They involve citizens in the goal of achieving the common good. They keep agencies accountable by letting them know that the public is monitoring their actions. And they promote good decisions by requiring that agencies engage in a give and take with the public to reach a rational decision.

Of course, the civic republican ideal can never be fully attained. For one thing, while civic republicanism views the common good as objective and ascertainable, that does not mean it can be easily ascertained. Even if it could, executive branch agencies, and thus participants in the public process, are constrained by laws that sometimes define the public interest more narrowly than public-minded citizens might if left to their own devices. Thus, for example, land use planning on U.S. Bureau of Land Management and Forest Service land is subject to a multiple-use and sustained-yield mandate,[27] and federal agencies must generally ensure that their actions do not jeopardize the survival of endangered species, irrespective of other public interest values that might be implicated.[28]

Moreover, it is the rare public process that is able to engage a dedicated group of public-minded citizens in a sustained and meaningful way. Nonetheless, if public-minded agency officials accept the value of the civic republican ideal in promoting good government they will have a strong incentive to work toward that ideal. Perfection may not be attainable, and the common good may be difficult to see. But if agencies understand the core principles that embody civic republicanism and if they commit to using processes that promote meaningful engagement by public-minded citizens of all backgrounds, experiences, and interests, then the choices that agencies make—both on process and substance—will likely be impacted in profound and positive ways.

IV. Public Process and Government Action

A. Preliminary Considerations

This section describes and assesses the merits of particular public participation processes, focusing on how well they reflect the civic republican ideal. Several core principles of that ideal will help to inform this assessment. First, as argued above, the ultimate goal of any public participation process should be to promote decisions that reflect the common good. For this reason, where it is fairly obvious which decision will promote the common good, process is less important, especially if, as Buchanan and Tullock argue, the "dictator" is "benevolent."[29]

Second, regardless of the process used, good decisions are more likely if we attract smart, talented people to public service, who are capable of knowing the common good when they see it, and who genuinely support a meaningful role for the public. Public process is not likely to be useful if agency personnel are not meaningfully engaged with the public. Neither agencies nor the public can necessarily control who will be involved in public process, but agencies should involve their best people in addressing important and controversial problems, and they should reach out to talented, public-minded citizens who may be in a position to help inform and improve the agency's ultimate decision. For its part, the public must recognize its responsibility to marshal its talent to assist the agency in carrying out a meaningful process.

Third, the cost of ascertaining the common good will likely be proportional to the complexity of the problem. This suggests that agencies should define the problem carefully to maximize public engagement on those aspects for which public participation will be most useful. If the cost of process is too high relative to the importance of the problem, and if the agency's tolerance for changing its proposal is correspondingly low, a robust suite of public processes may not be worth the cost.

Finally, bad faith or a lack of candor on the part of agency officials or public participants is antithetical to the civic republican ideal. It will undermine public confidence in the process and might even make the process counterproductive. So, for example, agencies that promote process after a decision has essentially been made are deceiving the public and can jeopardize public confidence about the agency's willingness to consider public input on future proposals. With these general principles in mind, the value of particular processes will be assessed, focusing on how well they accommodate a civic republican approach to decision making.

B. Participation Processes

1. Notice and Comment

The most common method for engaging the public is providing notice and an opportunity for comment. It is required for most substantive rules and for all environmental impact statements, and it is common to many permit processes as well. It may be hard to see why providing the public with notice and an "arms-length" opportunity for comment would ever be ill-advised. Yet, because courts review agency decisions on the record, it is incumbent upon agencies to respond to all significant comments. Otherwise a reviewing court will not be in a position to assess whether the agency has acted in an arbitrary and capricious manner. Thus, the opportunity to comment often imposes a significant additional burden on agencies. For example, when the Forest Service issued a draft EIS on the original proposed "roadless rule" it received well over one million public comments. From these the Forest Service identified 2,450 separate comments, to which it responded in a 221-page volume included in the final EIS.

Notwithstanding the burden that notice and comment may impose on agencies, it is arguably the minimal process that should be afforded whenever unresolved policy issues are raised. It promotes the civic republican ideal by offering all commenters equal access to the agency, and it offers a forum—albeit a somewhat clunky forum—for interested parties to engage each other in vetting the issues. Because they are a matter of public record, the comments and the agency's responses to them also promote agency accountability. They help to illuminate the issues and the agency's thinking about those issues. This record is also essential to any future appeal or litigation over the agency's decision, and the very fact that it exists should help to imbue the agency with a sense of its responsibility to be accountable for its decisions. Good, rational responses may go a long way toward helping the agency avoid having its decision challenged in court.

While traditional notice and comment processes can promote civic republican values, they only rarely promote meaningful engagement between agency officials and the public. A few relatively minor changes could greatly improve the process. First, while it may seem trite, agencies should include in every request for comments a statement of their public interest mission and a plea to commenters to exercise "civic virtue." In lieu of further explanation, agencies should request that commenters explain how their comments reflect the public interest mission of the agency and not simply their own private interests.

Second, comment processes should be set up to allow more give and take among the participants and the agency. The Internet could easily facilitate such a process. For example, the agency could promote an iterative process with two or three rounds of comments. The first round would look much like the traditional process used today. But first round participants would also be allowed to participate in a second and, perhaps, a third round, responding to each other and to preliminary responses from the agency. A "threaded" on-line discussion "could be part of this process. This would allow agencies to promote a far more robust engagement of the issues at a minimal cost.

Finally, agencies could be far more aggressive during the comment period in meeting with experts and informed citizens to solicit their views and to encourage their further engagement in the public process. Personal meetings with interested parties will help promote a better understanding of the issues on all sides and help make comments more relevant and useful.

2. Formal and Informal Hearings

Formal and informal hearings are most common for appeals from adjudicative actions such as permitting decisions that involve particular factual issues. Because of their narrow focus and because participation rights are often limited to "interested" parties, they do not fit the classic model for public engagement in agency action. Nonetheless, adjudicative hearings almost always follow some sort of notice and comment process, often on an environmental assessment, and they can provide important vehicles for setting agency policy where, for example, they establish precedents that guide future agency actions.

The two key federal land management agencies follow markedly different procedures for handling appeals from their decisions. The Forest Service follows a hierarchical, line of authority process, whereby agency decisions may be appealed to the next highest line officer. Thus, decisions by a Forest Supervisor may be appealed to the Regional Forester, and then to the Chief of the Forest Service.[30] The chief complaint about this process is that line officers are rarely neutral observers and are often perceived by the public as biased in favor of the agency decision. By contrast, the adjudicatory decisions of the Bureau of Land Management are generally appealed either to an administrative law judge or to the Interior Board of Land Appeals within Interior's quasi-independent Office of Hearings and Appeals.[31] While the BLM process has the advantage of affording a neutral decision maker, appeals taken to the Board of Land Appeals can take well over a year, and often more than two years, to resolve.

Even when they are informal, appellate processes do not lend themselves very well to the engagement of a wide range of citizens. For one thing, appeals often involve technical, legal issues, which turn on narrow questions of statutory or regulatory interpretation. But appeals are often motivated, not by the legal issues that become the subject of the appeal, but rather by the policy choices that the agency made. Agencies should be more sensitive to this possibility and should ask whether the appeal reflects a fair concern that the original opportunities for engaging the public were inadequate. If the agency concludes that they were not adequate, they should welcome the opportunity that the appeal offers to reopen the process toward the goal of reaching a decision more in line with the common good.

Too often, agencies take a defensive posture to appeals and view winning the appeal as an indicator of the merits of their decision. Yet agencies often win appeals simply because hearing officers and judges are required defer to agency policy judgments. Thus, the appeal process offers little assurance that the public interest has been well served. This must be the continuing responsibility of the agency even when they win appeals.

3. The Town Hall Meeting

Town hall–style meetings were once commonly offered by natural resource agencies, but they have largely been abandoned in favor of the open house. While the reasons for this change in strategy are not entirely clear, several observations can be made. First, the public nature of these meetings means that the press is often interested in covering them, especially when the issues are controversial. Agencies are understandably nervous about how these controversies may play out in the press and whether the agency may be portrayed in a bad light. Moreover, the very nature of controversial proposals provides that some parties will perceive the proposal as contrary to their interests and, subsequently, may try to enlist the press to present their opposition in a more favorable light. This could further fuel the level of controversy over the proposal. On the other hand, a free, fair, and open debate over controversial issues is the very essence of the civic republican ideal, and the publicity that often results from these meetings offers a great opportunity to identify public-minded citizens who might be willing to participate in meaningful discussions about the issues.

A common problem with town hall meetings is not the form, but the fact that agency officials lack the skills necessary to conduct them successfully. For example, agency officials are usually too cautious and therefore reluctant to engage people at these meetings. Instead, they refuse to respond to the questions and concerns offered by citizens in any substantive or meaningful way. No doubt they fear misrepresenting agency policy, and equally cautious agency lawyers may advise them to avoid substantive comments. But engagement is the very essence of a town hall meeting. Public concerns are aired, and the agency's response to those concerns can be judged in an open forum on its merits. Further give and take can then occur, which also helps to assure that the agency is more accountable to the public for its final decision. Legal concerns can be easily addressed by setting appropriate ground rules for the meetings. This might include, for example, a statement that comments and responses offered by agency officials are for the purpose of promoting an open and fair dialogue and should not be understood as firm commitments from or positions of the agency.

The value of the town hall meeting can be most easily seen by experiencing a well-run meeting. A master of the town hall meeting format is former Interior Secretary Bruce Babbitt. As Secretary of the Interior, Babbitt relished the opportunity to engage the public, even when he understood that many people would disagree with him. He not only welcomed critical comments, he responded to them, sometimes pointedly disagreeing with the commenter, other times, acknowledging the commenter's concern and agreeing to address it before any final decision was made. He always responded to comments rationally and on their merits, and in this way disarmed even those who disagreed with him.

Babbitt was successful for several reasons. First, he is simply a talented politician who is comfortable engaging people on many levels. Second, he was always well versed on the subject of the proposals and thus able to respond to comments meaningfully and with specificity. Third, he was not afraid to use the forum as a means for improving the proposal. If a commenter made a good point, Babbitt agreed to work toward a fair resolution of the issue. Fourth, it was clear to everyone who attended a forum with Babbitt that he was responding openly, honestly, rationally, and even cheerfully. People might disagree with him but they would be hard pressed to find him disagreeable, or to see his position as unreasonable. Finally, while Babbitt may not have said so directly, it was clear to everyone involved that his ultimate goal was to act in the public interest, and he was committed to ascertaining the public interest as objectively as he possibly could.

Few people, of course, possess Babbitt's background, experience, and talent. But many public officials are very capable of meaningfully engaging the public at a town hall meeting in a manner that will lead to a more open government, better public relations, and ultimately, better agency decisions that reflect the common good.

4. Open Houses

A clear trend within the natural resource agencies is toward open houses, which, as noted above, seem to be offered in lieu of the town hall meetings. The open house typically involves an invitation to the public to come meet with individual members of the agency to discuss an issue. Posters and other visual aids are set up in the room and agency officials are scattered around the room to explain the posters and talk with members of the public about their concerns. While it is certainly possible to have meaningful conversations with agency officials in these settings, they are nonetheless among the least satisfying of any participation model. The reasons are simple. First, open houses are not in any real sense a collective enterprise. A member of the public interacts individually with one or more agency officials but is effectively cut out of any collective engagement with the agency, as well as engagement with another party or a group of parties with different points of view. Moreover, because the comments and the response to those comments are not a matter of public record the agency is accountable for neither.

A report prepared by the Forest Service promoting collaborative processes suggests the preference among agencies for the open house format over the town hall meeting. In this report, the agency assessed the processes used in several national forests in the western United States. For example, officials from the Medicine Bow National Forest described their open house process as follows:

> The open houses were organized in a round-robin format with six stations corresponding to the six draft alternatives. Each station had a map, a written summary of the alternative, a flipchart, and a Forest Service staff member to answer questions. Public participants were invited to provide comments on each alternative's map

and flipchart—which parts of the alternative they liked and which parts they didn't like.[32]

It is not clear from the assessment whether the Forest Service viewed comments received in this manner as meaningful, either from the public's perspective or their own, or whether they recorded the comments and formally addressed them in their decision. But the observation that follows the statement above is revealing: "Because the open houses did not have any chairs nor were they organized in a traditional 'town hall meeting' format, several individuals who merely wanted to 'grandstand' turned around and left the venue."[33] How the agency knew that these people wanted to "grandstand" is not indicated in the report, but the language shows the disdain that some people within the agency apparently have for members of the public who might want to meaningfully engage other parties in a public forum.

While the town hall format does offer organized groups an opportunity to rally around a particular issue or cause—and even "grandstand"—the town hall is more effective than the open house at engaging a wider audience in a communal setting. Moreover, as noted previously, the publicity that often occurs both before and after town hall events further helps to promote a wide-ranging discussion within the affected community and can thus help hold the agency accountable for its actions.

Agencies are often reluctant to acknowledge controversy and they are understandably wary of people who may react strongly to their proposals. But if the agency follows a thoughtful process and puts forth reasonable and well-developed proposals, the public will generally respond accordingly. Moreover, by effectively dismissing the views of those who prefer to "grandstand," the agency shows a willingness to essentially ignore the point of view of what might be a significant segment of the public. The summary of the experience on the Medicine Bow National Forest closes with a statement that "[o]ver 20,000 public comments were received on the draft plan and draft environmental impact statement." Approximately 340 people showed up at seven open houses. One wonders how many of these commenters failed to show up at the open houses because they too felt disenfranchised by the process.

5. Workshops and Consensus-Based Processes

Collaborative and consensus-based decision making are increasingly popular with administrative agencies, in part because they help allow the agency to defuse and even avoid criticism for their decisions. They can, however, be problematic to the extent that the participants fail to understand that their role is to promote the common good. Achieving such an understanding is especially difficult when the affected interests are divergent. Nonetheless, where the issues and the conflicts are sufficiently narrow, where all sides can be fairly represented, and where a public-minded mission is articulated and accepted by the participants, collaborative processes can lead to good decisions. Moreover, when done well, they can help build trust between the agency and the public, and can help foster cooperative problem solving.

Workshops, whether organized in conjunction with a collaborative process or as a stand-alone process, can also be useful as a means to level the playing field among participants and to promote a common understanding of the issues and problems. But as with other collaborative processes, they are not practical if the problems are too broad or complex. To take one extreme example, workshops on the "roadless rule" would be of dubious value; the issues raised by the rule encompass a wide range of local, regional, and national concerns, and it would be impractical, and perhaps even impossible, to engage all of the myriad points of view in a discrete series of workshops.

Workshops and collaborative processes also require a substantial commitment of time and resources, and this tends to favor professional organizations and concentrated, rent-seeking private interests that have a direct economic stake in the decision. It is far more difficult for interested individuals without a direct economic interest in the decision to justify the expenditure of time and money that these processes require. As described previously, equality of access is a basic tenet of civic republicanism, and such access may be difficult or impossible to assure in many collaborative processes. At a minimum, agencies must be prepared to subsidize the costs of some participants to assure that all appropriate segments of the community are engaged.

Collaborative processes favor "team players" and those willing to accept their legitimacy. If any considerable faction refuses to accept the process, is not invited to participate because it is perceived as unable to work well with others, or is unable to participate due to the associated costs, then a collaborative process will disenfranchise that faction, even if valuable insights are thereby lost. The threat of disenfranchisement can be exacerbated by the fact that statutorily mandated notice and comment processes may become less important to the decision maker, and thus less meaningful in their ability to influence a decision, if a consensus is achieved among the people who participated in the collaborative process. Thus, a collaboration that does not engage all significant points of view cannot hope to achieve its goal of a true consensus decision.

Collaborative processes have become increasingly popular within the U.S. Forest Service, especially in the development of forest-wide land use plans. On its face, this trend seems problematic. These forests are by definition "national" and collaborative groups often encompass primarily or exclusively local interests. Moreover, forest plans raise just the kind of complex, multifaceted problems that seem ill-suited to collaborative processes.

Fortunately, six case studies included in a 2005 Forest Service report, *The Utilization of Collaborative Processes in Forest Planning*, suggest that the Forest Service, rather than focusing on achieving consensus decisions, has been using collaborative processes to promote "mutual learning and understanding" and to build trust among the interested parties. For example, a description of the Dixie and Fishlake National Forest process in Utah notes that "[l]earning is a primary objective collaboration." Such collaboration might still exclude some interested parties from important discussions and deliberations, but if decisions are made independent of these processes, then a meaningful opportunity may still exist for other interested parties to become involved.

6. Personal Meetings

An often overlooked tool for engaging in meaningful discussions and influencing agency decisions is the personal meeting between agency officials and members of the public. Agency officials are usually open to meeting with members of the public, especially during the public comment period on a proposal. These meetings offer a great opportunity for participants to get to know one another and to better understand their respective positions and views. Officials are usually far more candid and more willing to engage in a meaningful discussion in these private meetings than they are in a more public forum. Although agencies typically make a record of these meetings as required by law, one-on-one meetings are not a substitute for notice and comment or other processes. They can, however, help inform those processes and they allow interested parties to develop their comments with a better appreciation of the issues and concerns facing the agency.

Personal meetings can, of course, promote the same type of rent-seeking behavior that is sometimes problematic in consensus-based processes. To address this problem, agencies may need to seek out certain parties to be sure they hear different points of view, and they may want to convene meetings that include more than one side of an issue in an effort to promote a healthy discussion and debate. At a bare minimum, agencies must be fairly accessible to all interested parties and meetings must be open and transparent, with records kept of the substance of the meetings and the people who attend them. Agencies should also provide parties a reasonable opportunity to comment or schedule their own meeting when issues are first raised during these personal meetings.

V.   Meaningful Engagement: The Future of Public Participation in Resource Management

Achieving the virtues of public participation as extolled by Amartya Sen and others, including educating policy makers and the public, assuring government accountability, and promoting civic engagement, requires that agencies adopt policies and practices that promote meaningful engagement and that avoid those practices that undermine it.

By simply recognizing and committing themselves to these principles, agencies will vastly improve their interactions with the public.
Several particular practices described in greater detail below will help
agencies achieve this goal. The need for legislative reform of the rulemaking and adjudication processes is also considered.

A. Acknowledging the Proper Role of Participation in Particular Decisions

Public participation is required by law in most resource decisions, but agencies retain wide flexibility in deciding the kind and
extent of participation to allow. Where the public's involvement can
help educate the agency and the public, promote government accountability, and give the public a sense of their civic responsibility,
the process should be open and robust. Conversely, however, where
these virtues cannot be fairly realized because the issues are well understood and the government's options are clear and constrained, either by law or the political dynamics of the issue, agencies should
publicly acknowledge these constraints and limit public process to
those aspects of the decision for which meaningful engagement can
still occur.

B. Making Public Engagement Meaningful

Meaningful engagement has been a recurring theme throughout this chapter because it is the touchstone for any successful public
process. As previously argued, engagement that is not meaningful is
an affront to the public and a waste of time and resources. Of course,
it will not always be possible to know in advance how much or what
kind of process a particular issue requires, and it will not always be
obvious how to carry out that process in a way that is meaningful.
But agencies that commit themselves to this goal will succeed far better than agencies for whom process is simply a legal burden that must
be tolerated.

C. Making the Process Equitable and Accessible

Among the difficulties with designing a meaningful process is the potential for the process to favor some parties over others. A process can be meaningful for parties that are afforded a special opportunity to influence the agency but meaningless for others who are cut out of the agency process. By their very nature, collaborative processes and workshops can only accommodate a limited number of people. They also favor people with the time and financial resources to participate. Too often, these are also concentrated interests with a financial stake in the outcome. While those with a financial stake are certainly interested parties with a right to participate, agencies should take care to design a process that treats all parties fairly. Simple notice and comment processes and town hall meetings are far more egalitarian, and if carried out in a robust manner with the possibility of follow-up discussions, they can promote engagement that is both meaningful and fair. Personal meetings with individuals and interest groups, when used in conjunction with these other processes, can afford the agency and the public an opportunity to better explain their thinking and ideas, and can also help fill in any gaps in engagement that may result from the other processes.

D. Making the Process Efficient

As previously acknowledged, process is not free. Agency resources expended on one process may limit the amount of resources available for another. For this reason, where agencies are going to provide public process they must take into account the costs, including the opportunity costs, associated with process. Moreover, the agency should consider not only its own time and resource commitments but also the likely expenditures by the public.

In considering how best to promote efficient processes that are still meaningful, agencies should consider an incremental approach that anticipates the possibility, and perhaps even the likelihood, of further processes that can help flesh out and inform the key issues surrounding a proposal. The "scoping" process required for major agency proposals under the National Environmental Policy Act offers an excellent model that can be adapted to other notice and comment processes such as rulemaking. Indeed, agencies often use an "advanced notice of proposed rulemaking" as a kind of scoping process for rulemaking proposals. One major advantage of such processes is that they occur sufficiently early in the development of a proposal to truly influence the agency's thinking. By soliciting public involvement early in the evolution of a proposal, the agency can get a good sense of the public's interest in the issue and the general nature of public concerns. This can help the agency tailor future processes to reflect the level and nature of the public's interest.

Agencies should also be encouraged to provide additional process later in the development of the proposal as well, particularly where new issues or new alternatives are identified as a result of the initial processes. It is far better for public relations and, in the long run, far less costly for the agency to fully address public concerns before the proposal becomes final. Efforts to get decisions out quickly, without an adequate opportunity for the public to air its views, are far more likely to be challenged in court and reversed on procedural grounds.

Finally, agencies should always be open to the desirability of reopening a matter even after a final decision has been made, especially where a legitimate substantive or procedural concern is raised that was not adequately addressed during the public process. The best indicator of a successful process is not whether the agency ultimately prevails in court or before an administrative appeal board, but rather whether the agency is able to implement its decision without triggering an appeal in the first place.

E. Rethinking Rulemaking

For many years, legal scholars have been writing about the problems associated with the rulemaking process.[34] Whatever one thinks of these critiques, the process as envisioned by the 1945 APA is plainly not working as it was designed. The statutory distinction between "formal" and "informal" rulemaking is antiquated and no longer meaningful. Formal rulemaking as provided under the APA is an anachronism. Yet informal rulemaking is anything but informal. Depending on the nature and scope of the rule, the "informal" rulemaking process of today is burdened with many process requirements, including requirements for environmental analyses,[35] a "regulatory flexibility analysis" of the impacts of the rule on small businesses,[36] an analysis of the impacts of the rule on state and local governments,[37] a cost-benefit analysis,[38] and an environmental justice analysis.[39] If the rules require recordkeeping or reporting, these issues may also have to be assessed.[40]

One result of this complexity is that agencies increasingly try to avoid APA rulemaking processes altogether by characterizing their rules as procedural or interpretive, and thus not subject to notice and comment.[41] This is unfortunate. Yet it is hard to see how agencies can accomplish their myriad and ever increasing responsibilities if they are constantly bogged down with rulemaking processes that become ensnared in a constant loop of process, litigation, and more process. While a comprehensive look at reforming the rulemaking provisions of the APA is beyond the scope of this chapter, it seems plain that the APA must be amended to reflect modern realities and to streamline the rulemaking process, especially for truly modest proposals. Even for more complex proposals, an iterative approach could allow agencies to tailor the process to the importance of the issues and the level of public interest, and perhaps, to implement proposals after a reasonable amount of process, even as they anticipate further refinements to the final rule.

F. Rethinking Adjudication

The problems with the adjudication provisions in the APA are almost exactly the opposite of those of the rulemaking provisions. Unlike rulemaking, the distinction between formal and informal adjudications remains important, sensible, and relatively clear. The processes for trial-type standards established for formal adjudications are explicit and well established, and they appear to work reasonably well. The processes to be followed for informal adjudications, however, are far more problematic. Indeed, the APA does not specifically address informal adjudication processes. The only standards agencies must follow for informal adjudications are those demanded by the Constitution, especially the due process clause, and those included in a general section of the APA entitled "ancillary matters."[42] This section allows interested parties to appear before agencies in any proceeding and to be represented by counsel. It also requires agencies to respond to requests within a reasonable time, and if a request is denied, to provide a brief statement of the grounds for denial.

As with rulemaking, this chapter does not attempt a comprehensive assessment of the problem. Nonetheless, the differences between the informal adjudication processes of the Forest Service and the BLM illustrate the need for better legislative guidance. Informal appeals that run through the chain of command, as happens within the Forest Service, are far less likely to lead to changes in the decision. This is because those who supervise the decision maker are almost always familiar with important decisions made by lower level officials before they are made and in many cases have tacitly approved them before the appeal is filed. By contrast, review by the Interior Board of Land Appeals is generally acknowledged to be independent of the decision maker, and thus far less likely to be influenced by officials at the agency who made the decision or who supervised the decision maker.

While it may be too costly for other agencies to adopt a formal appeals process for all or even most of their informal decisions, some basic principles of fairness should be required for all informal orders involving natural resources. At a minimum, appeals should be heard by parties who are independent from the agency officials making the decision. A clear explanation of the obligation that agencies have to explain their reasons for denying an appeal would also be helpful. Courts have generally made clear that agencies must provide a response sufficient to allow a reviewing court to carry out its review function.[43] Ideally, this will ensure that agencies offer a specific response to each issue raised in the appeal.

VI. Conclusion

Public participation in resource decisions will continue to play a prominent role. But the role will not be meaningful unless agencies understand the potential advantages and exercise their authority to promote meaningful processes that are tailored to the particular proposals involved. Agencies are stressed by limited resources, and they are understandably wary of any public process that might expose flaws in their proposals and decisions. But if agencies view process as a means for fulfilling their role as guardians of the public interest and improving their decisions, they will have a strong incentive to use process effectively and meaningfully. The civic republican tradition offers a model for agencies to follow and offers our best hope for meeting Ben Franklin's challenge for keeping the republic.

Timber Demand and Supply Study: Medicine Bow National Forest

The Medicine Bow National Forest is located near Laramie, in southeastern Wyoming. Medicine Bow Peak, the highest point on the forest, tops out at just over 12,000 feet. In the mid- to late 1980s, Friends of the Bow (FOB), a small local group that included several current and former faculty members at the University of Wyoming (including the author), organized to promote more environmentally protective management of the forest. Friends of the Bow did not have a budget, let alone a paid staff, but it met with some early success in stopping the proposed expansion of the Mountain Meadows Guest Ranch and in securing protection of the Snowy Range area, which included Medicine Bow Peak, from the threat of mineral development. The focus of much the group's work, however, was on logging. Major timber mills were operating adjacent to the forest in Laramie, Sarasota, and Encampment, and a fourth mill in Foxpark, Wyoming, had only recently closed. From the perspective of FOB, the mills were demanding far more timber from the forest than could reasonably be sustained.

In 1988, in response to pressure from the logging industry, Forest Service officials agreed to prepare a "timber demand and supply study" that would assess the timber demand and determine the amount of timber that could be supplied from the forest consistent with federal law and the Medicine Bow forest plan.

Over the course of the many months that FOB had been working with the Forest Service, they had faced many conflicts with the agency but they were also developing a reasonably good working relationship with several high-ranking officials within the forest supervisor's office. Moreover, while the environmental assessments that the agency had prepared for some of the early disputes were—from FOB's perspective—fairly weak both analytically and substantively, the agency was clearly beginning to do better work as a result of the heightened level of public scrutiny. The public process seemed to be vindicating one of the key reasons for public participation–accountability.

The Forest Service had made clear in its public announcements about the study that it was prepared to reduce logging levels if the evidence did not support sustaining current logging levels. Nonetheless, Friends of the Bow was skeptical of the timber demand and supply study and worried that it would be used to justify increased levels of logging. Accordingly, the group decided to participate in the study by submitting comments and attending public and private meetings.

The focus of the study, and of much of FOB's work, was on the "suitable timber base"—essentially that land within the forest that was available for logging. The 1985 Medicine Bow forest plan had found 830,000 acres of forested land within the forest, of which 630,000 acres were potentially available for commercial logging. Restrictions in the forest plan were thought to eliminate another 180,000 acres from logging, which left 450,000 acres. Based on this figure, the forest plan had projected that the forest could sustain logging of approximately 28.4 million board feet (mmbf) of timber per year over the initial planning period of 10 to 15 years. If the suitable timber base was substantially larger than the 450,000 acres that had been assumed in the forest plan then additional logging could probably be sustained. But if the suitable timber base was smaller, then either logging levels would have to be reduced or the forest plan would have to be changed.

In May 1991, with the study well under way, Friends of the Bow complained that the public had been left out of the early development of the study, but its members nonetheless continued to be engaged. FOB member Don Duerr submitted extensive comments to the agency, arguing that hundreds of thousands of acres should be removed from the suitable timber base due to a wide range of technical and practical restrictions on logging mandated by either the forest plan or federal law. In September 1991, Duerr wrote a follow-up letter complaining that the agency had failed to respond to the detailed comments he had provided in May. By then it was becoming clear, however, that the Forest Service was reaching much the same conclusion as FOB. The forest could not sustain the logging levels that had been approved in the forest plan. In a brief memorandum written in December 1991, the agency indicated that the study would be completed in about six weeks more.

Then, in early 1992, after most of the work had been completed and the conclusions were clear, the Forest Service announced that it was abandoning the study in favor of commencing immediate efforts to revise the forest plan. The agency argued that the study had revealed the need to begin work on plan revisions without delay, and that any additional work on the nearly completed study would distract the agency from revising the forest plan. During this interim period, the forest would continue to be managed under the 1985 forest plan that was now plainly out of date.

Friends of the Bow and others in the conservation community were shocked and furious. After expending hundreds of hours of their own time providing detailed comments to the agency, and after the preliminary results of the study were plainly indicating that the suitable timber base was far too high, the agency was now abandoning its promise to let the study determine future logging levels.

Whatever trust the Forest Service had managed to build with the conservation community was shattered by this decision. In an effort to repair some of the damage, the Forest Service called a public meeting in May 1992 at which the preliminary results of the study were revealed. Ron Olsen, who was then the Deputy Forest Supervisor, chaired the meeting and indicated that the preliminary results of the study suggested that the forest could sustain less than 25 percent of the logging allowed under the 1985 plan—about 7 mmbf rather than the 28.4 mmbf authorized by the plan. He suggested that lifting some of the restrictions in the 1985 plan could increase that number to 10 or 11 mmbf, but plainly the forest could not sustain what the agency had thought it could sustain in 1985, even if the plan was changed.

Even the promise to commence work on a forest plan revision without delay was broken. The Medicine Bow forest plan was not finally revised until a federal court ordered its completion in December 2003, more than 11 years after the timber demand and supply study was abandoned.[44]

Most of the people involved with Friends of the Bow have now moved on. But the loss of trust between the agency and the public from this particular experience will likely color future encounters between its members and government agencies for many years to come.

In hindsight, it is important to ask why the public process failed in this case. Perhaps it was just that the agency's decision to prepare a timber demand and supply study and to engage the public in the development of the study was a mistake. Yet the results of the study plainly illustrate that further analysis of logging levels was needed. Much of the blame for the failure of the process has to be placed squarely with the agency. It was the agency, after all, that reneged on the commitment it had made when it embarked on the study. As is often the case, however, this was not a situation where the agency had deliberately designed the process to deceive the public. Most likely, it was simply a process that led to an unexpected conclusion—a conclusion that was just too difficult politically for the agency to accept.

Perhaps the agency's more fundamental mistake was its failure to recognize even before it undertook the study that significant declines in logging levels were inevitable. Had the agency anticipated this trend it could have so informed the local logging industry and given them an appropriate amount of time to adjust their operations. In fact, notwithstanding the decision to abandon the study, the facts that it revealed could not be ignored and logging on the Medicine Bow National Forest has declined dramatically. Ironically, this result came about despite, not because of, public process.

Notes

1. Sierra Club v. Morton, 405 U.S. 727 (1972).
2. 5 U.S.C. §§ 501–706.
3. 5 U.S.C. §§ 551(7), 554–556.
4. 5 U.S.C. § 551(4).
5. 5 U.S.C. § 552(b).
6. 42 U.S.C. § 4332(2)(E) (emphasis added).
7. 40 C.F.R. § 1501.4.
8. 16 U.S.C. § 1536.
9. 16 U.S.C. § 470f.
10. 16 U.S.C. § 1604(d).
11. 43 U.S.C. § 1712(a).
12. 16 U.S.C. § 668dd(e)(1)(A)(ii), (e)(4)(B).
13. 42 U.S.C. § 7661a(b)(6).
14. 33 U.S.C. § 1344(a).
15. 33 U.S.C. § 1342(b)(3).
16. Amartya Sen, *Democracy as a Universal Value,* 10 J. Democracy 3, 11 (1999) (emphasis in original).
17. James M. Buchanan & Gordon Tullock, The Calculus of Consent: Legal Foundation of Constitutional Democracy 3.8.6 (1962).
18. J.W. Hampton, Jr. & Co. v. United States, 276 U.S. 394, 409 (1928).
19. *See, e.g.,* A.L.A. Schecter Poultry Corp. v. United States, 295 U.S. 495 (1935); Panama Ref. Co. v. Ryan, 293 U.S. 388 (1935).

20.   Yakus v. United States, 321 U.S. 414 (1944).

21.   Mark Seidenfeld, *A Civic Republican Justification for the Bureaucratic State*, 105 HARV. L. REV. 1511 (1992).

22.   GIFFORD PINCHOT, BREAKING NEW GROUND 326, 353, 505 (Island Press 1998) (1947).

23.   42 U.S.C. § 7409(b)(1).

24.   Indus. Union Dept., AFL-CIO v. Am. Petroleum Inst., 448 U.S. 607, 642 (1980).

25.   Cass Sunstein, *Beyond the Republican Revival*, 97 YALE L.J. 1539, 1544 (1988).

26.   KENNETH ARROW, SOCIAL CHOICE AND INDIVIDUAL VALUES (1951).

27.   16 U.S.C. § 529; 43 U.S.C. § 1712(c)(1).

28.   16 U.S.C. § 1536(a)(2).

29.   BUCHANAN & TULLOCK, *supra* note 17.

30.   36 C.F.R. pt. 215.

31.   43 C.F.R. pt. 4.

32.   SAM BURNS & ANTONY S. CHENG, THE UTILIZATION OF COLLABORATIVE PROCESSES IN FOREST PLANNING 122 (U.S. Forest Service, Dec. 2005).

33.   *Id.*

34.   *See, e.g.*, Mark Seidenfeld, *Demystifying Deossification: Rethinking Recent Proposals to Modify Judicial Review of Notice and Comment Rulemaking*, 75 TEX. L. REV. 483 (1997); Thomas O. McGarity, *Some Thoughts on "Deossifying" the Rulemaking Process*, 41 DUKE L.J. 1315 (1992).

35.   42 U.S.C. § 4332(2)(C).

36.   5 U.S.C. §§ 601 *et seq.*

37.   2 U.S.C. §§ 1501 *et seq.*

38.   Exec. Order No. 12,886, 58 Fed. Reg. 51,735 (Oct. 4, 1993).

39.   Exec. Order No. 12,898, 59 Fed. Reg. 7629 (Feb. 16, 1994).

40.   44 U.S.C. §§ 3501 *et seq.*

41.   *See* 5 U.S.C. § 553(b)(3).

42.   5 U.S.C. § 555.

43.   City of Gillette v. FERC, 737 F.2d 883, 886 (10th Cir. 1984).

44.   Biodiversity Assocs. v. U.S. Forest Serv., 226 F. Supp. 2d 1270 (D. Wyo. 2002).

9

Inventorying the Public Lands

Why Naming and Labeling Matter in Natural Resources Law and Management

James Rasband

Planning mandates are pervasive in natural resources law. The National Forest Management Act (NFMA) requires the Secretary of Agriculture to "develop, maintain, and, as appropriate, revise land and resource management plans" for all of the national forests.[1] The Federal Land Policy Management Act (FLPMA) requires the Secretary of the Interior to do land use planning for the public lands by tract or area. The Coastal Zone Management Act likewise presses states to develop coastal zone management plans.[2] The National Wildlife Refuge Improvement Act of 1997 requires the preparation of comprehensive conservation plans.[3] And the Magnuson-Stevens Fishery Conservation and Management Act depends upon the development of fishery management plans.[4]

That planning is pervasive and will likely remain so into the future should not be particularly surprising. At least in theory, most would agree that in order to manage a resource wisely, it helps to have data about the quantity, location, and nature of the resource: Is it scarce or plentiful? What are its potential uses? (For example, does it have recreation, aesthetic, cultural, commodity, or ecosystem service value? Will a particular resource use be compatible with other uses or limit future options?) Planning is a particularly important tool in multiple-use management regimes because it is the process by which agencies and the public can consider the relative values of different land uses.

Natural resource planning on our public lands typically occurs in three stages. The first stage in the planning process is some form of inventory. Section 201 of FLPMA, for example, obligates the Interior Department to "prepare and maintain on a continuing basis an inventory of all public lands and their resource and other values."[5] The second stage in the planning process is the creation of a resource management plan. This generally involves notice and the opportunity for comment. In simple terms, a resource management plan zones the public lands by describing what sorts of activities and uses may be allowed for particular lands and inventoried resources. While the management plan typically describes what uses are *allowed* on particular lands, it does not guarantee that any particular proposal for an allowed use will be permitted. Thus, the third stage of the planning process occurs when a particular permit proposal—e.g., to build a road, engage in timber harvest, or offer a mineral lease—otherwise allowed by a resource management plan, must be vetted by a site-specific analysis under other applicable laws such as the National Environmental Policy Act (NEPA) and the Endangered Species Act (ESA).

The focus of this chapter is on the first step in the planning process—the inventory. At first blush it may seem as though an inventory would be relatively uncontroversial and that the real fighting would begin with the zoning process. In fact, the inventory process turns out to be quite controversial and quite important. It is hard enough as a matter of disinterested science to catalogue how many elk inhabit a particular habitat, whether an area is actually roadless, or the oil and gas potential of a particular formation, but when so much can ride on the classification, the scientific uncertainty tends to be magnified. To make matters even tougher, inventorying requires not just quantifying and describing existing natural resources, but also involves viewing those resources through a particular legal or policy lens—deciding, for example, whether a particular area has wilderness quality or is suited to recreation. Classifying an area as having particular qualities or values doesn't necessarily make the decision about how the area will be managed, but it goes a long way in that direction.

Consider a few related questions. If the legal rules governing the management of public lands do not change, does the label assigned to those lands influence the way in which the rules are applied? Would it matter, for example, if we renamed "national forests" as "national timber-management areas," even if both areas were governed by the same organic act? Or are the terms of the law the only driver of policy? Is the real driver of natural resource policy simply change in presidential administrations and agency priorities? Or, do the labels we use to describe the public lands actually constrain presidents and agencies in ways that go beyond applicable statutes, regulations, and handbooks? Does the choice between the terms "swamp" and "wetland" make any difference in the way the Corps of Engineers or the courts might interpret the appropriate application of Section 404 of the Clean Water Act?

This chapter suggests that names and labels have always mattered in public land law and policy and will continue to matter. The labels "park," "wilderness," "monument," and "refuge" impact policy and public perception beyond the proscriptions of law and regulation, as do alternative labels like "multiple use," "recreation area," or "special management area." The chapter illustrates that the concern over classifications and labels remains alive and well in public land law. It does so by considering the "wilderness" label that has been the focus of so much energy and angst during the last thirty years of effort by the Bureau of Land Management (BLM) to inventory, and then reinventory, its lands in Utah. Before telling the story, however, a bit of background on public land planning and wilderness inventorying will be useful.

I.   A Brief History of Public Lands Planning

The first century of U.S. history saw very little land use planning, at least not the type we would recognize today. The rectangular survey system imposed a rudimentary land use plan with its division of the public domain into 36-square-mile townships and one-square-mile sections. But the survey treated each section as fungible, whether it contained gold, redwoods, sagebrush, or a lake. Other than the occasional consideration given to mineral-bearing lands, little thought was given to managing land with reference to the resources on that land until well into the nineteenth century.

One point from which to trace the birth of resource planning might be the report of the 1879 Public Land Commission.[6] Strongly influenced by John Wesley Powell who was a member of the Commission, the report concluded that public land policy must reflect the nature of land. The public lands, the report suggested, should be inventoried and classified according to the resources they contained. Different laws and management regimes should then be developed for different resources.

The report's recommendations were not immediately embraced, but over the succeeding decades at least some classification did occur. Public lands were set aside for preservation and recreation as national parks and monuments; bird refuges were created to protect the wildlife resource; lands valuable for their supply of timber were reserved as national forests; and lands "chiefly valuable" for grazing were set aside under the Taylor Act, albeit pending future disposal. But beyond this general classification, there was not much in the way of planning. This was particularly true for the national forests and BLM lands, which tended to be managed for commodity production purposes.

Because the land use decisions of the BLM and Forest Service seemed so frequently captured by special interests, so often directed at the commodity use of public natural resources, and so infrequently dictated by careful science, Congress, beginning in the 1960s and accelerating in the 1970s, decided that management changes were needed. Part of the legal response was a renewed emphasis on planning. Congress began refocusing public land management on what it termed *multiple use* and *sustained yield*, passing the Multiple-Use Sustained-Yield Act for the Forest Service in 1960 and the Classification and Multiple Use Act in 1964 for the BLM. Although the Forest Service already had such authority, the idea was that the agencies should begin to think more broadly about the alternative uses of the natural resources on the public lands and more deeply about the sustainability of particular uses. The method of implementing these concepts of multiple use and sustained yield—the way of mediating between the various public land interests—was to be planning.

This emphasis on multiple use and planning continued with the adoption of the two organic acts that govern the BLM lands and national forests today: the Federal Land Policy Management Act (FLPMA) for the BLM and the National Forest Management Act (NFMA) for the Forest Service. As indicated in FLPMA's definition of "multiple use," the object of multiple-use planning was to enable

> management of the public lands and their various resource values so that they are utilized in the combination that will best meet the present and future needs of the American people; making the most judicious use of the land for some or all of these resources or related services over areas large enough to provide sufficient latitude for periodic adjustments in use to conform to changing needs and conditions; the use of some land for less than all of the resources; a combination of balanced and diverse resource uses that takes into account the long-term needs of future generations for renewable and nonrenewable resources, including, but not limited to, recreation, range, timber, minerals, watershed, wildlife and fish, and natural scenic, scientific and historical values. . . . [7]

As revealed in this statutory definition, which allows the agencies to decide upon some "combination of balanced and diverse resource uses," multiple-use management gives the agencies wide latitude in choosing how the public lands will be used. As a result, the public lands managed by the BLM and the Forest Service have precipitated frequent disputes as different interests have worked to encourage the agencies to exercise this broad discretion in favor of particular resource uses and values. Commodity and extractive interests have urged the agencies in one direction, preservation interests have pushed in another, and recreation and other interests have tugged in still more directions. The same tensions have arisen within the agencies themselves as different presidential administrations have emphasized different multiple-use values.

II. Inventorying BLM's Lands for Potential Wilderness Designation

As previously noted, the first step in the multiple-use planning process is an inventory. The story of this chapter has as its backdrop the inventory requirements of FLPMA, but the basic obligation to begin with an inventory is common to other natural resource planning regimes. FLPMA sets forth its basic inventory requirement in Section 201 of the statute, which obligates the Secretary of the Interior to prepare and maintain a continuing inventory of "all public lands and their resource and other values."[8] In addition to this continuing inventory requirement, Section 603 of FLPMA required the Secretary to conduct a special review of the BLM's lands for areas with wilderness characteristics and to then make a recommendation to the president about which of those lands was suitable for preservation as wilderness. This separate review, which came to be called the BLM's "wilderness inventory," was to be concluded "within fifteen years" of FLPMA's passage.[9]

A. A Brief History of Wilderness Inventories

The requirement that the BLM's lands be searched for potential wilderness did not spring full-blown from the mind of Congress for the first time in FLPMA. By 1976, wilderness reviews had some history. Congress had first called for a search of public lands with wilderness qualities in the 1964 Wilderness Act. Although today there are approximately 107 million acres of wilderness, the original Wilderness Act designated as wilderness only 9.1 million acres of land, consisting of areas that had previously been set aside by the Forest Service as "wilderness," "wild," or "canoe" areas.[10] However, the Act also provided for a review, to be completed within ten years, of the wilderness potential of all areas within the national forests that had previously been designated as "primitive areas," as well as a review of "every roadless area of 5,000 contiguous acres or more in the national parks, monuments and other units of the national park system and every such area of, and every roadless island within, the national wildlife refuges and game ranges."[11]

Although the Wilderness Act on its face seemed to confine the wilderness inventory in national forests to those areas previously designated as primitive areas, in the end the Forest Service inventoried all of the national forests for acreage that might qualify as wilderness. How this happened is a fascinating story that wends its way through various judicial opinions, and encompasses RARE (Roadless Area Review and Evaluation) I and RARE II, as well as the Clinton administration's roadless area rule and the subsequent tussle between the Bush administration and the courts over changes to that roadless rule. Although a fascinating story, it is not the story of this chapter.

B. FLPMA's Wilderness Inventory

Hewing to the old adage that the public lands managed by the BLM were the lands no one wanted, the Wilderness Act ignored them. Congress decided to rectify that omission when it passed FLPMA in 1976 and called for BLM to conduct its own wilderness inventory and review. That special wilderness inventory was imposed on top of FLPMA's continuing inventory requirement, just as the roadless area review under the Wilderness Act was added to the underlying inventory obligations of the Forest Service, Park Service, and the Fish and Wildlife Service. And similar to the Wilderness Act's call for its roadless area review to be completed within 10 years, FLPMA called for BLM's wilderness inventory to be completed within 15 years.

As mentioned above, FLPMA provided that the Secretary was to recommend to the president, and the president, in turn, to Congress, which BLM lands identified during the inventory as having wilderness characteristics should be included in the national wilderness preservation system. The kicker was that the areas identified by the Secretary as potential wilderness—what are now known as "wilderness study areas" or "WSAs"—were to be managed by the Secretary, and therefore the BLM, for nonimpairment of their wilderness characteristics until Congress decided to either designate the wilderness study areas as part of the wilderness preservation system or release them for multiple-use management.[12]

Like the RARE process for the national forests, the inventory of the BLM's lands for wilderness proceeded on a state-by-state basis. By the conclusion of the initial wilderness inventory in November 1980, out of almost 174 million acres surveyed, the Secretary identified 919 WSAs covering some 24 million acres.[13] Throughout this inventory process there was significant controversy about whether the Secretary had identified enough acres with wilderness characteristics. From the environmental community's perspective, BLM had hearkened too closely to the wishes of its traditional extractive industry constituency and had improperly failed to classify as WSAs parts of the public lands that had real wilderness quality. This criticism grew even louder when BLM recommended to the President that only a portion of the areas classified as WSAs were actually suitable for wilderness designation.

In the years following completion of the inventories, the question of what BLM lands should have been classified as having wilderness characteristics has remained largely stalled, although not entirely: Congress has added 6.7 million acres of BLM lands to the National Wilderness Preservation System. In broad strokes, western Republicans in whose states the wilderness study areas lie have proposed state-by-state wilderness bills that largely track the BLM's wilderness recommendations. At the same time, congressional Democrats and like-minded Republicans have proposed wilderness bills that include not just the BLM's recommended wilderness, but also all the WSAs included within BLM's initial wilderness inventory, as well as areas outside these WSAs that preservation advocates believe have wilderness quality.

At first glance, the stalemate might seem odd—why not at least designate as wilderness those areas on which the two sides agree? One prominent source of the stalemate is disagreement about "release" language. "Soft release" language in wilderness legislation removes wilderness study area status from nondesignated land but does not prohibit the area from being designated as wilderness in the future. "Hard release" language bars nondesignated areas of the state from being considered for possible wilderness designation forever or for some fixed period of time. In essence, hard release language is designed to eliminate wilderness management from the range of uses available to the BLM in its land use planning. For preservation advocates it makes little sense to compromise on release language when wilderness study areas must already be managed for nonimpairment of their wilderness characteristics.

This congressional stalemate sets the stage for a story about the wilderness inventory in Utah. That story, of course, is not just about Utah. It is also about the important role of inventorying in the planning process, and more generally, about the importance of labeling, naming, and classifying in public land policy making.

III. The Utah Wilderness Inventory

At the end of the BLM's wilderness inventory in Utah, the BLM had identified 82 wilderness study areas that included approximately 3.2 million acres of land. As was the case with many of the BLM's other state inventories, the environmental community believed the BLM had vastly understated potential wilderness in Utah. In February 1985 they formed the Utah Wilderness Coalition and sent their members into the field to perform their own review. In 1990, after thousands of hours of work, the Coalition concluded that Utah actually contained 5.7 million acres of wilderness. The tension between the two views was exacerbated when BLM recommended to the President that of the 3.2 million acres of WSAs it had inventoried in Utah, only about two million were suitable for designation as wilderness.

Over the next few years, competing Utah wilderness bills were advanced in Congress. Utah Representative Jim Hansen introduced a series of bills proposing to designate first 1.4 million acres and later 1.9 million acres as wilderness. Alternative bills, supported by the Clinton administration, were introduced relying on the work of the Utah Wilderness Coalition and proposing 5.7 million acres of wilderness. None of the bills could garner sufficient support for passage, partly because Congress and the presidency were divided throughout the 1990s.

IV. The Utah Wilderness Reinventory

In an effort to break this deadlock, the Clinton administration decided on two different administrative approaches to wilderness in Utah. The first was to use the Antiquities Act to proclaim the Grand Staircase-Escalante National Monument. Most of the 1.7 million acres proclaimed as part of the Grand Staircase-Escalante National Monument had been identified as potential wilderness in the 5.7-million-acre wilderness bill in Congress. Although a monument proclamation is not the same as wilderness designation, it was similarly designed to protect the area from resource development.

The administration's second effort to change the terms of the wilderness debate was to begin a "reinventory" of the BLM's lands in Utah. In this effort, the administration had some help from an unlikely source. During an April 1996 oversight hearing before the House Committee on Resources, Interior Secretary Bruce Babbitt and Utah Representative James Hansen, then the chair of the committee, tussled over the competing Utah wilderness bills and the differing perspectives of the Utah delegation and the Clinton administration about how much wilderness there really was in Utah.

MR. HANSEN:. . . Mr. Secretary, various entities fought with us out in Utah on H.R. 1745, which is the wilderness bill. You recently were quoted by Vice President Gore as saying it had to be 5 million acres. We both know what the definition of wilderness is under the 1964 Wilderness Act.

With that in mind, I would appreciate somebody finally acknowledging the things that we have said that are asking where is the additional acreage? Your man on the ground at the time that BLM did what the law provided was Mr. Jim Parker, who has since retired.

Mr. Parker stated the figure, after 15 years, after $10 million of the taxpayers' money, came up with 1.945 million. You have gone up to 5 million acres. All I am respectfully asking is where is it that fits it?

I have been on this for 19 years now. I have been on every inch of that ground. I think I am very acquainted with the definition of wilderness, and I would be very desirous of hearing from you or your designee as to where is that ground that the Vice President talked about, that you talked about, that the extreme environmentalists talk about? Where is it?

I would ask you respectfully if you could furnish me with that information.

MR. BABBITT: Mr. Hansen, I do not support, this administration does not support, and I disavow, the opinion of Mr. Parker. 1.945 million acres was the figure submitted in a previous administration. I respect their right to do that, but it does not and has never represented the position of this administration.

Now, what is the right number? That is obviously the subject of a give-and-take debate. I do believe that there are in fact 5 million acres that are suitable for wilderness, and I would be happy to respond in writing, because I believe that from my own experience, from my knowledge, from the work of the land specialists in this Department that there are in fact 5 million acres.

MR. HANSEN: I have no argument with your opinion. All I am saying is to re-inventory it, tell us where you are coming from. . . .

MR. BABBITT: Mr. Hansen, would you like the Department to re-inventory it?

MR. HANSEN: I would have no heartburn with that.

MR. BABBITT: Well, I have not taken that step, but if you have no objection to it, I would certainly consider formally rescinding the prior inventory and beginning a new one. . . .

MR. HANSEN: As the Secretary of the Interior, you surely have the right to disavow it, and you have the right to do it. I am just saying that I keep hearing these comments about all this additional acreage, but I have yet to see the criteria; I have yet to see the first acre of ground, Mr. Secretary, that says here is where it is. . . .

MR. BABBITT: I will consider that as a request to revoke the prior study and begin anew. I will proceed to do that.

MR. TAUZIN: The gentleman's time has expired.[14]

Taking Representative Hansen up on his challenge, three months later Secretary Babbitt announced that the BLM would reinventory its lands in Utah to determine whether lands with wilderness characteristics had improperly been excluded from the original inventory. Basically, Secretary Babbitt proposed to find out whether the Utah Wilderness Coalition's estimate of 5.7 million acres of wilderness was right. If Secretary Babbitt could find more potential wilderness than the areas identified in the BLM's initial inventory, it would give a leg up to the advocates of the larger wilderness bill. The Secretary presumably also hoped that any areas with wilderness potential identified during the reinventory could be classified as wilderness study areas and managed for nonimpairment of their wilderness characteristics.

Although the Hansen–Babbitt colloquy was a fun bit of political theatre, it is likely that Secretary Babbitt had already been moving toward a reinventory because it had been under discussion within the Department.[15] Nevertheless, the invitation from Representative Hansen made for good sport because almost as soon as the Secretary began the reinventory, Representative Hansen came out in opposition to it.

A. Utah's Lawsuit Against the Wilderness Reinventory

Concerned that the reinventory might restrict development on additional BLM lands beyond those already classified as wilderness study areas, the State of Utah, Utah's School and Institutional Trust Lands Administration, and the Utah Association of Counties (collectively "Utah") sued Secretary Babbitt seeking an injunction against the reinventory.

Utah argued that Secretary Babbitt did not have authority to conduct a reinventory of Utah's BLM lands in a search for more wilderness. In Utah's view, the time for wilderness inventories had ended, along with the Secretary's authority to designate wilderness study areas for nonimpairment management, when the 15-year period specified in Section 603 of FLPMA had expired. Thus, Utah alleged that it would be illegal for the Secretary to begin managing for nonimpairment lands identified in the reinventory as having potential wilderness quality. In fact, Utah asserted that the Secretary was already doing so, pointing to a November 1, 1993, Memorandum in which the Secretary had directed the BLM to give "careful attention" to areas identified by the Utah Wilderness Coalition as potential wilderness before allowing any development proposal to go forward.

The Secretary responded that regardless whether the BLM had authority to conduct the reinventory under FLPMA's 15-year wilderness inventory provision, it certainly had authority to do so under the act's continuous reinventory requirement. The Secretary also objected that Utah lacked standing to challenge the wilderness reinventory because the reinventory itself worked no injury to Utah. It was, after all, just labeling lands as potential wilderness; it didn't actually decide how the lands were to be managed.

The Tenth Circuit agreed with the Secretary that Utah lacked standing to challenge the wilderness reinventory, but opined that Utah had standing for its claim that the BLM was improperly affording nonimpairment management to lands outside of the original wilderness study areas.[16] Under Section 302 of FLPMA, noted the court, the BLM is required to manage the public lands in accordance with its land use plans.[17] In theory, therefore, to the extent that the BLM's existing land use plans had zoned as open to leasing and development areas identified by the Utah Wilderness Coalition as potential wilderness, BLM was supposed to manage those areas as if they were open for leasing and development unless it amended its existing land use plans. Although the Tenth Circuit saw little evidence of such *de facto* wilderness management, it remanded that issue to the district court.

Following the Tenth Circuit's remand, Utah's lawsuit lay dormant for several years. In the meantime, the reinventory went forward, and the Interior Department found that in addition to the 3.2 million acres originally identified as wilderness study areas, another roughly 2.6 million acres of BLM lands in Utah had wilderness quality, just as the Utah Wilderness Coalition had suggested. Interestingly enough, about this same time preservation groups in Utah completed another inventory and suggested that Utah actually had 9.1 million acres of potential wilderness. The latest version of the America's Red Rock Wilderness Act, introduced by Representative Hinchey in April 2007, seeks designation of 9.4 million acres of wilderness.[18]

The additional 2.6 million acres of potential wilderness found during the reinventory were divided into what the BLM called "wilderness inventory areas" or "WIAs." This moniker was used to distinguish these reinventoried areas identified under the BLM's continuing inventory authority from the wilderness study areas (WSAs) identified during the original inventory conducted within the 15-year window provided in Section 603 of FLPMA. The issue for the BLM was whether these new wilderness inventory areas could be managed for nonimpairment of their wilderness characteristics just as if they had been identified as wilderness study areas during the initial inventory. The hurdle for the BLM was that the existing land use plans had effectively zoned many of these wilderness inventory areas as open to development, and FLPMA required that the BLM manage its lands in accordance with existing land use plans. So, what happened?

In April 1999, the Department of the Interior Solicitor issued a directive that the BLM should use the National Environmental Policy Act (NEPA) to give "careful attention" to any proposal for development within a wilderness inventory area, including consideration of a "no action" alternative to preserve the area's wilderness characteristics. Then, on January 10, 2001, BLM adopted a new Wilderness Inventory and Study Procedures Handbook, which provided that the wilderness inventory areas could be designated as wilderness study areas in amended land use plans, after which they would be managed for nonimpairment until Congress made a decision on the areas or until the land use plan was amended yet again to remove the WSA designation. The handbook provided that the amended land use plans could designate as new wilderness study areas not only the wilderness inventory areas found during the reinventory but also other "lands included in proposed legislation, or land within externally generated proposals" that were determined to have wilderness characteristics in the land use planning process.

Based on the new handbook's guidance, on August 20, 2001, the Utah BLM State Director instructed all Utah field office managers to manage wilderness inventory areas so as to prevent any change that might prevent their future designation as wilderness. Thereafter, BLM field office managers in Utah declined to offer leases or allow road work within wilderness inventory areas despite the fact that almost all such areas were open to leasing under the relevant land use plans.

This approach ripened Utah's argument, for which the Tenth Circuit had suggested Utah still had standing, that the BLM was improperly affording WSA-type nonimpairment management to non-WSA lands despite FLPMA's requirement that the public lands be managed in accordance with existing land use plans. Of course, the Solicitor had only instructed the BLM to give "careful attention" to such areas, which was likely legitimate guidance to the BLM as it evaluated site-specific proposals. However, the Utah State Director's guidance went further and seemed to impose a specific nonimpairment management obligation pending revision of the land use plans.

B. The Utah Settlement Agreement

Although Utah's argument was ripening, it was not until the Clinton administration left office and the Bush administration had taken over that Utah decided to reinvigorate its lawsuit. In the early months of 2003, Utah amended its complaint and alleged that the BLM's adoption of the new Wilderness Inventory and Study Procedures Handbook and the guidance from the Utah BLM's State Director had improperly adopted a wilderness management standard for the wilderness inventory areas without having amended the relevant land use plans.

When Utah sent its proposed amended complaint to President Bush's Department of the Interior, the department recommended that the two sides attempt to settle the dispute. In April 2003, the Department of the Interior announced that it had settled the case with Utah. In the settlement agreement, the department agreed to rescind the new Wilderness Handbook and promised not to manage its wilderness inventory areas as if they were wilderness study areas. The agreement provided, however, that

> [N]othing herein is intended to diminish BLM's authority under FLPMA to prepare and maintain on a continuing basis an inventory of all public lands and their resources and other values, as described in FLPMA Section 201. These resources and other values may include, but are not limited to characteristics that are associated with the concept of wilderness. . . .

[N]othing herein shall be construed to diminish the Secretary's authority under FLPMA to utilize the criteria in Section 202(c) to develop and revise land use plans, including giving priority to the designation and protection of areas of critical environmental concern.[19]

Under the settlement agreement, therefore, the BLM remained free to conduct wilderness inventories pursuant to its continuous inventory authority and it was free to revise its land use plans and adopt a plan that protected an area's wilderness characteristics. What it was not free to do was to name or label those areas "wilderness study areas." The BLM's authority to manage wilderness inventory areas for nonimpairment was further confirmed by the settlement agreement's confirmation of the BLM's authority to designate wilderness inventory areas, or any other area of the public lands, as "areas of critical environmental concern," so-called ACECs. FLPMA defines these as follows:

areas within the public lands where special management attention is required (when such areas are developed or used or where no development is required) to protect and prevent irreparable damage to important historic, cultural, or scenic values, fish and wildlife resources or other natural systems or processes, or to protect life and safety from natural hazards.[20]

Under FLPMA, the BLM is supposed to give priority to both the identification of these ACECs during its continuing inventory process[21] and the designation and protection of such areas in the development and revision of its land use plans.[22]

The settlement agreement with Utah produced cheers from the public land development community and an uproar among preservation advocates. Both seemed to perceive the agreement as a significant legal change to the meaning of FLPMA rather than a reflection of a new presidential administration's public land priorities. This reaction was curious. Both before and after the agreement, the BLM was free to allow development, such as offering oil and gas leases, within wilderness inventory areas or on lands identified as having wilderness quality by a citizen group, as long as it acted in compliance with the existing land use plan and complied with NEPA. Likewise, both before and after the agreement, the BLM was free to identify wilderness under its continuing inventory authority and to amend its land use plans for such areas to provide for the protection of wilderness characteristics.

The settlement agreement changed only two things. First, the Clinton Interior Department's 2001 Wilderness Inventory and Study Procedures Handbook was rescinded. But the handbook was just a statement of the Clinton administration's position about how it planned to treat wilderness inventory areas. The handbook had not been adopted with notice and comment and wasn't controlling authority. So in essence, the repudiation of the 2001 handbook was simply an announcement of the new land use planning policy that the BLM intended to apply in Utah and in other states under similar circumstances. It is certainly understandable that there would be angst about this change in multiple-use management policy, which was another manifestation of the Bush administration's emphasis on oil and gas leasing and development over wilderness protection. But it is the nature of multiple-use management that different administrations choose to emphasize different uses and values in their land use planning.

The second change reflected in the settlement agreement was the Bush administration's agreement with Utah that FLPMA did not allow the "wilderness study area" label to be assigned to areas with wilderness qualities unless those areas had been classified as wilderness study areas under the original Section 603 wilderness inventory process. This part of the settlement agreement will not likely bind future administrations because the agreement's status as a consent decree was vacated in a later proceeding.[23] Nevertheless, even if it were binding on the current and future BLM, the settlement agreement was clear that such areas could still be called "areas of critical environmental concern" or given some other multiple-use management label such as "special recreation management area." (In fact, some of the wilderness inventory areas have ended up as ACECs in the revised resource management plans being prepared by the Utah BLM.)

Given that the BLM is free to give the same legal protection to a reinventoried area regardless of whether it is labeled a "wilderness study area" or an "area of critical environmental concern," one might believe that the "wilderness study area" label is important as a matter of law because WSAs must be managed for nonimpairment until Congress determines otherwise, whereas ACECs and other areas designated for protective management are only protected for as long as the management plan remains unchanged. But the requirement of nonimpairment management pending congressional determination only applies to WSAs established under the original Section 603 wilderness inventory. By contrast, areas with wilderness quality discovered during the continuous inventory process and labeled as WSAs during the land use planning process would have remained subject to change in a subsequent land use plan, just as would an ACEC.

Ironically enough, when the Southern Utah Wilderness Alliance (SUWA) challenged the settlement agreement, the district court held that SUWA lacked standing to challenge the agreement because it could not show injury. The BLM was still free to identify wilderness as part of its continuing inventory authority and to protect the wilderness characteristics of any areas so identified under its land use planning authority. As the court put it: "any lands found to have wilderness characteristics could in the exercise of the BLM's discretion be managed so as to be given protection essentially identical to that afforded a WSA".[24] Just as Utah had been denied standing to challenge the wilderness reinventory because of the Tenth Circuit's conclusion that the inventory did nothing more than rename areas on the public lands, SUWA's concern about the loss of the "wilderness study area" label fell on deaf ears because it would not, in theory, require any change in on-the-ground management.

Aside from the constitutional inquiry about what constitutes actual injury for standing purposes, upon which the courts properly focused, were the courts right in their broader message? Does changing the label assigned to particular areas of the public lands really not matter as long as the underlying legal management discretion remains the same? If public lands with wilderness characteristics can be protected as areas of critical environmental concern, special primitive recreation areas, or under some other appellation, how much does it matter that the BLM has agreed not to label the areas as "wilderness study areas"?

Was the Utah settlement agreement really worthy of the ecstatic cheers and derisive jeers it received? The answer to this question lies in how much one believes naming and labeling matter in natural resources law. Given the energy expended on the issue, the answer appears to be quite a bit, which is part of the reason why the process of inventorying and classifying is such an important step in the land use planning process.

V.   Why Naming and Labeling Matter in Public Land Law and Policy

So why does it matter that public lands with wilderness qualities might be labeled an "area of critical environmental concern" rather than a "wilderness study area"? Labels generally—and in the Utah dispute, the "wilderness study area" label particularly—matter because they have an effect on agency decision making. Labels send messages about how particular lands are valued and how they should be managed. Consider the BLM in Utah. The BLM had the same authority over wilderness reinventory areas and citizen-nominated areas before and after the settlement agreement. Yet, before the agreement it routinely refused leasing in these areas, and after the agreement it has been quicker to open them for leasing. Although the primary explanation for this change is the policy differences of the Clinton and Bush administrations, it is also plausible that the change in the perception of these areas as potential "wilderness study areas" has impacted the BLM's approach to leasing.

For a BLM field officer, it may well be more efficient and less risky to manage by label rather than to manage with reference to the individual characteristics of a particular area. In simple terms, if an area is a potential wilderness study area, protect it; if an area is open to multiple use, open it up to development. It's not that a wilderness inventory area with potential to be a wilderness study area couldn't be leased under the terms of existing land use plans; it's not that multiple-use management means open to development; it's just that managing according to categories and classifications is a whole lot easier and more efficient. That's part of the reason why multiple-use management doesn't often result in wilderness protection.

Names and labels also have meaning to courts. Even after the adoption of the settlement agreement, a federal district court enjoined 16 oil and gas leases offered within areas identified during the reinventory as having potential wilderness characteristics.[25] Relying upon the Supreme Court's decision in *Marsh v. Oregon Natural Resources Council*, which held that federal agencies must supplement their NEPA analysis if "new information" shows a potentially significant environmental impact "not already considered," the district court decided that BLM had not performed an adequate NEPA analysis before offering these areas for lease because it had failed to account for the significant new information about the wilderness qualities of these areas provided by the reinventory.[26] In light of the fact that the physical characteristics of the areas had not changed, one might ask whether it was really significant new information about the areas or the significant new label that produced the result? Most likely, it was some of both.

Labeling and naming can also make a difference to the budgets of federal agencies. Consider Secretary Babbitt's June 2000 creation of the National Landscape Conservation System (NLCS) within the BLM. In theory, the NLCS was just a grouping of certain land units managed by the BLM, including national monuments, wild and scenic rivers, national scenic and historic trails, wilderness, and wilderness study areas. It did not create any new legal protections. Similar to the designation of world heritage sites on an international scale, the primary purpose of the NLCS grouping was to increase public awareness of the resource values of these units. Increasing public awareness may seem rather inconsequential but it creates a constituency for the NLCS and gives the system greater leverage in the budgeting process. In fact, the NLCS is now a separate line item on the Department of the Interior's budget requests and a bill enacted by the 111th Congress made the NLCS permanent. Notably, although wilderness study areas are included in the NLCS, areas of critical environmental concern are not.

Over the last thirty years, the term "wilderness study area" has developed a powerful preservation connotation, partly because of the meaning associated with the word "wilderness" and partly because the associated management regime has been the nonimpairment mandate of Section 603 of FLPMA. Both supporters and opponents of the Utah settlement agreement understood that the perceptions of the public, the BLM, and the courts would be impacted by whether a reinventoried area was labeled a "wilderness study area," an "area of critical environmental concern," or simply as available for multiple use, even if the same management could legally be accomplished under any of those labels. This means that the debate about the wilderness reinventory and the Utah settlement agreement was primarily about capturing the rhetorical flag of wilderness—a flag that turns out to be quite important.

Notes

1. 16 U.S.C. § 1604(a).
2. 16 U.S.C. § 1452(3).
3. 16 U.S.C. § 668dd.
4. 16 U.S.C. § 1853(a).
5. 43 U.S.C. § 1711.
6. Report of the Public Lands Commission, H.R. Exec. Doc. No. 46, 46th Cong., 2d Sess. V–XLVII (1880).
7. 43 U.S.C. § 1702(c).
8. 43 U.S.C. § 1711(a).
9. 43 U.S.C. § 1782.
10. 16 U.S.C. § 1132(a).
11. 16 U.S.C. § 1132(c).
12. 43 U.S.C. § 1782(c).
13. 45 Fed. Reg. 77,574 (Nov. 14, 1980).
14. *Interior Department Review and Budget: Oversight Hearing before the Committee on Resources,* 104th Cong., 2d Sess. 27 (Apr. 24, 1996).
15. *See, e.g.,* 143 Cong. Rec. E2259, E2266 (Nov. 9, 1997) (Majority Report on Grand Staircase-Escalante National Monument Creation includes a March 29, 1996 e-mail from Linda Lance to T. Jensen, et. al. proposing a meeting at the Interior Department where "[w]e'll push them on new wilderness inventory . . .").
16. Utah v. Babbitt, 137 F.3d 1193 (10th Cir. 1998).
17. 43 U.S.C. § 1732(a).
18. H.R. 1919, 110th Cong., 1st Sess. (2007).

19. First paragraph of quotation is cited in Utah v. U.S. Dept. of Interior, 535 F.3d 1184, 1190 (10th Cir. 2008). Settlement agreement is on file with author.

20. 43 U.S.C. § 1702(a).

21. 43 U.S.C. § 1711.

22. 43 U.S.C. § 1712(c)(3).

23. Utah v. Norton, 2006 WL 2711798, at *5 (D. Utah 2006).

24. *Id.* at *28.

25. S. Utah Wilderness Alliance v. Norton, 457 F. Supp. 1253 (D. Utah 2006).

26. Marsh v. Or. Natural Res. Council, 490 U.S. 360 (1989).

10

Saving Special Places

Trends and Challenges for Protecting Public Lands

Robert B. Keiter

The federal public lands have served multiple purposes throughout our history, primarily as a storehouse for the nation's bountiful natural resources. Since the creation in 1872 of Yellowstone National Park—the world's first national park—one of those purposes has been to preserve landscapes from private disposition or commercial development. During the ensuing 135 years, the nation's commitment to preservation has grown significantly along with its populace and economy. Today more than 200 million acres, or nearly one-third of the public domain, is in some form of protective status (see table below).

The preservation of our public landscapes has occurred through the political process, often by citizen-led campaigns. Over the years, we have created multiple protected land systems that include national parks, wilderness areas, wildlife refuges, wild and scenic rivers, and a new national landscape conservation system. Each of the four principal federal land management agencies—the National Park Service, U.S. Fish and Wildlife Service, Forest Service, and Bureau of Land Management (BLM)—now has responsibility for overseeing various preserved lands. There is no reason to anticipate that the public's interest in protecting federal lands will diminish in the years ahead, nor should we expect the political nature of the preservation process to abate.

Federal Protected Lands, 2008

Agency	Acres (millions)
National Park Service	84
U.S. Fish and Wildlife Service	95
U.S. Forest Service (wilderness)	35
Bureau of Land Management (NLCS lands)	40
Total	254

Note: This table illustrates the acreage on public lands in federal protective status, as a national park, wildlife refuge, national forest wilderness area, or as part of the BLM's National Landscape Conservation
System (which includes national conservation areas, national monuments, wilderness areas, and wilderness study areas). More than two-
thirds of the National Park Service and Fish and Wildlife Service
acreage is located in Alaska. The BLM's acreage figure may slightly
overstate the protected acreage, because of overlapping designations.
Between the four agencies, the total acreage in federal ownership is
approximately 635 million acres.

Both the purposes and strategies for federal land preservation have
changed over time, while the amount of protected acreage has grown.
The purposes of preservation have evolved from aesthetic monumen-
talism and scenic protection to include biological diversity and ecosystem conservation. The lead strategic role that Congress has ordinarily
taken in protecting public lands has now also been assumed by the
President, the agencies, and even the courts. Although predicting the
future is always difficult, we can reasonably expect that even more
acreage in new and different designations will be transferred into the
protected category in years to come. The following discussion first
examines the evolving rationales for protecting public lands, then
analyzes the array of available protective strategies, and concludes
with reflections on what the future may hold.

I.   The Preservation Impulse

The philosophy underlying the administration of public lands has
steadily evolved with the passage of time. In the beginning, there was
no scarcity of wilderness, and the early pioneers devoted themselves to

taming wild nature. The prevailing ethic was to dispose of the publicly owned lands by transferring them into private ownership, which was done quite effectively through homesteading, mining, and other laws designed to attract new settlers into the western wilderness.

But as the years passed and the nation's natural heritage was increasingly subject to plunder, the idea surfaced that some of these lands should be retained in public ownership and managed to conserve their resources. Thus were born the concepts of the national park and forest reserve, both of which represented a fundamental shift in how we viewed the public domain. This shift in management philosophy continues yet today. With wild and relatively undisturbed places rapidly disappearing, the American public is engaged in saving our remaining undeveloped lands and is even beginning to restore the worst excesses of our profligate past.

The first federal foray into land preservation found expression in the national park idea. In 1872, Congress was persuaded to set aside more than 1.5 million acres of the storied Yellowstone country "as a public park or pleasuring-ground for the benefit and enjoyment of the people," withdrawing these lands from private disposition and thus establishing a new land management precedent.[1] This original designation was soon followed by other park designations, including Yosemite, Sequoia, Mount Rainier, Crater Lake, and Glacier.

By 1916, Congress had concluded that these fledgling parks should be incorporated into a new national park system. This was accomplished that year with adoption of the National Park Service Organic Act, which contained a distinctive mandate that instructed the new National Park Service "to conserve the scenery and the natural and historic objects and the wildlife therein and to provide for the enjoyment of the same in such manner . . . as will leave them unimpaired for the enjoyment of future generations."[2] According to historian Alfred Runte, American cultural nationalism inspired the incipient national park movement and focused early preservation efforts on protecting the young nation's unique scenic attractions and natural heritage.[3]

Wildlife conservation also figured prominently in early preservation campaigns. Several of the first national parks were created to provide a sanctuary for the nation's rapidly dwindling wildlife populations, which were being decimated by market hunters driven by profit. Not content to rely upon Congress to safeguard the nation's wildlife resources, President Roosevelt took it upon himself in 1903 to proclaim the country's first wildlife reserve at Pelican Island, thus creating another new protective designation that has evolved into the national wildlife refuge system.

Tourism and recreation were also important elements in these early preservation campaigns. The National Park Service Organic Act instructed the Park Service to provide for public enjoyment of the parks, and the first director quite intentionally encouraged the construction of hotels and roadways inside the parks to promote visitation.[4] Hunting and fishing advocates not only played a prominent role in creating the wildlife refuges, but they provided all-important financial support through license fees and taxes on their equipment. Once designated, the new national parks were often linked to the welfare of nearby "gateway" communities that offered visitor accommodations and services, thus establishing an important but sometimes perverse economic bond between the two.

As the nineteenth century drew to a close, Congress was persuaded to create new forest reserves to protect the western forest lands from the fate that befell timber lands further east, which had been badly cut over as the wave of settlement swept across the country. In 1891, Congress authorized the President to establish forest reserves, an invitation that a succession of presidents readily accepted, withdrawing more than 120 million acres into reserve status. In 1897, with passage of the Organic Administration Act, Congress instructed that the new forest reserves were to be managed for productive purposes, thus distinguishing these conserved lands from the national parks, which were protected from commercial exploitation.[5] A few years later the Forest Service was established to administer the new forest reserves, setting the stage for an interagency rivalry with the later-created National Park Service—a rivalry that continues yet today.

Notwithstanding its utilitarian origins, the Forest Service is responsible for introducing the wilderness concept, based on the idea that untrammeled and unmanaged nature merits protection for recreational and other purposes. During the 1920s, Aldo Leopold and other visionary Forest Service employees convinced the agency to set aside several large tracts of undeveloped forest lands as primitive areas exempt from logging or other industrial activities. Protective regulations soon ensued. However, following World War II, when the Forest Service began to invade these administratively protected areas for timber, wilderness advocates realized that only congressional legislation would ensure permanent protection for these undeveloped lands.

In 1964, Congress responded by adopting the Wilderness Act, which defined "wilderness" as "an area of undeveloped Federal land retaining its primeval character and influence, without permanent improvements or human habitation, which is protected and managed so as to preserve its natural conditions."[6] The act also created seven million acres of "instant" national forest wilderness and instructed the Forest Service, Park Service, and U.S. Fish and Wildlife Service to inventory their respective lands and recommend potential wilderness areas for legislative designation. In 1976, with the passage of the Federal Land Policy and Management Act, the BLM was given similar wilderness inventory and management responsibilities.[7]

By the latter part of the twentieth century, biodiversity and ecosystem conservation emerged as important preservation goals. Faced with an accelerating extinction rate and an increasingly destructive human presence across the landscape, scientists warned that our biological heritage (along with its incalculable medical and other benefits) was imperiled. Congress reacted with laws like the Endangered Species Act (ESA)[8] and the Wild and Scenic Rivers Act.[9] The ESA extended federal protection to imperiled species facing potential extinction, and it empowered the U.S. Fish and Wildlife Service to designate critical habitat on both federal and private lands to help safeguard protected species. The Wild and Scenic Rivers Act extended federal protection to ecologically important river corridors in an effort to protect these sensitive areas from dams and other development pressures. Underlying these new federal preservation programs was recognition that science had an important role to play in making protective decisions.

The nature preservation idea has also been extended to embrace cultural preservation as an important related federal management responsibility. Where early preservation campaigns focused on protecting landscapes in a natural condition without human uses or intrusion, more recent protective efforts have recognized preexisting human activities and sought to incorporate them into the protective designations. This is reflected in the Alaska National Interest Lands Conservation Act's subsistence provision,[10] the King Range National Conservation Area multiple-use provisions,[11] and in various national heritage area designations, such as the Blue Ridge National Heritage Area.[12] The concept of cultural preservation is also an acknowledgment that a human presence and economic activity are not always incompatible with preservationist objectives.

In short, the preservation impulse is now an amalgam of motivations, with biodiversity and ecosystem conservation assuming an ever more important role. But it is not always easy to translate these science-based concerns into a compelling political argument to support protecting ecologically sensitive public lands in wilderness or other protective designations. Ecological preservation proponents, therefore, must not discount the emotional and political appeal of aesthetic, spiritual, and recreation arguments that can be tied to biodiversity conservation objectives.

II.   Federal Preservation Strategies

The basic strategies employed to protect special public lands have not changed. Decisions regarding the public lands have long been shaped in political venues, and politics therefore figures prominently in nearly every preservation decision. As a result, the nature conservation movement has long relied upon a strong grassroots citizen-activist network. Put simply, preservation cannot be divorced from politics, which means public support is key to protecting sensitive public lands and resources.

A. The Congressional Role

Under the Property Clause in the U.S. Constitution, Congress is given power to "make all needful Rules and Regulations respecting the . . . Property belonging to the United States."[13] Vested with this authority, Congress has historically played a major role in federal land preservation, assuming primary responsibility for designating national parks, wilderness areas, wild and scenic rivers, and many wildlife refuges. Congress has also adopted organic acts—like the National Park Service Organic Act and the Wilderness Act—to govern the major land preservation systems, as well as separate enabling acts for individual protected areas, which may occasionally deviate from the overarching organic mandate. Further, Congress can override the land preservation decisions made by others; it may, for example, reverse a presidential national monument designation decision.

Given this prominent congressional role, preservation decisions have generally reflected a bipartisan consensus of national and local interests. Compromise provisions are thus evident in many national park enabling statutes, as well as in the Wilderness Act of 1964, which contains various grandfather provisions and other exceptions that were incorporated into this otherwise powerfully protective statute.[14] Over the past 40 years, however, the politics of preservation has devolved, as reflected in the shrinking scope and size of most recent wilderness bills and the increasing need within the bills to accommodate nonpreservation local needs, such as community economic development. Since the mid-1980s, with only a few exceptions, wilderness bills have addressed only one or two proposed designations in a single state; prior to that time, Congress had regularly legislated wilderness on a regional or statewide basis. Compare, for example, the 20 separate state wilderness bills that Congress passed in 1984, which created more than six million acres of new wilderness lands, with the Northern California Coastal Wild Heritage Wilderness Act of 2006, which was focused on a specific region and designated just 275,000 acres of new wilderness.[15]

B. The Use of Executive Authority

The President has also long played an important role in protecting public lands and sensitive resources. In the Antiquities Act of 1906,

Congress delegated explicit land-preservation authority, empowering the President to create national monuments in order to protect "objects of historic or scientific interest."[16] Many of the nation's most cherished national parks—Grand Canyon and Zion, for example—were originally protected by presidential decrees as national monuments, and only later gained national park status when Congress was persuaded to grant it. In addition, the President can withdraw public lands or resources from exploitation or development. This inherent withdrawal authority is derived from the President's constitutional executive powers, which Theodore Roosevelt relied upon to create unilaterally the nation's first wildlife refuge at Pelican Island in Florida. This withdrawal authority now has an explicit statutory basis in the Federal Land Policy and Management Act, which authorizes the Secretary of the Interior to withdraw public lands—a power that has regularly been used to protect sensitive areas from development pending a more definitive preservation decision.[17]

The federal land management agencies have utilized their own administrative powers to protect roadless or sensitive lands. The Forest Service first employed this strategy to create primitive areas in 1924 and then to adopt regulations limiting commercial activity in these areas. More recently, under the Clinton administration, the Forest Service used its general rulemaking authority to promulgate a controversial national forest roadless area rule that protected more than 58 million acres of undeveloped, roadless forest land from further timber harvesting, mineral leasing, or road building. (See the sidebar for a more detailed description of the Forest Service's roadless area rule and its subsequent history.) The Federal Land Policy and Management Act authorized the Bureau of Land Management (BLM) to designate wilderness study areas that enjoy significant statutory protection pending a final congressional wilderness designation decision.[18] The same statute authorizes the BLM to designate Areas of Environmental Concern, which can be used to protect sensitive landscapes and resources.[19] Moreover, most commentators agree that the land management agencies have the legal authority under their general rulemaking power to regulate threatening activities on adjacent privately owned lands, though political considerations have deterred the agencies from utilizing this authority aggressively.

The federal agencies can also employ other administrative strategies to protect sensitive lands or resources from intensive development. These strategies are linked to the agencies' general organic mandates and their planning responsibilities, as well as other laws, such as the Endangered Species Act, that superimpose explicit resource-protection obligations on them. Drawing upon this authority, the Forest Service has adopted the Northwest Forest Plan, which created special old-growth reserves to protect the northern spotted owl, and the Sierra Nevada Framework Plan, which established old-forest emphasis areas to limit logging. The Forest Service has also designated various Research Natural Areas to preserve baseline conditions in order to better understand forest ecology, and the U.S. Fish and Wildlife Service has invoked its authority under the Endangered Species Act to make critical habitat designations that limit logging, mining, and other industrial activities.[20] Though these administrative decisions do not have the same legal stature as legislative national park or wilderness designations, they have effectively expanded the scope and breadth of protected acreage on the public lands.

C. The Land Exchange Option

The land exchange represents another strategy that can be employed—either legislatively or administratively—to expand and safeguard protected areas. Land exchanges can be used to "block up" federal landholdings, to alleviate inholdings and related access problems, and to address difficult boundary management issues. In recent years, Congress has approved several large-scale federal land exchanges, such as the Utah School and Lands Exchange Act of 1998, which eliminated state trust land holdings from within Utah's national parks, national forests, and the new Grand Staircase–Escalante National Monument, thus enabling federal managers to better protect these areas from access roads and industrial activities.[21] However, whether initiated by the agencies or by Congress, land exchanges can pose difficult and sometimes controversial valuation issues, because the exchanges must be for equal value.

D. Judicial Intervention and Oversight

During the past several decades, the federal courts have played an increasingly important role in protecting undeveloped public lands until Congress decides whether to make a wilderness or other protective designation. Even before the Wilderness Act was adopted, federal courts intervened to safeguard unroaded lands. In *McMichael v. United States*, the court upheld the Forest Service's primitive area regulations limiting motorized access.[22] Under the Wilderness Act, the Federal Land Policy and Management Act wilderness provision, and other laws, the courts have proven willing to protect roadless areas pending a final congressional wilderness designation decision. In *California v. Block*, for example, the federal courts relied upon the National Environmental Policy Act to stop the Forest Service from opening roadless lands that it did not regard as wilderness-worthy in its second roadless area review process.[23] In addition, the courts have blocked the agencies from opening protected areas to development. In *California ex rel. Lockyer v. U.S. Forest Service*, for example, a federal court recently enjoined the Forest Service from logging in the Giant Sequoia National Monument.[24]

III. Management and Preservation

Simply putting federal lands into national park, wilderness, or other protective status, however, does not ensure that the area will be fully protected from human activities and their impacts. Indeed, some of the most vexing questions that agencies and the preservation community face today involve management of protected areas. How these management issues are addressed and resolved can—and undoubtedly will—influence future strategies for designating and protecting public lands. The answers could either promote or retard protective efforts.

First is the question of whether national parks, wilderness areas, or other protected areas should be actively or passively managed.

What degree of human intervention, if any, is appropriate to ensure the area's resource values are protected or restored? More specifically, should park managers extinguish wildfires to protect park resources, or should naturally ignited fires be allowed to burn despite damage to forest landscapes and scenic vistas? Should park managers manipulate wildlife populations, for example, by culling excess elk or deer from local herds, or should nature be allowed to take its course and weed out the most vulnerable animals? How these questions are answered is also affected by the proximity of the protected lands to nearby communities and private lands that might be adversely affected by runaway wildfires or excessive ungulate populations. The fear that these threats may not be controlled adequately has frequently fostered opposition to protected area designation proposals.

A second management question involves the potential conflict between protecting the landscape and permitting recreational access. Given that most protected areas are also designed to provide recreational opportunities, managers must decide how many visitors can be accommodated and what types of activities are appropriate. There is little dispute over the authority of park and wilderness managers to control entry and limit visitation, though visitors sometimes resent being turned away from popular areas or told that to enter they must use public transportation rather than their own private automobile. Much more disagreement persists over whether off-road vehicles, snowmobiles, and personal watercraft should be permitted in national parks and other recreational areas, as well as how such vehicles should be regulated. In fact, wilderness and other protective designation proposals have regularly foundered because of opposition from off-road enthusiasts concerned that such a designation will deny them access to a popular recreational site.

A third and relatively recent question involves the need to integrate effectively the multiple-use concept into the management of protected areas. This is a question that has surfaced in the aftermath of the Clinton-era multiple-use national monument designations, such as the Grand Staircase–Escalante National Monument in southern Utah, which is generally off-limits to mining, energy, and logging but open to livestock grazing, hunting, and various recreational uses. Most of the other BLM-managed national monuments contain similar provisions in their enabling proclamations, requiring the agency to preserve monument resources while allowing some intensive and potentially damaging activities to continue. Despite the obvious management challenges this type of arrangement raises, ensuring that locally important activities are not prohibited can help promote local political support for a protective designation. Given the political nature of preservation decisions, any approach that reduces local opposition to such designations will ultimately help facilitate the protection of federal lands. The challenge for agencies is to meet their resource protection responsibilities while still accommodating compatible human activities on the landscape.

A related fourth issue raises the question whether it is legal or appropriate for federal agencies to relinquish management responsibility for a protected area to a nonfederal or private entity. One strategy for garnering local support for federal land preservation is to enable local communities or citizens to play a meaningful role in managing the area. This is what the National Park Service did with the Niobrara National Scenic River in Nebraska when it adopted a management plan empowering a citizen council to oversee administration of the river corridor. In *National Parks Conservation Ass'n v. Stanton*, however, a federal district court ruled that the Park Service had unlawfully delegated its management duties to a nonfederal entity that did not share the same national preservation vision and was not bound by federal environmental and other laws.[25] More recently, a similar proposal involving the U.S. Fish and Wildlife Service and the Salish and Kootenai Indian Tribes for sharing management of the National Bison Range in Montana stalled over concerns that federal officials have given the tribe too great a role in the refuge's management. Federal officials in most instances must retain final decision-making authority.

Put simply, the threshold preservation decision cannot be divorced from related management issues. Important legal questions and political concerns must be addressed by preservation advocates as part of the calculus over whether and how to protect sensitive federal lands or resources. How these questions are answered will increasingly either advance or impede protective efforts.

IV. Reflections on the Future

What does the evolution of preservation policy and strategy suggest about the future? With the usual provisos about the hazards of prediction, several observations seem in order, recognizing that the contentious political nature of federal land preservation requires a long-term perspective and occasionally leads to the unexpected.

A. Contemporary Tensions

Traditionally, the preservation debate has been cast as pitting development against conservation. The turn of the century Muir-Pinchot face-off over construction of the Hetch Hetchy Dam in Yosemite National Park epitomizes this debate. The same conflict continues today, as reflected in the controversy over energy leasing and development in sensitive locations such as the Rocky Mountain Front, Otero Mesa, Roan Plateau, and elsewhere across the intermountain West. The current debate finds national energy concerns arrayed against coalitions of local residents and other groups intent on protecting special areas from industrial development. These political alignments are quite different from those that have ordinarily contested federal land preservation proposals, namely, national conservation groups opposed by local interests wedded to extraction-based economic development.

It is no longer accurate (if it ever was) to suggest that a preservation decision inevitably portends adverse economic consequences for nearby communities or local citizens. Rather, such a decision may promote tourism, recreation, and real estate activities, and thus offer different but nonetheless positive economic incentives for nearby residents. But tourism and recreation, along with the second-home development that the presence of protected lands can stimulate, are not ecologically benign activities. They can bring hordes of people, trails, roads, and new construction to the area, which can fragment the landscape, disturb human-sensitive species, and adversely effect riparian and other sensitive areas. These consequences can be every bit as environmentally damaging as those associated with logging, mining, and other industrial uses.

The preservation–utilization debate has become more complicated as recreational use of the public lands has continued to grow, diversify, and assume ever greater economic importance. Early on, we relied heavily on the marriage between preservation and recreation to secure support for protective designations and to limit industrial uses. But over time, that traditional alliance has frayed. Old and new recreation constituencies now regularly find themselves at odds over the types of recreational activities—off-road vehicles, mountain bikes, base jumping, and the like—that should be permitted in a protected area. Is mountain biking, for example, consistent with the preservation goals for a national park or wilderness area, where such activities are generally prohibited? These differences can pit an assortment of recreational constituencies against one another over the purpose, designation, and management of proposed protected areas.

Though the primary motivations for public land preservation have long been aesthetics and recreation, public concern over the environment has elevated biodiversity and ecosystem conservation on the preservation agenda. This new emphasis on ecological science, however, has called into question the original enclave theory of nature conservation, which held that setting aside designated national parks, refuges, and wilderness areas was sufficient to protect the biological and other resources found within these areas. But we now understand that the linear boundaries used to define these sanctuaries do not adequately safeguard them from such natural forces as wildfires or from external influences, such as adjacent logging or residential development. Because nature regularly ignores the legal boundary lines we have drawn on maps, we must begin to plan and manage across jurisdictional boundaries in order to achieve lasting conservation objectives.

Moreover, the island metaphor that has long been used to characterize national parks and other protected areas has taken on new meaning. Most of the early national parks, refuges, and wilderness areas were located in remote areas removed from most human habitation. As a result, these protected areas were regarded as island sanctuaries, generally well buffered by surrounding undeveloped public or private lands. But that is no longer the case. Nature loving citizens now regularly seek the beauty, solitude, and recreational opportunities found near these protected lands, and residential development is sprawling right up to the boundary lines. This is creating evident frictions between federal protective management objectives and the interests of neighboring property owners. Our protected areas, in short, are becoming isolated islands amidst human-dominated landscapes.

B. Thinking on a Large Scale

With public land preservation efforts increasingly linked with biodiversity and ecosystem conservation goals, there is a gathering consensus that protected areas must be both large and interconnected to provide adequate habitat and migration corridors. Most scientists now agree that current national parks and other nature reserves are too small to sufficiently protect many species or to allow historical ecological processes to operate unimpeded. Not only have native species been extirpated from national parks over the past century, but others are imperiled, as reflected by the many endangered species listings and the growing impact of climate change. The answer, according to conservation biologists, is to expand and connect protected areas in order to facilitate migration, dispersal, and gene exchange, and to provide protection against catastrophic events like runaway wildfires, flooding, and earthquakes.

Several efforts have already been undertaken to pursue these large-scale ecological preservation goals. At the governmental level, these include: the Northwest Forest Plan and its interlinked late-successional reserves; the Sierra Nevada Framework's old forest emphasis areas; the now-defunct Interior Columbia Basin Ecosystem Management Project, with its protected nature reserves; the creation of the Giant Sequoia National Monument adjacent to Sequoia National Park; and the Forest Service's 2001 roadless area rule, which originally placed more than 58 million acres off limits to logging, mining, or roadbuilding. Nongovernmental groups have advocated other large-scale land protection initiatives, including the Greater Yellowstone, Crown of the Continent, and similar regional or "greater ecosystem" management proposals; the Yellowstone to Yukon continental-scale conservation initiative extending along the spine of the Rocky Mountains; the multistate Northern Rockies Ecosystem Protection Act legislative proposal, with its expanded and connected wilderness areas; and the expansive Wildlands Project with its regional nature reserve and connective corridor proposals. Other such concepts include the northern Great Plains Buffalo Commons and the Great North Woods, both of which seek to protect vast swathes of public and private lands.

The common thread uniting these large-scale conservation initiatives is recognition of the need to stitch the fragmented landscape together. Effective preservation efforts focused on biodiversity and ecosystem conservation must integrate publicly and privately owned lands into a functional system of interconnected nature reserves. The traditional strategies for doing this include land exchanges, conservation easements, coordinated management, targeted financial incentives, and regulatory constraints. This also could include fusing natural and cultural preservation objectives, with a view toward preserving (and perhaps restoring) the landscape while incorporating local residents and communities into the reconfigured landscape.

One way to expand and connect protected areas is to create new ecosystem or biodiversity reserve designations based on the principle of sustainability. These reserves would be designed to achieve specific ecological preservation objectives while integrating nearby communities into the conservation effort and allowing some economic activities to continue. More specifically, local residents might be afforded a meaningful role in managing the protected area, offered conditional financial incentives geared toward promoting compatible economic activities, or provided nonimpairing economic opportunities within the reserve itself, such as ecotourism concessions or bioprospecting. The key is to secure local support for the designation and for the ensuing conservation effort.

Some examples of these types of hybrid conservation arrangements already exist in several locations. They include the Clinton-era multiple-use national monuments, the United Nations' biosphere reserve program, and the various national heritage area designations.[26] Moreover, Congress has passed several bills that combine wilderness designations with other conservation and economic development provisions, including the Steens Mountain Cooperative Management and Protective Area Act, which added 150,000 acres to BLM's wilderness inventory, authorized several strategic land exchanges, and established an advisory citizens' management council;[27] and the White Pine County Conservation, Recreation, and Development Act of 2006, which designated more than 500,000 acres of new wilderness while authorizing various land transfers and sales.[28] Yet other such legislative proposals are pending; these include the Owyhee Initiative Implementation Act, which would designate 517,000 acres of wilderness in southwestern Idaho, create a travel plan limiting motorized access, and establish a panel of experts to review federal livestock grazing decisions,[29] and the Washington County Growth and Conservation Act, which would designate nearly 265,000 acres of wilderness in southwestern Utah, establish two new national conservation areas, authorize the sale of 9,000 acres of local federal lands for development purposes, and create new off-highway vehicle recreational trails.[30] In each instance, the legislation is designed to address local economic and other concerns while expanding the federal preserved land base.

With the ubiquitous and growing presence of people and homes on the landscape, an expanded ecological conservation agenda will have to accommodate (or at least tolerate) a greater human presence either in or immediately adjacent to protected areas. This marks a significant departure from the original goal of the Yellowstone legislation and the Wilderness Act, which sought to preserve natural areas free from any permanent human presence. But it does not diminish the need to increase and enlarge protected areas on the public lands to provide adequate sanctuary for at-risk species and to allow basic ecological processes to operate without regular disruption. The challenge is to stitch the landscape together into a sustainable whole, and thus meet human needs and ensure the long term viability of our natural heritage. Put simply, an expanded nature reserve system must be both ecologically and politically tenable.

C. Preservation and Restoration

The traditional view of wilderness and other protected area designations has been to preserve relatively undisturbed landscapes, but there is no reason why future nature reserves could not be fashioned from once-harvested timber lands and other disturbed landscapes. During the early twentieth century, under the Weeks Act of 1911, the federal government reacquired depleted eastern and midwestern forest lands and then spent the next several decades restoring these cut-over landscapes.[31] Today these national forest lands provide valuable open space, wildlife habitat, recreational opportunities, and wilderness retreats for a large segment of the public. Similarly, the Great Smoky Mountains and Shenandoah national parks were each cobbled together with depleted private lands that were eventually restored to a more natural condition.

Drawing upon the field of restoration ecology, we might consider creating new restoration reserves to extend and diversify the preservation effort across the landscape. Over recent years, restoration ecologists have gained significant insights into how to restore damaged landscapes, while conservation biologists now have much greater understanding of the value of particular landscapes for biodiversity and other ecological purposes. New restoration reserves could provide an opportunity to expand the effective boundaries of existing national parks and wilderness areas, and it would lay the groundwork for an entirely new network of protected areas that would realize their full potential over time. Given that many of our logged-out timber lands or overgrazed range lands are located at low elevations where few protected areas have been established, this restoration reserve strategy could provide important ecological diversity to the suite of preserved federal lands, many of which are located at higher elevations. It also could provide local employment opportunities for displaced loggers and other workers, and help address local fire management concerns. And with proper planning, this approach could serve as a proactive response to the potential impact of global warming on the public lands and native biodiversity.

D. The Funding Quandary

A major hurdle to contemporary preservation efforts is the lack of adequate financial resources to acquire sensitive lands that are in private ownership. This has traditionally been done using funds from the Land and Water Conservation Fund, which consists of offshore oil and gas royalty revenues. But these monies are not available unless Congress actually appropriates the funds. With current federal budget concerns and deficits, Congress has not been inclined to allocate substantial amounts for nature conservation. Instead, land exchanges can be arranged to acquire strategic private lands in some instances; but this strategy depends on identifying mutually agreeable lands that can be exchanged and that meet the equal value statutory exchange criteria.

Is it possible, therefore, to create a dedicated public land preservation funding source removed from the vicissitudes of every day politics? Some potential, though controversial, options for new funding sources include: earmarking federal on-shore oil and gas or new mineral royalties for land conservation purchases; establishing a new tax on outdoor recreational equipment for federal land acquisition purposes; directing a portion of national park entrance or other user fees for in-holding and adjacent land purchases; and creating a federal income tax checkoff for land conservation similar to the presidential election campaign checkoff option. If one or another of these new funding sources could be created, then Congress also must be persuaded to ensure that the funds would be dedicated to land preservation. But getting Congress to relinquish control over federal expenditures is always difficult, because control over funding equates to political power. A new funding source would thus require a strong, bipartisan effort, and would almost certainly prompt lawmakers to ask whether federal land acquisition authority would include condemnation authority or just be limited to voluntary transactions.

Any significantly expanded federal public land conservation effort will also raise questions about how to offset lost resource-production revenues for the states and local communities. The traditional method that Congress has used to address this issue is the Payment in Lieu of Taxes (PILT) funds that are dispersed to counties based upon the amount of federal acreage within their borders. While these PILT funds were ordinarily linked to timber and other resource production levels, Congress has recently sought to decouple PILT payments from commodity production, recognizing that the connection created perverse incentives that often ran contrary to federal land management goals. In addition, Congress could actually use the PILT system to encourage private land conservation by conditioning PILT payments on adoption and implementation of local land-use plans that meet clearly defined federal conservation standards. This would provide a local economic incentive for private land conservation consistent with adjacent federal land conservation strategies, and thus could help stitch the fragmented public and private landscape together into a sustainable ecological whole.

E. Preservation Politics Revisited

Public land preservation decisions are fundamentally political decisions, whether made at the congressional, presidential, or agency level. Though difficult to gauge accurately, there seems to be widespread public support for protecting environmental values on public lands and for adding to the protected lands inventory. The challenge is to translate this generalized support into the political consensus necessary to achieve wilderness or other protective designations.

The need for public consensus then poses the question: should federal land preservation decisions be made at the national, state, or local level? For the most part, these decisions have been made at the national level, either by Congress, the President, or the agencies, which is what the Forest Service did with its sweeping 2001 roadless rule, described in the sidebar. The logic of this national approach is evident: these are publicly owned lands with significant nationwide constituencies; ecosystem-scale conservation requires a regional or multijurisdictional perspective; wilderness and related preservation issues have traditionally been addressed at the national level; and history has repeatedly demonstrated that parochial interests can crater or dilute even the most well-intentioned local conservation effort. Besides, the Constitution vests Congress with final authority over the public lands.

History also suggests, however, that state and local support is ultimately necessary to secure congressional endorsement of preservation proposals. This has proven true for new wilderness designations, as well as for presidential or agency protective designations, such as presidentially-decreed national monuments that may merit elevation to national park status. A purely national approach to preservation can overlook important local concerns, which can help foment ongoing local resistance (and perhaps even sabotage) to the conservation effort. Local knowledge of on-the-ground conditions can also be helpful in shaping an effective conservation initiative. This may explain why Congress, where state and local interests are represented and regularly heard, has long been the principal decision maker for public land preservation issues in our federal system. But when Congress either cannot or will not act and when important resource values are at risk from local intransigence, the President and the agencies have sufficient authority to protect these lands, at least until Congress steps forward. And they, like Congress, can be held accountable through the political process.

Another question—addressed in more detail in chapter 8—is whether and how the public should be involved in federal land preservation decisions. History demonstrates that grassroots citizen activism has regularly served as the catalyst for protective designations, thus supporting the notion of robust public involvement in these decisions. But the level and type of public engagement may well vary depending on the decision-making entity. Given the predominant congressional role in such decisions and the generally transparent nature of the legislative process, the public has ample opportunity to make its views known in this arena. The same is not true, however, when the President acts unilaterally under the Antiquities Act or invokes his withdrawal authority, though this power is generally used only when resources face imminent damage or local interests have persistently blocked otherwise popular preservation proposals in Congress. If the President miscalculates, then Congress can always intervene and override his decision, and the President is himself politically accountable to the national electorate. When an agency, through its planning or other processes, contemplates making a protective designation, as the Forest Service did during the Clinton years with its roadless rule, it must adhere to National Environmental Policy Act and other public involvement requirements. This process not only affords the general public (including local residents) an opportunity to express its views, but also means the agency's decision-making process can be subjected to judicial review. The public, thus, has one or more venues available to assert itself, which should protect against unbridled agency unilateralism.

Yet another question is whether administrative protective designations are secure once political power shifts from one party to another, as it inevitably will. The answer is clearly no, as illustrated by the Bush administration's prompt and significant revisions to the Clinton administration's national forest roadless area conservation rule, as explained in the sidebar. Although Congress can always intervene in such agency rulemaking matters, such intervention requires a strong political consensus that can be difficult to muster. The courts can be brought into the fray, as has occurred with both the Clinton- and Bush-era roadless area rules, though judicial intervention has provided mixed and uncertain results thus far. Nonetheless, when Congress has repeatedly defaulted on an important national conservation issue, agency action—through rulemaking or otherwise—may be the only avenue available to protect sensitive lands or resources. Though sometimes problematic, these agency decisions can be both bolstered and legitimized through inclusive collaborative strategies designed to build broad-based public support for the protective measures. Not only can such a collaborative strategy help prevent future challenges to the action, it may even induce Congress to adopt legislation confirming the negotiated arrangement.

V. Conclusion

This brief excursion through federal land preservation law and policy highlights the political nature of public land preservation decisions and the need to seek consensus over such matters in our federal system. That said, federal land protection efforts have expanded dramatically over the past century and show no sign of abating. The general public plainly supports the notion of preserving our shared natural heritage, a sentiment that is only growing stronger as natural landscapes continue to disappear at an alarming rate. The rising concern over biodiversity and ecosystem conservation is forcing us to rethink our preservation efforts, drawing upon the compelling scientific evidence that we need larger and more interconnected nature reserves to ensure this precious heritage. In response, we have seen Congress, the President, and the responsible agencies take some initial steps toward new landscape-scale conservation initiatives and hybrid protective designations. As we enter this new era in land conservation, these efforts might include new ecosystem or biodiversity reserves, as well as restoration reserves to remediate our past excesses. The ultimate goal, as it has been all along, must be to marry politics and ecology in the name of preservation.

Epilogue

In early 2009, Congress passed and the President signed into law the Omnibus Public Land Management Act of 2009 that cumulatively protects more than two million acres of new wilderness areas on federally owned lands. The Omnibus Act, an amalgam of over 160 separate bills addressing the public lands and related conservation concerns, has been widely hailed as the most significant piece of conservation legislation passed in the last 15 years. Besides creating new wilderness areas, the bill added nearly 1100 miles to the National Wild and Scenic River System in seven states, increased the National Trails System by more than 2800 miles, and established several new national monuments and national conservation areas. It also formalized the Bureau of Land Management's National Landscape Conservation System, giving the BLM explicit legal responsibility for over 26 million acres of protected public lands consisting of national monuments, wilderness areas, national conservation areas, areas of critical environmental concern, and wilderness study areas. With this landmark legislation, Congress has clearly inserted itself back into the public land preservation process and signaled its willingness to review and confirm carefully negotiated preservationist legislation.

The Omnibus Act created 15 new or expanded wilderness areas in nine different states: California, Colorado, Idaho, Michigan, New Mexico, Oregon, Utah, Virginia, and West Virginia. Driven by persistent citizen activists, many of the bills incorporated into the Omnibus Act represented local compromises between divergent interests that not only designated new wilderness lands but also addressed community development and expansion concerns. Notably, the legislation included the Owyhee Public Lands Management Act and the Washington County Growth and Conservation Act, both of which employed hybrid conservation arrangements to establish new BLM wilderness areas in Idaho and Utah. The Omnibus Act also contained several bills that stopped short of new wilderness designations, but still limited development in sensitive areas; the Wyoming Range Legacy Act, for example, withdraws wildlife-rich national forest lands in western Wyoming from any further energy leasing without giving them any additional formal legal protection. The diverse compromises that make up this composite legislation reconfirm the inherent political nature of the preservation process and provide yet more models for advancing the preservation agenda.

The National Forest Roadless Rule

Depending on one's point of view, the Clinton administration's national forest roadless area conservation rule represents either a visionary effort to protect diminishing sensitive landscapes or an audacious executive branch power grab that usurped congressional prerogatives over the public lands. Few, however, would disagree that the expansive roadless national forest lands contain a plethora of both tangible and intangible valuable resources and have long served as a primary battleground over the wisdom of preserving or developing these resources. The roadless rule is only the latest chapter in this saga, which has consumed the Forest Service, Congress, the courts, and the various partisans for nearly a century, with no end in sight.

The Clinton administration's roadless rule and the Bush administration's revised roadless rule raise as many questions as they answer about appropriate strategies and forums for pursuing nature conservation objectives on the public lands. Should nature conservation decisions be treated primarily as scientific or political matters? At what scale—regional, landscape, ecosystem, species, or local—should nature conservation be pursued? At what level—national, state, or local—should nature conservation decisions be made? Who should make those decisions? Congress, the federal agencies, or state or local officials? How, if at all, should the public be involved in these decisions? And what role, if any, should the courts play in these matters?

The current roadless rule is not the first instance in which the Forest Service has used its administrative authority to protect its sensitive, undeveloped lands. By 1929, the agency had classified some of its forest lands as natural, primitive, or wilderness areas, and promulgated regulations designed to preserve these primitive conditions for public education and recreational purposes. By 1939, the Forest Service had designated more than 14 million acres as protected primitive areas and adopted new regulations prohibiting any commercial activities on these lands. But shortly after World War II, the pressure was mounting to open some of these areas for timber harvesting, which the agency began to do over the strenuous objection of preservationists, who then sought more permanent protection for these undeveloped lands.

Thus was borne the Wilderness Act of 1964, which both vested Congress with the power to designate new wilderness areas and extended permanent legislative protection to more than seven million acres of national forest lands. Twice since then the Forest Service has undertaken roadless area reviews of its still-undeveloped lands with the goal of making further wilderness recommendations to Congress, and twice the federal courts have found the agency's review process legally flawed.[32] In the meantime, Congress has proceeded to gradually add federal acreage to the nation's wilderness preservation system, and more than 35 million acres of national forest lands are now classified as official wilderness, though not without heated controversy that has stalled much wilderness legislation over the years and frustrated preservation advocates.

Indeed, the Forest Service's remaining roadless lands have become the primary battleground over preservation versus development on federally owned lands. Formally managed under the agency's Multiple-Use Sustained-Yield Act mandate, these roadless lands have long been coveted by preservationists as additions to the wilderness system, while timber companies and other commodity producers have argued that these lands should be put to productive use and not "locked up" as wilderness.[33] Although the Forest Service left many of these areas undisturbed through its National Forest Management Act–mandated forest planning process, it also opened some areas to logging, road building, and other commercial activities.[34] This forest-by-forest decision process satisfied almost no one, frequently resulting in more controversy, litigation, and even congressional intervention on occasion.

To address this problem, in early 2001, the Clinton administration adopted a national forest roadless area conservation rule that placed nearly 60 million acres of unroaded forest lands off limits to most timber harvesting, road building, and other such activities.[35] According to the Forest Service, the affected lands covered 31 percent of the national forest land base, but accounted for less than 7 percent of the available timber. They served as "biological strongholds for terrestrial and aquatic plants and wildlife and as sources of high-quality water," and sheltered more than half the ESA-listed species found on the national forests. Further, the agency noted: "A growing number of people value Federal lands as a repository of biodiversity and conservation. Many people appreciate national forest system lands more for their inherent naturalness than for the commodities, such as timber, mineral, and grazing, that they can provide." And, in fact, the overwhelming sentiment among those who commented on the original roadless rule proposal supported it.

This executive-level preservation decision unleashed a firestorm of protest among some western states, rural communities, and traditional forest users. Although the Ninth Circuit Court of Appeals sustained the rule against an attack by the state of

Idaho, a Wyoming federal district court invalidated the rule, finding NEPA procedural violations and that the Forest Service had de facto usurped Congress's wilderness designation role in violation of the Wilderness Act.[36] At this point, the Bush administration not only retracted the original roadless rule, but promulgated its own quite different rule that empowered state governors to petition the Forest Service for roadless protection on some or all of the originally designated acreage. To support this change in direction, the agency explained that state involvement "allows for the recognition of local situations and resolutions of unique resource management challenges within a specific State . . . [and] helps ensure balanced management decisions."[37] In a lawsuit initiated by four western states, however, a California federal court ruled that the new Bush administration roadless rule violated NEPA analysis and ESA consultation requirements and enjoined its implementation.[38]

Meanwhile, relying upon the Bush administration's new roadless rule, several states submitted their own roadless area petitions to the Forest Service, which is currently reviewing them under its general administrative authority. Some states created citizen advisory committees to help prepare their roadless petitions, others convened public hearings to secure citizen input, and others chose not to solicit much public comment. Significantly, several states (including California, Oregon, New Mexico, Virginia, and North Carolina) have petitioned the Forest Service to reinstate the Clinton-era roadless area protections on local national forests, while others (including Idaho and Colorado) have submitted less sweeping roadless area petitions that nonetheless would extend administrative protection to substantial acreages. At the same time, Congress has acted piecemeal on various local wilderness designation proposals, such as the Northern California Coastal Wild Heritage Wilderness Act.[39]

The advantages of a national roadless area rule are perhaps evident: it affects all citizens; it demonstrates the wisdom of pursuing ecological conservation objectives on a broader landscape or ecosystem scale; its comprehensiveness helps neutralize the controversy that has for decades plagued agency management of these lands; and it preserves the uniformity that has been a hallmark of the national forest system. The disadvantages are also evident: it does not take account of local needs, concerns, or differences; it disregards or overlooks local knowledge about resource values; it may foment local resistance and undermine cooperative management possibilities; and it will only shift the area of conflict to adjacent lands that buffer the new roadless areas. Of course, just as it has in the past with similar administrative designations, the Forest Service can always independently reverse itself and re-open these lands to industrial activity. The critical substantive question, then, is whether these lands have become more valuable in their undisturbed status or for their productive potential.

The critical procedural question is whether such preservation decisions should be made by Congress, the President, the agencies, state officials, or local entities. Although Congress reserved for itself wilderness designation power in the Wilderness Act, both the President and the agencies have a long history of protecting sensitive or valuable lands, as reflected in the Forest Service's early twentieth-century primitive-area designations and related regulations. Besides, the Forest Service's roadless area rule falls well short of a de facto wilderness designation and can be best understood as a multiple-use management decision that gives priority to wildlife, fish, and recreation, all of which are well within the agency's statutorily delegated authority. Although recent experience with the Bush administration's state petition roadless rule suggests this may be changing, the traditional state and local view toward protective management of national forest lands has been one of resistance linked to lost jobs, tax revenues, and other short-term economic concerns.

As the general public's view of the national forests and other public lands continues to evolve, the trend toward more protection and less industrial use will only grow. This intensifying support should assist agency officials inclined to stretch the limits of their administrative authority through such devices as the national roadless area rule, and it should send a message to Congress as it deliberates over proposed wilderness designations. Besides, the courts have proven willing to intervene to ensure the agency is accountable for such protective decisions, that it has met basic NEPA analysis, ESA consultation, and public engagement legal requirements. Once that has occurred, executive authority seems like an eminently sensible way to preserve natural landscapes without precluding alternative uses if future needs or demands change.

Notes

1.   16 U.S.C. §§ 21–22.
2.   16 U.S.C. § 1.
3.   Alfred Runte, National Parks: The American Experience 11–32 (2d ed. 1987).
4.   Richard West Sellars, Preserving Nature in the National Parks 58–66 (1997).
5.   Organic Administration Act of June 4, 1897, 30 Stat. 35 (codified at 16 U.S.C. §§ 473 et seq.).
6.   16 U.S.C. § 1131(c).
7.   43 U.S.C. § 1782.
8.   16 U.S.C. §§ 1531–43.
9.   16 U.S.C. §§ 1271–87.
10. 16 U.S.C. §§ 3111–26.
11. 16 U.S.C. § 460y.
12. 117 Stat. 1241 (2003).
13. U.S. Const. art. IV, § 2.
14. 16 U.S.C. § 1133(d).
15. Northern California Coastal Wild Heritage Wilderness Act of 2006, Pub. L. No. 109-362, 120 Stat. 2064 (2006).
16. 16 U.S.C. § 431.
17. 43 U.S.C. § 1714.
18. 43 U.S.C. § 1782.
19. 43 U.S.C. § 1712(c)(3).
20. 16 U.S.C. § 1533(b)(2).
21. Utah School and Lands Exchange Act of 1998, Pub. L. No. 105-335, 112 Stat. 3139 (1998).
22. McMichael v. United States, 355 F.2d 283 (9th Cir. 1965).
23. California v. Block, 690 F.2d 753 (9th Cir. 1982). See also Utah v. Andrus, 486 F. Supp. 995 (D. Utah 1979) (protecting BLM wilderness study area lands);

and Parker v. United States, 448 F.2d 793 (10th Cir. 1971) (prohibiting logging on unroaded national forest lands adjacent to a designated wilderness area).

24.   California *ex rel.* Lockyer v. U.S. Forest Serv., 465 F. Supp. 2d 942 (N.D. Cal. 2006).

25.   Nat'l Parks Conservation Ass'n v. Stanton, 54 F. Supp. 2d 7 (D.D.C. 1999).

26.   *See generally* National Heritage Area Partnership Act, S. 278, 110th Cong., 1st sess. (2007).

27.   16 U.S.C. § 460nnn.

28.   White Pine County Conservation, Recreation, and Development Act of 2006, Pub. L. No. 109-432 § 301 et seq., 120 Stat. 3032 (2006).

29.   Owyhee Initiative Implementation Act, S. 802, 110th Cong., 1st sess. (2007).

30.   Washington County Growth and Conservation Act, S. 2834, 110th Cong., 2d sess. (2008).

31.   Weeks Act of 1911, Pub. L. No. 61-435, 36 Stat. 961.

32.   *See, e.g.,* Wyoming Outdoor Council v. Butz, 484 F.2d 1244 (10th Cir. 1973); California v. Block, 690 F.2d 753 (9th Cir. 1982).

33.   16 U.S.C. §§ 428–31.

34.   16 U.S.C. § 1604.

35.   66 Fed. Reg. 35,918 (July 10, 2000).

36.   *See* Kootenai Tribe of Idaho v. Veneman, 313 F.3d 1094 (9th Cir. 2002); Wyoming v. U.S. Dept. of Agric., 277 F. Supp. 2d 1197 (D. Wyo. 2003).

37.   70 Fed. Reg. 25,654, 25,655 (May 13, 2005).

38.   California *ex rel.* Lockyer v. U.S. Dept. of Agric., 459 F. Supp. 2d 874 (N.D. Cal. 2006).

39.   Northern California Coastal Wild Heritage Wilderness Act, Pub. L. No. 109-362, 120 Stat. 2064 (2006).

11

Dam Building and Removal on the Elwha

A Prototype of Adaptive Mismanagement and a Tribal Opportunity

William H. Rodgers, Jr.

I.   Introduction

[A great experiment in restoration ecology awaits us at points] past the dam and the reservoir and into the hills and canyons of the Olympic National Park. . . . It is still wild and nearly pristine, having been protected for over fifty years by the Olympic National Park.
> —Jim Lichatowich, *Salmon Without Rivers: A History of the Pacific Salmon Crisis*

Dams on the Elwha River in Olympic National Park provide the classic case of enduring, illegally constructed dams.
> —David R. Montgomery, *King of Fish: The Thousand-Year Run of Salmon*

The prospect of the removal of the Elwha River dams—the Elwha Dam at river mile 4.9 and the Glines Canyon Dam, further upstream at river mile 8.0—is remarkable for several reasons. The perpetrators who illegally built the dams did so through a devious wave of law-breaking that can only inspire warm thoughts of corrective justice. The dams destroyed 10 magnificent runs of anadromous fish—among them the famed Elwha River chinook salmon, un-

282

equaled in size and strength. Removal of the dams presents a significant opportunity for a scientific study of restoration that has experts raring to go. Moreover, given its importance to Native American fishing rights, corrective action will be celebrated far beyond the Lower Elwha Indian reservation that sits at the base of the Olympic Peninsula in the Straits of Juan de Fuca.

From a biological perspective, the expected payoffs for fisheries restoration are high—and have been for decades. If there is such a thing as low-hanging fruit in this business of building a better world, the Elwha is the place to find it.

But from an engineering perspective the Elwha dam removals are far from a trivial undertaking. These were major works to build, and it will take major work to remove them. Glines Canyon is 210 feet high—taller than any of the hundreds of small dams removed in the United States in recent years. The structures are rickety and dangerous. Weather is bad. Slopes are steep. Accumulations of sediment are enormous—far beyond mere nuisance levels. This will prove to be a difficult, costly, and prolonged job.

Legally, the Elwha dams offer another package of precedents. Some questions were answered—and new ones raised—by the 1992 congressional "settlement" of this matter, the Elwha River Ecosystem and Fisheries Restoration Act.[1] In addition, the downstream Lower Elwha Klallam Tribe has valuable fishing rights reserved by the 1855 Treaty of Point-no-Point.[2] Regionally, these tribal fishing rights are known as the "Boldt fishing rights," named after the rulings of federal district judge George Boldt that made them secure. Generally, tribes are entitled to up to 50 percent of the harvestable portions of anadromous fish runs passing through their usual and accustomed areas. Recently, a federal district judge in Seattle added further legal muscle to these treaties by ruling that they require removal of highway culverts that obstruct fish passage.[3] Under this rationale, the Elwha dams are monstrous culverts.

In a 1989 brochure the Lower Elwha River Tribal Council described the situation thus:

> In the case of the Elwha River the United States has allowed private hydroelectric developments to stop a treaty-guaranteed

reservation fishery for 75 years. It has permitted exploitation of the river at the expense of the families who can least afford to underwrite it, increased the poverty of the Tribe by drastically reducing its principal economic resource, caused the depletion of reservation beaches, and forced the Tribe to live downstream from an unsafe Dam.

II. Timeline

This chapter is organized around seven "adaptive management moments," a term that I describe in greater detail in part III, below. The first of these was the long period of adamant and formal fish protection that ran from 1848 to 1915 in Washington territory and state. Next came the dramatic legal phase-changes that took place on the Elwha in 1914 and 1915, when fisheries management authorities chose to accept the dam with a hatchery as compensation for fish losses, first in the particular case of the Elwha and then in all similar cases.

The third and fourth moments took place in 1992, when Congress launched the restoration of the Elwha by making crucial policy choices to acquire the dams and effect removal with public funds, and to do so only after all affected parties had received satisfactory mitigation.

Moments five through seven look ahead to the restoration of the Elwha. The work will take place against an institutional background of scientific uncertainty and waffling goals, which I also call the baseline question (moment five); international conflict, manifested in the Pacific Salmon Treaty of 1985 (moment six); and political opportunism, which I will call the declaration of success (moment seven).

A description of the events that make up these adaptive management moments is provided in the timeline below.

1848   Congress adopts no-obstruction law for fisheries in the Territory of Oregon[4]

1855   Governor of Washington and tribal leaders sign Point-No-Point Treaty

1859   U.S. Senate ratifies Point-No-Point Treaty, securing tribal fisheries

1881   Before statehood, the Washington territorial legislature makes it a crime to place "any obstruction" in rivers frequented by salmon for spawning without constructing a "suitable fishway"[5]

1889   Washington becomes a state

1889–90   The Washington state legislature reenacts the 1881 protective measure[6]

1894   Thomas T. Aldwell secures a "homestead" on the Elwha with power site potential and makes plans for a hydroelectric dam and reservoir

1910   Aldwell and his partner, George A. Glines, form the Olympic Power and Development Company; construction of the Elwha Dam begins

1912   Enormous fish losses occur; foundation of Elwha Dam blows out

1914   Olympic Power Company signs agreement to build a fish hatchery because dams were built in violation of laws requiring fish passage

1915   Washington Fisheries Code repeals fishway requirements, allows hatcheries in lieu of fishways[7]

1922   State abandons fish hatchery at the Elwha

1926   Construction of Glines Canyon Dam at river mile 8.0 begins

1934   Approximately 30 tribal families living on or near Ediz Hook (14 families were assigned land at the Lower Elwha); other tribal families forced off Ediz Hook

1936   United States purchases land under the Indian Reorganization Act of 1934[8] for the Lower Elwha tribe along the Elwha River

1938   Congress creates Olympic National Park

1946   Ernie Brannon, a 51-year employee of the Department of Fisheries, catches 70-pound chinook salmon

1968	Federal government recognizes Lower Elwha Reservation
1975	Lower Elwha Klallam Tribal fish hatchery opens for business
1987	Federal government builds set-back levee in the lower valley
1992	Lower Elwha becomes a self-governance tribe
1992	President George H. W. Bush signs Elwha River Ecosystem and Fisheries Restoration Act
1995	In June, National Park Service publishes Final Environmental Impact Statement for Elwha River Ecosystem Restoration
1995–1999	Congress appropriates $37.9 million to fund acquisition of the two dams by the Department of Interior
2000	Congress appropriates $22 million for the first phase of the Elwha River Restoration Project
2000	Commemorative Declaration occurs
2000	Department of Interior purchases two dams from Fort James
2000–2004	Congress appropriates $74.9 million for Elwha River Restoration Project
2009	$54 million in Obama administration stimulus money becomes available and pushes projected start of removal work from 2012 to 2011[9]

III. Adaptive Management Defined

Most contemporary definitions of adaptive management focus on incremental adjustments, learning over time, and improvement.[10] I would like to focus instead on the Darwinian aspects of the definition that treat an "adaptation" as a behavioral or characteristic change of an entity as a result of outside selection pressures. Adaptive management, as I see it, is a steering of the enterprise safely through a particularly challenging environment. On this view, adaptive management is less a matter of learning through experience and more a matter of just getting by, avoiding trouble, and running to daylight.

This more desperate version of adaption has no perfection, admiration, or improvement within it. Indeed, quite the opposite is true:

> One of Darwin's enduring demonstrations was that adaptations are usually not marvels of perfection at all, but historical compromises. On closer examination they usually turn out to be jerry-built contraptions—products of unique, opportunistic history.[11]

What is good, then, for the agency or for the Congress, might not be good for the fish or the tribes. These "adaptations," therefore, can have policy "maladaptations" written all over them—what Machiavelli described as the unfortunate distractions of "current necessities." Each of the adaptive management moments described in this chapter represents this kind of compromise.

IV. Evaluating the Moments of Adaptive Management on the Elwha

A. Adaptive Management Moment Number One: Environmental Laws Without Enforcement

> We're matchless at making new social conventions, creating intricate laws to enforce them—and then finding all sorts of ways to evade them.
> —Marvin Minsky, *The Emotion Machine: Commonsense Thinking, Artificial Intelligence, and the Future of the Human Mind*

What is most remarkable about the fall of the fisheries on the Elwha is how it was achieved so easily and with such flimsy justification. The sixty-year regional prohibition on obstruction of salmon streams was overcome by the entirely legalistic assertion that the dam would facilitate the capture of fish that could be used in a hatchery enterprise. In the mind of Washington Fisheries Manager Leslie Darwin, this faulty rhetoric meant that the dam would not be a bad obstruction, but a good one. The Olympic Power Company revised its initial plans and proposed a hatchery along with the dam; this clever expediency (two developments, not one) brought the Elwha Dam in and put the protective laws out. But within two years, as huge and grotesque losses already were being recorded from the early construction, supplicant Thomas Aldwell convinced Fisheries Manager Leslie Darwin to solve the Elwha fisheries crisis by a remarkable application of win-win, making it appear as though two antagonistic aims were simultaneously achievable.

We cannot get inside Leslie Darwin's head. But we can say that the "dam for hatchery" deal gave him a face-saving way to argue—to himself as well as to others—that nonenforcement could produce better results (dams *and* fish) than mere enforcement (fish alone). For Fisheries Manager Darwin, at least, that was true: the dam-for-hatchery arrangement certainly appeared to be the more beneficial route for him.

Indeed, let's credit Leslie Darwin with one of the great win-win discoveries that has swept into modern times: environmental laws *without* enforcement. Perhaps because of the often "perfect" conflict between development and environmental protection, discovery of a fictional reconciliation of the two has proven to be one of the more robust breakthroughs in the history of adaptive management. For managers in all walks of life, this particular deceit is likened in significance to the discovery of fire, upright gait, and early speech in human evolutionary history.

Let me mention two rather startling features of the win-win of environmental laws without enforcement.

The fall of the Elwha in 1912–1914 was not a case of a magnificent hydroelectric project attacking fish-protection laws at points most vulnerable, or of the nibbling away of protections on marginal streams by urgent development. On the contrary, this was a terrible project on one of the best fish runs. The experience is an advertisement, perhaps, of the inherent weaknesses of environmental laws. The law that got run over on the Elwha was longstanding, clear, well accepted, and decisive in its mandates. But it was, to be sure, very fragile.

The second lesson of the "have laws, don't enforce" mentality apparent on the Elwha is that the win–win is triumphant in perception only. On the Elwha, the original "hatchery" that served as a consideration for the destruction of fish was nine parts myth. The power company never made the payments expected of it. Nobody ever paid for a facility to house the hatchery manager, and the hatchery itself was repeatedly washed out by flooding. By 1922 it was functionally gone from the scene.

B. Adaptive Management Moment Number Two: Hatcheries in Lieu of Habitat Protection

> Hatcheries offered a win–win temptation politicians could not resist: river development and fish production. All could be overcome by "promising fish for everyone."
> —Joseph E. Taylor III, *Making Salmon: An Environmental History of the Northwest Fisheries Crisis*

The Elwha hatchery-for-dam deal began so auspiciously that Washington Governor Ernest Lister and his fisheries man, Leslie Darwin, moved quickly to extend the advantage. In 1915, the Washington State Legislature made it official by repealing the fish passage requirements and by allowing hatcheries in lieu of fishways for all dams and in all rivers.[12]

This hatcheries-for-habitat compromise—adaptive management moment number two—was another win–win for participants. It was sustained by the stubborn mythology that Washington could have development and maintain the fish too.[13] Politicians loved the idea of having it both ways, and fisheries managers welcomed the challenges and exploited their new opportunities. Scientists still believed that they could do the impossible.

The win–win myth has been thoroughly shattered,[14] and convincing histories of regret have been written. Development at the expense of fish was possible—the impossible part was sustaining the fish without the habitats that had been so knowingly and confidently sacrificed.

The Lower Elwha Tribe has lived through two of the uglier chapters of this hatcheries-for-habitat charlatanry. The first was the 13-year quest of the Attorney General of Washington to separate the tribe from hatchery fish on the theory that an 1855 treaty right of taking "fish" could not possibly have envisaged the white man's future inventions. The second is the ongoing campaign to defeat or moderate anadromous fish Endangered Species Act (ESA) listings on the theory that the numbers—if not the long-term biology of the affair—look better when you count hatchery fish.

Both of these much-contested "legal" propositions are utter nonsense. But a robust and convincing win-win compromise doesn't have to be true or durable or validated over time. Its capacity to appear to be true and to collapse over time is what makes it serviceable as a win-win. The imagined productivity of hatcheries has served a purpose. And it still does.

The Washington Department of Game also embraced the myth that hatcheries were better than habitat protection. The Department refined the myth, practiced it, extended it, and drove itself to extinction believing in it—a clear case of a deliberately undertaken measure of adaptive management that proved dreadfully maladaptive.[15]

C. Adaptive Management Moment Number Three: Removal of the Elwha Dams—A Public Financial Responsibility

The Elwha River Ecosystem and Fisheries Restoration Act authorizes the Secretary of Interior to acquire the Elwha and Glines Canyon projects upon a determination "that removal of the Project dams is necessary for the full restoration of the Elwha River ecosystem and native anadromous fisheries."[16] The Act declares that consideration for acquisition of the projects "shall be $29.5 million and no more," and it directs the Secretary to prepare a report on the acquisition of the projects and "plans for the full restoration of the Elwha River ecosystem and the native anadromous fisheries."[17]

The report was issued in June 1994 and concluded that removal of the dams is the only alternative that would result in "full restoration" of the Elwha River ecosystem. The report presented an Elwha River Restoration Project Schedule that would include preparation of an environmental impact statement. The environmental impact statements are done. Money has been appropriated. The dams have been acquired by the United States. All that needs to be done is to remove the dams.

It is important to understand the commitment made by the United States. It comes in four parts: The United States must pay full value to the private project owners ("$29 million and no more") to acquire the projects. The United States assumes all costs and liabilities associated with dam removal and restoration. The United States must find the funds to do this within the normal budget appropriation process. And finally, private owners get a full and complete release from the United States from the consequences of 90 years of destructive management:

> [Acquisition of the projects] shall be conditioned on a release of liability providing that all obligations and liabilities of the owner and the local industrial consumer to the United States arising from the Projects, based upon ownership, license, permit, contract, or other authority, including, but not limited to, project removal and any ecosystem, fish and wildlife mitigation or restoration obligations, shall, from the moment of title transfer, be deemed to have been satisfied. . . . [18]

One wonders in this urgent age of privatization how liability on the Elwha could be saddled so completely and decisively on the United States. It happened because the United States, so long ago, had established a remote and extravagant homesteading policy that threw open dam sites to opportunistic seizure by the likes of Thomas Aldwell. In any event, it is possible to surmise that the United States, burdened with this responsibility, could "gather the expertise" and "demonstrate the model" for dam removal and restoration that would then rebound fruitfully throughout the economy at the behest of entrepreneurs who would flock to do this sort of work.

But the Elwha example could very well go the other way. No visions of Atomic Energy Commission grandeur or NASA extravagance cloud this endeavor. There is a long line of prospective dam removals that will get even longer if removal must always await U.S. funding. Federal agencies will tire quickly of "buyback" strategies. The U.S. Park Service already is feeling the pinch as healthy portions of its operations budget are siphoned off for the good cause of Elwha Dam removal. There is no finer recipe for the status quo than the linking of changes to government funds and the simultaneous recognition that none are available.

The Elwha model of "U.S. liable" is completely oblivious to the Superfund model of "owner and operator" liable. "Polluter pays" is as good in one context as it is in another. Owners and operators of dams, like the monarchs of hazardous substance sites, make many incremental choices to charge the land and the waters with their unwanted costs. They run the place down for profit and inspire many others to bring it back up in the name of "restoration." Lest this model of owner-and-operator liability be forgotten completely, I sketch below what a "Damfund" law might look like:

> Section 107 of the Damfund Law, 42 U.S.C.A. § 9607(a) (imaginary):
>
> Notwithstanding any other provision or rule of law [and subject only to limited defenses]—
>
> > (1) the owner and operator of a fish-destructive dam;
> >
> > (2) any person who at the time of fish destruction owned or operated the dam;
> >
> > (3) any person who by contract, agreement, or otherwise acquired energy from a fish-destructive dam, shall be liable for—
> >
> > > (A) all costs of removal or remedial action incurred by the United States Government or a State or an American Indian tribe;
> > >
> > > (B) any other necessary costs of response incurred by any other person; and
> > >
> > > (C) damages for injury to, destruction of, or loss of natural resources, including the reasonable costs of assessing such injury, destruction or loss.

This was the road not taken on the Elwha.

The road that was taken is adaptive management moment number three: a public-private partnership where the public assumes all risks and costs while private entities enjoy all profits and benefits. This was a successful adaptive move for all concerned on the Elwha. It was a win-win for regional political leaders who designed the deal, and all objecting parties were held harmless or bought off. It was the only feasible way for the Lower Elwha Tribe to get rid of the dams. Environmentalists went along because it was a way to get rid of two bad dams while the question of embarrassing precedent was left for another day.

D. Adaptive Management Moment Number Four: No Dam Shall Be Removed Unless and Until All Affected Parties Are Held Harmless and Made Harmless by Preemptive Mitigation

The Elwha River Ecosystem and Fisheries Restoration Act extends an extraordinary mantle of protection to third parties who may be injured economically by restoration efforts. Section 4 of the Act directs the Secretary to take actions "necessary" to implement "protection of the existing quality and availability of water from the Elwha River for municipal and industrial uses from possible adverse impacts of dam removal." It reads as follows:

> The definite plan . . . must include all actions reasonably necessary to maintain and protect existing water quality for the City of Port Angeles, Dry Creek Water Association, and the industrial users of Elwha River Water against adverse impacts of dam removal. The cost of such actions, which may include as determined by the Secretary, if reasonably necessary, design, construction, operation and maintenance of water treatment or related facilities, shall be borne by the Secretary. *Funds may not be appropriated for the removal of the dams unless, at the same time, funds are appropriated for actions necessary to protect existing water quality.*[19]

This sort of arrangement is unheard of in the annals of environmental law. I call this preemptive mitigation because the mitigation must precede the project, not follow in its wake. Historically, of course, "mitigation" follows the project—usually never catching up. Environmental law offers thousands of examples of mitigation postponed, passed over, and forgotten in the urgent necessities of getting on with the job.

Environmentalists will stand in awe upon hearing that the mitigation on the Elwha will happen *before* the dams are removed. (This may also be the first known environmental case where mitigation actually happens.) Practically, the City of Port Angeles will get an alternative water supply before dam removal (and its accompanying release of sediments) commences. The cart precedes the horse.

Of course, there is a down side for the Elwha. Protection of the city water supply is proceeding with the helpful assistance of knowledgeable consultants holding the highest of gold-plated ambitions. The source of the funds is the same source of funds that later will provide for dam removal. Would it be conceivable for the city to get its new water supply and then *oppose* removal of the dam in principle? Stranger things have happened.

Thus, under this theory of preemptive mitigation all inquiry into comparative fault is abandoned. Complete protection is extended to all entitlements associated with fish-destroying projects, including water rights, power-generation capacities, and all values associated with "incidental kill" of fish and destruction of habitat. All present beneficiaries of the projects are treated as victims, to the extent that the dams cannot be removed without concurrent mitigation.

This transaction amounted to nearly instant justice for the City of Port Angeles. At least it offered concurrent justice. The deal was very protective of people discommoded by the return of fish. The Indians would have liked as much when they were removed along with their fish at Celilo Falls on the Columbia. Mitigation took a bit longer in those days—about 53 years.

Time will tell whether preemptive mitigation is so soothing, generous, and painless that it will make dam removal and fish restoration all but impossible.

E. Adaptive Management Moment Number Five: The Dancing Baseline

The "baseline" is the restoration goal for environmental laws—the striving backwards to where we once were. Different laws and different folks have different baselines. Almost certainly, the baseline toward which the Lower Elwha Tribe is striving is 1855—the Year of the Treaty of Point-No-Point.

What is the baseline identified in the 1992 Restoration Act? *Full restoration.* It was not otherwise defined, codified, or elaborated upon. Undoubtedly, the undefined term of "full restoration" was a highly adaptive ambiguity for many of the principals. Not saying something has always been the best way to agree. Under the ample tent of full restoration can be brought the Lower Elwha Klallam Tribe, with their extravagant ambitions, and others whose idea of "full restoration" might mean just a few more fish or any improvement after completion. Once the baseline became a beacon of reform for environmentalists, the goal of the opposition became baseline diminishment, achieved through baseline obliteration: the conscious avoidance of understanding the way things were and opposition to all monitoring and study that could identify preexisting conditions. Perpetuating ignorance on such subjects would be adaptive for any party hoping to diminish restoration goals or discourage convincing evaluations of success or failure.

Is the Lower Elwha Klallam Tribe free to pursue the goal of full restoration to 1855 conditions? Yes. The tribe is aided in a number of ways by the Act—securing a 99-year lease of lands on Ediz Hook[20] and an appropriation to acquire lands "for housing, economic development, and moorage for the Tribal commercial fishing fleet."[21] The tribe received particularized consultation rights under the Act,[22] along with the boilerplate—though important—assurance that the Secretary is obliged to act in ways "consistent with" the "rights of any Indian tribe secured by treaty."[23] The United States' "release of liability" to third parties does not extend to liabilities owed to the tribe. The tribes will see no Indian trust damage claim for failures in some of the bolder hopes for fisheries restoration. But the Lower Elwha Klallam Tribe has its treaty and its high expectations.

In many ways, the tribe is on its own as it pursues the content, meaning, and working reality of full restoration. It is important to remember that Senator Slade Gorton, one of the architects of the Elwha River Restoration Act, made a career of splashy opposition to all things related to Indian treaty fishing. He devoted his political life to the goal of making nothing of the treaties. It would be a luscious irony if the Lower Elwha Klallam Tribe succeeds in giving full restoration an aboriginal baseline of 1855 plenty.

F. Adaptive Management Moment Number Six: The Consensus Accord

If the restoration miracle is completed on the Elwha and the fish come back, there is a serious question whether the recovery will be sustainable. One problem is that 25 percent or more of ESA-listed chinook are taken by Canadian fisheries. In 2005 a Biological Opinion on Puget Sound fisheries acknowledged that Canadian harvest of Nooksack River–origin chinook (north Puget Sound) "is well above the rate necessary to rebuild that population."[24]

The legal vehicle for scrutinizing this problem of cross-boundary fish interception is the Pacific Salmon Treaty, which is the United States–Canada bilateral treaty on the topic.[25] Like much of international law, this arrangement can be described as a consensus accord, or, in other words, a jovial accord among parties who agree to agree, notwithstanding their broad areas of ignorance, inability to control entities they represent, and fundamental conflicts of interest.

Consensus accords are strongly adaptive for principals whose goals do not look past the accord. Diplomats are fond of celebrating agreements without worrying about troublesome implementing details.

It has been difficult to implement the Pacific Salmon Treaty. To put these difficulties in context, consider two quotations from William Ruckelshaus, the chief U.S. negotiator at one of these treaty sessions. Said Ruckelshaus on an early occasion, "Global Management today involves converting scientific findings into political action . . . trying to get a substantial portion of the world's people to change their behavior."[26] Years later, he opined further, "I don't personally believe you can force the individual to change the way they interact with the environment through government."[27]

These are the two views on the power of law to change behavior. It might happen. It might not. But neither outcome can stand in the way of a consensus accord.

G. Adaptive Management Moment Number Seven: The Duplicative Law

In responding to the Indian treaty fishing ruling holding that the State of Washington is duty-bound to repair highway culverts that block fish passage, Governor Christine Gregoire stated that the State was "obviously disappointed."[28] This raises the question: Why would a governor who has a bold new measure to clean up water pollution in Puget Sound and bring back the salmon be "obviously disappointed" with a Treaty ruling that could make these things happen? Perhaps it was that this so-called culvert decision was too strong, too determined, and far too likely to bring about the goals declared.

Governor Gregoire has received substantial political mileage from a clean-up-Puget-Sound-law entitled the Puget Sound Partnership.[29] It was promoted, among other ways, by promising "fishable, swimmable, and diggable waters by the year 2020."[30] Those of us with long memories have heard this story before. The Federal Water Pollution Control Act Amendments of 1972 pledged the elimination of the discharge of pollutants into navigable waters by 1985,[31] and before that (July 1, 1983) the achievement of "fishable" and "swimmable" waters.[32]

Fool me once, it was said, and the shame was on you. Fool me twice and the shame is on me.

Without belaboring the details of Governor Gregoire's Puget Sound Partnership, it does suggest yet another model of adaptive management. This model I call the Duplicative Law; that is, a law that expresses the identical goals, objectives, purposes, and measures of an earlier law but adds no meaningful substance or process to facilitate realization of those ends.

Duplicative Laws are adaptive for the principals. They are ingenious inventions of the politics of treading water. An astute political leader can get all the benefits of a new law with none of the costs, and a healthy lag between law one and law two allows the promoter to win a new generation of supporters. Opponents of the second instance are quieted by reminders that "this is already the law."

I cannot claim complete "duplication" between Governor Gregoire's 2007 Puget Sound Partnership and preexisting law, but there is some. As with all duplicative laws, efforts will be made to make it better than the last one and the one before that. But if the Governor's version of cleaning up Puget Sound is incompatible with the tribe's celebrated victory in the culvert case, then we have discovered yet another example of adaptive management that stands in the way of the boldest restoration project on the face of the earth.

V.   Conclusion

In the ambitious reaches of Elwha River restoration, in the sweeping demands to bring back Puget Sound, and now in the ever more urgent challenges of global warming, political conviction, decisive choice, and firm law are needed. The Elwha was humbled in the past by the many variants of political adaptation. It is now dangling in time as the cynical details of calculated stalemate assert themselves—18 years after Congress boasted of a "Fisheries Restoration Act," 15 years after the final environmental impact statement, 10 years after a "Commemorative Declaration" was signed. Still, not a brick has been removed, and generations of the tribal people have grown weary of waiting.

Hope is dwindling that the Elwha restorations will set the precedents and bring the satisfaction and knowledge expected of them. But restoration, closer now than in the past, is within reach and can be achieved.

Much will be forgiven and forgotten when these great fish are allowed to return home once again.

Notes

1. Elwha River Ecosystem and Fisheries Restoration Act, Pub. L. No. 102-495, 106 Stat. 3173 (Oct. 24, 1992). For background, see Russell W. Busch, *Tribal Advocacy for Elwha River Dams Removal on Washington's Olympic Peninsula*, The West's Aging Dams: Retain or Remove, 2 Golden Gate U. Envtl. L.J. 5 (2008).

2. Treaty of Point-no-Point, 12 Stat. 963 (Jan. 26, 1855). For background on the treaties, see JOSEPH C. DUPRIS, KATHLEEN S. HILL AND WILLIAM H. RODGERS, JR., THE SI'LAILO WAY: INDIANS, SALMON AND LAW ON THE CO-LUMBIA RIVER (Carolina Academic Press 2006) [hereinafter 2006 SI'LAILO WAY], *reviewed by* Oliver Houck, *Species and Culture at the Edge of Survival*, Envt'l Forum, March/April, 2009, pp. 8–9.

3. United States v. Washington, Civ. No. C70-9213, Sub-Proceeding No. 01-01 (Phase II-Culverts), Order on Cross -Motions for Summary Judgment (W.D. Wash., August 22, 2007) (Ricardo S. Martinez, J.), described in WILLIAM H. RODGERS, JR., ENVIRONMENTAL LAW IN INDIAN COUNTRY § 1:3 at 84–86 (Thomson/West 2005).

4. OR. TERRITORIAL CONST. § 12, 9 Stat. 323, 328 (Aug. 14, 1848).

5. Territory of Washington, Code of 1881, § 1173.

6. 1889–90 WASH. SESS. LAWS 107, § 8 ("said dam or obstruction may in the discretion of the court, be abated as a nuisance").

7. WASHINGTON LAWS OF 1915, ch. 31.

8. Indian Reorganization Act of 1934, Pub. L. No. 73-383, 48 Stat. 984 (1934).

9. Warren Cornwall, *Stimulus money will speed Elwha removal*, SEATTLE TIMES, April 23, 2009.

10. *See, e.g.,* Alfred R. Light, *Tales of the Tamiami Trail: Implementing Adaptive Management in Everglades Restoration*, 22 J. LAND USE & ENVT'L L. 59, 90 (2006) ("Adaptive Management participants learn to treat 'management' as a series of experiments to be consciously observed, evaluated, and acted upon"); J. B. Ruhl, *Regulation by Adaptive Management—Is It Possible?* 7 MINN. J. LAW, SCI. & TECH. 21, 31 (2005) ("[I]n order for adaptive management to flourish in administrative agencies, legislatures must empower them to do it, interest groups must let them do it, and the courts must resist the temptation to second-guess when they in fact do it").

11. RICHARD MILNER, THE ENCYCLOPEDIA OF EVOLUTION: HUMANITY'S SEARCH FOR ITS ORIGINS 3, 4 (1990).

12. Washington Laws of 1915, ch. 31.

13. *See generally* John M. Cobb, U.S. Bureau of Fisheries, Pacific Salmon Fisheries, App. III to the Report of U.S. Commissioner of Fisheries for 1916, Department of Commerce, Bureau of Fisheries 94 (Bureau of Fisheries Document No. 839, 1917) ("an almost idolatrous faith in the efficacy of artificial culture").

14. *See generally* Press Release, Dr. Robert Paine, University of Washington & Dalhousie University, Policy Review in SCIENCE Calls for Bush Administration to Protect Wild Salmon (March 25, 2004) ("[S]cience is clear and unambiguous; as they are currently operated, hatcheries and hatchery fish cannot protect wild stocks.").

15. The sad end of this policy appears in California State Grange v. Nat'l Marine Fisheries Service, — F. Supp. 2d —, 2008 WL 4755610 (E.D. Cal. Oct. 27, 2008) (upholding ESA listings of five populations of West Coast steelhead over various objections; this was the species that would be denied to the Indians at any cost.); For background, *see* 2006 SI'LAILO WAY ch. 19.

16. Pub. L. No. 102-495, § 3(a), 106 Stat. 3173, 3174.

17. Pub. L. No. 102-495, § 3(b), (c), 106 Stat. 3173, 3174.

18. Pub. L. No. 102-495, § 3(b), 106 Stat. 3173, 3174.

19. Pub. L. No. 102-495, § 4(b), 106 Stat. 3173, 3176 (emphasis added).

20. Pub. L. No. 102-495, § 6(b), 106 Stat. 3173, 3177.

21. Pub. L. No. 102-495, § 7(a), 106 Stat. 3173, 3178.

22. Pub. L. No. 102-495, § 3(d), 106 Stat. 3173, 3175.

23. Pub. L. No. 102-495, § 8(b), 106 Stat. 3173, 3178.

24. Quoted in Salmon & Spawning & Recovery Alliance v. Gutierrez, 2006 WL 2620421, at *5 (W.D. Wash. 2006) (but finding no standing to challenge continued excessive harvest under the Pacific Salmon Treaty).

25. Treaty Between the United States and Canada Concerning Pacific Salmon, T.I.A.S. No. 11091 (1985), *ratified by* Pacific Salmon Treaty Act of 1985, 16 U.S.C. §§ 3631–44, with Commentary by Michael C. Blumm and F. Lorraine Bodi, in *The Northwest Salmon Crisis: A Documentary History* 274, 276 (Joseph Cone & Sandy Ridlington eds., 1996).

26. William Ruckelshaus, *Whose Common Future? Reclaiming the Commons,* THE ECOLOGIST 129 (1993).

27. Quoted in Warren Cornwall, *Huge Task Faces Puget Sound's Anointed Savior,* SEATTLE TIMES, May 20, 2007.

28. SEATTLE POST-INTELLIGENCER, Aug. 23, 2007.

29. *See* Puget Sound Partnership, at http://www.psp.wa.gov/.

30. *See* programming for Puget Sound, "Visions for Restoring Puget Sound, October 30, 2007 ("Governor Christine Gregoire shares her vision of a fishable, swimmable and diggable Puget Sound and what it will take to make that happen by the year 2020") *available at* http://www.pugetsound.org/learn/adults/psv/07/; *Washington governor wants $220 million for Puget Sound cleanup,* U.S. WATER NEWS ONLINE, Dec. 2006, *available at* http://www.uswaternews.com/archives/arcquality/5washgove12.html ("Gregoire, a former state Ecology department director, promised to help make Puget Sound 'fishable, diggable, and swimmable' by 2020."); Joel Connelly, *Gregoire leads Rossi in new poll, though Rossi is close,* SEATTLE POST-INTELLIGENCER blog, Nov. 8, 2007 ("The Gregoire administration has launched a series of initiatives, from an

effort to provide all the state's children with health insurance to a cleanup of Puget Sound. It is designed, in Gregoire's words, 'as a legacy to our children to make the Sound fishable, swimmable, and diggable.'"), *available at* http://blog.seattlepi.com/seattlepolitics/archives/125372.asp.

31.   Federal Water Pollution Control Act of 1972, § 101(2), 33 U.S.C.A. § 1251(2).
32.   Federal Water Pollution Control Act of 1972, § 101(1), 33 U.S.C.A. § 1251(1).

12

The Future Public Law
of Private Ecosystems

Merging a Mantra, a Metric, and a Method

J. B. Ruhl

The enactment of the Endangered Species Act (ESA) in 1973 marked a turning point in the law of ecosystems.[1] For one thing, the ESA used the word "ecosystems" in its stated purpose—to "provide a means whereby the ecosystems upon which endangered species and threatened species depend may be conserved."[2] From there, however, the story becomes quite complex, particularly with respect to private lands. The ESA has become neither what anyone in 1973 thought it would be, nor what anyone since then has hoped it would be.

The origins and legislative history of the ESA are well documented. This chapter traces the emergence and development of three themes since passage of the law: (1) the implementation of the ESA and its importance as the *mantra* of the law of ecosystems; (2) the growing importance of the concept of biodiversity as a *metric* for the health of ecosystems and the performance of ecosystem law; and (3) the adoption of ecosystem management as the *method* for implementing ecosystem policy goals. A fragmentary history of each theme is provided, followed by thoughts and observations offered about their past interrelationship and their future coevolution.

302

I.   The Three Paths of Ecosystem Law

I've been pondering the connections between the ESA, biodiversity, and ecosystem management since the 1990s, with some early thoughts laid out in a 1995 issue of the *Colorado Law Review* in an article titled "Biodiversity Conservation and the Ever-Expanding Web of Federal Laws Regulating Nonfederal Lands."[3] Oliver Houck took the topic a giant step farther in his landmark 1997 *Minnesota Law Review* article, "On the Law of Biodiversity and Ecosystem Management."[4] This essay revisits the topic a decade later, with the benefit perhaps of some hindsight, but with no better power to predict the future.

A. The Endangered Species Act—An Old Mantra Grows Out of Tune

The ESA hit its apogee in 1978 with *Tennessee Valley Authority (TVA) v. Hill* and the decision's famous lines that the statute "afford[s] endangered species *the highest of priorities*" and is intended to "reverse the trend toward species extinction—*whatever the cost*."[5] When a dam bursts, the immediate effects are quite spectacular, but over time the water spreads out and recedes; the effects, while lasting, can be tolerated. This is largely the story of the ESA since *TVA v. Hill*. The statute has never been implemented—not by Congress, not by the agencies, and not by the courts—in a way that lives up to *TVA v. Hill*. To be sure, it is powerful, but almost all interest groups with a stake in the ESA are content to live with it as is, with minor adjustments here and there from agencies and courts, despite the statute's misfit in the modern ecosystem era. The idea of changing it in Congress opens too scary a Pandora's box.

This slow but tangible erosion of the statute is apparent in the historical evidence:

- amendments in 1978 adding the "God Squad" extinction exemption process

- amendments in 1982 adding the incidental take authorization provisions in section 7 and section 10

- repeated judicial rulings that the so-called conservation duty that federal agencies must fulfill pursuant to section 7(a)(1) is discretionary

- the erosion of the "best scientific data available" standard through court rulings that have rendered it little different in practical effect from the default rules applied under the Administrative Procedure Act

- the administrative reforms instituted under the tenure of Bruce Babbitt as Secretary of the Department of the Interior—habitat conservation plans, safe harbors, candidate conservation agreements, and no surprises—which, while putting up a good defense against an aggressive congressional threat on the statute, considerably softened the "pit bull" bite of the section 9 take prohibition

- the Supreme Court's *Sweet Home* decision in 1995, followed by many lower court decisions since, that have interpreted the take prohibition as limited by tort-like proximate cause principles and placed the burden of proof on the plaintiff[6]

- the critical habitat wars, beginning in the Babbitt era and going strong today, which exposed the weaknesses of the critical habitat mechanism

- efficiency-minded reforms in the Bush administration, such as conservation banking and joint counterpart regulations, which have further transformed the statute into a plain-vanilla environmental permitting law

- concerns over the politicization of the listing and critical habitat designation processes

- 25 years of congressional inertia

In short, the ESA has become a narrow, technical, litigation-driven statute administered primarily by the courts. To be sure, depending on what yardstick one uses, the statute has accomplished much—it has halted projects that activists opposed, it has provided models of market-based environmental regulation, and, more important, very few species that have come under its protective wings have taken the final step into oblivion. The pit bull may have fewer teeth, but those remaining must still be reckoned with. Yet it has by no measure become "a means whereby *the ecosystems* upon which endangered species and threatened species depend may be conserved," and this is particularly so with respect to private lands. It may be, as Oliver Houck has suggested, an effective means to "convene the meeting and draw a bottom line," as it has done in the Klamath River Basin (see the sidebar at the end of this chapter), but it has not been and is highly unlikely ever to become the means for comprehensively managing ecosystems over significant landscape scales. These days it doesn't look much different from any other environmental law in this respect.

B. Biodiversity—A New Metric in Search of a Home

The concept of biodiversity (or biological diversity, or natural diversity) has been around in science for at least thirty years. It became a household word in the early 1990s with E. O. Wilson's 1992 publication of the elegant *The Diversity of Life*, which established biodiversity as something science studies and measures and which many ecologists believe ought to be important to policy. Ecologists since Wilson, particularly C. S. Holling, Lance Gunderson, Carl Folke, and Simon Levin, have emphasized the importance of biodiversity to ecological resilience—the ability of an ecosystem to recover from perturbations. The Nature Conservancy's publication in 2000 of *Precious Heritage: The Status of Biodiversity in the United States* beautifully demonstrated the power of biodiversity and resilience as metrics of ecosystem health.

Indeed, biodiversity has picked up steam as a metric in ecosystem law as well. Law was actually ahead of the science curve in one rare example—the biodiversity management provision of the National Forest Management Act of 1976.[7] In 1992, the Convention on Biological Diversity was adopted. Bill Snape's edited volume, *Biodiversity and the Law*, was published the same year, providing a thorough account of where biodiversity had and could become part of the legal fabric. In the 1997 case *National Association of Home Builders v. Babbitt*, one judge on the D.C. Circuit suggested that impacts to biodiversity resulting from loss of the habitat of an intrastate endangered species are of such ubiquitous importance as to immunize the ESA from *Lopez*-style Commerce Clause challenges.[8] Legal scholarship has grown impressively on the topic, going from zero articles using the phrase "biodiversity" as of 1985, to just six as recently as 1990, to more than 5,000 articles by 2007 (albeit many references are to party names in cases).[9]

The Environmental Law Institute's 2007 publication, *The Biodiversity Conservation Handbook*, surveys legal developments at federal, state, and local levels. Much ground is covered in its 37 chapters, but is there really a law of biodiversity? If there is, its development path is the opposite of the path the ESA is taking: biodiversity law is struggling to build itself up from bits and pieces of other environmental laws, whereas the ESA is struggling not to fall too far from its auspicious beginnings as *the* environmental law.

C. Ecosystem Management—A Method Caught in the Middle

The last path in the story is ecosystem management, which hit the scene in the 1990s as a central topic in the debate over public lands management. Vice President Gore's reinvention initiative included a call for federal agencies to develop "a proactive approach to ensuring a sustainable economy and a sustainable environment through ecosystem management." Edward Grumbine's landmark 1994 article, "What Is Ecosystem Management?" truly put the concept into play as a complex policy implementation method by questioning whether the management of resources on ecosystem scales is meant primarily for nature or for humans.[10]

In the 1990s, ecosystem management—along with its cousin, adaptive management—firmly took hold as a policy goal in the federal public land management agencies, as well as in the EPA and the Fish and Wildlife Service's ESA Division.

In 1993, the Northwest Forest Plan, a large-scale ecosystem management program, was initiated. And in 1994, the FWS adopted an ecosystem management policy for ESA implementation.[11] That same year, the EPA issued its *Edgewater Consensus on an EPA Strategy for Ecosystem Protection*, calling for a more "place-driven" approach to implementing pollution control statutes. Legal scholarship on ecosystem management also exploded. In 1990 only 14 articles had mentioned the term. Yet by 2000, 600 articles referenced the term, and by 2007 more than 1,300 did.

Yet ecosystem management is not without its detractors from both ends of the spectrum. Compare, for example, the position of Canadian law professor Bruce Pardy, as voiced in an ongoing debate with me in four issues (so far) of the *Pace Environmental Law Review*, in which he characterizes ecosystem management as too soft,[12] versus the scathing attack Allan Fitzsimmons launched from the property rights perspective in his 1999 book *Defending Illusions: Federal Protection of Ecosystems*, in which he alleges it is too hard.[13] Perhaps the pragmatism of ecosystem management makes it too malleable to suit the tastes of those whose focus is fixed on species rights or property rights, but the complexity of ecosystems, particularly as they fit within biocentric and anthropocentric dimensions, seems to demand the more adaptive method ecosystem management has to offer.

II.   Future Trajectories

Biodiversity and ecosystem management are powerful concepts that respond to the set of problems we are likely to face in the next several decades as we muddle our way through non-point-source pollution, climate change, invasive species, fisheries collapse, and so on—that is, large-scale, complex, cumulative effects problems that have replaced contaminated sites and dirty discharges as the agenda. Unfortunately, these concepts have yet to be operationalized in hard law. The ESA's species-specific focus has prevented the law from fully integrating the features of biodiversity and ecosystem management, and consequently the ESA itself is becoming less and less relevant. A species-specific focus is not the answer to climate change or

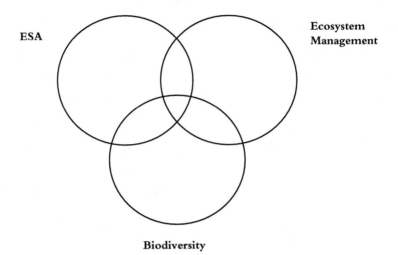

any of the other problems just mentioned. It has been a rare case, therefore, when the three themes overlap in application—when they meet in the sweet spot of a Venn diagram (shown above)—though it has been accomplished on occasion through programs such as regional habitat conservation plans and multispecies recovery plans.

So, how do we "tighten" the circles to enlarge the sweet spot? I leave for others the exercise of devising grand reform proposals. Rather, assuming Congress will not be moving the circles or drawing in new ones for the foreseeable future, I make the following suggestions:

- *Explore all nooks and crannies of the ESA.* As the Babbitt-era reforms suggested, the ESA is remarkably flexible and provides the agencies considerable leeway to move the circles. There is probably more room in the statute, particularly for programs using market-based instruments, to squeeze out more uses of biodiversity and ecosystem management principles. Conservation banking has some promise, as does the emerging concept of "recovery crediting," through which proactive steps that promote recovery of species reduces the regulatory burden on landowners. Some form of performance track program—for example, rewarding "beyond compliance" with expedited permitting—could also prove effective.

- *State and local governments can draw more circles.* The ESA could be more effectively integrated with other state and local programs that can and do use biodiversity and ecosystem management principles. An example is Florida's Rural Land Stewardship Act, which rewards landowners who set aside natural areas, including listed species habitat, with transferable development rights.[14]

- *Bulk up the science.* The species-specific focus of the ESA does not preclude using an ecosystem-based approach to questions of take, jeopardy, and recovery. The problem is that the science of the ESA is not sufficiently developed to *require* taking an ecosystem-based approach. Further advances in the science of complex systems in application to ecosystems, and of the role of biodiversity in ecosystem resilience, will help increase the overlap between the ESA, ecosystem management, and biodiversity.

- *Look elsewhere.* Ultimately, the ESA can only operate where listed species roam, and thus can only carry biodiversity and ecosystem management that far. But other concepts and programs may integrate well with them. The ecosystem services concept provides a new angle on ecosystem management, one that plugs it in more directly to market economies and business realities. And even the common law is beginning to have some play as an ecologically relevant institution.

In short, many small steps taken on many different fronts may add up to significant traction. One can hope that climate change, invasive species, and the suite of "wicked problems" on the horizon will prompt meaningful new legislative initiatives, and that Congress and state and local legislatures will lean heavily on biodiversity as a metric and ecosystem management as a method. Until then, however, moving the circles and pulling in others will happen one small step at a time.

III. Conclusion

Back in 1995, I closed my initial foray into this topic with the following observation:

> A strong federal presence in shaping our national response to bio-diversity conservation clearly is needed. The present federal system for defining that policy, however, is in danger of disintegrating as a result of uncoordinated regulatory efforts and overzealous application of unbridled regulatory powers. . . . We cannot afford, in terms of money, environmental health, and political stability, to allow federal biodiversity conservation policy for nonfederal lands to be carried out any longer by the present structure. Its myopic emphasis on regulation through coercive mechanisms will not produce meaningful biodiversity conservation without an unacceptable human-factor cost.[15]

A year later, Oliver Houck closed his commentary with a different perspective:

> The law of diversity and ecosystem protection is at a crossroads. Looking back over our shoulders we can see that single species management has been fairly effective—in some cases wildly effective—in promoting the success of individual species and the habitats on which they depend. This approach has begun to lose its steam, however, as more species and more habitats come into view. The temptation to shed our concerns for individual species in favor of conservation on a more holistic, landscape level is strong. All the more so where single species protections require us to make specific and difficult accommodations, while landscape conservation can be assigned to the realm of planning and discretion. At bottom, species-based protection is law. Ecosystem management, as currently promoted, is politics with a strong flavor of law-avoidance.[16]

There is truth in both observations. First, the ESA has been able to breathe some life into ecosystem management—and keep breathing itself—through innovation, not through harder regulation. The ESA would not be alive and well today without habitat conservation plans (HCPs), regional HCPs, safe harbors, candidate conservation agreements, "no surprise" policies, conservation banking, and all the rest of the administrative reforms Babbitt started. In addition, these administrative reforms advanced the formation of ecosystem management principles. Yet the regulatory arm of the ESA remains our bottom line commitment device in ecosystem law. And as such it is essential for the continued development of biodiversity and ecosystem management as policies, as they have yet to find any other home in the law. The fit between the three remains at a crossroads ten years after they first found each other, and is as poorly tailored and mismatched as it was in the 1990s. But they are still all the clothes we've got. We need to keep trying to make them look good.

The Endangered Species Act and Ecosystem Management in the Klamath River Basin

It would be difficult to identify a better example of the uneasy relationship between Endangered Species Act (ESA) law, biodiversity science, and ecosystem management policy than the Klamath River Basin in southern Oregon and northern California. Stretching 263 miles through its 12,100-square-mile watershed, the Klamath River has become the symbol of all that is right and wrong with the ESA as a mechanism for shaping biodiversity and ecosystem management policies. To be sure, the ESA convened a meeting and defined baseline management of the river, but from there it has proven the limitations of species-specific management of ecosystem-wide challenges.

The Klamath has only recently enjoyed national notoriety in this regard. Prior to European settlement, several Native American tribes built their cultures around the river and its bounty of salmon and sucker fishes. This relative tranquility was rocked in the early 1900s as the U.S. Bureau of Reclamation (BuRec) began impoundment and irrigation projects to supply agricultural water to farmers lured to the area by the federal government's promise of water. Eventually the dammed Upper Klamath Lake reservoir would supply water to more than 1,400 farms, irrigating more than 200,000 acres of crops. Elsewhere throughout the basin other farmers drew water directly from tributaries and grazed livestock to their banks, hydropower dams added to the interruptions of river flow, federal wildlife refuges added to the demand for water, and logging denuded riparian habitat.

Though remote and largely agricultural, by the year 2000 the basin could only be described as a human-dominated ecosystem driven by one overarching limit—water—and inevitably headed for a collision between the interests competing for it. Water was the one thing the basin was not getting more of, yet farmers, tribes, power companies, recreationalists, and emerging urban centers all demanded an increasing supply. And don't forget about the fish—they were there first.

Indeed, while most eyes were on the multiparty water rights adjudications underway in Oregon, the fish were the time bomb waiting to explode. In 1988, the U.S. Fish and Wildlife Service (FWS) listed two species of suckers residing in the upper basin above the BuRec dam as endangered under the ESA. And in 1997, the National Marine Fisheries Service (NMFS) listed a population of coho salmon residing in the lower basin as threatened. Among factors in the species' mutual declines were the obvious: the suckers had lost downstream habitat below the dam; the coho had lost upstream habitat above the dam; and all had lost an ecologically viable water supply. Pursuant to the ESA, the listings required BuRec to compile annual flow planning, dividing water in the lake between reservoir holdings (the choice of FWS), downstream releases (NMFS's vote), and irrigation supply (BuRec's preference).

The agencies' game of chicken ended in 2001, though it is still not clear which agency won. A severe drought that year led FWS and NMFS to inform BuRec that further irrigation diversions would jeopardize the protected fish. BuRec had no choice under the ESA—it had to curtail supplies. It took federal marshals to quell the ensuing civil protests, and ultimately the crop failures amounted to substantial economic and personal losses.

Round one thus went to FWS and NMFS, but round two was something none of the agencies expected. The Secretaries of

Commerce and the Interior asked the National Academy of Sciences, through its National Research Council (NRC), to convene a committee of experts to assess whether the agencies' biological opinions were consistent with the available scientific information. After careful study of extensive scientific reports and information, in an interim report released early in 2002 the committee announced its conclusion that there was a lack of scientific support for the central premise of *each* agency's position: FWS did not have a scientific case for its proposed higher lake levels, nor did NMFS for its proposed minimum river flows, nor did BuRec for its proposed flow regime. Round two thus was a draw.

This, to say the least, sparked yet more controversy. Some interests characterized the NRC findings as evidence that FWS and NMFS had used "junk science," a characterization the NRC committee vehemently rejected. Other interests immediately set out to challenge the committee's findings about lake levels and minimum flows. The committee's findings had everyone's attention, and over the next few months the committee toured the basin, held public meetings, and studied mountains of research.

The final NRC committee report in 2003 confirmed the interim findings and exposed the limitations of the ESA in addressing what was a far more complex set of questions than had been in play until then. For one thing, the BuRec's irrigation diversions accounted for only 57 percent of diversions from the system. Agricultural diversions abounded in the tributaries, usually with no screens to protect sucker and coho fry. Why hadn't the ESA been directed there, and what else could be used to manage those diversions? Moreover, water released from the BuRec reservoir was warm and accounted for only 10 percent of supply at the mouth of the river. The Trinity River, which enters the Klamath just 40 miles upstream from the Pacific and can release cool water right where and when it is needed, is far more important in defining conditions where salmon enter and leave the river, yet it has also been degraded by agricultural uses and extensively diverted to supply water to California's Central Valley. Why had the ESA not been directed at the Trinity, and what else could be used to manage its important role in the Klamath basin? These and many other questions led the NRC committee to question the effectiveness of single-minded reliance on the ESA and to suggest the need for a broad-based ecosystem management approach.

Many interests took the final report to heart and began focusing on restoration at ecosystem scales. Yet events have prevented the NRC report and its ecosystem approach proposal from gaining consensus. In September 2002, just prior to the release of the committee's report, a significant die-off of chinook (and some coho) salmon occurred at the mouth of the river as the fish were gathering for their upstream migration just when water temperatures began to rise beyond tolerance levels. This unfortunate event immediately became evidence supporting the assertions that the NRC committee had underestimated the importance of releases from the BuRec reservoir and that BuRec had acted recklessly in response to the report's findings. Although the NRC committee was able to address the event in the final report, explaining its view that the die-off was caused by a "perfect storm" of adverse factors and that release of warm water from the lake would not have helped, the die-off has remained a rallying point for those who advocate curtailment of irrigation diversions to save the salmon. Indeed, five years later the die-off was back in the news, as revelations in the *Washington Post* that Vice President Dick Cheney had weighed in on the Klamath, even to the point of orchestrating the call for the NRC to become involved, led to congressional hearings in July 2007 to get to the bottom of his role in the "fish kill."

Since then the Klamath has been active on many fronts. Farmers deprived of water have sued the federal government for takings. Proposals to remove the hydropower dams have been put on the table. Oregon has moved forward with controversial water rights adjudications. The various water rights stakeholders have engaged in protracted settlement negotiations. And along the way federal dollars have flowed into the basin. The only thing that has not changed is the water—there's no more of it and still too little to go around. The ESA hasn't changed that.

Although in many ways the Klamath has looked like a three-ring circus, complete with civil unrest and political intrigue, it is truly a tragedy of resources management. The ESA had focused all eyes on three fish and one dam, whereas the underlying problems were chronic and pervasive throughout the basin. Clearly, a focus on basinwide biodiversity and ecosystem management is needed in the Klamath. Yet, while the NRC process surely moved the ball toward viewing and managing the basin as a whole and getting outside of the ESA box, even that was initiated because of the ESA. Alas, the ESA started the Klamath conversation, but by no means will the ESA end it.

Notes

1. 16 U.S.C. §§ 1531 *et seq.*
2. 16 U.S.C. § 1531(b).
3. J. B. Ruhl, *Biodiversity Conservation and the Ever-Expanding Web of Federal Laws Regulating Nonfederal Lands*, 66 U. Colo. L. Rev. 555 (1995).
4. Oliver Houck, *On the Law of Biodiversity and Ecosystem Management*, 81 Minn. L. Rev. 869 (1997).
5. Tenn. Valley Auth. v. Hill, 437 U.S. 153, 154 (1978) (emphasis added).
6. Babbitt v. Sweet Home Chapter of Cmtys. for Great Or., 515 U.S. 687 (1995).
7. 16 U.S.C. § 1604(g)(3)(B).
8. National Association of Home Builders v. Babbitt, 130 F.3d 1041 (D.C. Cir. 1997).
9. Biodiversity even has its own law school casebook: John Nagle & J. B. Ruhl, The Law of Biodiversity and Ecosystem Management (2d ed. 2006).
10. Edward Grumbine, *What Is Ecosystem Management?* 8 Conservation Biology 27 (1994).
11. 59 Fed. Reg. 34,271 (July 1, 1994).
12. For a summary of the series, see J.B. Ruhl, *The Pardy-Ruhl Dialogue on Ecosystem Management, Part IV: Narrowing and Sharpening the Questions*, 24 Pace Envtl. L. Rev. 25 (2007).
13. Allan K. Fitzsimmons, Defending Illusions: Federal Protection of Ecosystems (1999).
14. Rural Land Stewardship Act, Fla. Stat. 163.3177(11)(d).
15. Ruhl, *supra* note 3, at 672.
16. Houck, *supra* note 4, at 974–75.

13

Water Law and Management

An Urbanizing and Greener West Copes with New Challenges

David H. Getches and A. Dan Tarlock

The "truths" of western water law have changed significantly in the recent past, and with this has come new challenges. Until the last quarter of the twentieth century, water users held to several fundamental beliefs: (1) that federal government would continue to backstop sacred state water rights by the construction of carryover storage reservoirs; (2) that the West's historic, variable climate cycles would not significantly change in timing or amplitude; (3) that the main competitor for the water traditionally shared among the triad of irrigation, municipal–industrial use, and hydropower generation would be American Indian tribes, not fish—except perhaps in some specially protected streams; and (4) that irrigated agriculture would continue to be the primary use of water. All of these assumptions were severely eroded in the past three decades. The new realities will influence the evolution of western water policy in the decades to come.

Four recent developments have stressed the region's variable water supplies. The recent transition from the reclamation era to an era of reallocation has been marked by a diminished federal role, climate variability, fishery protection, and urban growth. These trends were palpable when *Natural Resources Policy and Law* was published in 1993.[1] Now they have become even more pronounced, and responses have inevitably evolved as the consequences of the trends have emerged.

The stresses on water management driven by modern phenomena have important consequences for water institutions and laws that were created early in the twentieth century to promote irrigation in the West. But the West's responses to modern stresses are fragmented. These responses range from using the law to jump-start creative processes, to using law to resist change. The greatest creativity is coming from cities that face rapidly growing demands for water and must turn to irrigated agriculture for new supplies.

In addition, throughout the West there is an array of ad hoc, often localized efforts to solve specific problems within relatively fixed water budgets using "outside-the-box" approaches. Increasingly isolated voices argue for a return to the golden age of dam building.

With one exception—a return to major dam building—all of these efforts have some traction. The United States is unlikely to see a return to the scale of dam building that characterized the first six decades of the twentieth century. However, continued population growth and the risk of decreased supply caused by global climate change will create pressure to build new, although smaller and "smarter," reservoirs. These factors could also increase demand to open dam sites on rivers in the federal wild and scenic rivers system or in similar state programs.

In this chapter, we focus on three emerging responses to the stresses felt today in western water management. First, rapid urban growth is forcing cities and developers to take a more aggressive role in water supply planning and acquisition as legislatures and courts impose new risk analysis mandates on them. Second, the collapse of the imperial federal water bureaucracy and the slow pace of the states to fill the vacuum, especially on issues of river restoration, have led to the rise of "outside-the-box solutions." Third, the law of prior appropriation remains viable despite premature reports of its death. There are, however, subtle but increasingly significant changes in the formal doctrine and in its application on and under the ground.

I.   A Venerable System Under Stress

A. Farewell to the Reclamation Era?

The reclamation era has ended, and the role of the federal government has dramatically shrunk, limiting options for future supply development and thus stressing western water management. Supply augmentation is no longer the primary objective of federal and state water policy. As the 2005 *California Water Plan Update* dryly observed, "[S]tate and federal projects have not expanded as originally expected, in fact, diversions have been reduced in recognition of environmental needs."[2] More generally, the prospects for building large, new, multipurpose projects are dim everywhere but China. For example, the influential *Report of the World Commission on Dams*, published in 2000, recommended a more rigorous assessment of proposed new dams, increased focus on the reoperation of existing dams and irrigation systems, and urged the promotion of more sustainable water storage and use technologies.[3]

B. Chronic Climate Variability Meets Global Climate Change

The West's variable climate, which is likely to become more variable due to global warming, is the second stress. The possibility that the greenhouse effect will alter traditional snow pack and runoff patterns thrusts an additional element of uncertainty into already intense competition for the region's variable supplies, especially in the arid Southwest.[4] In many areas, spring runoffs may occur earlier in the year, and increased evaporation will decrease available supplies and base flows during periods of peak summer demand. The 2005 *California State Water Plan* advises that a change of 2.1 degrees Celsius, which is well within the range of current models, could result in a 52 percent reduction in the vital April–July snowpack runoff. With changed flow regimes in rivers, dams built to store water based on historical patterns of runoff and use may no longer serve their intended purpose.

C. Fish Power Drives River Restoration

Fisheries conservation is now a powerful proxy for the whole range of aquatic environmental values. A series of influential studies in the United States, Europe, and the Middle East, has recently led to the radical idea of managing river systems to maximize ecological functions to recreate "normative" rivers.[5] The developing science of conservation biology furnishes the technical underpinnings for new management paradigms. Conservation biology posits that all river systems—modified and "natural"—must be seen as ever-changing, dynamic, functioning ecosystems that provide a variety of services, from the maintenance of consumptive uses to the sustenance of valuable ecosystems. The current focus is on river restoration because so many large systems have been modified.

D. The West Urbanizes

The final pressure is caused by continued urban growth in areas with highly variable and vulnerable supplies. The region is capturing a significant share of the nation's absolute population growth and continues to urbanize or, more accurately, "ex-urbanize."[6] Alone among the major industrialized (or post-industrialized) countries, the United States' population is rapidly growing, and the West is the beneficiary of that growth. Populations are attracted by jobs in cities made livable by air conditioning and imported water. One theory suggests that this growth was stimulated by federal policies put in place during World War II. With both coasts vulnerable to Axis attacks, "essentially, the federal government promoted the restructuring of the natural-resource-based colonial economy into a technologically oriented and service economy stimulated by massive federal expenditures."[7] Federal spending and subsidies surely helped the West to develop as a series of urban oases fueled by investments in federal and military activity and private industrial and distribution centers. These have now morphed into more widespread archipelagos of human settlement and "lifestyle" exurban areas, increasingly less dependent on traditional commodity production activities and large-scale water projects. The ultimate irony of the post-"cowboy" West is that aridity, once thought to be a barrier to sustainable settlement, is a major growth magnet.

E. Implications for a Stressed West: Reallocation

The four stresses discussed above have animated a theme of reallocation to replace the theme of development that dominated water policy and management in much of the twentieth century. The end of the large-scale, subsidized river basin development era means that in the future, the competition for water resources will become more rather than less intense. Rapidly growing cities are competing with irrigated agriculture for limited supplies, and environmental interests are competing with all major consumptive uses, as well as the hydroelectric power industry, for increased instream flows or more "natural" hydrologic regimes.

Future competition will also be messier than it has been in the past because the once "imperial" water agencies have less power to mediate conflicts and to participate in the politics of the distribution of resources. For instance, the U.S. Bureau of Reclamation and Corps of Engineers are increasingly assuming a passive role in water conflicts; neither agency has much to bring to the table as Congress has put them on a maintenance diet. The U.S. Department of the Interior's *Water 2025*, unveiled by Secretary Norton in 2003, illustrates the once mighty Bureau's diminished power. Formally, the plan announced that the Department would concentrate its resources on ten hot spots in the West, but the underlying message was that the western states could not expect the Department to build new projects for them or to supply much policy leadership, because policy had always been tied to congressional support for pouring concrete. The Bureau, of course, still has considerable leverage on the Colorado River and in the operation of existing reservoirs and projects. Today, however, the most important role of the Bureau and the Corps is to participate in "outside-the-box solutions."

The shift from supply augmentation to reallocation increases the demand for water transfers, especially from existing to new uses, and for aggressive management to meet new demands of growing population and the rise of new societal values, primarily environmental protection. Most modern transfers will move water relatively short distances. They will not be massive interregional and international schemes like those proposed by visionary engineers and politicians in the past. Nonetheless, many of these transfers will be extremely controversial because they threaten to disrupt established economic and cultural patterns, stress ecosystems, and raise long-standing fears about the monopolization of water. In general, states have either de jure or de facto delegated water-planning responsibility to lower levels of government or let it pass by default to the federal government.

An era characterized by reallocation suggests profoundly important roles for cities, local grassroots efforts, and a more flexibly applied prior appropriation doctrine. Each of these means is being mobilized to respond to the stresses plaguing the West today.

II. A New Role for Cities: Water Supply and Land Use Planning Slouch Toward Integration

During the reclamation era, the states, Congress, and the federal water agencies managed much of the West's waters. Cities were the incidental beneficiaries of this management but had limited responsibility for water supply planning or management as opposed to contracting. As a result, water supply planning (and project construction) was completely divorced from any land use planning. Cities assumed that they had a public duty to supply water to all new residents. This duty was fulfilled by water doctrines that gave cities super-preference to water rights and the construction of federal and state reservoirs. In short, unlimited urban growth was a manifestation of faith in technology's ability to overcome any barriers to settlement imposed by the region's harsh landscape and climate.

In the reallocation era, management responsibility is drifting downward to cities and land developers as secure, dependable, dry-year water supplies become harder to obtain, yet are demanded as a precondition to continued urban development. The time has ended when powerful state engineers, such as the late Stephen Reynolds of New Mexico, could dominate water allocation in a state and lubricate development with new projects. The future belongs to those who can keep water flowing to cities by navigating through the minefields of markets, social equity, and environmental protection. Urban dwellers in Arizona and California now assume that the existence of an adequate, long-term, drought-proof supply of water is a consumer entitlement. This expectation places considerable responsibility on local governments charged with providing water, a task made harder by mounting concerns about the effects of global climate change.

Arizona was forced to begin integrated consideration of water and land use planning as the price for construction of the long-sought, federally funded Central Arizona Project (CAP). The state agreed to stop mining water from deep aquifers that were being tapped primarily for agricultural irrigation. In order to support inexorable and exponential urban growth, the state adopted the 1980 Groundwater Management Act.[8] Despite intense opposition, the state adopted rules mandated by the Act, which require all new developments in four groundwater basins included within designated Active Management Areas (AMAs), and thus on their municipal suppliers, to guarantee that "sufficient water will be physically available to satisfy the applicant's 100-year projected water demand."[9] The rules are structured to eliminate groundwater mining as a means of assuring an adequate water supply.

Initially, the rules set off a scramble to acquire agricultural water rights in remote counties, but more recently municipal suppliers began paying the high CAP rates for Arizona's underused Colorado River entitlement. This price shock was alleviated by the creation of the Central Arizona Groundwater Replenishment District, which allows members to store and withdraw groundwater.

Growth has continued outside the metropolitan areas, beyond the reach of the Groundwater Management Act. Until recently there was no consensus as to how to address the environmental impacts of the growth. The Arizona State Department of Water Resources reviews building plans to determine whether the water supplies will last 100 years, but their determination has no legally binding effect. A review of state records in 2005 revealed that 35 percent of the applications reviewed since 2001 were returned with an "inadequate water supply" finding, but most of those projects proceeded anyway. As a result, many subdivisions in rural Arizona are constructed with tenuous and unreliable water sources. In 2007, the legislature required state approval of "the adequacy of the water supply" to meet the projected needs of new subdivisions outside of AMAs.[10]

California's approach shifts even more responsibility to developers to find adequate supplies and imposes stringent risk assessment duties on suppliers. The policy of "leave it to Sacramento" began to change in 1993. The then "green" board of the East Bay Municipal Utility District (EBMUD), which serves a booming region of the San Francisco Bay Area, opposed an 11,000-unit development in Contra Costa County. EBMUD obtained a trial court verdict stating that the county had to consider the availability of an adequate water supply, but the case was settled on appeal. After a weak law failed to pass the legislature in 2001, California enacted a tougher law prohibiting the approval of tentative subdivision maps, parcel maps, or development agreements for subdivisions of more than 500 units unless there is a "sufficient water supply."[11] Sufficient supply is defined as the total water available during a "normal single-dry, and multiple dry years within a 20-year projection."[12] To calculate these amounts, the supplier must include a number of contingencies such as the availability of water from water supply projects, and "federal, state, and local water initiatives such as CALFED and water conservation."[13] Enforcement is tied to the duty of water suppliers to prepare urban water management plans.[14] Water supply assessments must either be consistent with these plans or meet the available water supply criteria set forth by the California Water Code.[15] Assessments may trigger a duty to acquire additional water supplies.

The planning requirement will be enforced primarily under the California Environmental Quality Act (CEQA).[16] The process, fully and honestly administered, will allow objectors to probe the underlying assumptions and reliability of the data on which the assessments are made. In the past, courts have aggressively used CEQA review to force cities and other providers to prove that their water supply projections were based on actually available water—wet, not "paper water"—and to prove that they have taken into account risks such as potentially adverse environmental impacts.[17]

State water supply projects in California provide much of the water for new growth. Contracts for water from these projects, however, can only guarantee water that is available in a particular year. In 2003, to settle litigation, the state agreed, *inter alia*, to drop the word "entitlement" from state water project supply contracts and to prepare more accurate supply and delivery forecasts.[18]

In 2007 a California Supreme Court decision substantially increased the disclosure requirements for municipal water supply plans. Plans must explain how a city's long-term water needs will be met, the uncertainties—such as global climate change—involved in the calculations and their likely impacts, and how the impacts will be mitigated.[19]

Climate change will become a larger factor in land use planning and regulation in California, and this will reinforce the duty to provide drought-proof urban water supplies. In 2006, the California Legislature enacted A.B. 32, which seeks a 25 percent reduction in greenhouse gases by 2020. This has already spawned litigation. In November 2006, a nongovernmental organization filed a lawsuit against a city to overturn the approval of a 1,500-home development. The suit alleged that the project will result in large emissions of carbon dioxide, a greenhouse gas, because the project will increase vehicle trips, and that the environmental impact report prepared for the project under CEQA failed to analyze those emissions or associated global warming impacts. In April 2007, the same organization filed another suit challenging a county's new general plan. The county updated its plan to accommodate a projected 25 percent increase in the county's population by the year 2030. The state Attorney General, who joined the suit on the side of the plaintiff, contended that "despite the enactment of A.B. 32, the FEIR [Final Environmental Impact Report] on the General Plan update . . . makes no attempt to analyze the effects of those [greenhouse gas emissions] increases on global warming or the greenhouse gas emissions reductions required by A.B. 32. . . ." In August 2007, Attorney General Brown and the County of San Bernardino settled the lawsuit; the county agreed to develop a greenhouse gas emissions reduction plan that will include its discretionary land-use authority to achieve reductions.[20]

The impacts of global climate change may not, at least in the foreseeable future, slow the westward population tilt. Nevertheless, the response of some states is beginning to press cities to become more active participants in all aspects of water policy, including small and large-scale watershed conservation processes.

III. Problem Solving Moves Outside the Box

Policymaking is for problems that can be approached broadly. In water management, we have lacked consensus for major policy changes requiring sweeping legislation. This is partly because entrenched law is the foundation for allocations that create expectations and rights that abrade emerging values, and without reconciliation between these values and expectations, a policy shift would be inappropriate. Thus, this section discusses the ways in which policy evolution is occurring without sweeping legislative modification of the essential doctrine of prior appropriation. In this section, we look at a number of practical responses to modern conditions that do not amount themselves to "policy" but which manifest a coalescing de facto policy of place-based solutions to problems.

Federal reclamation policy has changed largely by atrophy. Funding for large water project construction has dwindled, and there is no political will to continue the old development-oriented policy. Moreover, other federal mandates and programs, not under the banner of water policy, are contrary to the practice of damming streams, flooding lands, and fueling growth patterns that depend on subsidized water supplies. Today, there is major political resistance to construction or activities that would curtail fish spawning, pollute pristine streams, fill or flood wetlands, or otherwise destroy the habitat of terrestrial or aquatic species that depend on streams. The kind of extirpation of species that has occurred in the past is not only unacceptable but the Endangered Species Act bars it. Other harms are prohibited by federal laws, like the Clean Water Act and the Fish and Wildlife Coordination Act, as well as state laws with similar policy aims.

The silent change in policy that implicitly inhibits future development of major water projects also affects existing projects, practices, and conditions. Communities see rivers depleted and degraded by past water uses. Developers and local governments are told that they will not be able to use land or pursue economic development because of fish habitat or pollution problems. Consequently, they have joined with others, such as federal and state regulators and environmental organizations, to find tailored, often novel solutions. The solutions range from river restoration to removal of dams. They can be pursued locally or throughout an entire watershed.

A. Collaborative Restoration

Throughout the West there are examples, both large and small, of local citizens and public officials addressing problems caused by past water development and mitigating the effects of future water or land use otherwise inhibited by protective environmental laws. In most cases, they are joined by federal agency representatives who have an essential duty to ensure that any solution will produce a result consistent with the law. In addition, there may sometimes be federal funding available for these efforts.

Hundreds of groups in the West have formed to deal with local issues. In Colorado, the Animas Stakeholder Group was created by local residents coming together after the state Health Department declared the Animas River contaminated by heavy metals, such as cadmium and lead, from years of mining activity. Some wanted to avoid the stigma or potential liability of a Superfund designation. Others wanted to improve the fishery. The participants included fishermen and environmentalists, a mining company, an American Indian tribe, landowners, and several local governments. The U.S. Environmental Protection Agency, then officially supportive of local watershed efforts, hired a facilitator. The group worked for many months, developed monitoring programs to deal with causes of pollution, and organized various cleanup efforts.

In northern California, the San Pedro Creek Watershed Coalition was formed with the mission to restore the health of the San Pedro Creek and its watershed and with plans to involve the watershed's 10,000 residents in this major undertaking. Pollution, invasive species, and barriers for migrating fish were the main challenges the Coalition faced. Thus far, numerous efforts have improved the creek's condition, including educating the community on methods to improve water quality, organizing groups to remove invasive species and replant natives, restoring wetlands, enhancing riparian habitats, and replacing existing culverts with bridges that allow passage of migrating fish. The Coalition's endeavors are ongoing, and its continued success relies on the unrelenting support provided by a local network of concerned citizens, various organizations, and government members.

A remarkably complex example of a multiparty project to deal with serious environmental and social issues arose on the Truckee River in Nevada. The Truckee River terminates in Pyramid Lake, which is surrounded by the reservation of the Pyramid Lake Paiute Tribe. Early in the twentieth century, the U.S. government built a reclamation project to take water from the river to an adjoining watershed and deliver it to non–American Indian farmers. Over time, water depletions from the project lowered the lake level to the point that two species of fish were imperiled. One of the species was listed as endangered under the Endangered Species Act. In addition, the fishery, essentially destroyed, had been the Paiute Tribe's traditional source of livelihood. Although the tribe claimed the government had infringed its water rights, solving the problem was not as simple as turning off the diversion of water. Of course, the non–American Indian farmers had become dependent on the water provided to them for more than 70 years by the federal government, and the drainage of the irrigation system was sustaining a National Wildlife Refuge that was habitat to large numbers of migratory birds. Questions of equity and politics and the rights or expectations of others frustrated any simple solution pursued by invoking the law.

Decades of litigation followed with no conclusion. Eventually the parties got to the negotiating table, where they were joined by others; the Truckee River was of interest to many. Neighboring cities of Reno and Sparks were concerned with future water supplies. The Fallon Paiute-Shoshone Tribe asserted its water rights. And a power company wanted to use water for hydropower generation. An ongoing dispute over the amounts of Truckee River water that California and Nevada were entitled to use added another dimension to the negotiation.

The Truckee River matter was settled by agreement, and provisions were embodied in federal legislation that provided for a wide variety of actions, such as water rights purchases for wetlands maintenance, water storage and exchanges to optimize uses, and water conservation requirements, including at a nearby military base.[21]

B. Undamming the River

Perhaps the most revolutionary approach to reversing the damage to rivers is to remove the source of the problem. The idea is controversial in concept because dam building has traditionally been viewed as essential to social and economic progress. Yet, we are starting to see dams demolished or breeched in order to restore fish habitat. Some of the notorious examples include the Edwards Dam in Maine, which obstructed salmon passage for almost as long as the United States has existed as a nation, and the Elwha Dam and Glines Canyon Dam in Washington. The latter two dams were owned by a power company. When the company's license to operate the dams was being considered for reauthorization, a dispute ensued concerning the jurisdiction of the Federal Energy Regulatory Commission (FERC) to issue such licenses; it lasted almost two decades, until President George H.W. Bush signed the Elwha River Ecosystem and Fisheries Restoration Act into law, staying the FERC licensing process.[22] Responding to numerous reports recommending the removal of both dams in order to meet the Act's goal of restoring the Elwha River ecosystem, the federal government acquired the dams in early 2000, and in 2004 entered into an agreement with the City of Port Angeles and the Lower Elwha Klallam Tribe, providing for the dismantling of the dams starting in early 2008. The demolition is expected to take two and a half years; thereafter, biologists predict it will take another 15 to 25 years for the fish runs to recover fully. See chapter 11 for more discussion of the Elwha River restoration initiative.

A particularly intriguing proposal to deal with one of the most vexing conflicts between fish survival and water use arises on the Snake River. Several large dams were built on this major tributary to the Columbia River. The Snake River, though a great source for generating hydropower, was historically habitat for copious salmon runs. Since the construction of dams, beginning in the mid-twentieth century, the fishery has declined. Now, it is seriously depleted and some stocks are gone or nearly so. Litigation invoking the Endangered Species Act resulted in courts chastising the federal government for its failure to take effective action. In addition, the fulfillment of tribal treaty fishing rights has been frustrated by the destruction to the fishery. These events led to proposals to breach four dams on the upper Snake River in order to facilitate the fish passage that is necessary for spawning migration.

In 2005, the National Wildlife Federation brought suit against the National Marine Fisheries Service (NMFS), challenging its 2004 biological opinion, which found that dam operations on the Snake and Columbia Rivers would not jeopardize 13 threatened or endangered salmonid species, nor adversely affect their habitat. The district court invalidated the opinion, as a violation of the Endangered Species Act, and ordered specific spill requirements for the salmon.[23] The Ninth Circuit Court of Appeals affirmed the decision, but remanded on the issue of whether the order needed to be modified.[24] The district court's response was direct: The NMFS had one year to issue a new biological opinion, consistent with the court's previous order.[25] The decision led the *Vancouver Columbian* to label the presiding judge, James Redden, "the best friend of endangered fish in the Northwest." As for the future of the dams, Judge Redden noted that his order "requires [NMFS] and the Action Agencies to be aware of the possibility of breaching the four dams on the lower Snake River, *if all else fails.*"[26] In April 2007, the Ninth Circuit Court of Appeals affirmed the decision.[27] Only time will tell the fate of the Snake River's dams and dwindling salmon runs.

Short of tearing out a dam or taking it out of service, a reservoir can be operated in ways that minimize harm. Releases of water from a hydroelectric dam, for instance, can be scheduled to minimize the harmful consequences of operating it. "Reoperation" has been advanced as a means of continuing to derive utility from a dam while reducing or mitigating the harmful effects. The most obvious reoperation technique is bypassing water that would otherwise be stored. Large dams straddling major rivers can release water to create flows in amounts and at times when fish most need it. Many years ago, when environmental and recreational interests challenged the operating regime for Glen Canyon Dam, it resulted in a temporary change that was largely accepted in new rulemaking following a major study. Instead of operating the dam to produce the maximum amounts of power when the prices are the highest, the new regime sacrifices some revenues from power generation for the benefit of protecting habitat and recreational opportunities. A more dramatic reoperation of Glen Canyon has been suggested as a way of ameliorating the far-reaching environmental impacts of the dam—and as an alternative to decommissioning the dam altogether, as desired by some environmental interests. The Department of the Interior also has considered reoperation of dams on the Colorado River in order to recover populations of endangered fish.

What makes outside-the-box solutions so remarkable is that they are not the products of institutional decision making or official government programs. Although the federal agencies have provided support through funding, lending technical advice, and participation, outside-the-box efforts are mostly grassroots efforts. In fact, the most significant role the government can play is to create the pressure to take some action. The Colorado River example is different in that the government itself took the action, although it was in response to public pressure. Outside-the-box approaches typically address problems when and in ways that state water law and institutions are unable to solve them. It is predictable, and desirable, that use of these collaborative and creative problem-solving approaches will expand.

IV. No Eulogy for "Prior"; Maybe a Makeover

A. All (Relatively) Quiet on the Legal Front

For more than a century, experts have opined that to serve the West well the doctrine of prior appropriation required modification.[28] And, in recent decades, prior appropriation has been harshly criticized by many environmentalists and economists for locking water into low value uses, drying up rivers, and perpetuating the status quo. In 1991, Charles Wilkinson wrote allegorically of the demise of one "Prior Appropriation."[29] Yet it appears that "Prior" continues to live as he enters his third century. The great Samuel Weil would recognize most of the features of the doctrine that he explicated in his early treatise on water law, despite his prescient warnings that the law would have to adapt to changing conditions.[30]

Though alive, Prior is increasingly marginalized as an anachronism, a bit out of touch with the times but with some bite as well as bark. Courts continue to recite the catechism of intent to appropriate, relation back, priority, and beneficial use. But on the ground, users are working around the doctrine through transfers, water banks, and other new sharing arrangements, and courts make incremental doctrinal adjustments. Ironically, to the dismay of hard-core riparianists, reverse colonization is occurring. As the East turns to regulated riparianism, eastern state legislatures, regulatory agencies, and courts are also finding that the protection of prior users is essential for any allocation regime.[31] It is simply too late in the day to impose substantial disruption on the settled expectations of economic interests.

Western water rights add an interesting footnote to the famous Coase theorem. Ronald Coase won the Nobel Prize in economics for positing that, absent transaction costs, conflicts over resources will be resolved through the market regardless of the initial assignment of property rights.[32] Water transfers show that even with high transaction costs, markets will move toward efficiency. Water continues to move from low- to high-valued urban uses, as well as to support instream flows. Western water players have always known that water flows uphill to money.

Reallocation coexists with the static, formal doctrine of prior appropriation, for at least three basic reasons. First, the embedded wealth supported by the doctrine runs into the billions. The endurance of prior appropriation is neither surprising nor an indictment of the doctrine. Doctrines such as prior appropriation are justified not for their baroque form but because they induce widespread patterns of investment needed to maintain a reasonable level of security and a correspondingly low level of unanticipated change. But change happens nonetheless, as the stresses described here illustrate, even as the West has sought to provide the maximum possible level of security to users. Beginning in the 1970s, states invested millions of dollars in McCarran Act adjudications, with the false hope that by quantifying federal reserved water rights the system would be made perpetually secure.[33]

The second reason for the coexistence of reallocation and prior appropriation is that the latter continues to serve as a useful default rule because security and change are not necessarily incompatible. Prior appropriation is a relatively adaptable system compared to other relics of nineteenth-century public land law. Prior appropriation could function, for example, as a climate change adaptation system. Shortages induced by global climate change would simply be another risk that junior right holders face. The losers in this scenario would be fish and junior groundwater users, among others, whose rights would be subordinated to senior surface users. Prior appropriation also remains a useful rule among small users and as a default rule in permit systems.

The third strength of prior appropriation is in its ability to function as a shadow or hammer rule. Parties recognize it as the formal rule that would apply if users decide to "stand on their rights," but in many cases, users seek to avoid its actual application because the consequences can be harsh, inefficient, and highly disruptive of long-held investment-backed expectations, reasonable or not. The efforts of the Upper Basin Colorado River states to avoid an actual call by the Lower Basin by equalizing the levels of water stored in Lakes Mead and Powell, is an example of this dynamic at work.

B. Subtle Risk Adjustment

Despite the continued relevance of prior appropriation, a law designed for a developing irrigation economy must inevitably change as that economy diminishes in importance and the law must serve an ever-urbanizing, whitewater West. In an era when dependable water supplies are becoming harder to secure, new interests will seek a competitive advantage over older ones, who in turn will try to hold off change. Courts are mediating these battles by continually readjusting risks among users.

The law of prior appropriation has always been a risk allocation and sharing regime. Users have long faced the risks of a variable climate, preemptive calls by senior users, and third party challenges that water is being used wastefully or that rights have been abandoned in whole or in part. Moreover prospective and existing rights are subject to societal needs and the imposition of the public trust. Thanks to generous federal and state subsidized infrastructure investments in carryover storage, as well as informal sharing, the extent of these risks, and often-lax administration, were masked. In addition, unrestrained capture rules for groundwater in some states and the lack of any responsibility for aquatic degradation allowed appropriators to shift the burdens and impacts of overuse to the public, fish, and future generations by diminishing the water available for existing nonconsumptive uses and future consumptive and nonconsumptive demands.

As the West changes and the region must live within its constrained water budget, this cozy "deal" is unraveling. Courts are imposing new risks on users to squeeze more water out of available supplies, to promote the long-standing tradition of sharing within the user community, and to preserve the status quo. This tradition of sharing faded as appropriative rights were made more exclusive and the rhetoric of western water law took on a Lockean cast.[34] Risks can be shifted in any direction. Recent risk shifting includes the application of the public trust doctrine, a modest reinvigoration of the beneficial use doctrine, heightened application of the populist bias against speculation, efforts to curtail the super-preference that cities have long enjoyed, and a greater recognition of the need to protect existing users of instream flow rights.

1. Decreasing Risks of Environmental Degradation
to Future Generations

Western water users have been able to shift the costs of environmental degradation far downstream and into the future with little blowback. By contrast, recognizing a public trust obligation in water allocation is a way to shift some of these costs and the risks of shortages back to current users. Since the famous Mono Lake case, the public trust has hovered over all western water rights like an inchoate lien. But, it has remained primarily just that, an inchoate threat, except in Hawaii, where the state supreme court has made the public trust a major factor in water allocation to a greater extent than any other state, including California. The court has applied the Mono Lake decision to the reallocation of water rights abandoned by the collapse of the state's sugar cane and pineapple plantation economies, and it imposed potentially higher environmental protection duties than the California Supreme Court did post–Mono Lake.[35] Agency trust decisions are not entitled to a full presumption of validity because the public trust requires the affirmative protection of public rights such as instream flows. In other states, the trust continues to play a significant role in protecting public rights in old-fashioned navigable waters cases,[36] but there are countertrends, such as Idaho's reflexive anti–federal reserved rights jurisprudence, which aims to protect irrigators against the possibility of disruption by federal reserved rights.[37]

Colorado has limited the risks to which state–held instream flow appropriative rights may be subject to the impacts of later development pursuant to a plan for augmentation. A municipal appropriator claimed that its proposed plan would allow it to divert water when its junior water rights were out of priority regardless of the impact on a senior state instream flow right. The Colorado Supreme Court held that the state's instream flow program creates property rights, which are on the same footing as all appropriative rights, and thus, the non-injury requirement applies to plans for augmentation and reflects a legislative intent to balance preservation of the state's natural habitat with the consumptive use of water.[38] To prevent the frustration of the legislature's objective and protect its right to the stream conditions at the time of the instream flow appropriation, the state, as a junior appropriator, "may resist all proposed changes in time, place, or use of water from a source which in any way materially injures or adversely affects the decreed minimum flow in the absence of adequate protective conditions in the change of water right or augmentation decree."[39] Colorado has also allowed nonstatutory instream flow appropriations by asserting the fiction that channeling the instream flow is sufficient control to constitute a diversion.[40]

2. Beneficial Use and Beyond

Beneficial use became an integral part of western water law, thanks in part to the necessity of enforced settler cooperation among Mormons settling Utah. However, for decades its potential far exceeded its implementation. In recent years, courts have increasingly invalidated appropriations because applicants could not prove that water would be put to beneficial use,[41] and have shown a willingness to uphold cancellation of applications for failure to put water to a beneficial use.[42] This shifts more risks to existing, primarily agricultural users, except in Colorado. Colorado has taken beneficial use a step further and articulated a populist, antispeculation doctrine, which focuses on the proposed use of the water to give agricultural users a possible way to oppose transfers. The antispeculation doctrine applies to new appropriations and changes in use, and it also adds a level of judicial scrutiny beyond that provided by the markets.[43]

One iron rule of modern water law is that cities almost always win because they have superior financial resources and enjoy the benefit of a number of doctrines that add up to a super-preference. Except in Colorado, cities face almost no risk of loss by holding water rights for long periods of time.[44] There have been some modest efforts to curb the super-preference for urban growth. The most striking is New Mexico's rejection of the much disputed pueblo rights doctrine.[45] Washington trimmed the so-called "growing cities" doctrine by holding that beneficial use, not the capacity of a municipal water system, is the measure of a water right.[46] An intermediate Oregon court of appeals held that municipalities were not exempt from the statutory requirement that water be put to beneficial use within five years of the issuance of a permit.[47] However, in the last two examples, the state legislatures intervened to put an end to this heresy of treating cities like any other water users.[48]

3. Groundwater Users Brought into the System

With some exceptions, such as New Mexico and Colorado, groundwater users have been able to pump with impunity. The artificial separation of ground from surface water in state law has allowed groundwater pumpers to extract water regardless of the impacts on surface users, who generally hold senior rights. This is changing quite rapidly as courts are imposing new curtailment risks on groundwater use—some of which have materialized. Texas remains a holdout,[49] but Arizona,[50] California,[51] Montana,[52] Nebraska (to a lesser extent),[53] and Washington[54] have all imposed liability on groundwater pumpers who interfere with senior or riparian surface rights. Colorado has had formal integration, and the Colorado courts have held rigidly that priority meant priority, regardless of the source of water.[55] As a result, Colorado shut down numerous wells along the South Platte, imposing heavy burdens on groundwater users to rebut alleged interference with senior surface users.

4. California Rediscovers Prior Appropriation

In California, where a mix of riparian rights and prior appropriation has always existed, the courts are rediscovering and applying the formal doctrine. California historically substituted money for priority enforcement or used physical solutions to maximize the amount of water available to competing users. While Coloradans fought over miner's inches and fractions of acre-feet, California moved around large blocks of water and tolerated a very uncertain dual system of riparian and appropriative water rights. In the twentieth century, California spent billions of dollars to backstop water rights and create surplus supplies in the arid southern part of the state. The era of mega projects came to an end in the 1980s when the North Coast rivers were designated as federal and state wild and scenic rivers. Governor Schwarzenegger is currently trying to revive a more modest dam building program as the state navigates the reallocation era with a growing population and stressed supplies.

It is not surprising that existing users are starting to stand on their water rights to shift the risks of scarcity to other claimants. In the main, California is shifting the risks to municipalities rather than to farmers and fish. In 2000, the California Supreme Court surprised many by holding that a trial court could not impose a physical solution on a groundwater basin that increased slightly the risk that prior agricultural pumpers would not be able to take their full entitlement, even though the plan had been accepted by a majority of pumpers, including municipal suppliers.[56] The courts have also held that there is an equal protection dimension to priority. Senior rights holders cannot subsequently be subjected to conditions to which juniors are not. The California Water Resources Control Board approved the assignment to a water district of a state appropriation with a 1927 priority, but it required the water district to curtail its diversions whenever the Bureau of Reclamation or the State Water Project released stored water to meet the Sacramento–San Joaquin Bay Delta water quality standards. Because the same condition was not imposed on junior right holders, "the Board's action contravened the rule of priority, which is one of the fundamental principles of California water law . . . ."[57] Obviously, there are market responses to these decisions. Risk must be managed with investments in senior water rights.

V. Conclusion

With the venerable doctrine of prior appropriation showing vitality in latter-day applications and with substantial alterations that adapt it to modern realities, there is little doubt that the old "Prior" is here to stay for the foreseeable future. Continued evolution will ensure the doctrine's adaptation, and its apparently rigid application will encourage market transfers. But its relevance is, nevertheless, in decline.

The prior appropriation system cannot be counted on to respond adequately to all the modern stresses that bear on water management in the American West, as is apparent in Idaho's efforts to balance surface and groundwater rights with highly valued, junior groundwater uses (see the sidebar to this chapter). The system is particularly ill-equipped to deal with environmental issues that often focus on the publicly supported demand to maintain fisheries and fish habitat. There are federal and some state laws that champion environmental protection, but these laws can clash with prior appropriation concepts. The safety valve preventing the doctrine from being seriously threatened by its own inadequacy is the now well-established practice of self-help in the form of outside-the-box solutions. Parties would rather craft their own solutions to problems that are, in the first place, localized in nature. Environmental interests and federal agencies struggling with the unpopular results of enforcing laws are finding better ways to accomplish their purposes in multiparty, multi-interest negotiations. Complex issues are bound to be aggregated for customized solutions, tailored through negotiations to specific local needs while promoting the larger goals of environmental protection.

The critical issue of how to deal with population growth in the West remains. Major water development will be rarer. With the disappearance of easy federal money for water projects, states have passed responsibility for water supply to the source of demand growth: cities. Appropriately, this has sometimes been in the guise of land-use planning law. In leaving the future of water planning largely in the control of cities, some states have begun to freight the responsibility with requirements to consider the possible impacts of climate change. In this milieu, cities will build some small and agile projects. But they will weigh the enormous investments needed for large water projects and the risks inherent in climate change against options with dramatically lower water demand. They will likely choose the latter options, such as planning for new urban growth based largely on transfers of senior agricultural rights and development of housing in planned, higher density communities.

The common thread connecting the stresses challenging western water management and the solutions that are emerging is the same pragmatic streak that led to creation of water laws and the avoidance of water wars throughout history. The adaptive use of prior appropriation, the localized creation of outside-the-box solutions to coalesce varied goals, and the shifting of burdens to cities, which are, after all, the centers of water demand and wealth creation, are all common-sense approaches. Their emergence is a cause for optimism.

Conjunctive Use in the Snake River Plain: From In to Out of the Box

Idaho's Snake River Plain (SRP) is one of the West's most productive irrigated areas. It is also overappropriated and struggling with the tension between the demands of senior surface appropriators and junior groundwater pumpers. Along with Colorado and New Mexico, Idaho has tried to implement the teachings of hydrologists that groundwater and surface water are often a single source and therefore should be managed conjunctively. However, it is proving difficult and costly to fit conjunctive use into prior appropriation box, which was not designed for the hydrological complexities and scale of the SRP. As lawyers and administrators struggle with untested aspects of prior appropriation, the state is finding that the doctrine is more useful as a catalyst to spur out-of-the-box solutions than as the basis for modern water rights administration.

In the nineteenth and early twentieth centuries, irrigators in Idaho and elsewhere in the West relied almost exclusively on surface water sources except in a few artesian areas. Surface diversions were the only choice for the seniors because the technology for high-capacity wells did not develop until after World War II. Groundwater use came after a large surface irrigation system was in place. Pumping was possible from these wells even when surface water was unavailable and groundwater use diminished the overall supply of water in the Snake River basin. Many SRP irrigators switched to groundwater to protect their uses. Today, more than three million acres are currently under irrigation in the Snake River Plain, much of the area supplied by groundwater. Although some of this irrigation is by senior appropriators who converted their surface rights to groundwater rights; many other long-used groundwater rights are junior to the much older senior surface rights.

The SRP is a classic example of the false dichotomy between ground and surface water. Most of the groundwater is pumped from the Eastern Snake Plain Aquifer, which is hydrologically connected to the river. This scientific reality is fully appreciated today, but that was not always the case. Among the western states, only New Mexico got a head start on conjunctive management and has long maintained the water budget of the Rio Grande by conditioning new groundwater appropriations on the retirement of senior surface rights. Early on, Colorado integrated groundwater uses that affected—that is, are "tributary" to—surface streams with its prior appropriation system. Idaho, along with other states, allowed two separate systems to develop and is now playing catch-up. Idaho has long applied prior appropriation to groundwater, but is only now confronting the difficulty of real integration of two water sources that were long treated as separate.

It is not easy to integrate surface water and groundwater management, especially after uses have become complicated with longstanding practices and expectations. Even in the best case, prior appropriation was designed for surface diversions and is more difficult to administer in applying it to groundwater. A junior's upstream surface diversion can have an immediate and quickly remedied adverse impact on a senior's use of water. Headgates can be shut. When this occurs on small ditches and canals, the "justice" in enforcing priorities is generally understood and accepted. Prior appropriation rightfully blames the junior for the senior's injury. But the justice of selectively shutting down junior wells believed to be the culprits in affecting senior surface use or groundwater pumping is subject to skepticism and argument. Causation, masked as it is by time and distance, is not so easy to determine. All groundwater pumpers can mutually injure one other by collectively lowering the water table.

Idaho, along with other states, has rejected protecting early pumpers against a decline in aquifer levels or impacts on pump lift (causing greater expense to pump from deeper wells) because such a rule of absolute protection would preclude all future groundwater use. Instead, states like Idaho impose the prior appropriation doctrine to protect senior water users—of surface or groundwater—against "material injury." The justice of shutting wells to protect senior surface users is theoretically more acceptable but in practice is highly contested. It takes time (sometimes a long time) for the effects of reducing pumping to be felt by surface users or even many other well users. Idaho was able to avoid the conundrum for many years by viewing ground and surface water as separate sources of rights, despite calls for conjunctive management to recognize hydrologic reality.

The increasing sophistication of groundwater models undercut this "out of sight, out of mind mentality" as the costs of ignoring reality began to mount. Idaho, as the largest supplier of potatoes for McDonald's, paid part of the costs for a Big Mac and fries by tolerating depleted aquifers, springs, and river flows. Finally, the state began to embrace more aggressively conjunctive management in the 1990s, only to discover that the principles of prior appropriation look better on paper than they do on the ground. In theory, a junior groundwater pumper is just another junior right that must yield to a senior in a dry year. However, junior pumpers have the incentive and power to resist the theory's literal application. But groundwater pumpers have considerable historical equities and economics on their side. Not surprisingly, courts and administrators are beginning to step back from the view that prior appropriation is a fair and easy-to-administer system and is as imperative for the West as it was when the California and Colorado courts created the doctrine out of whole cloth. As the Idaho Supreme Court put it, "[w]hile the Constitution, statutes and case law in Idaho set forth principles of the prior appropriation doctrine, these principles are more easily stated than applied. These principles become especially more difficult, and harsh, in their application in times of drought."[58]

Idaho has been flirting with well shutdowns since the 1990s but has so far avoided them. This is in contrast to Colorado, which has recently shut wells in the South Platte. In 1993, senior surface irrigators in Idaho's Hagerman Valley made a call on junior pumpers, but the call was avoided when enough irrigators agreed to reconvert their rights to surface diversions.

The most recent trouble arose in 2005 when trout farms in the Magic Valley, in the south central part of the state, made a call and rejected an initial offer of 45,000 acre-feet of replacement water. The Idaho Department of Water Resources eventually threatened to shut pumps for 41,000 acres and several towns and industries in the valley. In addition to invoking the economic dislocation of shutting down irrigation, the groundwater users asserted the "futile call" doctrine, which holds that junior rights should not be shut down if the water called for will not actually reach the senior. The state's initial conjunctive use rules incorporated futile call principles to give the Department sufficient discretion to decide when to honor a call. A trial judge struck down the rules because they imposed too high a burden on senior surface delivery calls and thus were inconsistent with the constitutional right to appropriate. The state supreme court then reversed. Later, the Idaho pumpers obtained an injunction against enforcing the order until the Department could makes a scientifically based decision about the extent of injury to seniors.

Once again, the junior well users made mitigation efforts, but when they were refused by a fish farm with senior rights the Department again ordered a shutdown of pumping. On the eve of the shutdown in March 2009, the pumpers offered a new mitigation plan and once again the Department decided to stay its shutdown order. Administrative proceedings grind on.

Three tentative, broader lessons can be drawn from Idaho's experience so far. First, when prior appropriation creates a large class of losers and the economic stakes are high, there are pressures on courts and administrators to make a crude cost-benefit analysis and to ease strict enforcement by finding the seams in the doctrine that diminish its severity. Second, as the costs of applying the catechism of priority rise, out-of-the-box solutions will emerge, such as land retirement and set-aside pools. Third, to fund these solutions water users will partially shift the costs of mitigation to state and federal taxpayers. Idaho has created an $80 million program that it hopes will be matched by federal funds for fallowing and land retirement payments.

It's no longer your grandfather's prior appropriation doctrine.

Notes

1. Natural Resources Policy and Law: Trends and Directions (Lawrence J. MacDonnell & Sarah E. Bates eds., 1993).

2. California Water Plan Update 2005. Department of Water Resources Bulletin 160–165 (December, 2005).

3. The World Commission on Dams, Dams and Development: A New Framework for Development (2000), *available at* http://www.dams.org/report/.

4. *E.g.,* National Research Council, Colorado River Water Management: Evaluating and Adjusting to Hydrologic Variability (2007).

5. National Research Council, Water for the Future: The West Bank and Gaza Strip, Israel and Jordan (1999).

6. William Travis, New Geographies of the American West (2007).

7. Gerald Nash, The Federal Landscape: An Economic History of the Twentieth Century West (1999).

8. Groundwater Management Act, Ariz. Rev. Stat. § 45-576.

9. Arizona Department of Water Resources, R12-15-703(b) (Feb. 7, 1995).

10. Arizona House Bill 2321, amending Ariz. Rev. Stat. § 45-108 (2007).

11. Cal. Govt. Code § 66473.7(b)(1).

12. Cal. Govt. Code § 66473.7(a)(2).

13. Cal. Govt. Code § 66473.7(a)(2)(D).

14. Cal. Water Code § 10910.

15. *Id.*

16. California Environmental Quality Act, Cal. Pub. Res. Code §§ 21000–21177.

17. Planning & Conservation League v. Dept. of Water Res., 83 Cal. App. 4th 892 (2000), *appeal denied sub nom.* Santa Clarita Org. for Planning the Env't v. County of Los Angeles, 2003 Cal. LEXIS 291 (Feb. 27, 2003) (unpublished).

18. Settlement Agreement (May 5, 2003), *available at* http://www.montereyamendments.water.ca.gov.

19. Vineyard Area Citizens for Responsible Growth v. City of Rancho Cordova, 40 Cal. 4th 412, 150 P.3d 709 (2007).

20. Settlement Agreement (2007), *available at* http://ag.ca/cms-pdfs/press/2007 -08-21San_Bernardino_settlement_agreement.pdf.

21. Fallon Paiute-Shoshone Truckee-Carson-Pyramid Lake Water Rights Settlement Act, Pub. L. No. 101-618, 104 Stat. 3289 (1990).

22. Elwha River Ecosystem and Fisheries Restoration Act, Pub. L. No. 102-495, 106 Stat. 3173 (1992).

23. Nat'l Wildlife Fed'n v. Nat'l Marine Fisheries Serv., 2005 WL 1398223 (D. Or. June 10, 2005).

24. Nat'l Wildlife Fed'n v. Nat'l Marine Fisheries Serv., 422 F.3d 782 (9th Cir. 2005).

25. Nat'l Wildlife Fed'n v. Nat'l Marine Fisheries Serv., 2005 WL 2488447 (D. Or. Oct. 7, 2005).

26. *Id.* at *3 (emphasis in original).

27. Nat'l Wildlife Fed'n v. Nat'l Marine Fisheries Serv., 481 F.3d 1224 (9th Cir. 2007).

28. *E.g.,* Moses Lasky, *From Prior Appropriation to Economic Distribution of Water by the State,* 1 ROCKY MTN. L. REV. 161 (1929); 1 ROCKY MTN. L. REV. 248 (1929); 2 ROCKY MTN. L. REV. 35 (1929).

29. Charles F. Wilkinson, *In Memoriam, Prior Appropriation 1848–1991,* 21 ENVTL. L. no. 3, pt. 1 (1991).

30. SAMUEL C. WEIL, WATER RIGHTS IN THE WESTERN STATES § 57 (3d ed. 1911).

31. Edmundson v. Edwards, 111 S.W.3d 906, 910 (Mo. Ct. App. 2003).

32. Ronald Coase, *The Problem of Social Cost,* 3 J.L. & ECON. 1 (1960).

33. A. Dan Tarlock, *General Stream Adjudications: A Good Public Investment?,* 133 WATER RESOURCES RESEARCH 52 (May 2006).

34. *See* David B. Schorr, *Appropriation as Agrarianism: Distributive Justice in the Creation of Property Rights,* 32 ECOLOGY L.Q. 3 (2005).

35. *In re* Water Use Permit Applications for the Waiahole Ditch, 94 Haw. 97, 9 P.3d 409 (2000); Mono Lake State Water Resources Control Board Cases, 39 Cal. Rptr. 3d 189, 267–72 (Cal. Ct. App. 2006).

36. In the Matter of Sanders Beach, 147 P.3d 75, 85 (Idaho 2006).

37. United States v. Idaho, 23 P.3d 128–29 (Idaho 2001).

38. Colo. Water Conservation Bd. v. City of Central, 125 P.3d 424 (Colo. 2005).

39. 125 P.3d at 440.

40. City of Thornton v. City of Fort Collins, 830 P.2d 915 (Colo. 1992) (boat chute); State Engineer v. City of Golden, 69 P.3d 1027 (Colo. 2003).

41. *E.g.,* Central Delta Water Agency v. State Water Res. Control Bd., 124 Cal. App. 4th 245, 20 Cal. Rptr. 3d 898 (2004).

42. Natural Energy Res. Co. v. Upper Gunnison River Water Conservancy Dist., 142 P.3d 1265 (Colo. 2006).

43. *E.g.,* High Plains A & M, LLC v. Southeastern Colo. Water Conservancy Dist., 120 P.3d 710 (Colo. 2005).

44. Pagosa Area Water and Sanitation Dist. v. Trout Unlimited, No. 06SA338 (Colo. Oct. 27, 2007).

45. State v. City of Las Vegas, 135 N.M. 375, 89 P.3d 47 (2004).

46. State Dep't of Ecology v. Theodoratus, 135 Wash. 2d 582, 957 P.2d 1241 (1998).

47. Water Watch of Or., Inc. v. Water Res. Council, 193 Or. App. 87, 88 P.3d 327 (2004), *vacated*, 339 Or. 275, 119 P.3d 221 (2005).

48. OR. REV. STAT. § 537.230 (2005).

49. Sipriano v. Great Springs Waters of Am., 1 S.W.3d 75 (Tex. 1999).

50. *In re* General Adjudication of Gila River Sys., 857 P.2d 1236 (Ariz. 1993); 9 P.3d 1069 (Ariz. 2000).

51. N. Guaala Water Co. v. State Water Res. Control Bd., 43 Cal. Rptr. 3d 821 (Cal. Ct. App. 2006).

52. Mont. Trout Unlimited v. Mont. Dep't of Natural Res. & Conservation, 331 Mont. 483, 133 P.3d 224 (2006).

53. Spear T Ranch v. Knaub, 691 N.W.2d 116 (Neb. 2005).

54. Hubbard v. State, 86 Wash. App. 119, 936 P.2d 27 (1997).

55. Empire Lodge Homeowners Ass'n v. Moyer, 39 P.3d 1139 (Colo. 2002).

56. City of Barstow v. Mojave Water Agency, 23 Cal. 4th 1224, 99 Cal. Rptr. 2d 294, 5 P.3d 853 (2000).

57. El Dorado Irrigation Dist. v. State Water Res. Control Bd., 142 Cal. App. 4th 937, 48 Cal. Rptr. 3d 468, 473 (2006).

58. Am. Falls Reservoir Dist. v. Idaho Dep't of Water Res., 154 P.3d. 433 (Idaho 2007).

14

The Future of Mineral Development on Federal Lands

John D. Leshy

In this chapter I discuss both the energy minerals—coal, oil, gas, oil shale, geothermal, and uranium—and the more valuable "hardrock" minerals like copper, gold, silver, lead, zinc, and molybdenum. Beyond my scope are the fertilizer minerals (potash, sodium, phosphate) and more ubiquitous substances like building stone, sand, gravel, and clay.

Several facts shape the context for my speculations. First, federal lands are currently important national sources of many of these minerals, particularly oil, gas, and coal. One reason for this is the sheer size of the federal estate, which includes about one-third of the nation's uplands, and almost all of the submerged lands off the coasts—those extending three to 200 miles offshore. (The federal Submerged Lands Act of 1953[1] gave the coastal states title to the submerged lands and minerals in the first three miles or, in a few places, the first three leagues.) A second reason is the location of these lands, concentrated as they are in regions geologically favorable to the occurrence of certain minerals: for example, hardrocks are plentiful in the Rocky Mountains, the northern Great Plains are rich with coal, and the Outer Continental Shelf (OCS) in the Gulf of Mexico contains large amounts of oil and gas.

Federal lands have been supplying an increasing proportion of coal, oil, and gas. They were responsible for 10 percent of the nation's domestic coal production in 1976, 20 percent in 1985, 30 percent in 1993, and nearly half today. This federal coal is produced mostly from nine huge strip mines located in Campbell County, Wyoming. The trend to western federal lands was underscored recently when Peabody, the world's largest coal company, announced it was divesting itself of its private properties in Appalachia and concentrating its U.S. operations on federal lands in Wyoming.

Oil and gas production has undergone a similar shift, almost as dramatic. Federal lands accounted for about 10 percent of the nation's crude oil production in 1959; today, they supply about 33 percent. Federal lands accounted for about 10 percent of the nation's natural gas production in 1964; today, they supply nearly 40 percent. Federal oil and gas production has also increasingly moved offshore. The OCS now supplies about five-sixths of the federal oil and more than two-thirds of the federal gas produced. More than twice as much federal acreage is now leased offshore (nearly all of it in the Gulf of Mexico) than onshore.

In the future, federal lands are also likely to be important, perhaps predominant, sources of uranium, geothermal energy, tar sands, and oil shale, if—and it is a very big if—technology and policy favor production of such resources.

The importance of federal lands for hardrock mineral production is a more complicated story. The government keeps no relevant statistics. While nearly all domestic production of hardrock minerals is in the western United States where federal lands predominate, a good deal of it is on land that has passed out federal ownership, thanks to the privatization (patenting) feature of the Mining Law. A Government Accountability Office (GAO) survey of mineral operators in the early 1990s indicated that approximately three-quarters of the total hardrock mineral production in the 12 western states came from nonfederal land.[2]

Even so, federal land mineral policy remains important to hardrock mineral production. Many large hardrock mines are on a mixture of federal, state and private ownerships, often in bewilderingly complex patterns. Federal policy toward the federal portion can control or at least influence what happens on the state and private lands. Also, large modern mining operations typically need vast amounts of land for waste dumps, tailings piles and processing facilities, and federal lands may be the only ones available for this purpose. Finally, federal lands are important future sources: that same GAO report estimated that the federal lands contained about $65 billion in hardrock mineral reserves.

I. Some Basic Propositions

Several propositions—which, I believe, are mostly obvious and undisputed—are relevant to forecasting the future for federally owned minerals. First, the future of federal mineral production, particularly energy minerals, is very much tied up with national energy policy. Today national energy needs are met primarily with fossil fuels. More than one-third of the energy consumed in the United States is derived from oil, and about one-quarter each from natural gas and coal. If national energy policy discourages the use of coal, demand for federal coal will be dampened. If national energy policy promotes nuclear power, demand for federal uranium may increase. And so forth.

So, what will that very influential national energy policy be? A strong consensus is emerging that efforts to slow emissions of greenhouse gases must drive our energy policy. Major corporations, including some big energy companies, are climbing aboard what looks increasingly like a bandwagon. Indeed, we may be (hopefully) on the threshold of some very fundamental changes in national energy policy to come to grips with greenhouse gas emissions. Such changes will have a major impact on federal mineral production. But the contours of that policy is, as of this writing, anyone's guess. The political process works toward compromise and something-for-everybody solutions, suggesting that national energy policy could include such seemingly dubious goals as promoting corn-based ethanol and coal-to-liquid processing, as well as subsidies for softer paths like wind and solar. One can hope that the national policy will be bold, recalling the turtle that only makes progress when it sticks its neck out. Only time will tell.

The future of non-energy minerals presents an even more murky and variegated picture. Demand for industrial metals is closely linked to overall health in the economy, and demand for certain materials may benefit from greenhouse gas emissions controls. For example, every Toyota Prius hybrid automobile contains 50 pounds of copper. Future demand for molybdenum is linked to the health of the oil industry, which is a heavy consumer of moly-hardened steel. Eighty percent of oil wells drilled today are at least 8,000 feet deep, and each one requires hundreds of tons of steel. Future demand for gold, whose principal use—85 percent of demand—is for jewelry rather than investment, is harder to predict because it is driven by psychological forces. Growing jewelry demand in developing countries like China and India has been a big driver of gold prices in recent years.

The market for most minerals is now a global one. Venezuelan or Saudi policy toward oil production, or Zambian policy toward copper production, or Australian policy toward uranium production, may have as much or more to say about demand for federal minerals as federal mineral policy. The exceptions are coal and natural gas (at least until more ports to accommodate liquefied natural gas vessels are licensed and built), because not much of either moves across U.S. borders.

In this global marketplace, the relative stability of governments and the amount of protection they afford investment in capital-intensive mineral development ventures are important factors. The United States has long been favored because of these factors. Canada's Fraser Institute annually surveys leading mining company executives to rate hardrock-mineral-rich jurisdictions around the world on their friendliness to mining as measured by such factors as government stability, infrastructure, labor, tax, and regulatory policies. Western U.S. states usually rank at the top—Nevada was number one several years in a row—along with Canadian provinces and Australian states.[3]

Globalization has also helped fuel consolidation in many of these industries. A handful of hardrock mining companies now dominate. The four biggest gold mines—all in Nevada, which boasts 12 of the 15 largest mines—account for well over half the total U.S.

production, and the 30 biggest mines account for well over 99 percent. Production of copper, molybdenum, lead, silver and zinc is also concentrated in relatively few mines.

Many see less reliance on foreign sources of energy and minerals as highly desirable. Canada, which now supplies the United States with a significant amount of oil from tar sands (2–3 million barrels a day) and natural gas, is an exception. Nevertheless, the facts overwhelmingly support the proposition that domestic production, even from an all-out effort to develop sources on federal lands, cannot liberate us from foreign sources. Consider oil: while the federal estate's relative contribution to domestic oil production has steadily grown, the percentage of U.S. oil demand met from all domestic sources has steadily diminished.

The culprit is a combination of rising demand and, more recently, declining production. From 1948 to 1972, domestic oil production from all federal and nonfederal sources nearly doubled, from 5.5 million to 9.5 million barrels per day. Because demand grew so much faster, however, the percentage of oil imports more than tripled over the same period, from less than 10 percent to about 33 percent. Since 1972, imports have nearly doubled again, and now account for more than half of U.S. consumption. Over that same period, domestic oil production has declined in absolute terms.

The picture seems particularly bleak for onshore federal lands. While today federal lands onshore and offshore cumulatively supply about one-third of domestic oil production, onshore federal lands comprise less than one-fifth of that, or only about 6 percent of the total domestic oil production, and less than 3 percent of our total oil consumption. The picture for natural gas is much the same: Of the 85 percent of total U.S. natural gas consumption that is produced domestically (almost all the rest comes from Canada), only about 10 percent comes from onshore federal lands. About twice as much, or 20 percent, comes from the federal OCS.

History teaches that technological breakthroughs, though very hard to predict, have huge effects on federal mineral supply and demand. The shift in federal oil and gas production to the OCS over the last 30 years has capitalized on major advances in technology, allowing oil and gas deposits in offshore water several thousand feet deep to be located and tapped safely—a remarkable achievement given that the industry did not begin a serious move offshore until well into the second half of the twentieth century. Just in the last 15 years, perfection of techniques for extracting natural gas from coalbeds, where gas was long considered a nuisance, have sparked a booming industry on federal lands in Wyoming and elsewhere. In the last few years, improvements in hydraulic fracturing and horizontal drilling techniques have led to rapid expansion in hydrocarbon rich shale formations, especially in regions of the country without much federal land.[4] Gold production from federal lands went up dramatically when cyanide heap-leach mining and the development of massive earth-moving machines enabled extraction of highly disseminated fine-particle gold. Comparable developments have occurred several times in the past; for example, the development of the froth flotation process for extracting copper and other minerals from lower grade deposits a century ago ushered in giant open-pit mining on federal land.

Federal mineral production is big business. The investments and potential profits are huge, and they can carry comparable political weight, encouraging governments to look favorably on federal policies promoting mineral production. The direct revenues to government from federal mineral production dwarf those derived from all other uses of federal lands (such as recreation, timber harvesting, and livestock grazing) combined. In fact, the Interior Department's energy mineral leasing program is the third biggest federal revenue generator after the Internal Revenue Service (federal income tax) and Social Security/Medicare tax. In fiscal year 2008, the Minerals Management Service reported that the federal government was paid rents, bonus bids, and royalties totaling about $24 billion from coal, oil, and gas leases on federal and American Indian lands and on the Outer Continental Shelf.[5]

Some of this revenue is shared with the states, which get 50 percent of onshore federal oil, gas, and coal revenues (except for Alaska, which gets 90 percent of oil and gas revenues). Federal mineral revenue sharing is a significant part of the state budgets of Alaska, Wyoming, and New Mexico. There was, until recently, no sharing of federal offshore oil and gas revenues with the states, but that is changing with enactment of the 2005 Energy Policy Act[6] and the Gulf of

Mexico Energy Security Act of 2006.[7] States also levy severance taxes on federal energy minerals over and above the share of federal revenues they get directly. The commerce clause of the Constitution has not proved a significant barrier to such taxation.[8] The revenue picture is distinctly different for hardrock mineral production on federal lands, for which the federal government levies no royalty or other charges. The states can and do derive revenues from federal hardrock mineral production through severance taxes.

Jobs tied to federal mineral production are important in some local areas, but the minerals industry has become a much more efficient user of manpower. Today the entire direct payroll of the Wyoming coal industry—which produces nearly half the coal in the entire country—numbers about 5,000. Labor efficiency is a very big reason why the industry has migrated west. Unit output per job in the hardrock mining industry went up much faster than in other industries in the 1970s and 1980s. The total number of mining and smelting jobs in the Rocky Mountain West was slashed in half in the early 1980s, and has continued to decline marginally.[9] Fewer jobs, no matter how well-paying, translate into reduced political clout locally and regionally.

Onshore mineral development tends to be an intensive land use, and can pose serious threats to water and air quality, fish and wildlife habitat, and scenic beauty. Some of these impacts can be controlled or mitigated satisfactorily, but some cannot. Some impacts are localized, but some are not. The U.S. Environmental Protection Agency's annual Toxics Release Inventory (TRI) shows that hardrock mines are responsible for about one-quarter by weight of all toxic substances emitted by U.S. industry. In 2005 these mines released nearly 400 million pounds of lead, more than 170 million pounds of arsenic, and nearly four million pounds of airborne mercury. Processing facilities associated with giant Nevada gold mines account for an estimated one-quarter of all mercury air emissions west of Texas. Acid mine drainage from mines that ceased production many decades ago still fouls water bodies across the West. Historic mining areas like Butte, Montana and Globe, Arizona are permanently scarred. Total cleanup costs for abandoned hardrock mines across the West have been estimated at dozens of billions of dollars.[10]

Although the onshore petroleum industry has developed various drilling techniques to reduce its footprint on the landscape, its impact can be major, especially if associated road-building is considered. Coal-bed methane, a relatively low-grade energy source, requires a lot of land and a large number of wells for each unit of gas extracted. Overall, petroleum development may be the most important current cause of wildlife habitat fragmentation and disruption in the intermountain West. Still, mineral development directly disturbs a much smaller area of federal land (only a few million acres) than livestock grazing (found on more than a quarter of a billion federal acres), timber harvesting, and many other federal land uses like motorized recreation.

II. The Legal Framework for Federal Mineral Development

The basic legal framework has remained the same for several decades. Most mineral development on federal lands is carried out by private industry under federal supervision, with the government reserving the authority to decide where and under what conditions federal minerals are developed. It was not always so. After an early nineteenth century experiment with mineral leasing, U.S. federal land mineral policy generally favored open, unrestricted exploitation, best exemplified in the "come and get it" free access policy of the Mining Law of 1872.[11] A titanic struggle—triggered by Teddy Roosevelt's aggressive policy of "withdrawing" from availability substantial amounts of federal mineral land in the early twentieth century—culminated in the enactment of the Mineral Leasing Act of 1920.[12] This landmark law put all federal energy minerals (except for uranium) under a leasing system where the government (a) retains substantial control (if it wants to exercise it) over whether and how the federal minerals are developed; and (b) receives a direct financial return in the form of bonus bids, rentals, and a royalty on production. The details of these systems vary somewhat on ordinary federal lands, acquired federal lands, and the outer continental shelf, but the basic elements are the same.

Hardrock minerals are the big exception. They remain generally subject to the Mining Law of 1872, under which the government has less control over when and how minerals are developed, and the mining companies make no direct payments to the federal treasury. This law has stubbornly resisted repeated attempts to repeal or fundamentally change it. Another such effort is underway in the 111th Congress, with reform bills pending in the both the House (HR 699) and Senate (S796 and S140) as of this writing.

Another legacy of the progressive era of a century ago is divided ownership of about sixty million acres of land, mostly in the northern Great Plains and the Southwest. During that time, the federal government began reserving to itself, when it transferred lands out of federal ownership, both the title to the minerals and the right to develop them. These "split-estate" lands have, predictably, sparked controversy when the federal government's mineral policies conflict with the wishes of the surface owner.

III. Some Near-Term Predictions

Building on these facts and observations, I fearlessly offer some rather specific predictions. But perhaps there is not much to fear. Despite John Kenneth Galbraith's famous assertion that "if all else fails, immortality can always be assured by spectacular error," bad forecasts, even colossally bad ones, are usually not remembered. Recall the "paperless office" touted by electronic gearheads? The average worker now goes through 12,000 sheets a year.

My first prediction does seem really safe: Climate change and U.S. policies to address it are huge wild cards that could trump practically everything else affecting future use of federal minerals. While the shape of the United States' response to the challenge is only dimly discernable as of this writing, the specter of climate change makes some things fairly clear. For example, despite the fervent hopes and predictions of its champions, oil shale will never, absent some huge technological breakthrough, achieve commercial production; it is simply too carbon-rich and requires too much water and energy to produce. Oil shale, so an industry saying goes, is the energy source of the future, and it always will be.

The long-term future of coal, another carbon-rich source of energy, is almost as cloudy, as it depends on whether any of various technological bets being placed on controlling its greenhouse emissions will pay off. Known coal-to-liquids processes consume a lot of energy, and the feasibility of carbon capture and sequestration by underground injection is not yet proven on the vast scale required for coal to become truly climate-change-friendly. As George W. Bush gave way to Barack Obama, the Bureau of Land Management was assuming that coal could be "fixed" in a world conscious of greenhouse gas emissions; it was preparing to put several billion more tons of federal coal in northeast Wyoming up for lease over the next few years.

Oil and gas will likely remain an important transition fuel, but over the long term, substantial conservation efforts, prompted by tougher vehicle fuel-efficiency standards (so-called CAFE, or Corporate Average Fuel Economy, regulations), may dampen demand. And as the price of fossil fuels increases, electricity-generating alternatives like solar and wind look better and better.

More directly pertinent to the public lands, the early twenty-first century reenactment of the nineteenth century's "Gilded Age"—giving industrial interests free access to much of the public domain—may be ending. Its high water mark may have come with approval of the Energy Policy Act of 2005, which unabashedly favored traditional energy industries. One of its more notable features directed the federal agencies to throw a big party for oil shale commercialization.[13] It is still an open question whether anyone will show up.

Historians may mark the beginning of the end of this epoch at the short but fierce battle in late 2005 and early 2006 over the brazen Pombo-Gibbons proposal to put the antiquated Mining Law on steroids. By renewing patenting and liberalizing its terms, the proposal (passed by the House but stymied in the Senate) would have opened the door to privatizing millions of acres of federal land. The 2006 fall elections, in which Mr. Pombo was defeated and the Democrats resumed control of both houses of Congress, dramatically changed public lands politics. In addition to enacting overwhelmingly conservation-oriented omnibus public lands management legislation in early 2009,[14]

Congress—driven in part by the need to raise revenue to close the budget deficit, and as part of a fundamental, climate-change-induced reexamination of national energy policy—has begun reexamining sweeteners handed out in the 2005 energy bill, which were rather shameless, even by Washington, D.C., standards.

Conservationists and their allies will continue to advocate protection from mineral—principally oil and gas—development for some special wild areas of the onshore public lands. The coastal plain of the Arctic National Wildlife Refuge will likely continue to be the "poster child" for such efforts, because, despite some close calls, it has not yet been leased. The strenuous battle waged over the last three decades to protect it raises an interesting if unanswerable question: would more special places in the lower 48 have been saved if conservationists had diverted some of their resources to protect them, or did the massive campaign to protect the Arctic Refuge's coastal plain lay the groundwork for Congress to protect at least some of the others?

The loose coalition of farmers, ranchers, hunters, anglers, cultural and historic preservation advocates, tribes, and conservationists, which formed to fight the aggressive onshore federal lands energy initiatives of the George W. Bush administration, will likely hold together and grow more influential, at least for the next few years. It has been effective in waging campaigns to protect some special places whose names—if not yet household words—are much more familiar than they were a few short years ago. This coalition has scored some signal successes. In the Rocky Mountain Front and New Mexico's Valle Vidal, close congressional election battles in 2006 helped turn normally prodevelopment members of Congress (Conrad Burns, Heather Wilson, Pete Domenici) into protection advocates, and Congress followed their lead.

As protection campaigns picked up supporters, they began at last to slow, in its waning days, the Bush administration's relentless push for more leasing and development. Politicians from the West became bolder advocates of protection. Representative John Salazar opposed BLM's push to build roads and lease lands in roadless areas of the HD Mountains in western Colorado. New Mexico Governor Bill Richardson opposed further oil and gas leasing on the Otero Mesa, even going so far as to file suit to stop it. The late Senator Craig Thomas, a conservative Republican, opposed new leasing in the Wyoming Range south of Jackson (and Congress in 2009 enacted legislation to protect it[15]) and expressed some misgivings about aggressive plans to issue new leases in the Red Desert. These middle-of-the-road voices on the side of conservation have turned "war on the West" rhetoric upside down. The Obama administration will likely be more favorable to such entreaties.

For its part, the hardrock industry—aided by favorable geology and a hospitable regulatory climate in Nevada and Arizona—has mostly been fenced out of pristine landscapes over the past couple of decades. Nearly every large new mine proposed outside of established mining areas in the western states has encountered significant opposition and been bogged down. The proposed giant Pebble Mine on state land in Alaska may be a key test of whether the industry can change that pattern. This is a far cry from yesteryear, when governments and western communities never saw a proposed mine they didn't like.

The minerals industry might be able to operate in some of these areas by reducing its footprint and exploiting more environmentally friendly techniques like directional drilling. But—especially barring significant advances in various kinds of *in situ* mineral extraction—such efforts can only take the industry so far. To many conservationists and their allies, the industrialization that accompanies mineral development cannot be reconciled with protecting scenery and habitat. It seems likely, then, that more and more federal lands will be put off-limits to significant mineral development by a variety of formal and informal mechanisms.

From a long-range perspective, this continues a trend that goes back to the Yellowstone National Park Act of 1872,[16] and that has seen national parks, monuments, wildlife refuges, conservation areas, wilderness and wilderness study areas generally put off-limits to mineral activity. The effect is an ever-increasing geographic concentration of federal mineral development; for example, the gold industry in Nevada, the copper industry in Arizona, the coal industry in the northern Great Plains with outposts in Colorado and Utah, and the coalbed methane industry in the Powder and San Juan River basins.

Looking to federal resources offshore, political debate is intensi-fying over how much to expand the search for oil and gas resources on the Outer Continental Shelf, including in "frontier" areas. Over the last 40 years, an alliance of conservationists and not-in-my-backyard (NIMBY) advocates along the coasts have forged a strong bipartisan consensus that has fenced off most OCS areas from new federal leasing. The petroleum industry is seeking to change that and has been making progress. Its case for opening up these areas is bol-stered by the fact that offshore oil and gas development has had a practically unblemished record of spill prevention in U.S. waters since it perfected techniques to prevent blowouts and spills in the wake of the 1969 Santa Barbara oil blowout. More frequent and severe hurri-canes (if some climate change experts are correct) may provide more of a challenge, but even though the industry's sprawling Gulf of Mexico operations suffered major hurricane damage in recent years, relatively little oil spilled. Of course, OCS development can have substantial onshore impacts from concomitant industrialization, and the Louisiana Gulf Coast has suffered substantial loss of wetlands, owing in part to offshore oil and gas activity (along with interruption of renewing sediments as a result of Army Corps of Engineers' reen-gineering the Mississippi River). The industry and its allies seek to assuage coastal state environmental concerns by sharing federal reve-nues with them. In February 2008, under the Bush administration, the industry scored a big success with a large lease sale (netting the government nearly $3 billion in bonus bids) in the Arctic Ocean off northern Alaska, although litigation has so far stymied drilling.[17]

There is considerable irony in the fact that the United States has restricted OCS oil and gas development in part to protect the com-mercial fishing industry, and yet stood by while that industry plun-dered and essentially destroyed productive fishing grounds. I recall, during my service in the Carter administration, accompanying my boss, Interior Secretary Cecil Andrus, as he got an earful from Sena-tor Edward Kennedy about how oil and gas leasing off Massachusetts would destroy one of the world's most valuable fisheries, at Georges Bank. We acceded to the Senator's request and shelved leasing plans, but within a couple of decades the Georges Bank fishery was history, destroyed by overfishing.

For decades, mining enterprises effectively controlled the political machinery in many western states, which were little more than cheerleaders for mineral development. Many states even enacted industry-sponsored laws preempting local governments from regulating mining through land use laws, changing the normal rule that land use regulation was a prerogative of local government. Today the situation is much changed. States are becoming more aggressive about participating in federal mineral decision-making, and their regulatory programs are improving, as they respond to demographic and economic changes. (For an example of this, see sidebar at the end of this chapter.) The amenity and economic value of wide open spaces is increasingly recognized across the political spectrum, drawing on studies documenting how, for example, western counties with more protected wilderness have healthier economies.[18] This has made many local areas more hesitant to embrace mining activities and associated industrialization

State regulatory programs that apply to federal mineral development still vary substantially in rigor, but even Nevada—along with Arizona, historically the friendliest to hardrock mining—has begun to pay some attention to mercury emissions from the giant gold mines in the state. Water is a somewhat different story. Water needed for mineral operations on federal lands is obtained under state, not federal law, and mineral extraction can have major hydrologic impacts. Coalbed methane (CBM) extracts large quantities of groundwater as a necessary byproduct, and the giant open pits common to large hardrock mines often require constant dewatering, drawing down regional groundwater supplies. In both cases groundwater is usually discharged on the surface, and is often of lower quality than the surface water it mixes with. States with CBM production, most notably Wyoming, and states with large hardrock mines, like Nevada and Arizona, have done relatively little to control or to mitigate these impacts. Although the western states have long and fiercely defended their right to manage water within their borders, this big perturbation in the hydrologic system so far seems to be little managed.

By contrast, most states are increasing demands for financial assurance for reclaiming lands disturbed by mining. To some extent this is to make up for past spectacular failures (for example, Summitville in

Colorado and Zortman-Landusky in Montana), where hardrock mining companies declared bankruptcy and saddled state and federal taxpayers with large cleanup bills. States are also enacting or considering laws to provide more protection to private surface owners in split-estate situations, and are beginning to assess state and local infrastructure costs associated with mining more realistically, doubtless motivated at least in part by the desire to maintain the pipeline to federal revenue-sharing. Colorado, for example, recently estimated that state and local governments will incur billions of dollars in energy-impact costs over the next couple of decades.

Offshore, states do not regulate activities on OCS lands under federal jurisdiction, but they do have nearly plenary authority over the onshore impacts of OCS development. Spurred by the nightmarish experience with Hurricane Katrina, where coastal land loss was exacerbated by decades of oil and gas development, Louisiana is leading a charge to tap revenues from federal leases and is making some headway.

At the federal level, both industry and environmental interests have long criticized the regulatory processes under which federal minerals are developed. Federal mineral decision-making tends to proceed through familiar pathways like the National Environmental Policy Act (NEPA) and, when imperiled species may be affected, the Endangered Species Act (ESA). Also, federal land and resource planning processes used by the Bureau of Land Management and the U.S. Forest Service help guide the extent to which federal lands are made available for mineral activities. A considerable body of opinion across the political spectrum regards the NEPA and planning processes as not functioning very well in guiding federal mineral development. But there is no consensus on how to improve them. Conservationists tend to advocate that these processes focus more on the big environmental and policy issues and on tighter controls. They also want to maintain the opportunity to challenge plans in court. Industry, which had the support of the Bush administration but likely not its successor, wants to streamline the processes using simplification devices like "categorical exclusions," and to reduce litigation opportunities. Perhaps climate change will provide the catalyst to achieve significant reform, but I am not holding my breath: I suspect the current situation is not so bad as to tempt either conservation or development interests to use up much political capital to fix it.

In the last couple of decades green consumer and corporate campaigns have begun to show some political traction. Mineral extraction being a visibly dirty business, campaigns to change the industry's corporate behavior and attitude toward federal minerals policy reforms could have growing influence. In the last few years, influenced by concerns over "blood diamonds" used to foment violence in Africa, a group of jewelers led by Tiffany and Company have begun to advocate for more responsible mining practices by the precious metals mining industry. This "no dirty gold" campaign helped put reform of the antiquated 1872 Mining Law back on the congressional agenda. Similar campaigns might take root in other segments of the minerals industry and might help temper industry opposition to tougher regulation of their practices, especially on public lands.

Regarding reform of the antiquated Mining Law of 1872, hardrock mining continues to argue that reform could drive it off federal lands. But it remains true that (1) the industry has a sweeter financial deal on those lands—paying no royalty on production— than it has just about anywhere else on the planet, and (2) industry health is much more influenced by commodity prices than by other factors. Any reform legislation would likely phase in royalty payments for existing mines, if it did not exempt them entirely, so it seems unlikely that reform, if it comes, will have much effect on federal land mineral production.

IV. Federal Mineral Development in 2029—A Hypothetical Status Report

Federal coal production has remained strong, still concentrated in Wyoming's huge beds of strippable, low-sulfur coal. Demand has not dried up because technology to capture and sequester much of its carbon has been developed and implemented, thanks to huge federal subsidies. The power of big coal has proved the equal to big agribusiness and big pharma.

Federal oil and gas production continues, though at an ever-dwindling rate. While clever new technologies continue to wring more resource out of declining fields, even they are incapable of getting blood from a turnip. Meanwhile, the boom in "shale gas" production continues, but largely off federal lands. Petroleum production from onshore federal land is now concentrated in a few "sacrifice" areas and in some other places under stringent limitation regarding road-building, directional drilling, and other measures to reduce the industry's footprint on the landscape. The coalbed methane development boom is largely over, as the supplies in large coal seams are rapidly being exhausted. In its wake are depleted aquifers and some lingering surface water pollution, a scarred landscape that is slowly healing, and some formerly booming communities gone bust.

In the meantime, a number of special places where drilling proposals were hotly disputed have been protected, either by wilderness designation or other special legislation, by executive branch national monument proclamations or other withdrawals, or simply by executive branch inaction on drilling proposals. For some of these places, protection was accompanied by compensation (from public or private funds or a combination) to existing leaseholders.

Offshore, federal oil and gas production in the deepwater Gulf of Mexico continues apace, with Texas, Louisiana, Mississippi and Alabama now reaping substantial revenue-sharing benefits. A vigorous natural gas industry emerged off Virginia and the Carolinas after federal leases were issued on the OCS there starting in 2014. Florida is being ringed with OCS development after a deal struck in 2018 allowed the state, with federal funds derived from OCS royalties, to offer free prescription drugs to all 34 million of its senior citizens. Leases were issued and drilling was finally under way on the OCS off the New England coast, soon after the last Kennedy left Congress in 2020. Alaska is also experiencing an offshore petroleum boom, as much of the OCS around the state (all now free of ice year-round) is under lease. California, meanwhile, remains bitterly divided about offshore oil development, but happily, widespread telecommuting and the emergence of tiny fuel-cell driven cars has reduced its previously insatiable demand for gasoline. Oregon and Washington, meanwhile, are still considering whether to accept a congressional proposal to allow leasing on the OCS off their shores, in return for guaranteed federal dollars to operate the hatcheries that are now the sole supply of salmon in their states' rivers.

A small uranium mining industry is operating on federal lands in eastern Wyoming and eastern Utah, helping fuel a rejuvenated domestic nuclear power industry, which has also been bolstered by large federal subsidies. The industry is successfully operating under the Uranium Mineral Leasing Act of 2010, which had removed uranium from the old Mining Law of 1872. Congress's more general overhaul of the Mining Law didn't come until late in Hillary Clinton's Administration, in 2019. The breakthrough came on a deal that limited the application of the Mining Law to the state of Nevada and a handful of other specific geographic areas in the West that had long been the scene of mining activity. Everywhere else, hardrock minerals are now subject to a leasing system, and so far almost no new leases have been issued because "cappuccino cowboy" towns that dominate the rural West rose up to defeat leasing proposals in the few places they were made. Even in some places where the old Mining Law still applies, such as historic copper mining towns in Arizona, hordes of retirees successfully organized to limit operations that threatened the amenities that brought them there. Meanwhile, "in situ" mining techniques are beginning to show promise, although concerns about their effects on groundwater quality have not been entirely assuaged.

V. Conclusion

These speculations are made with full awareness that the history of federal mineral development offers little confidence about predictions. A few decades ago almost no one would have forecast that the nation's coal industry would shift to federal lands in the West, that the domestic petroleum industry would shift to the deepwater Gulf of Mexico, or that northern Nevada would be transformed by the rise of heap-leach mining of fine-particle gold. I content myself with the observation that in our recent Gilded Age, remarkably little professional consequence seemed to follow from being wrong, as illustrated by CEOs who ran their companies into the ground and made off with handsome compensation packages voted by compliant boards of directors. I won't have, nor hopefully will I need, such luck.

The Fight Over Drilling on Colorado's Roan Plateau

Western Colorado's 9,000-foot-high Roan Plateau has been the scene of one of the new millennium's battles over federal mineral development. Almost 75,000 acres of federal land in the area had been withdrawn as a Naval Oil Shale Reserve in 1912, but in 1997 it was transferred to the U.S. Bureau of Land Management (BLM). Ever since, BLM has been working to lease and develop the area for oil and gas. Complicating the picture is the presence of many acres of private land in the area, much of it owned by Encana Energy.

BLM estimated that the Roan Plateau contains one-third of Colorado's and 4 percent of the Nation's natural gas reserves. It is also a rich wildlife and recreation resource, popular with hunters, anglers, and other recreationists. The government had to decide whether to protect the top of the Plateau to preserve its wildlife and other wild values. Some of the area's resources could be tapped by lateral drilling from neighboring lands, even if it were leased under stipulations prohibiting the land surface from being occupied. Assuming some surface development was allowed, the government needed to determine its pace and intensity, including road building, well spacing, reclamation, and the like.

Conservationists helped assemble a coalition of hunters, anglers, local outfitters, and other rural residents to oppose development. They found the ear of Representative John Salazar, his brother, Senator Ken Salazar, and newly elected Colorado Governor Bill Ritter. Governor Ritter proposed a plan that would have kept more land off-limits to direct drilling and leased the land in phases over several years, which he argued would ultimately generate more revenue.

BLM rejected Ritter's proposal, although it did include no-surface-occupancy stipulations in some leases, required well pads to be spaced at least a half-mile apart, and limited road building. The BLM plan projects 13 well pads and 210 wells on top of the Plateau, with an additional 180 pads and 1360 wells in the general area.[19] In September 2008 it proceeded to lease several thousand acres on the Plateau, the auction generating $114 million in revenue.

Conservationists challenged the leases in federal court, and after the change in presidential administrations, the Obama administration initiated settlement talks, with now–Secretary of the Interior Ken Salazar describing the effort as a way to better protect the resource and value to the taxpayers. No settlement has been announced as of this writing. In a related move, Colorado's Oil and Gas Conservation Commission, the state agency regulating oil and gas activities, adopted new rules in March 2009 implementing new laws adopted by the state legislature and requiring more consideration of the environment, wildlife, and public health and safety when approving gas and oil development. The Legislature approved the laws in 2007 and then the Commission's new rules in 2009. The oil and gas industry strongly opposed the new rules and has filed a lawsuit challenging them. Meanwhile, on July 1, 2009, the state agency, the U.S. Forest Service, and BLM reached agreement as to their applicability to federal lands.

Notes

1. 43 U.S.C. §§ 1301–1315.
2. U.S. GENERAL ACCOUNTING OFFICE, MINERAL RESOURCES: VALUE OF HARDROCK MINERALS EXTRACTED FROM AND REMAINING ON FEDERAL LANDS, GAO/RCED-92-192 (Aug. 1992).
3. See http://www.fraserinstitute.org/researchandpublications/publications/6534 .aspx.
4. See, e.g., U.S. DEPARTMENT OF ENERGY, MODERN SHALE GAS DEVELOPMENT IN THE UNITED STATES: A PRIMER (April 2009) available at http://www.gwpc .org/e-library/documents/general/Shale%20Gas%20Primer%202009.pdf .
5. See Minerals Management Service, Disbursements and Reported Royalties, http://www.mrm.mms.gov/MRMWebStats/Disbursements_Royalties

.aspx?report=AllReportedRoyaltyRevenues&yeartype=FY&year=2008&
datetype=AY.

6. Energy Policy Act, 42 U.S.C. § 15802.

7. Gulf of Mexico Energy Security Act, 43 U.S.C. § 1331.

8. Commonwealth Edison v. Montana, 453 U.S. 609 (1981).

9. TOM POWER, LOST LANDSCAPES AND FAILED ECONOMIES (1996); TOM POWER
    AND RICHARD N. BARNETT, POST–COWBOY ECONOMICS: PAY AND PROSPER-
    ITY IN THE NEW AMERICAN WEST (2001).

10. *See, e.g.*, Patricia Nelson Limerick et al., Cleaning Up Abandoned Hardrock
    Mines in the West: Prospecting for a Better Future, http://www.centerwest
    .org/publications/pdf/mines.pdf.

11. 30 U.S.C. §§ 21–54.

12. 30 U.S.C. §§181–241.

13. Pub. L. No. 109-58, § 369.

14. Pub. L. No. 111-11; *see also* http://www.whitehouse.gov/the_press_office/State-
    ment-from-the-Presidents-signing-statements-on-HR-146-the-Omnibus
    -Public-Lands-Management-Act/.

15. Pub. L. No. 111-11, §§ 3201-03.

16. 16 U.S.C. § 21.

17. *See, e.g.,* http://wilco278.wordpress.com/2009/03/09/9th-circuit-vacates
    -shell-beaufort-sea/.

18. *E.g.,* SONORAN INSTITUTE, PROSPERITY IN THE TWENTY-FIRST CENTURY
    WEST: THE ROLE OF PROTECTED PUBLIC LANDS (2005).

19. GLENWOOD SPRINGS FIELD OFFICE, BUREAU OF LAND MANAGEMENT, RE-
    CORD OF DECISION FOR THE APPROVAL OF PORTIONS OF THE ROAN PLATEAU,
    http://www.blm.gov/rmp/co/roanplateau/record_of_decision.htm.

15

The Future of America's Forests and Grasslands

Globalization, Crowded Landscapes, Change, and the National Environmental Policy Act

Federico Cheever

I.   Introduction

We are entering what I will call the "fourth phase" in our national quest to manage wisely the natural resources of our forests and grasslands. This fourth phase will be shaped by an emerging climate change crisis, the globalization of natural resource production and use, and the continued expansion of human population on the once sparsely settled western landscape. It will be accompanied by a collision between the established traditions of public land management, local land-use planning and regulation, and public and private land conservation transactions. These developments will impose new stress on the always problematic distinction between publicly and privately owned forests and grasslands. The only statutory tool we have to plan for the future of these lands together is the National Environmental Policy Act of 1970 (NEPA).[1] Yet, unfortunately, that law is under assault.

Whatever happens in the future of American natural resources law will happen, largely, on forests and grasslands. Forests and grasslands together make up most of the landscape of the North American continent. According to the U.S. Department of Agriculture's Economic Research Service, of the 2.3 billion acres in the United States

367

(including Alaska), 651 million acres (28.8 percent) are forest use lands, 98 million acres (4.5 percent) are forestland in parks and other protective designations, and 587 million acres (25.9 percent) are grassland: pasture and range.[2]

Of the United States' roughly 749 million acres of forestland, more than 246 million acres are in public, primarily federal, ownership. Statistics gathered by the U.S. Bureau of Land Management reveal that, of the 587 million acres of grassland and range, roughly 239 million acres are in federal ownership.[3]

Obviously, forest and grasslands are enormously important, providing an array of ecosystem services and traditional commodities. Forests stabilize landscapes by protecting soil and helping soil retain moisture. Forests cycle nutrients necessary for many plant and animal species. By preserving watersheds, they regulate both the quality and quantity of water. They stabilize climate at both local and regional levels. At a global level, they limit climate change by sequestering enormous quantities of carbon in a stable form. They also produce timber and an extraordinary range of recreational opportunities. Grasslands also help maintain the composition of the atmosphere, biological diversity, weather modification, and soil conservation. They too create recreational opportunities, and they produce forage, which, in turn, helps produce meat, milk, leather, and wool.

The United States has divided control of forests and grasslands between private owners and public managers. In the aggregate, roughly one-third of forests and grassland are in public ownership. The rest is private property. The aggregate figure can be deceptive because the public-private mix varies dramatically in different regions of the country. Still, even in the 11 western states dominated by public ownership (12 if you include Alaska), public forests and grasslands are usually islands in a matrix of privately owned land. The public lands are like the chocolate chips in a chocolate chip cookie.

This division becomes more interesting when one considers that we have made no similar division regarding other significant land uses. Of the 442 million acres (19.5 percent) of the United States identified as cropland by the Department of Agriculture, no significant portion is in public ownership. There may be corn and soybean subsidies and the Conservation Reserve Program, which famously pays farmers not to grow crops, but there is no national cropland system in public ownership. Similarly, with the exception of parks, roads, and public buildings, and a few public housing projects, very little of the 60 million acres of urban land in the United States is in public ownership.

Conservative thinkers have asserted that significant public ownership of forests and grasslands (not to mention everything else) is a terrible mistake.[4] One can argue that partial public ownership of forests and grasslands in the United States is a historical accident: a side effect of the history of the development of land use patterns in United States. To some degree this is plainly true. Public ownership of forests and grasslands is the result of episodic periods of national concern centering around issues and policies now largely forgotten. The durable fact of ownership almost inevitably outlasts the policy that inspired it.

However, the existence of similar public-private divisions of forests and grasslands in other common law countries suggests that the ownership pattern is not accidental. The vast majority (more than 90 percent) of Canadian forests are in public ownership, with about 77 percent owned by the provincial governments, and about 16 percent belonging to the federal government. However, a small but significant portion (about 7 percent) of Canadian forests are in private hands. In Australia, Victoria has 3.4 million hectares of state forest. Tasmania's state forests covers 1.5 million hectares. New South Wales' forests cover 2.8 million hectares.

It seems more likely that public ownership of forests and grasslands is the result of the occasional, if not consistent, recognition of the public values these ecosystems embody. The statutes that provide authority for the management of publicly owned forests and grasslands recognize the importance of the public interest in the administration of these lands. The Yellowstone Act of 1872, the National Forest Creation Act of 1891, the National Forest Organic Act of 1897, the National Park Service Organic Act of 1916, the Taylor Grazing Act of 1934, the Multiple-Use Sustained-Yield Act of 1960, the Federal Land Management and Policy Act of 1976, the National Forest Management Act of 1976, and the National Wildlife Refuge Improvement Act of 1997 are dramatically different laws spanning almost half of

American history. Nevertheless, they all share one common theme: the value of the land managed and preserved for the American people.

This does not suggest that privately owned forests and grasslands are without public significance. Privately owned forests and grasslands often embody the same public values and serve the same public functions that publicly owned forests and grasslands do. They are subject to a range of public regulation and benefit from a range of public subsidies.

Public ownership suggests a qualitatively different level of public concern, but this can be an illusion. Public concern attaches to the values forests and grasslands embody and the functions they fill, not to the soils, trees, and grass themselves. Public forests are more likely to be managed with the public interest in mind, but the public interest does not end at the border of the public land and never has.

II.   The Fourth Phase for Forest and Grasslands

There is a very good argument that we are entering a "fourth phase" in the history of American management of forests and grasslands, both public and private, and of natural resources in general. However, before we launch into discussing this fourth phase, we need to consider the three phases that preceded it.

A. The First Phase

As Sally Fairfax, Helen Ingram, and Leigh Raymond remind us in chapter 1, private development dominated the first phase of forest and grassland management. From the end of the Revolutionary War until long after the reservation at Yellowstone in 1872, forests and grasslands were logged and grazed, cleared and burned, and used as mine supports and railroad ties by private concerns.

In *Federalist No. 7*, Alexander Hamilton argued in favor of a strong federal government as necessary to resolve continuing disputes about the western lands. Pointing out that "territorial disputes" had been responsible for "[p]erhaps the greatest proportion of wars that have desolated the earth," Hamilton wrote, "[t]his cause would exist among us in full force. We have a vast tract of unsettled territory within the boundaries of the United States."[5] Accordingly, the language of the "Property Clause" is among the most unqualified in the Constitution and has been interpreted through two centuries of federal court decisions as "without limitation."[6] Yet, despite this powerful constitutional platform, Congress did as little as possible with the public domain for almost 100 years.

Through most of the nineteenth century, as settlement progressed across the woodlands and prairies of the Midwest, through the Deep South, and into the Great Lakes region, the system devised for establishing territories, selling land, and admitting territories as states with their own endowment of public land worked relatively well.

Throughout this era, the federal government's public land laws focused almost completely on the process of disposing of that public land. The federal government devised a bewildering variety of statutory methods for turning land into money while at the same time endeavoring to protect the rights of "squatters," who almost invariably found a way to occupy land well ahead of the line of federal survey. Congress offered surveyed lands for sale in a many different ways, but it also passed "preemption" statutes designed to protect the rights of those already settled on the lands from having their claims sold out from under them when the survey crews and their attendant land speculators finally arrived. Preemption statutes granted actual settlers an option to buy the land they occupied should the federal government decide to sell it.

With the exception of military posts and the occasional fact-finding expedition, the federal government did not concern itself with managing the billions of acres technically in federal hands. "Mountain men" set forth to trap beaver and were replaced, in turn, by miners, settlers, and cattle, all with relatively little interference from the national government, which, in theory, owned almost all the land on which they roamed. The federal government required no trapping or grazing permits, collected few statistics on resource use, and, with the exception of occasionally keeping the peace, let well enough alone.

In 1862, the first of the homestead laws offered free land for settlers who could occupy, cultivate, and survive for the required five years, increasing the administrative profile of the government.[7] The United States eventually granted or sold more than 287 million acres to homesteaders and another 11 million acres under the 1877 Desert Lands Act.[8]

Still, the federal government tried hard to stay out of the day-to-day business of managing the public domain, leaving governance in the hands of the states and territories and their partially organized residents. In the mining laws of the 1860s, culminating in the General Mining Law of 1872, Congress set up a "perpetual motion" machine, whereby mining claims on the public domain could be "perfected" and exploited without the federal government making a decision or even knowing about the claim.[9] The law explicitly relies on local "regulations" made by "[t]he miners of each mining district" governing "the location, manner of recording," and "amount of work necessary to hold possession of a mining claim."[10]

When we examine the now largely defunct machinery of nineteenth- and early twentieth-century land management, it is easy to come to the conclusion that its purpose was the transfer of public rights into private hands. That is, after all, what the laws actually did and what the Supreme Court, in 1845, declared in *Pollard v. Hagan* that they were supposed to do.[11] However, disposal was not a purpose, it was only the means to achieve a variety of nineteenth-century policy goals. These policy goals are now largely forgotten.

Every western state contains thousands of acres that were once transferred into private ownership for nothing under the Homestead Act, and the Stock Raising Homestead Act (287,500,000 acres), and the Desert Lands Act (10,700,000 acres), or for almost nothing under the Timber Culture Act (10,900,000 acres) and the Timber and Stone Act (13,900,000 acres).[12] From 1862, a heady mixture of state donation-act tradition, an egalitarian National Land Reform Movement, and a desire to bind the West more closely to the Union during the Civil War prompted the federal government to give land away to claimants who had fulfilled residency requirements and submitted minimal paperwork.

Many, if not most, surveyed townships in western states still contain one, two or three sections of state land granted by the federal government for support of the common schools (77,630,000 acres), universities, hospitals, prisons and more (21,700,000 acres).[13] In most states, these sections now provide only a tiny amount of the money needed to run modern schools, land grant universities, and prisons. In November 2005 the Colorado State Auditor reported that fiscal year 2003 revenues from state school grant lands were projected to provide 29 million (1.1 percent) of Colorado's 2.7 billion state school budget.[14]

B. The Second Phase

The "first phase" in forest and grassland management did not end in 1872. There is an argument that it ended with the 1976 passage of the Federal Land Policy and Management Act, with its declaration that the public domain was here to stay and its repeal of a number of the laws that undergirded disposal of the public lands. There is also an argument that the first phase lives on through the continued leasing and sale of mineral interests across the United States. However, it is fair to say that, after 1872, something else began happening as well.

During this "second phase," public development—in the form of national forests, national parks, wildlife refuges, dams and reservoirs, and eventually grazing districts—emerged and provided an alternative to the continuing pattern of private development. Theodore Roosevelt, Gifford Pinchot (first chief of the U.S. Forest Service), and Stephen Mather and Horace Albright (first and second directors of the National Park Service)—to name just a few—divided the forests and grasslands, particularly in the West, into two imperfectly defined spheres of activity. The division between those spheres, at least in theory, was the border between private land and the public domain.

On March 1, 1872, President Ulysses S. Grant signed the Yellowstone Park Act and thereby had "reserved and withdrawn" two million acres of land "[f]rom settlement, occupancy or sale under the laws of the United States" as a "pleasuring ground for the benefit and the enjoyment of the people," with the additional provision that there was to be protection against "wanton destruction of the fish and game found within said Park."[15] As Robert Keiter discusses in chapter 10, the Yellowstone reservation was the beginning of a system of public development on public land, ostensibly for the public good.

The idea of preserving some of the nation's forests under government control also emerged onto the political landscape in 1872 when Franklin Hough addressed the American Association for the Advancement of Science, "On the Duty of Governments in the Preservation of Forests." Aware of private logging practices in New York State, Hough briefly discussed the vital role of forests in water conservation and "the economical value of timber, and our absolute dependence on it." Hough argued that laws were necessary "to regulate, promote and protect" them as they are for "any other great object of public utility."[16]

In 1897, Congress passed a three-page amendment to the Sundry Civil Act, the first law directly authorizing active management of portions of the federal public domain outside national parks.[17] The amendment—now generally known as the Forest Service Organic Act—built on the even shorter 1891 enactment authorizing the President to set aside Forest Reserves. The 1897 law authorized the Secretary of the Interior to promulgate "rules and regulations" and establish "such service as will ensure the objects of such regulation," managing the reserves.[18] (Authority would shift to the Secretary of Agriculture after the Forest Reserves moved to the Department of Agriculture in 1905.)

The activities taking place on public and private forest and grassland were not as different as we sometime suppose. "Conservation" was not limited to public, much less federal, land. Nor was "development" limited to private land.

On May 12, 1908, President Theodore Roosevelt and chief forester Gifford Pinchot hosted the National Conservation Conference at the White House. Forty-five state and territorial governors dined with the President. They had been invited to discuss the nation's natural resources and how long they were likely to last. Roosevelt informed the assembled notables that they had come together to discuss "the conservation and use of the great fundamental sources of

wealth of this Nation. . . . We cannot, when the nation becomes fully
civilized and very rich, continue to be civilized and rich unless the
nation shows more foresight than we are showing at this moment."[19]
When the conference adjourned two days later, the assembled governors issued a statement supporting the Roosevelt administration's
conservation policies.

The "conservation" of 1908 was not the subtle and diverse
thought of later decades. It did not reflect the complexities of the
"land organism" that Aldo Leopold described in *Round River* in the
1940s. It did not involve biotic communities or endangered species.
Conservation, in the first decade of the last century, had a hard political edge. "Conservationists" promised that government control of the
public land would make life better now and in the future. They
warned that a continuation of current policies without "Conservation" would result in a host of catastrophes likely to destroy civiliza-
tion itself.

In 1910, Gifford Pinchot published *The Fight for Conservation*, in
which he declared the United States the "most prosperous nation of
to-day" because "our forefathers bequeathed to us a land of marvel-
ous resources still unexhausted."[20] He made it clear that should those
resources be exhausted "disaster and decay in every department of
national life follow as a matter of course."[21] He chided Americans for
applying the "stupidly false" adjective "inexhaustible" to natural resources,[22] and predicted coal famine, timber famine, oil and gas
shortage, iron ore shortage, soil exhaustion, a shortage of clean water
and a shortage of grazing land.

Conservation, according to Pinchot, "stands for development . . . [t]he recognition of the right of the present generation to
the fullest necessary use of all the resources with which this country is
so abundantly blessed."[23] How was development to be reconciled with
Pinchot's repeated dire warnings of resource famine? Through "prevention of waste."[24] Waste, according to Pinchot, was rampant in the
coal fields, in the oil and gas fields, in hardrock mining, in range management, and in forestry. In response, Pinchot offered, "[t]he out-
growth of conservation, the inevitable result, is national efficiency."[25]

The assumption of "efficiency" and absence of "waste" that
Hough, Roosevelt, and Pinchot associated with public management

may surprise those who have lived through the recent political era, in which almost everyone has assumed that efficiency was the exclusive province of private activities and markets. In retrospect, it seems obvious that the assumption that any type of human organization has a monopoly on efficiency is simplistic.

The public land managers of this great age of the American Public Lands defined their goals—rightly or wrongly—in contrast to what they perceived as the often shortsighted, unsustainable, and downright rapacious pattern of development on private land. As Eric Freyfogle points out in chapter 5, this division between public and private development really never worked well. However, a century ago in the West, land was sufficiently plentiful and settlement was sufficiently sparse so that public land managers were not forced to deal with the interrelationship between the public land tradition they were creating and the private land use they used as negative inspiration and cautionary tale.

C. The Third Phase

The "third phase" in the history of the management of American forests and grasslands altered the nature of development on both public and private land. The emergence of environmental awareness in the 1960s eventually required both public and private land managers to consider a range of values that they had traditionally ignored.

Remembering back to the time before Earth Day 1970, former Wisconsin Senator Gaylord Nelson wrote: "It was a time when people could see, smell, and taste pollution. The air above major cities such as New York and Los Angeles was orange, Lake Erie was declared dead, and backyard birds were dying from a chemical known as DDT."[26] Environmental awareness is founded on the horrifying realization that change in the biochemistry of nature outside human bodies has a significant and often unavoidable effect on human health.

In the preface to his history of the environmental movement in the United States, *Fierce Green Fire*, Philip Shabecoff, long-time *New York Times* environmental correspondent, recalled the environmental problems the nation confronted in 1970:

Environmental issues were frequently in the news, and the news was almost all bad. A river in Cleveland burst into flame when the chemical wastes oozing into its waters ignited. Beaches and coastal waters were being fouled with sewage and oil. The Great Lakes were dying from fertilizers and detergents. The air over urban and industrial areas was becoming choked with sulfur, carbon, lead, nitrogen, and a poisonous brew of industrial gases. A growing torrent of synthetic chemicals and radioactive materials was toxifying our land, air, and water—even our blood and body tissue and the milk in mothers' breasts.[27]

Unlike the "conservation" of Roosevelt and Pinchot, the issue at the heart of environmental awareness was not the threatened famine of available goods, but rather their uncontrolled multiplication. As Shabecoff observed: "[t]he flow of goods and products churned out for the seemingly insatiable appetite of an affluent consumer society was leaving a suffocating residue that littered our roads and countryside and had created an avalanche of garbage that threatened to bury us."[28]

What was missing, what was threatened, could not be boxed and shipped, or managed like coal, timber, or water. It could not be readily measured. It was quality of life, as well as health, and the clean environment that supported both. Careful management of resources owned by government would not solve the problem.

Shabecoff's observations illustrate vividly the core quality of 1970s-era environmental concerns: the overlap and frequent unity of issues affecting environmental degradation and the protection of human health. In almost every example Shabecoff presents, the poison pumped through nature's veins eventually ended up in a human body. Toxification of the land, air, and water contaminated our blood and breast milk. It was, and remains, a potent combination of issues.

This link between dangers to the environment and dangers to health provides much of the power in Rachel Carson's 1962 classic, *Silent Spring*. The book's title refers to the loss birdsong and the buzzing of bees caused by pesticide use. Carson begins with a haunting "fable of tomorrow" in which a town "in the heart of America" is showered with a white powder that kills the birds and insects, creating the eponymous silent spring.[29] At first, concerns about human health play no obvious role in the book. Yet, by the end of the book, the reader comes away with a vivid sense of the dangers pesticides pose for human health, indeed the reader's health. In her hair-raising later chapters, Carson examined "the ecology of the world within our bodies," illustrating that, where this sort of contamination is concerned, there is no boundary between people and the environment.

The publication of Stewart Udall's *The Quiet Crisis* in 1963 was a pivotal moment in the application of environmental awareness to forests and grasslands. *The Quiet Crisis* is an extraordinary book, not least because it was the work of a sitting Secretary of the Interior. It traces the history of the public lands, occasionally weaving in an excursion into environmental philosophy, and then broadens out into a general discussion of what would soon be recognized as environmental issues. Udall rejects the "myth of superabundance" in language reminiscent of Pinchot's *Fight for Conservation*.[30] In his final analysis he recapitulates the history of the public lands and public works. Then, in an abrupt shift of emphasis, he addresses problems of pollution, population, and urbanization. He supports the work of Rachel Carson and speaks in classic environmental terms: "our manipulations have multiplied waste products that befoul the land and have introduced frightening new forms of erosion that diminish the quality of indispensable resources and even imperil human health."

The passage of environmental laws like the Clean Water Act and Endangered Species Act have transformed the very nature of the public development contemplated in the conservation era. Dam building, road building, logging, mining, and cattle grazing have all been affected by the application of these statutory fruits of environmental awareness. Indeed, it's fair to say that the environmental laws passed between 1970 and 1980 have transformed and are still transforming the methods and values of the agencies that manage publicly owned forests and grasslands.

The ease with which we can identify the effects of new environmental consciousness in the tradition of public land development regularly leads us into the trap of assuming that environmental consciousness *only* affected public land management. In fact, the observations of Nelson, Shabecoff, Carson, and even Udall apply with just as much force to privately held forests and grasslands, though the effects are much more difficult to trace. Some examples of these effects include 20 years of litigation about the government-sanctioned application of pesticides on private grazing land, furors over bears and wolves in the northern Rocky Mountains, abortive property takings cases involving fish and spotted owls on timber lands,[31] and battles over fish and water in the Klamath River Basin.

D. The Fourth Phase

What do we know about the projected "fourth phase" in the management of American forests and grasslands?

First, as Lisa Heinzerling reminds us in chapter 3, the fourth phase will be played out against a background of potentially catastrophic climate instability. The U.S. Supreme Court 2007 opinion in *Massachusetts v. EPA* prominently featured the National Research Council's 2001 *Climate Change: An Analysis of Some Key Questions*, concluding that there may be significant regional transitions associated with shifts in forest location and composition in the United States due to climate change.[32] Climate change is likely to alter the geographic distribution of North American forests. Changes in temperature and precipitation are expected to change forest location, composition, and productivity. Climate change effects that influence tree growth will also alter rates of carbon sequestration in trees and soils. Increased carbon sequestration would remove more carbon dioxide (CO_2) from the atmosphere, whereas carbon losses through forest disturbances (for example, fire) would result in more CO_2 entering the atmosphere. Changes in forest disturbance regimes, such as fire or disease, could also affect the future of U.S. forests and the market for forest products, such as timber.

More generally, we know that—to an unprecedented degree—global issues will dominate the future: climate change and the resulting loss of biodiversity, and global markets for timber, energy, minerals, agricultural products and recreation. As John Leshy describes in chapter 14, the future demand for U.S. timber, coal, oil, and gas will be a function of decisions made in Asia, Europe, and Africa. Asian tourists will decide whether to visit the Grand Canyon or the savannas of the East Africa. American tourists will decide whether to spend their vacations at Yellowstone or Rotorua. The United Nations World Tourism Organization predicts continued dramatic growth in international tourism. International tourism revenue in 2003 supplied approximately 6 percent of worldwide exports of goods and services. And service exports alone provided nearly 30 percent of tourism exports. Americans, who left eastern cities and suburbs to telecommute from the edge of the Arapahoe and Roosevelt National Forests, may find the land cheaper and the views better in Tasmania. As the Tasmanian Department of Economic Development points out on its Web site, "[w]ith a comfortable climate, relaxed lifestyle and beautiful environment Tasmania is an ideal place to retire to [sic]." The first three phases in the history of managing U.S. forests and grasslands, different though they were, were played out, predominately, within the borders of the United States. The fourth phase will not be. To state the obvious, neither the climate change crisis nor global resource demands will make any distinction between public and private land.

We also know that the relative abundance of land and scarcity of people, which has allowed land managers, both public and private, to ignore neighboring land use, is gone. Conversations about the "wildland urban interface" have become ubiquitous in the American West. The population of the Rocky Mountain West grows faster (in percentages) than any other region in the United States. William Travis, David Theobald, and Daniel Fagre write in *Rocky Mountain Futures*: "Rocky Mountain population and economic growth is now tethered to two major geographic features. First, counties adjacent to metropolitan areas or within an hour's drive of them are the fastest-growing in the West. . . . Second, high-amenity areas removed from cities have become new Rocky Mountain growth poles."[33] That hundreds of Americans would take their dogs for morning exercise in the fragile alpine woodlands and meadows around the strip city of Vail, Colorado, in the until recently unsettled heart of the White River National Forest, was quite beyond the imagining of even the most prescient public land managers in the early twentieth century.

The explosion in "backyard wilderness" alters fundamentally what Americans can get from their public land and the dangers Americans pose to those lands. Travis, Theobald and Fagre report that "many regional analysts believe that this amenity boom, based on the region's natural qualities and enabled by the postindustrial economy, will endure and outlast previous booms. But, like previous booms, it too has the potential to remake Rocky Mountain landscapes in profound ways."[34]

From now on, management of forests and grasslands will not just be a conversation between environmental value and commodity-oriented development; it will also be a conversation between public land management and private land use planning and development. In the 1920s, cities across the United States began employing regulations to control the development of their "built environment." Even before it was ever enacted in an American city, Henry Morgenthau reported to the Conference of City Planning in 1909 that zoning had become "the prime instrument" of planning.

Zoning quickly became the chief instrument for ordering the urban environment and reforming its denizens. "The most important part of City Planning, as far as the future health of the city is concerned," declared Benjamin C. Marsh, one of New York's early zoning advocates, "is the districting of the city into zones or districts in which buildings" of certain heights, volumes, and uses would be confined.[35] Through zoning, planners could achieve the progressive vision of efficiency, rationalizing and controlling urban space by isolating homes, industries, and businesses into discrete districts dedicated to the fullest realization of a single use rather than mixed areas in which conflicting uses contended for dominance.

The 1916 New York zoning code established on its face what planning historian Seymour Toll calls a "hierarchy, a kind of fixed, developmental pecking order for every square inch of city land and every cubic foot of city building." This hierarchy, Toll claims, "was all summed up in the homely phrase, 'A place for everything and everything in its place.'" Nature, in any form, seemed to have nothing to do with land use planning for a surprisingly long time.

In recent years, land use planners' view of open space has changed dramatically. In their 2005 book, *Nature-Friendly Communities: Habitat Protection and Land Use Planning*, Christopher Duerksen and Cara Snyder embrace the idea of habitat conservation as an integral part of modern land use planning. The book includes case studies of 20 communities around the nation that have adopted an extraordinary range of land use planning and regulation strategies to protect natural landscapes within their borders.

The third thing we know about the fourth phase is that a new group will play an essential role on the landscape mosaic. The land trust community—public and private holders of property rights for preservation (variously described)—is the fastest-growing part of the conservation community and now controls millions of acres of land across the United States. The history of the land trust movement is long, involved, and maddeningly diffuse. The first identifiable private land trust in the United States was the Trustees of Reservations established in Massachusetts in 1891 by landscape architect Charles Norton Eliot. The term "conservation easement" did not emerge until half a century after Eliot's death in 1897. In the late 1950s journalist William Whyte advocated using private land use controls to accomplish landscape preservation. Whyte's plan centered on comprehensive planning, land use controls, and private land conservation. By the time Whyte coined the term "conservation easement," the property interest he described was already relatively well established. In the 1930s and 1940s, the National Park Service purchased easements encumbering almost 1,500 acres in Virginia and North Carolina to protect scenic vistas along the Blue Ridge Parkway and another 4,500 acres in Mississippi, Alabama, and Tennessee to protect scenic vistas along the Natchez Trace Parkway.

States began enacting legislation known as "easement enabling statutes," which authorized the use of conservation easements to accomplish a broader range of land conservation goals. The earliest easement enabling statutes were enacted by California in 1959 and New York in 1960. By 1979, 40 states had enacted easement enabling statutes. In 1981, the National Conference of Commissioners on Uniform State Laws promulgated the Uniform Conservation Easement Act (UCEA), which has since been adopted in 22 states. In 2005, Wyoming was the fiftieth state to adopt conservation easement legislation.

At the same time states were busy enacting easement enabling legislation, the Internal Revenue Service and Congress were announcing that federal tax benefits were available to landowners who donated conservation easements. In 1964, the IRS published a Revenue Ruling authorizing a federal charitable income tax deduction for the donation of a conservation easement protecting scenic land adjacent to a federal highway. In 1965, the IRS issued a news release advertising the availability of the charitable income tax deduction for the donation of scenic easements. In the conference report to the Tax Reform Act of 1969, the conferees indicated that donors of "open space" easements are eligible for charitable income, gift, and estate tax deductions. Then in 1976, Congress enacted an explicit statutory provision authorizing conservation easement donors to claim charitable income, gift, and estate deductions.

Today, the vast majority of conservation easements are granted "in perpetuity" because most land trusts accept only perpetual easements and the federal tax incentives are available to landowners only if their donated easements are perpetual. In addition, because most land trusts wish to attract easement donations, they take pains to retain their status as publicly supported charities (and, thus, as "qualified organizations"), and to use one or more of the four qualified conservation purposes listed above as the basis for their easement selection criteria.

As state after state enacted easement enabling legislation and the availability of federal and state tax incentives for easement donations became more widely known and understood, the number of land trusts increased dramatically. The best statistics are maintained by the Land Trust Alliance, which collects periodic census data with respect to the local, state, and regional land trusts operating in the United States (including government and quasi-governmental agencies that operate in a manner similar to land trusts, such as the Maryland Environmental Trust). In 1950, according to this source, there were only 53 land trusts extant, most of which operated in the Northeast. In 1985, there were 479 local, state, and regional land trusts operating in the United States. By 1990, that number had grown to 887; by the end of 2000, there were 1,263; and by 2005, there were 1,667 local, state, and regional land trusts operating nationwide.

The combination of statutory conservation easements, federal and state tax incentives, and well over a thousand land trusts has fundamentally altered the pattern of ownership on the American landscape. According to the Land Trust Alliance's 2005 land trust census, national, regional, and local land trusts have protected more than

37 million acres of land in the United States. The public-land-dominated American West is the fastest-growing region for land trust activity.

III. The Role of NEPA

So what law will guide us into this new "fourth phase" in the history of grasslands and forests? What law allows us to think across jurisdictions and disciplines, to balance commodity production and environmental quality at a national and global level? Perhaps most significantly, what law allows us to consider problems on public land and private land together? What law allows us to consider conservation acquisition and public land use planning as part of the same mosaic of land management?

The ambitious land management statutes of the 1970s will not. The overwhelming focus of the National Forest Management Act, the Federal Land Policy and Management Act, and similar legislation is on public forest and grassland. These acts have already proved inadequate in dealing with a range of land issues, both public and private. Their enforcement has been problematic at the best of times. Further, the recent assault on NEPA, discussed below, has had the effect of depriving the land use plans they generate of any binding force they may otherwise have had.

Absent dramatic changes in Washington, D.C., for better or worse, the key law at the federal level is the National Environmental Policy Act of 1970. NEPA, of course, was a harbinger of the coming of the "third phase" of natural resources development discussed above, but its language is broad enough to make it the most significant potential source of authority in dealing with the problems we will encounter in the "fourth phase."

Why is NEPA so important?

In his message transmitting the first edition of *Environmental Quality* to Congress in August 1970, President Nixon indulged in flights of environmentalist rhetoric representative of the times. "Man," the President noted "has been too cavalier in his relations with nature" and "unless we arrest the depredations that have been

inflicted so carelessly on our natural systems—which exist in an intri-
cate set of balances—we face the prospect of ecological disaster." The
"environment," Nixon continued, "is not an abstract concern or simply a matter of esthetics, or of personal taste . . . Our physical nature,
our mental health, our culture and institutions, our opportunities for
challenge and fulfillment, our very survival—all of these are directly
related to and affected by the environment in which we live."

The legislative history of NEPA contains similar overwrought
"third phase" language:

> By land, sea, and air, the enemies of man's survival relentlessly press
> their attack. The most dangerous of all these enemies is man's own
> undirected technology. The radioactive poisons from nuclear tests,
> the runoff into rivers of nitrogen fertilizers, the smog from auto-
> mobiles, the pesticides in the food chains, and the destruction of
> topsoil by strip mining are examples of the failure to foresee and
> control the untoward consequences of modern technology.[36]

So what was NEPA supposed to do to prevent the "depredations that
have been inflicted so carelessly on our natural systems" and the
"failure[s] to foresee and control the untoward consequences" lamented by Nixon?

NEPA has been variously called the "Magna Carta," the "Ten
Commandments," the "Bill of Rights," and the "Sherman Antitrust
Act" of American environmental law. In light of this rhetoric, it's
worth remembering a few historical facts: King John, signer of Magna
Carta, promptly rejected the document after he escaped from the bar-
ons at Runnemede, and it was centuries before the document attained its current unquestioned status in the constitutional tradition.
The meaning of the Bill of Rights has evolved dramatically in the
past two hundred years. The Ten Commandments did not receive an
immediate positive reception from all the Israelites. And the Sherman
Antitrust Act has been used at various times to suppress strikes, break
up great combinations of wealth and power, and proselytize neoclas-
sical economic thinking. In other words, you cannot always judge a
law's potential by its track record after enactment.

We all know, but cannot say too often, that NEPA is about a
great deal more than the technicalities of environmental impact

assessment, the length of the comment periods, the range of alternatives that must be considered in an environmental impact statement, or even the appropriate role of a categorical exclusion. As William Rodgers wrote in *Environmental Law*, "[t]he procedural side of NEPA long has overshadowed the substantive underside."[37] As Philip Michael Ferester noted, "[a] study of NEPA's legislative history and the scholarly and judicial interpretations glossing the original text reveals why this statute, written for laudable and even grandiose purposes, has subsequently been labeled a mere full disclosure bill."[38]

Borrowing Professor Rodger's taxonomy, NEPA embodies six general goals: (1) to fulfill the responsibilities of each generation as trustee of the environment for succeeding generations; (2) to assure for all Americans safe and healthful, productive, and aesthetically and culturally pleasing surroundings; (3) to attain the widest range of beneficial uses of the environment without degradation, risk to public health or safety, or other undesirable or unintended consequences; (4) to preserve important historic, cultural, and natural aspects of our national heritage, and maintain this heritage wherever possible in an environment which supports diversity and variety of individual choice; (5) to achieve a balance between population and resource use, which will permit high standards of living in a wide sharing of life's amenities; and (6) to enhance the quality of renewable resources and approach the maximum attainable recycling of the applicable resources.

NEPA section 102 directs all federal agencies "to the fullest extent possible" to undertake nine types of actions designed to fulfill the six objectives. Among these actions are the following:

> (A) utilize a systematic, interdisciplinary approach which will ensure the integrated use of the natural and social sciences and the environmental design arts in planning and decisionmaking which may have an impact on man's environment;
>
> (B) identify and develop methods and procedures in consultation with the Council on Environmental Quality . . . which will ensure that presently unquantified environmental amenities and values may be given appropriate consideration in decisionmaking along with economic and technical considerations;

(F) recognize the worldwide and long-range character of environmental problems and, where consistent with the foreign policy of the United States, lend appropriate support to initiatives resolutions and programs designed to maximize international cooperation in anticipating and preventing a decline in the quality of mankind's world environment;

(G) make available to states, counties, municipalities, institutions, and individuals advice and information useful in restoring, maintaining, and enhancing the quality of the environment.

And, of course, NEPA also directs agencies to prepare "detailed statements" for major federal actions significantly affecting the quality of the human environment.

NEPA is breathtakingly prescient. It urges federal agencies to consider the "global" nature and "long-range" character of the environmental problems they encounter. It urges federal agencies to work with states and municipalities—the primary jurisdictions for land use planning. At least arguably, it urges them to work with groups that operate in both the public and private sphere like the land trust community[39]— "institutions and individuals"—and provide them with information "useful in restoring, maintaining, and enhancing the quality of the environment." As the Council on Environmental Quality (CEQ) observed in its January 1997 report, *The National Environmental Policy Act: A Study of Its Effectiveness After Twenty-Five Years*: "NEPA set forth an inclusive, comprehensive vision for the environment. NEPA 25 years ago anticipated today's call for enhanced local involvement and responsibility, sustainable development and government accountability."[40]

Even for the NEPA skeptic, there really isn't anything else in U.S. Code that provides the authority to deal with the problems and opportunities we currently confront.

NEPA imposes significant substantive obligations on federal public land management agencies. They're not substantive in the sense that they prohibit certain activities, order priorities, or set on-the-ground management standards. They are substantive in the sense that they require broad cross-jurisdictional, environmentally sensitive, scientifically informed decision making.

Like it or not, the laudable goals of NEPA are imposed on federal agencies largely through the environmental impact assessment process. It is through the preparation of environmental impact statements, environmental assessments, and categorical exclusions that NEPA encourages federal agencies to alter their decision-making processes to meet its substantive goals. While the responsibilities for environmental impact analysis fall squarely on federal agencies, the scope of analysis regularly includes a broad range of private action. The analysis itself is almost always available to all interested parties.

The CEQ regulations, which govern the application of NEPA by federal agencies, focus the diffuse intent in the statute into a more comprehensible goal of insuring "that environmental information is available to public officials and citizens before decisions are made and before actions are taken" and "that the policies and goals defined in the Act are infused into the ongoing programs and actions of the Federal Government." The regulations go on to say that this goal is to be achieved through the generation of "action-forcing" documents, primarily environmental impact statements. Yet, the regulations caution, "NEPA's purpose is not to generate paperwork—even excellent paperwork—but to foster excellent action."[41]

As the Council on Environmental Quality's NEPA regulations make clear, as part of the "scoping process" federal decision makers are required to "[i]nvite the participation of affected Federal, State, and local agencies, any affected Indian tribe, the proponent of the action, and other interested persons (including those who might not be in accord with the action on environmental grounds)"[42] and in selecting alternatives to consider in an environmental impact statement, federal agencies must "[i]nclude reasonable alternatives not within the jurisdiction of the lead agency."[43]

IV. Undermining NEPA

This is not the best time to advocate NEPA's capacity to assist us in dealing with the complex world we face. Despite the recent change in federal administration, it still appears that NEPA's friends "lack all conviction" while NEPA's enemies are "full of passionate intensity." For the past half decade, at least, the executive branch and, to a lesser degree, the courts have been bashing holes in the structures that give NEPA meaning. While their attempt to reduce the "regulatory burden" NEPA imposes on federal agencies may have been undertaken in good faith, they have gone a long way toward depriving us of the only national tool we have to deal with many of the problems we will confront.

The environmental impact assessment process born in NEPA and now copied (and improved) everywhere in the world is currently subject to a concerted attack. The nature of the attack involves at least three powerful arguments.

First, there is a growing body of case law that suggests that NEPA is impossible to comply with, that its requirements of objectivity and its technical, procedural niceties are beyond the capacity of even the most gifted federal official. This argument is best illustrated in 2003 district court opinions regarding the roadless rule in Wyoming[44] and Idaho.[45] However, there have been a variety of earlier cases taking similar points of view. It seems that, in 2004, the federal government lost *International Snowmobile Association v. Norton* because a U.S district court judge did not believe that the Clinton administration could have engaged in a balanced NEPA process regarding snowmobiles in Yellowstone.[46]

A more cynical view of this attack is that NEPA—rather than being impossible to comply with—always provides a colorable argument for the opponents of any documented decision. The NEPA compliance process associated with the roadless rule took place on a heroic scale with millions of comments and hundreds of meetings. Still, a number of federal district court judges were able to find fault with its compliance.[47]

Second, there is a stubbornly held belief in the executive branch that NEPA only applies to decisions that will inevitably result in direct physical disturbance of the environment. Perhaps the best example is the U.S. Forest Service's categorical exclusion for land and resource management plans required by the National Forest Management Act.[48] Subject to this belief, regulations and even land use plans themselves do not require NEPA compliance. It is largely inconsistent with a history of NEPA and the Act's focus on decision making rather than direct environmental effect. In this belief, federal agencies have been abetted by the Supreme Court. In *Norton v. Southern Utah Wilderness Alliance*, the Supreme Court, following the Forest Service's lead, declared that the Bureau of Land Management's land use plan, developed under the Federal Land Policy and Management Act, was discretionary and therefore largely immune to NEPA.[49]

In recent years we have witnessed the spectacle of the Department of Justice simultaneously asserting that NEPA didn't apply to regulations, land use plans, and roadless rules because they did not result inevitably in direct physical disturbances of the environment, while at the same time failing to appeal injunctions based on hypertechnical readings of NEPA requirements applied to just such rules.

The third argument against NEPA, which the executive branch has asserted and many courts have accepted, is the argument that NEPA categorical exclusions can be applied universally to actions that rarely result in the preparation of environmental impact statements. Sometime in the late 1970s or early 1980s, the public interest natural resources community came to accept that an environmental assessment accompanied by a finding of no significant impact was adequate (if not ideal) environmental analysis for timber sales, small road construction, and a variety of other relatively routine but potentially extremely damaging activities on the public lands. In its 1997 report on NEPA, the Council on Environmental Quality observed that far more environmental assessments where being prepared than environmental impact statements required by NEPA "for major federal actions significantly affecting the human environment."[50] With every finding of no significant impact resulting from an environmental assessment, the agency that prepared the finding built a larger empirical base for excluding the type of conduct from NEPA analysis altogether.

Beginning with the 1983 publication of CEQ's Guidance on Agency Implementation of NEPA Regulations, pressure had been building to use the categorical exclusions from NEPA analysis authorized by CEQ's 1978 regulations to make NEPA more "efficient." Commenters on the CEQ guidance argued "that categorical exclusions were not adequately identified and defined," that "agencies were overly restrictive in their interpretations of categorical exclusions," and that "agencies were requiring too much documentation for projects that were not major federal actions with significant effects."[51] In 1985, the Forest Service adopted new NEPA policies creating ten broad, flexible categorical exclusions from NEPA analysis, including "Low-impact silvicultural activities that are limited in size and duration and that primarily use existing roads and facilities, such as firewood sales; salvage, thinning, and small harvest cuts; site preparation; and planting and seeding" and "Mineral and energy activities of limited size, duration, and degree of disturbance, such as preliminary exploration and removal of small mineral samples."[52] The regulations did not define phrases like "low-impact" and "limited size." In 2003, grand categorical exclusions began to emerge for large silvicultural activities.[53] Because hundreds of timber sales and road projects had resulted in no significant environmental impact, it was easy to argue that—absent extraordinary circumstances—no such project would result in a statutorily significant impact.

The empirically based categorical exclusions for timber sales and the like are, at least arguably, logically inconsistent with the "no need to do an EIS for forest plan" argument. Since timber sales on national forests, so far, have all been subject to land and resource management plans and the accompanying environmental impact statement, they provide less empirical support than the U.S. Forest Service suggests. Should the 2006 categorical exclusion for land and resource management plans come into effect, future timber sales will not be tied to an existing land management plan environmental impact statement.

V. Conclusion

In June 1970, six months after Richard Nixon signed NEPA into law, the Public Land Law Review Commission observed:

> The National Environmental Policy Act of 1969 . . . appl[ies] to all federal agencies in the performance of any of their responsibilities which may have an impact "on man's environment." Thus, [it provides] a statutory basis to bring environmental quality into planning and decision-making wherever gaps exist in previous laws,

even though an agency may have to obtain additional legislative authority before taking final action.[54]

Although many federal environmental laws have been passed since June 1970, history keeps creating "gaps" for NEPA to fill. As we enter a new, more complicated age in the management of natural resources, we need to take the substantive mandates of the National Environmental Policy Act more seriously. Rather than seeing it as a procedural impediment to our environmental decision-making (which may or may not be wise), we need to use it as a tool to help us make wise decisions. It is only through the sort of integrated decision making that NEPA mandates, that the federal government can continue to effectively resolve the "territorial disputes" about our forests and grasslands: the "unsettled territory within the boundaries of the United States" of which Alexander Hamilton warned us more than 200 years ago.

Notes

1.   National Environmental Policy Act, 42 U.S.C. §§ 4321–47.

2.   ECONOMIC RESEARCH SERVICE, U.S. DEPARTMENT OF AGRICULTURE, MAJOR USE OF LAND IN THE UNITED STATES, 2002 (May 2006).

3.   U.S. BUREAU OF LAND MANAGEMENT, 2004 PUBLIC LAND STATISTICS (2004), available at http://www.blm.gov/natacq/pls04/.

4.   See, e.g., TERRY L. ANDERSON, VERNON L. SMITH & EMILY SIMMONS, HOW AND WHY TO PRIVATIZE FEDERAL LANDS 2 (1999).

5.   THE FEDERALIST NO. 7, at 83 (Alexander Hamilton) (John C. Hamilton ed., 1869).

6.   See United States v. Gardner, 107 F.3d 1314, 1318 (9th Cir. 1997).

7.   Homestead Act of 1862, 43 U.S.C. §§161–284 (repealed 1976); see PAUL W. GATES, HISTORY OF PUBLIC LAND LAW DEVELOPMENT (1968).

8.   U.S. BUREAU OF LAND MANAGEMENT, 2007 PUBLIC LAND STATISTICS table 1-2 (2007), available at http://www.blm.gov/public_land_statistics/pls07/pls1-2_07.pdf.

9.   JOHN LESHY, THE MINING LAW: A STUDY IN PERPETUAL MOTION (1987).

10.   General Mining Law of 1872, 30 U.S.C. § 28.

11.   Pollard v. Hagan, 44 U.S. 212 (1845).

12.   Id.

13.   Id.

14.   https://www.lincolninst.edu/subcenters/managing-state-trust-lands/state/ed-funding-co.pdf.

15. Yellowstone Park Act, 42 Cong. Ch. 24, 17 Stat. 32, 33 (1872).

16. Quoted in MICHAEL WILLIAMS, AMERICANS AND THEIR FORESTS: A HISTORICAL GEOGRAPHY 400 (1992).

17. 16 U.S.C. § 476, 30 Stat. 35 (repealed 1976).

18. *Id.*

19. EDMUND MORRIS, THEODORE REX 500 (2001).

20. GIFFORD PINCHOT, THE FIGHT FOR CONSERVATION 3 (1910).

21. *Id.* at 4.

22. *Id.* at 6.

23. *Id.* at 42.

24. *Id.* at 44.

25. *Id.* at 50.

26. GAYLORD NELSON, BEYOND EARTH DAY: FULFILLING THE PROMISE 6 (2002).

27. PHILIP SHABECOFF, FIERCE GREEN FIRE xiii (2d ed. 2003).

28. *Id.*

29. RACHEL CARSON, SILENT SPRING 1 (1962).

30. STEWART UDALL, THE QUIET CRISIS 54–68 (1963).

31. Morris v. United States, 392 F.3d 1372 (Fed. Cir. 2004); Seiber v. United States, 364 F.3d 1356 (Fed. Cir. 2004).

32. Massachusetts v. EPA, 127 S. Ct. 1438, 1450 (2007).

33. WILLIAM TRAVIS, DAVID THEOBALD & DANIEL FAGRE, ROCKY MOUNTAIN FUTURES: AN ECOLOGICAL PERSPECTIVE 7 (Jill Baron ed., 2002).

34. *Id.* at 8.

35. *Quoted in* SEYMOUR TOLL, ZONED AMERICAN 124 (1969).

36. H.R. REP. NO. 91-378, at 3 (1969), *reprinted in* 1969 U.S.C.C.A.N. 2751, 2753 (quoting N.Y. TIMES, May 3, 1969, at 34, col. 2).

37. WILLIAM RODGERS, ENVIRONMENTAL LAW 802 (2d ed. 1994).

38. Philip Michael Ferester, *Revitalizing the National Environmental Policy Act: Substantive Law Adaptations from NEPA's Progeny*, 16 HARV. ENVTL. L. REV. 207, 207 (1992).

39. *See* Federico Cheever, *Public Good and Private Magic in the Law of Land Trusts and Conservation Easements: A Happy Present and a Troubled Future,* 73 DENV. U. L. REV. 1074 (1996).

40. COUNCIL ON ENVIRONMENTAL QUALITY, THE NATIONAL ENVIRONMENTAL POLICY ACT: A STUDY OF ITS EFFECTIVENESS AFTER TWENTY-FIVE YEARS 2 (Jan. 1997), *available at* http://ceq.hss.doe.gov/nepa/nepa25fn.pdf.

41. 40 C.F.R. § 1500.1

42. 40 C.F.R. § 1501.7(a)(1)

43. 40 C.F.R. § 1502.14(c).

44. Wyoming v. USDA, 277 F. Supp. 2d 1197, 1221 (D. Wyo. 2003).

45. Idaho v. U.S. Forest Service, 142 F. Supp. 2d 1248, 1262–63 (D. Idaho 2001).

46.   Int'l Snowmobile Ass'n v. Norton, 340 F. Supp. 2d 1249 (D. Wyo. 2004).

47.   *See* Wyoming v. USDA, *supra* note 44; Idaho v. U.S. Forest Service, *supra* note 45.

48.   National Forest Management Act, 75 Fed. Reg. 75,481 (Dec. 15, 2006).

49.   Norton v. S. Utah Wilderness Alliance, 124 S. Ct. 2373 (2004).

50.   COUNCIL ON ENVIRONMENTAL QUALITY, *supra* note 40, at 19.

51.   Guidance on Agency Implementation of NEPA Regulations, 48 Fed. Reg. 34,263, 34264–65 (July 28, 1983).

52.   50 Fed. Reg. 26,078, 26,081 (June 24, 1985).

53.   National Environmental Policy Act Documentation Needed for Limited Timber Harvest, 68 Fed. Reg. 44,598 (July 29, 2003).

54.   PUBLIC LAND LAW REVIEW COMMISSION, ONE THIRD OF THE NATION'S LAND 67–68 (June 1970).

Index

inventory obligation of, 235
National Landscape Conservation
   System, 249
SMCRA authority, 150
See also wilderness inventories;
   specific bureaus and services
International Boundary Waters
   Treaty, 148
International Panel on Climate
   Change (IPCC)
   Fourth Assessment Report, 32,
      35–36, 45
   statements on global warming, 39
International Snowmobile Ass'n v. Norton,
   389
Internet, and notice and comment,
   210
interstate commerce. *See* commerce
   clause
Inuit communities
   and global climate change, 36–37,
      39, 44
   and polar bears, 54, 59
inventories, history of, 231–32,
   233, 256. *See also* wilderness
   inventories
IPCC. *See* International Panel on
   Climate Change (IPCC)

Jamieson, Dale, 36, 38
Jay, John, 196
John R. Sand & Gravel Co. v. United
   States, 144
judicial intervention, role in
   preservation, 261, 273
just compensation, 6, 14, 141–42

Katrina. *See* Hurricane Katrina
Keeling, Charles, 31–32
Keiter, Robert, 188
Kelo v. City of New London, 85–86
Kennedy, Anthony, 132, 142
Kennedy, Edward, 358

King Range National Conservation
   Area, 257
Klamath River Basin, 305, 311–15,
   379
Kyoto Protocol, 33–34

labels, importance of, 231–32, 238,
   247–50
laissez faire, demise of, 103
lake governance, case study, 119–22
Land and Water Conservation Fund,
   149, 270
Land Ethic (Leopold), 41–43, 45
land exchanges, 260, 267, 268, 270
land grants, 5–6, 373
land trusts, 14–15, 382–84
land use planning. *See* planning
Leopold, Aldo
   Land Ethic, 41–43
   on nature's interconnectedness,
      68–69
   and primitive areas, 255–56
   Round River, 375
   Sand County Almanac, A, 29
Levin, Simon, 305
Lichatowich, Jim, 282
Light v. United States, 9
Lingle v. Chevron U.S.A., 143
Lister, Ernest, 289
Livingston, Henry, 111–12
lobbying, history of, 8
Locke, John, notions of ownership,
   11, 17, 21, 22–23
Louisiana, Gulf Coast, 358, 360, 362
Lower Elwha Klallam Tribe, 283–84,
   285–86, 290, 293, 295–96, 328
Lucas v. South Carolina Coastal
   Council, 14, 142
Lyng v. Northwest Indian Cemetery
   Protective Ass'n, 48, 151–52

Maas, Arthur, 7
Madison, James, 196